Allen –
for journeying & learning
together

Love, Claire
Christmas, 1983 –
New Years, 1984

THE AGES OF BRITAIN

THE AGES OF BRITAIN

Editor
PETER CROOKSTON

Consultant
JOHN KENYON

St. Martin's Press
New York

Book Design by Jo Dale

Library of Congress Catalog Card Number: 83-061036

ISBN 0-312-01401-5

First published in Great Britain by Hamish Hamilton Ltd.

First U.S. Edition

10 9 8 7 6 5 4 3 2 1

CONTENTS

INTRODUCTION

by John Kenyon

Britain is a land thronged with ghosts; not only the ghosts of men and women, but the ghosts of past events, and past life styles. Nor have the efforts of generations of planners, beginning as long ago as the 17th century, materially impaired our heritage.

The names of city streets – The Headrow, Fletchergate – recall lost trades, or, as in Great Russell Street or Southampton Row, famous families now much diminished. They remind us of vanished geographical features, as in Fleet Street (named after a river of that name), or even extinguished religions, as in Covent Garden. Names like this very rarely change; though in 1829 the residents of Grub Street, E.C., did succeed in having it renamed 'Milton Street'. Meanwhile, our suburbs have distended to absorb the sites of past battles, to envelop rural manor houses and even great mansions, like Woolaton and Temple Newsam. Charming country villages like Battersea, Kensington and Chelsea, Roundhay and Edgbaston, have become suburbs themselves.

On the moors to the north and west dolmens loom, and castles still guard fords and passes which long ago lost their strategic significance. The roads are like palimpsests, with layers of history imposed one upon another; the A 15 from Lincoln to the Humber was once the Saxon Ermine Street, but it was originally laid out by the Romans to carry their legions north to York. In the Midlands and the South main roads are punctuated every few miles by park gates, with the drives beyond curving off into the concealing woods, leading sometimes to a modest Victorian 'Holly Lodge', sometimes to a palatial extravaganza surviving from an age of greater splendour. Every village has its church, which may have been built in any century, from the ninth to the nineteenth. Modern signposts lure us down side lanes to villages with evocative, melancholy names: Langport, Flodden, Long Marston, Market Bosworth, Prestonpans. Even the pubs echo past glories. The multitude of 'Marquises of Granby' and 'Dukes of Cumberland' attest the veneration of demobilised 18th-century NCOs for their commanders in the German Wars. Our 'Royal Oaks' commemorate the famous tree at Boscobel which sheltered Charles II after his defeat at Worcester in 1651, and they were probably founded, or rechristened, by discharged veterans of Cromwell's army ten years later, who were more anxious than most to display their loyalty to the new regime.

And of course, every great house down to the present century has its treasures of paintings, porcelain, plate, furniture and books, often spilling over into our great museums and art galleries.

There is no lack of manuals, directories and guides to these relics of the past, but for the most part they are each devoted to one category or one locality. There are books on castles, on stately homes, on historic pictures, on roads and on towns; not to mention specialist works on architecture, painting, china, glass and so on for every period. There are a multitude of cultural guides to individual towns, counties, regions and countries. But none of these makes it easy to place the physical remains of our past civilizations in their proper context, or associate them with other artefacts of the same period. They miss the sweep of British history.

To correct that deficiency we have commissioned leading historians in their different fields to write about each 'age' in British history. Sometimes these 'ages' cover several centuries, sometimes barely a hundred years. They were asked to place special emphasis on those physical aspects of the past which survive into the present day, yet at the same time try to communicate something of the spirit or atmosphere of their particular period. In conjunction with our research team, they were also asked to point out buildings, museums or locations which are of particular interest or significance, and which you can freely visit. These are set out in the gazeteer section which starts on page 162 and the whole is illustrated by some splendid photographs, most of them specially commissioned by *The Observer* when 'The Ages of Britain' was published in its original form as a summer series in the magazine in 1981. We have also added a number of special sections dealing with the development of weapons, transport, agriculture and so on, right across the centuries; each of them written by an expert in the field and illustrated with line drawings.

It is, we hope, not just another guide book, but a new kind of guide, and one which it will be as pleasant to read and study at home as it will be helpful to you in your travels.

Professor Kenyon is Chairman of the Department of Modern History at the University of St Andrews and is the author of 'Stuart England', 'The Popish Plot' and 'Revolution Principles'.

CONTRIBUTORS

Barry Cunliffe
Professor of European Archaeology
University of Oxford

Professor Donald Earl
University of Hull

Professor Peter Sawyer
Department of Medieval History
Leeds University

Professor Henry Loyn
Westfield College
University of London

Dr. John Palmer
Senior Lecturer in Medieval History
University of Hull

Roger Lockyer
Senior Lecturer in History, Royal Holloway College
University of London

Professor John Kenyon
Chairman of Department of Modern History
University of St. Andrews

Professor John Cannon
Head of Department of History
University of Newcastle upon Tyne

Dr. Brian Harrison
Tutor in Modern History and
Politics, Corpus Christi College
University of Oxford

Roy Brigden *(Agricultural Implements) is Keeper of the Museum of English Rural Life, University of Reading*
Stephen M. Riley *(Maritime Transport) is Assistant Keeper, Department of Ships, National Maritime Museum, Greenwich*
Andrew Nahum *(Land Transport) is a curator of the Science Museum, London*
Jeffery Daniels *(The Chair) is Curator of the Jeffrye Museum, London*
Lyndon Cave *(The Small House) is an architect and author of The Smaller English House*
Dennis Knight *(Weapons) is a military historian whose most recent book is Harvest of Messerschmitts*
Mary Norwak *(The Household) is the author of The Farmhouse Kitchen and Kitchen Antiques*
Jane Tozer *(Costume) is Keeper of the Gallery of English Costume, City of Manchester*

THE
TRIBAL ISLANDS

by Barry Cunliffe

Stonehenge

Nowhere in Europe can the tangible remains of our distant past be seen to better effect than in Britain. Walk or drive through virtually any area of British countryside and, so long as you know what you are looking for, the signs of the activities of our prehistoric ancestors are everywhere to be seen. The countryside is indelibly impressed with the triumphs and follies of the past. Indelibly is perhaps too strong a word – all too often these days modern agricultural techniques and suburban sprawl are obliterating landscapes which have survived largely unaltered for thousands of years, and are replacing them with a new structure – an archaeology of the late 20th century. There has of course always been change in the landscape: what is different about our time is the *rate* of change. All the more important that we should be aware of that part of our heritage which is fast disappearing, so that we can ensure that the best is saved before the slate is wiped completely clean.

The story of our prehistoric past is an interweaving of many themes. But above all it is the story of man gradually bringing his natural environment under control, and of his response, through social and economic change, to the problems of a steadily increasing population. While this epic was being enacted many sub-plots were introduced – technological innovation, folk movements, warfare – but these pall into insignificance against the strength and drama of the main theme. This begins with a few bands of hunters following their game in the summer months to the unsubmerged part of the continental shelf that we now call Britain some time about 60,000 years ago, and ends with an urbanised society enjoying Mediterranean luxuries in the decades before the Roman invasion in AD 43.

Strictly, the story falls into three parts. It begins with a long palaeolithic prelude during which the small and isolated communities who used these islands were subservient to nature, depending for their livelihood entirely upon hunting and collecting and leaving very little trace of their presence on the landscape, apart from the occasional fire which might have destroyed part of the primeval forest.

The second episode begins in the fourth millennium BC when communities in Britain, now a group of islands, began to settle down – to till the soil, to grow their own food and to husband their domestic animals. It was at this time that the great religious monuments, which we shall describe, were erected.

The final episode is a short epilogue when the bowwave of Mediterranean civilisation broke on the British shores and in the last century and a half of freedom from Roman domination (c 100 BC–AD 43), the communities of the south east made rapid advances towards a more civilised, urban society with regular markets, coinage, writing and the emergence of a state system of government.

Of the palaeolithic prelude there is little to be seen, no great monuments to the dead or to the gods, and no

fortifications. Camps were temporary and shelters slight, but this is not to say that this long period of 60,000 years is totally anonymous – our museums are full of roughly fashioned palaeolithic stone implements like the general purpose hand-axe, useful for killing, skinning and grubbing up roots. Only very rarely are other remains, like a hard wood spear from Clacton or the skull fragments of Britain's earliest known inhabitant from Swanscombe, to be found.

It was later, in the upper paleolithic period that man began to inhabit what is to us a more recognisable landscape. Perhaps most dramatic are the cave sites like Kents Cavern near Torquay, Creswell Crags in Derbyshire and the Mendip caves of Cheddar, used as temporary shelters by bands of hunters (equipped with a more refined and specialised kit of flint tools) at various times throughout the period from 27,000 to 8000 BC.

But it would be wrong to give the impression that these people were cave dwellers; they would have used the caves only during the hunting season. At other times they would have inhabited temporary settlements in the open countryside, places like the coastal fringes around Portsmouth harbour or the upland promontory of Hengistbury Head overlooking the Solent, both within easy reach of shellfish and sea birds.

As the climate of Britain gradually warmed up and began to approximate to its present day range, from about 8000 BC onwards, so forest spread across the landscape and the hunting and collecting regimes became more specialised. Composite tools such as flint-barbed wooden arrows and harpoons with bone heads came more commonly into use.

We must imagine the hunting bands of this Mesolithic period having an intimate knowledge of their environment – far more detailed than ours. They would know when it was good to grub up roots, when to eat bracken shoots, the medicinal and nutritional value of every available herb, and above all they would have a precise knowledge of the behaviour of the animals and birds upon which they preyed, gearing their own migratory movements to those of their hunted beasts.

It was in this period, roughly 8000–4000 BC, that man first began to make an impression on the landscape, partially damming rivers to make fish traps and perhaps firing the forest to drive herds into the arms of the hunters. By constantly returning to the same seasonal camp sites on lake edges or forest fringes, wear on the natural landscape would have begun to show: clearings would have grown bigger. It was the start of the process of forest clearance which is still continuing today.

A major threshold in the development of British society was crossed during the course of the late fifth

Gough's Cave, in the Mendip Hills, Somerset, is one of the places where remains of palaeolithic hunters have been found. But caves were not permanent homes; they were used only as temporary shelters when hunting. Palaeolithic people preferred settlements in open countryside, usually within easy reach of the sea

millennium BC, when settlers from the European continent crossed the Channel to Britain bringing with them
their domesticated animals and supplies of seed corn to
sow: within a mere 1,000 years knowledge of cultivation
and domestication had spread to all parts of the British
Isles. The arrivals marked the beginning of a totally new
way of life – men were no longer at the mercy of the
natural world but had begun to exert some degree of
control over it.

There were two almost immediate effects: first, great
inroads were made on the forest cover and the small
clearings of the preceding period began to coalesce; and,
second, people were now tied to the land and communities could begin to grow in size. The way of life would, of
course, have been precarious – adverse weather or disease among crops and animals could have led quickly to
famine and to the disappearance of whole communities,
but the new economy was a sufficient improvement over
the old to survive all the initial difficulties.

We must not suppose that a stable farming landscape
appeared overnight: the reality would have been far
more haphazard. A family group might move into a
forest area, clear it by slash and burn methods, farm it for
a few years until fertility started to decline, and then
move off to clear a new area, returning to the first a
generation or two later to begin again. In this way and
with an increasing population large areas of Britain were
opened up and brought under cultivation. On some soils
overcropping and poor management eventually led to
permanent exhaustion. Many of our heath lands, like
the New Forest, had already been created by the middle
of the second millennium, while other more stable soils
like those on the chalk did not begin to show signs of
serious exhaustion until the late first millennium.

Technology was still based on stone-using (hence the
archaeological use of the term Neolithic 'new stone' to
describe this period) but a new range of skills were
developed including the polishing of stone, the mining
of flint nodules and the manufacture of pottery. The flint
mines are among the most impressive monuments of the
period. Massive shafts were dug down through the chalk
to a suitable band of flint, which was then followed in a
maze of galleries.

For the most part all one sees now is a hillside pock-
marked with hollows looking like shell holes, each representing a silted up shaft; Cissbury and Harrow Hill in
Sussex are good examples, but at Grimes Graves near
Thetford in Norfolk several shafts have been excavated
and can now be visited.

The digging of the flint mines implies a level of social
organisation, since it was an activity requiring a degree
of specialisation and the specialists had to be supported
by a surplus of food produced by others. The 'Neolithic'

economy not only allowed specialisation, but actually
encouraged it by allowing people to live in larger communities.

The earliest social monuments to be found are called
'causewayed camps' – archaeological jargon for an area
defined by ditches and banks dug in discontinuous
lengths. The best examples occur on the chalklands of
the South, but the camps are now known to have extended well into the river valleys of the Midlands. Just
what these monuments were built for is still a matter of
doubt and speculation. It is generally believed that most
of them served a social and communal function, perhaps
centres where the tribe could meet together to enact
laws, arrange marriages, reaffirm land boundaries, exchange goods and in general be reminded that they were
one people.

It is not difficult, on visiting the grass-grown banks
and ditches of one of the better preserved camps like
Windmill Hill near Avebury, to visualise it on one of
these communal occasions teeming with busy people –
like a rural medieval fair. The earthworks may have had
other uses. One scarp edge enclosure, Crickley Hill in
the Cotswolds, has produced clear evidence of its
ramparts being attacked with a hail of flint-tipped arrows
and then being burnt.

Radiocarbon dates for causewayed camps suggest that

**Previous page: Knowlton Circle, Dorset, a 4,000-year-old
Neolithic religious henge. A 12th-century Christian church was
built in the middle as a deliberate act of exorcism. The henge has a
surrounding ditch and two entrances**

they span the period from 3500 to 2500 BC. Much the same date range applies to the great long barrows in which the Neolithic communities buried their dead leaders. In southern Britain most of them are built of earth and rubble from flanking ditches up to 200ft long – the consolidated effort of a large sector of the community. The barrows made from gleaming white chalk must have seemed dramatic in the ancient landscape. Excavation has shown that the building of the barrow was the last stage in a complex ritual, which involved laying out the bodies for some time in a timber-built mortuary chamber possibly until the last member of the group had died.

Exactly the same idea of collective burial is shown by the contemporary chambered tombs found mainly in the west and north of Britain, where stone is plentiful. These contained a chamber built of large stone slabs, sometimes in combination with dry stone walling, embedded in a long mound of soil and rubble. When a member of the kin group died the chamber was opened, the bones of the previous occupant were packed away and the newly deceased laid out instead. After fires of purification and feasting the tomb would have been sealed again until another member was ready for burial.

The rituals, and the enormous amount of work which went into the building of the barrow, leave little doubt that these monuments were symbols of strength and

prestige – one can imagine one community vying with another to make its monument more magnificent than its neighbours'.

Long barrows and chambered tombs are widely distributed in Britain, from the north of Scotland and the Orkneys, to Wales, the Cotswolds and Wessex. Many of the chambered varieties like West Kennet near Avebury and Wayland Smithy on the Berkshire Downs, are open to the public and well worth a visit.

Overlapping with the period of building of causewayed camps and long barrows, and extending throughout most of the third millennium BC, another type of monument was erected widely throughout Britain – sites called henge monuments. These are ditched enclosures with the bank on the outer lip of the ditch broken by two or four entrance gaps. Inside there is often evidence of a massive circular structure composed of concentric settings of upright timbers.

Whether or not these structures were roofed is a matter of debate, as indeed is their function, but some

kind of social or ritual use is implied both by their size and by the fact that the bank-outside-ditch arrangement is hardly defensive. It has been suggested, quite reasonably, that the 'henges' replace the causewayed camps and carry on the same social functions – the dating at present available tends to support this view but evidence of use is notoriously difficult to come by.

The best known henge is the site from which the name came – Stonehenge. Paradoxically it is not the upright stones that are the typical henge (these came later) but the outer bank and ditch which most visitors pass through without noticing. The other famous Wessex henge – far more dramatic than Stonehenge – is the great monument of Avebury with a huge bank and ditch and stone settings inside.

Not far from Avebury is the even more puzzling 'one off' monument, the great artificial hill of Silbury erected some time in the late third millennium BC. Together, the henges, Silbury, the long barrows and the causewayed camps are a remarkable collection of structures: they demonstrate beyond doubt the strength, social cohesion and stability of our earliest farming communities, only a comparatively short time after their ancestors had crossed the Channel to colonise the British Isles.

Towards the end of the third millennium a new European cultural tradition begins to impose itself on the British Isles, quite possibly as the result of an immigration of new people – cosily referred to in the older literature as 'the Beaker folk'. This new cultural element is distinguishable by their very characteristic beaker-shaped pots. By the middle of the second millennium the Beaker phenomenon had spread throughout the whole country.

Where these new people came from is still hotly debated: an Atlantic coastal element is dimly distinguishable, but the most impressive similarities seem to have been with the Rhine area.

Single burial under round barrows now becomes widespread but, perhaps more important, with the Beaker immigrants came a knowledge of bronze working. The spread of bronze working was a revolutionary step, for not only did it offer a new and highly efficient material from which tools and weapons could be made, but it also meant that extensive networks of exchange had to be set up so that plentiful supplies of copper and tin could be made available. Those communities who could dominate the trade routes could grow rich on the proceeds, as did the chieftains of Wessex in the first half of the second millennium BC. Many of their bodies, adorned with gold and amber, were found by the excavators of the last century, engaging in the gentlemanly sport of Sunday afternoon barrow digging.

Crickley Hill, Gloucestershire, a Neolithic causewayed camp covering nine acres in the Cotswolds, has steep natural defences falling away to the north and south. Archaeologists have found evidence that its ramparts were attacked with a hail of flint-tipped arrows.

This is the biggest man-made mound in Europe – Silbury Hill, Wiltshire, a 130-foot high artificial hill built in the late third millennium BC which still puzzles archaeologists

The round barrows (*tumuli* on our Ordnance Survey maps) are the most prolific field monuments of the second millennium BC. Many thousands are known in Britain, particularly in the south of the country, and many hundreds still survive in tolerable condition, although later communities, impressed by the continuing sanctity of the location, frequently inserted their own dead into the mound. Barrows are quite simply mounds of soil and rubble, often from a circular ditch, piled up over a primary burial. They are often found in rows, and it is tempting to see in such arrangements the orderly growth of the cemetery of a dynasty, a new barrow being added to the row every time a worthy member of the community died.

Barrows were clearly meant to be seen and to impress by their dominating position. If you examine the sitings in detail you will find that they are often not on the actual summits of hills but some little way down from the crest on what would be the skyline when viewed from the lower land – a nice point which the 18th century antiquary William Stukeley was first to note.

While the round barrow and its embedded concept of individual burial marks a sharp contrast with the indigenous long-barrow/collective burial tradition, there was a degree of overlapping, and other aspects of the culture of the second millennium show an impressive continuity. The henge monuments, for example, continued to be used, but grafted on to the ancient tradition was a new concept involving the erection of standing stones, the stone circles and stone rows so plentiful in western parts of the British Isles from Cornwall to Orkney.

In reality there may not be all that much of a difference in tradition, for the stone may only be the survival, in landscapes where stone occurs naturally, of the standing timber used in areas where there is no suitable stone. This is not much different from the massive timber structures found in the earlier henges.

Both Stonehenge and Avebury provide very clear examples of the two traditions merging, with stone circles erected in already ancient henge monuments.

Stonehenge reached its final form after many generations.

A great deal has been written recently about the astronomical potential of these stone circles and stone rows. The arguments are complex, but most archaeologists would now accept some degree of relationship between the planning of some of these monuments and celestial phenomena such as the rising of the moon or prominent stars. All that would be required of the people was the ability to record these events over a period of time and some basic knowledge of measurement. Precise measurement and complex geometry were not necessarily involved.

It is easy to see how primitive people became interested in these matters. Farmers whose livelihood depended upon their ability to act in harmony with the seasons would have had to develop some method of measuring time so that sowing, for example, could be regulated. The movement of the stars and the moon provided a ready means of doing this. Stone circles, therefore, come down to us as a vivid reminder of man's relationship with his natural environment.

The middle of the second millennium marks a turning point in the development of prehistoric society in Britain – the old order dies away and gradually there emerges a very different society bereft of its great prestigious monuments. Why this should have happened is very difficult to say.

There is no evidence of catastrophe or revolution, no new invaders, just gradual but perceptible social and economic change. It's as though the old social order had outlived its usefulness and new structures were developing to cope with new situations as the population continued to increase. Dead were disposed of by cremation, the ashes often being buried in urns in small cemeteries while the people lived in isolated farms or hamlets dotted about among their fields apparently without need of prestigious social monuments to cement the group together.

The principal monuments that survive from the second half of the second millennium are field systems and the earthworks of the farmsteads – where these delicate remains have survived the ravages of more recent agriculture. They are best preserved in upland areas like Dartmoor, Wales and the north where stone occurs naturally and modern clearance has been far more limited.

The moors of Dartmoor and Bodmin present a remarkable picture of this mid-late Bronze Age landscape complete with reeves (boundary walls) dividing territories, field systems and hut circles, all of which owe their preservation to the fact that slight climatic deterioration soon after 1000 BC made the land too wet to use and led to the formation of blanket bog. So much is now preserved beneath a light mantle of peat that the moors can fairly be regarded as a unique textbook of archaeology.

By about 1000 BC changes in annual rainfall, which made some settled land unworkable, and pressure from the rise in population, caused signs of aggression. Weapons occur in greater quantity and defended hilltop enclosures begin to be built in various parts of the country. Some hillforts built in the early part of the first millennium appear not to have been intensively used, but soon after the middle of the millennium there was a spate of refortification and rebuilding, particularly in the area stretching from North Wales through the Welsh borderland to Wessex.

It was at this time that huge fortifications like Maiden Castle and Cadbury Castle were nearing completion – with multiple rings of defence and with gates heavily protected by outworks. There can be little doubt that forts like this were designed against attack and served as places where the rural population could find shelter along with the hillfort dwellers in times of unrest.

Each one is centred in a block of land 20–30 square miles, within which there were many small communities. Defence was certainly needed against aggressive neighbours – the Roman historian Tacitus described the Britons as 'distracted between the jarring factions of rival chieftains'.

Only one of the developed hillforts, Danebury in Hampshire, has been excavated in sufficient detail to begin to tell us what hillfort life was like. Here, by the second century BC, the space within the defences was packed with houses and storage structures, laid out with some degree of order along well-maintained metalled roads. The houses tended to be grouped around the periphery of the central area in the shelter of the ramparts with the store buildings and silos placed along the roads, while in the centre was a cluster of rectangular buildings, possibly shrines or temples.

By this stage, the fort was a manufacturing centre – raw materials like salt, bronze, iron, stone and Kimmeridge shale (for bracelet manufacture) were arriving and were being divided up or turned into consumer durables for the rural population. In return agrarian products were coming into the fort from the countryside. The fort appears to have had all the functions of a small town. But the emphasis was on defence. Ramparts and ditches were kept in good order, the gates were continually being replaced and great hoards of ammunition – sling stones – were kept ready.

The kind of warfare involved was not the long-term aggression of more recent times but swift, almost casual, raids. This is the picture the classical authors, writing about the Celts, give us. There was no need for the forts to prepare themselves for long-term siege, but they had to be strong enough to withstand the kind of invasion that was a short sharp shock.

Why society should have developed these warlike attributes is a fascinating, if unanswerable, question; but in any community, insect or animal, rigid territoriality and aggression increases when the population approaches the holding capacity of the land. This may well be the situation in Iron Age Britain – the archaeolo-

Maiden Castle, Dorset, greatest of all ancient British hill forts. Behind its multiple rings of defence a fort like this had all the functions of a small town and provided shelter for the surrounding population in times of inter-tribal warfare

gical evidence suggests a great increase in the number of settlements and Caesar actually remarks on the densely settled nature of the British landscape.

The hillfort-dominated landscape we have been considering does not cover the whole of the British Isles. The east of England has very few forts of this date, while in the western parts of the country the emphasis is on the strongly defended homestead or hamlet: in Cornwall they are called 'rounds', in Wales 'raths', but they are essentially the same – a strong earthwork enclosing a cluster of buildings.

Not all settlements were protected in this way. In the extreme west of Cornwall, for example, clusters of well preserved stone houses survive without enclosing earthworks. These can be seen still largely intact at Chysauster and Carn Euny. They give the strange feeling of having been only recently abandoned. Clusters of unenclosed houses also pepper the Welsh mountainsides. The dichotomy may represent some kind of social divide: only those of high status being allowed to defend themselves, much as they were later on in medieval England.

Scotland has its own distinctive types of defended homesteads, called 'duns' and 'brochs' – the duns are more spacious, much like the raths and rounds, while the brochs are a very specialised type of tower-like house, now usually standing in dramatic isolation in the north and west of Scotland and as far north as Orkney and Shetland. They were the centres of small Iron Age

communities, representing perhaps a local chief and his followers.

The later part of the first millennium (the Iron Age, in old-fashioned archaeological parlance) is, then, particularly rich in field monuments redolent of the strengths and tensions of the age.

The final stage – the epilogue – is relevant only to the south-east. To understand it we must look briefly to the Continent to see what was happening. In 123 BC the Romans moved into the south of France and established the *Provincia Romana* – Provence as we now know it. This was a beginning: the end of the process came in 51 BC when Caesar completed the conquest of Gaul, bringing France, Belgium and Southern Holland firmly under Roman control.

These events cannot have failed to have had their effects on Britain. The first sign we have, about 100 BC, is that Roman wine was beginning to reach Southern Britain, carried in durable ceramic wine *amphorae*, imported through ports like Hengistbury Head. A few years later Caesar made a limited foray into the south-east in 55 and 54 BC, and after this, until the time of the Roman conquest of Britain beginning in AD 43, the south-east became more and more Romanised through exotic imports and political allegiances.

West Kennet long barrow, Wiltshire, one of the biggest Neolithic burial sites in Britain. Inside this mound of chalk 350 feet long were five stone chambers containing the remains of 46 people

The development of long-distance trade between Britain and the Roman world caused great dislocations in the social and economic structure of the south-east – metals, hides, hunting dogs and slaves were exported in return for the luxuries of civilised life. To cope with it, society had to reorganise: the old hillforts were abandoned in the south, and new defensive *oppida* were built at route crossings. It was here that traders would cluster, coins would be minted and the law enacted. Many of these places – Canterbury, St Albans, Colchester – became major towns in the Roman period and have continued to thrive ever since.

By the time of the Roman invasion in AD 43 an urban structure had spread over most of the south-east of Britain up to a line joining Lincoln to Exeter. Significantly it was this line that the Romans chose in AD 43 or 44 to be the frontier of the province of Britannia, marking it with a frontier road – the Fosse Way – much of which survives today. Their intention was to contain the civilised part of the island and leave the rest of the barbarians to their own devices. The policy soon broke down and the armies were forced to conquer the north and west, but even after nearly 400 years of Roman rule the land beyond the old Fosse frontier line was barely civilised. In other words the prehistoric pattern determined the course of the Roman occupation.

There is still a great deal to be seen of our prehistoric heritage, the great neolithic monuments, the barrows, and the later hillforts, but it is a wasting asset. The last 20 years has seen the destruction of thousands of archaeological sites. No one could fairly argue against this so long as some of the best are preserved, but the pitifully inadequate funding made available by successive governments for the archaeological recording of sites about to be destroyed is little short of a national disgrace. The entire annual budget is about equivalent to the sum lost by British Steel in a single afternoon.

Let us hope that a greater awareness of our remarkable heritage will shame those in power into responsible action before it is too late.

AGRICULTURAL IMPLEMENTS

by Roy Brigden

For thousands of years, from the beginnings of farming to the accession of Queen Victoria, man relied entirely upon his own labour and that of his animals to till the soil and harvest the crops. Many of the rudimentary tools that performed basic tasks in the tribal age retained the same recognisable form through to the 19th century when some mechanisation replaced human or animal muscle.

Most of the hand tools known to Victorian farmers were used by their Roman counterparts in this country. Corn, for example, was first cut with the balanced sickle in the Iron Age and threshing with the jointed flail can be traced at least as far back as the later Roman period of the fourth century AD. Neither tool had been fully extinguished from British farm practice by the end of the Victorian period. Similarly, the characteristic designs of billhooks, mattocks and hoes excavated from Roman sites can be seen repeated in the 19th century catalogues of Sheffield tool makers. The real distinction was in the material of manufacture, for metallurgical advances in the industrial age made new steels widely available in the production of tougher and harder wearing edge tools.

Alongside this strong thread of continuity, evolutionary stages both gradual and rapid can be discerned. Comparatively few complete examples of implements used before the 19th century have survived so the story has in many cases to be pieced together with the additional help of illustrations and contemporary descriptions from the period concerned. By these means, it is clear the plough underwent a long phase of development: the Iron Age ard which at worst did little more than scratch the surface of the soil was refined by the Romans to cut a furrow slice and push it to one side. It was further modified from the 11th century when ploughs were first equipped with mouldboards that turned the slice over and buried the surface vegetation. These were sturdy implements drawn often by four oxen and capable of ploughing the heavy lands that had been brought under cultivation. Further understanding of the mechanics of ploughing from the 18th century resulted in the steady emergence of lighter, more efficient ploughs that could be pulled at a faster pace by a pair of horses even on the heavier soils.

Before the 19th century, the production of farm equipment was entirely in the hands of small groups of craftsmen scattered through the villages and market towns. Timber formed the basic raw material with harder wearing parts being fashioned out of wrought iron or wood with an iron casing. The implement maker was highly skilled in the versatile properties of wood: the springiness of ash made it first choice for horse shafts, while oak, with its tightly packed grain, possessed the strength necessary for the spokes of cart wheels. When selecting timber, the experienced eye picked out the gently curving bough that had naturally taken the shape of a plough beam or the forked branch that could with little difficulty be fashioned into a sturdy pitch fork.

Every item was a one-off, individually made and with the detail of shape and dimension dictated by the material from which it was fashioned. Replacements for worn or broken parts also had to be individually made and could result in a time-consuming return of the implement to its maker. As the market served by each craftsman was local, the equipment he produced reflected the traditions and geographical conditions of the area as well as the prejudices of his customers. Regional variations, therefore, abounded both amongst the smaller hand tools as well as the ploughs and other larger implements.

The rate of technological development in farming quickened dramatically after 1750, and over the following 100 years change, rather than continuity, became the

Medieval peasant using a sickle to cut corn. From an agricultural calendar of the 14th century

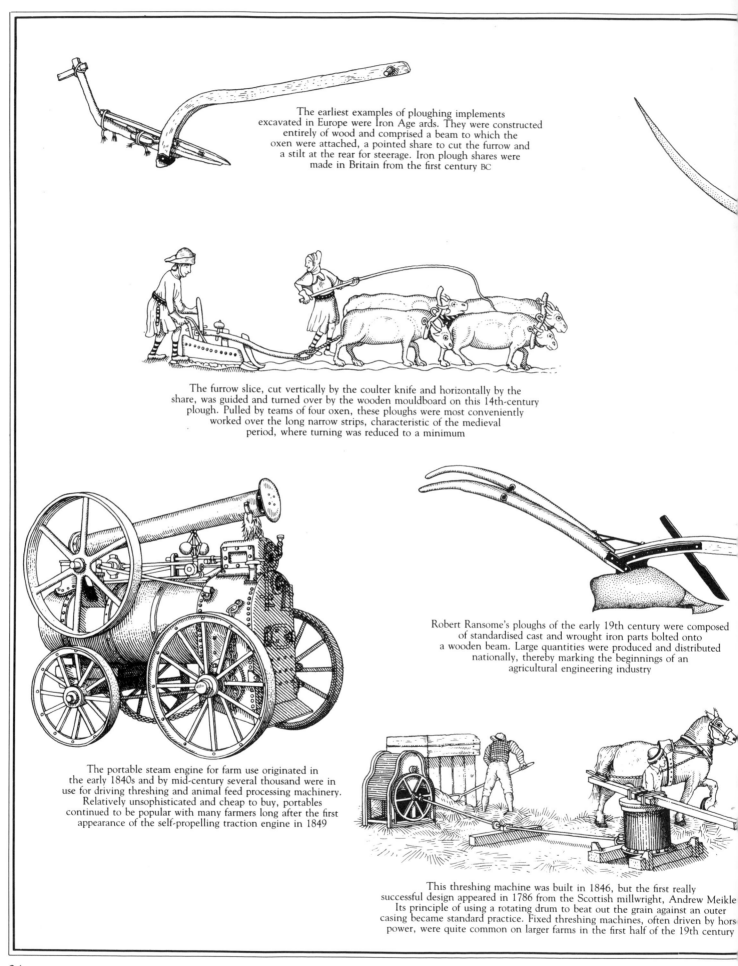

The earliest examples of ploughing implements excavated in Europe were Iron Age ards. They were constructed entirely of wood and comprised a beam to which the oxen were attached, a pointed share to cut the furrow and a stilt at the rear for steerage. Iron plough shares were made in Britain from the first century BC

The furrow slice, cut vertically by the coulter knife and horizontally by the share, was guided and turned over by the wooden mouldboard on this 14th-century plough. Pulled by teams of four oxen, these ploughs were most conveniently worked over the long narrow strips, characteristic of the medieval period, where turning was reduced to a minimum

Robert Ransome's ploughs of the early 19th century were composed of standardised cast and wrought iron parts bolted onto a wooden beam. Large quantities were produced and distributed nationally, thereby marking the beginnings of an agricultural engineering industry

The portable steam engine for farm use originated in the early 1840s and by mid-century several thousand were in use for driving threshing and animal feed processing machinery. Relatively unsophisticated and cheap to buy, portables continued to be popular with many farmers long after the first appearance of the self-propelling traction engine in 1849

This threshing machine was built in 1846, but the first really successful design appeared in 1786 from the Scottish millwright, Andrew Meikle Its principle of using a rotating drum to beat out the grain against an outer casing became standard practice. Fixed threshing machines, often driven by horse power, were quite common on larger farms in the first half of the 19th century

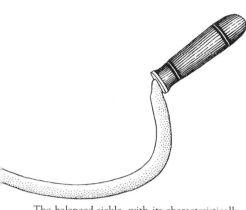

The balanced sickle, with its characteristically curved, serrated blade, first appeared in this country towards the end of the Iron Age. Its role as the principal tool of the corn harvest was not seriously challenged until the 19th century

Beating or threshing the grain from the ears of corn with a flail was known in Roman times. It remained in widespread use, representing one of the most labour intensive occupations on the farm, right through to the Victorian period. The ash staff was swung back over the head and then the short beater rod brought sharply down upon the corn spread on the barn floor

The reaper built by Patrick Bell of Scotland in 1828, while still a divinity student, was the first practical British machine for harvesting corn. Mechanised reaping spread quickly during the second half of the century after the American machines of Cyrus McCormick and Obed Hussey had aroused widespread interest at the Great Exhibition of 1851

The Grantham firm of Richard Hornsby & Sons started production in 1892 of the oil engine developed by a brilliant young engineer, Herbert Akroyd Stuart. It provided a cheap, reliable and durable power source for machines of all kinds. This was the beginning of the internal combustion engine revolution which, in the guise of the tractor, has transformed farming in the 20th century

**Farmworker of 1830 using
a harrow not much different
from some still in use today**

dominant feature. This was a period characterised by enclosure of farmland, rise in population, particularly in the non food producing urban sector, and inflation of farm prices during the Napoleonic Wars. All these factors acted as inducements to the introduction of quicker, less labour intensive and therefore more productive cultivation methods.

At the end of the 18th century, from his small foundry in Ipswich, Robert Ransome overcame the brittle qualities of cast iron to make it applicable to agriculture. This opened the way for large-scale production of standardised implements that soon could be distributed over a national market at low cost through the means of an expanding railway network. By 1850 a new industry of agricultural engineering had emerged with a large number of firms competing for the farmer's custom and in the process maintaining the momentum of mechanical innovation and improvement.

Some of these new enterprises had their roots in small family firms of blacksmiths and wheelwrights that had expanded and profited from the potential offered by agricultural machinery. They, for example, were responsible for making the threshing machine and seed drill, both inventions of the eighteenth century, progressively more widely available after 1800. The portable steam engine, suitable for use around the farm to drive processing machinery, appeared from the same sources in the late 1840s and underwent considerable refinement over the next 30 years to improve its efficiency and reduce running costs. Steam power did not quite fulfil all its early expectations for it proved to be too complicated and costly as a means of direct cultivation on any but the larger arable holdings. Sets of steam threshing tackle, however, whether owned or hired by the farmer, were a common sight in the second half of the century and for many provided the first enduring image of industrialised agriculture.

Although Patrick Bell demonstrated the feasibility of reaping corn by machine in the late 1820s, the real push towards mechanical harvesting came after 1850. Here American ideas and expertise, prompted by efforts to open up the vast grain producing prairies with scant labour resources, heavily influenced the British market. Both the reaper, in the form generally adopted in this country, and its successor the binder were essentially of transatlantic pedigree even though many were manufactured in this country by native firms. The horse-drawn binder, incorporating relatively sophisticated mechanisms to not only cut the corn but also tie the bundles automatically into sheaves, became popular here towards the end of the Victorian period by which time machines were accounting for the harvest of most of the country's corn crop.

At the same time a new inanimate workhorse, the internal combustion engine, was progressing from the purely experimental stage and beginning to feature in agricultural practice. It quickly developed as an indispensable small power source around the farm for driving a range of equipment from feed processing machinery and cream separators to saw benches. The next step was to use the engine as a light but powerful self-propelled unit capable of hauling cultivating implements across the field. The success of the tractor, however, and the revolutionary effect it had upon associated farm equipment, has been a phenomenon of the 20th century.

THE
ROMANS

by Donald Earl

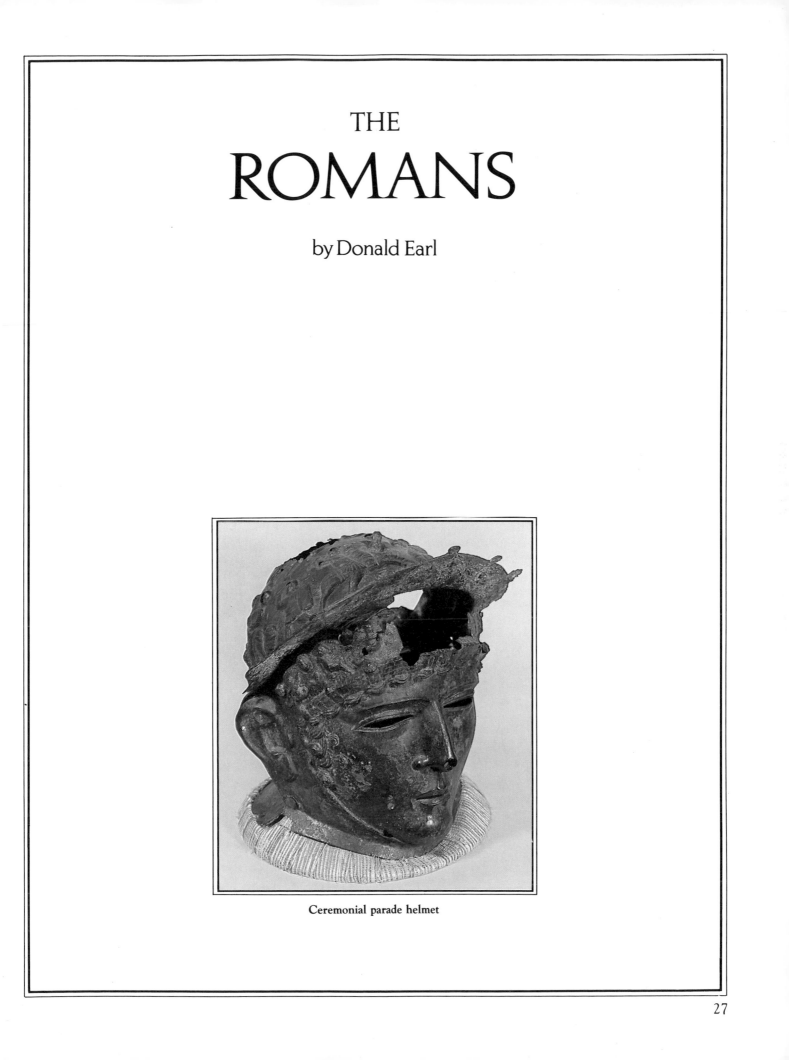

Ceremonial parade helmet

The first Roman to invade Britain with an army, wrote the historian Tacitus, was the deified Julius, 'but although he terrified the natives by winning a battle and got control of the coast, he may be seen as having drawn the island to the attention of posterity rather than as having handed it on to them as a possession'. The ancient sources generally agree with Tacitus in depreciating Caesar's two brief raids in 55 and 54 BC. Whether or not he had in mind the eventual conquest of at least the lowland parts of Britain, Caesar's immediate achievements were distinctly limited and in 54 he seems to have taken the initiative in offering acceptable terms in order to extricate his army before the onset of the equinoctial gales of late September. His claim to have received the submission of the islanders is hardly justified by the taking of hostages and the fixing of an annual tribute.

But what he had done was in one respect crucial: by his raids he had drawn Britain into the *imperium Romanum*, a hazy and imprecise concept which covered not merely the established and administered provinces, but all those areas in which Rome claimed to exercise power, authority or influence in however indirect or nebulous a manner. After Caesar, Britain was, at least potentially, an area of Roman interest.

Interest could be manifested or exploited in many ways. Augustus is credited with planning invasion on three occasions, and the Augustan poets assume and celebrate his intention to conquer the whole island as part of the subjection of the world to Roman control. In the event, in Britain as elsewhere, Augustus exercised influence through diplomacy, recognising some native chieftains as clients and receiving two, Tincommius and Dubnovellaunus, as refugees at Rome. Dubnovellaunus had been ejected by Shakespeare's 'radiant Cymbeline', Cunobelinus, who built up considerable power in southern Britain.

It was Claudius who finally took in hand the matter of Britain. The normal Roman impulsion to military glory was magnified in his case. Treated as a fool in the imperial household, despised by the upper classes, his accession to the imperial power in 41 BC was unexpected. The conquest of Britain offered military glory, prestige and an opportunity to impress the legions. The death of Cunobelinus and the expansionist policy of his sons provided the pretext. Claudius was to participate in person. Four legions, plus auxiliary troops (about 40,000 men in all), assembled at Boulogne. Some mutinied at the prospect of being sent beyond the Ocean, the boundary of the known world. Eventually the fleet landed, certainly at Richborough, possibly also at Dover and Lympne.

After several defeats, the Britons fell back on the Thames, 'near where the river flows into the ocean and forms a pool at high tide', which the Romans eventually crossed, perhaps near Westminster. Here the army halted to await the emperor. Claudius arrived in style with elephants and the Praetorian Guard to attend the capture of Camolodunum (Colchester). He stayed only about 16 days and then travelled slowly back to Rome, where he celebrated a triumph and in AD 51 erected a triumphal arch, on which he claimed to have been the first to have brought barbarian tribes beyond the Ocean under Roman control (so much for Caesar!) and to have received the surrender of 11 British kings. Further advance was greatly assisted by three British rulers in particular: Prasutagus of the Iceni, who became a client of Rome and whose widow, Boudicca (the name means 'Victory'), raised her revolt when the Romans decided upon the annexation of her husband's kingdom after his death in AD 60; Cartimandua, queen regnant, unique among the Celtic peoples, of the Brigantes, who betrayed Caractacus and whose matrimonial adventures (her name meant, perhaps, 'sleek filly') led to the Roman occupation of Yorkshire; and Cogidubnus, a loyal client of Rome, who was given Roman citizenship by Claudius, ruled at Chichester and perhaps occupied the magnificent palace at Fishbourne.

By the end of Claudius' reign the northern frontier of the Roman province stretched, roughly, diagonally from Lincoln to Caersws in Wales, and Exeter had been reached in the south-west. Once begun, the advance pressed remorselessly onwards, though not without setbacks and revolts, of which Boudicca's rebellion, with the sacking of Colchester, London and St Albans and the massacre of 70,000 inhabitants, was the most spectacular. But by AD 74 the Brigantes had made their last stand at Stanwick near Scotch Corner; by 78 Wales was pacified and legionary fortresses established at Caerleon and Chester. In 78 too there arrived the most famous of all the Roman governors of Britain, Cn. Julius Agricola, father-in-law of the historian Tacitus, who wrote his biography.

Agricola was an expansionist. In 79 he advanced to the Tyne–Solway line; the following year to that of the Forth and Clyde and reconnoitred as far as the Tay. Two years later he invaded south-west Scotland and in 83–84 came a push to the Spey, the establishment of a legionary fortress at Inchtuthill, the battle of Mons Graupius, in which Calgacus and 30,000 Caledonians were defeated, and the circumnavigation of Britain.

Agricola was recalled in 85. Thereafter attention turned to consolidation. The troops were progressively withdrawn from Scotland and the frontier established on the line of the Tyne and the Solway.

Then in AD 122, almost 80 years after Claudius' invasion, another Roman emperor came to Britain. Hadrian 'made for Britain, where he corrected many things and was the first to draw a wall along the length of 80 miles to separate the barbarians and the Romans'. Hadrian's Wall remained, despite a brief advance to the Forth–

Hadrian's Wall, Northumbria – a wonder of the Roman world, and one of its greatest feats of military engineering. It runs across rugged terrain between the Tyne and the Solway and marked a fixed frontier to Rome's British province

Clyde line by Antoninus Pius, which lasted less than 20
years, the definitive northern frontier of the Roman
province.

Behind this frontier the Romanisation of Britain,
begun haphazardly as a result of Caesar's raids, continued. To the Romans the essence of civilised and cul-
tured life lay in towns. It is clear that when they first
came to Britain they found nothing, whatever the existing pattern of settlement, that they could recognise as
a town. Even today it is broadly true that if the manufacturing towns which arose in the Industrial Revolution
are removed from the map of England the remaining
settlement pattern is that established under the Romans.

A first example to the natives was set under Claudius
by the deliberate foundation in AD 49 of Camolodunum
(Colchester), a *colonia* of retired Roman legionaries, on
the site of an abandoned legionary fortress. Towards the
end of the first century AD two more such *coloniae* were
established at Lincoln and Gloucester, again on the sites
of abandoned legionary fortresses. Later, with the spread
of urbanisation, the title *colonia* became honorary and
existing towns were promoted to the grade.

By AD 237 the prosperous civilian settlement which
had grown up across the river Ouse from the legionary
fortress at York had become a *colonia*. The status of
Londinium is unknown, but it seems unlikely that the
largest town in Britain, which became the provincial
capital and the seat of the diocesan vicar, did not
become a *colonia*. Below the *coloniae* ranked the
municipia, towns with Latin rather than full Roman
rights. The only probable example in Britain is
Verulamium (St Albans), plus, possibly, Londinium.

Different again were those towns now commonly referred to as *civitas* – capitals. On occupying new territory
the Romans preferred, if possible, to base administration
upon the already existing institutions and divisions.
Thus in Gaul and Britain the pre-Roman tribal structure
was retained and formed the foundation of the civilian
administration of the country. Each tribal area was given
local self-government as a *civitas* with a constitution and
careful prescription of rights and duties. Towns emerged
as administrative centres of such *civitates*.

By the mid-second century AD there were some 15 of
them. The earliest appear to have been Canterbury and
Verulamium, with Chelmsford. Between AD 60 and 80
there were added Caistor St Edmund, Chichester, Winchester and Silchester. In the 80s came Exeter,
Cirencester, Dorchester, Wroxeter and Leicester. Caerwent and Carmarthen in Wales and Brough-on-Humber
and Aldborough in Yorkshire reflect troop movements
after Hadrian's establishment of a permanent frontier.

All of these towns were essentially native in population, as were the numerous smaller settlements about

Defensive ditch which was part of the Antonine Wall near Falkirk.
The wall, between the Forth and the Clyde, extended Roman
domination into Scotland for about 20 years

which little is now known, although the village of Wall on Watling Street near Lichfield, Great Casterton and Ancaster on Ermine Street and Horncastle in north-east Lincolnshire still show remains typical of such posting-stations, small market towns and settlements attracted by the Roman road system. Similarly the *vici*, civilian settlements which naturally grew up around the military forts, have mostly disappeared from view, save at House-steads and Vindolanda (Chesterholm).

Such informal settlements differed radically from what we may call the towns proper. To a Roman a town was not a mere collection, however large, of houses. He had a clear and specific conception of the nature and function of a town. It lay within its own territory and this land formed an essential part of the town: hence the possibility of large displacement of the native population by the establishment of a veteran *colonia*. But the town was not merely a home for agricultural workers or a market centre for their produce: it functioned also as the administrative centre of its area. Thus a developed Roman town is characterised by certain specific and typical buildings.

The civic centre and market, the forum, was a large court surrounded by colonnades. At one end would be the basilica, a long hall for the administration of justice. Today Roman forums tend to lie buried beneath the centres of later towns, but Wroxeter does still show the column stumps of the long portico that bordered the east side of the Roman forum. Wroxeter also exhibits the best surviving example of another Roman civic amenity: the suite of public baths.

Bathing was to the Romans an indispensable necessity. Every town, villa and fort came to have its bath-house, sometimes very elaborate. The principle was akin to that of the Turkish bath.

Public baths tended to become the social centres of their towns and could, so our censorious sources inform us, become dens of every imaginable vice unless the authorities were vigilant. The best preserved military bath is that of the cavalry fort at Chesters on Hadrian's Wall. The sumptuous establishment at Bath was entirely *sui generis*; a sacred spring was developed by the Romans into a spa of great magnificence. Nearly the whole sequence is now on show and forms perhaps the most impressive monument to the Romans in Britain after such military works as Hadrian's Wall and the forts of the Saxon shore.

Roman hydraulic engineering was superb, but Britain, perhaps unfortunately for later ages, did not call for the great arched aqueducts which form such striking monuments in Spain, Gaul and North Africa. Water was brought into the towns in channels of simple construction which followed the contours of the ground, as can be seen most clearly at Wroxeter and Dorchester.

Sewers, too, were normal, running under or beside the main streets. A splendid example, over 150ft in length, 4–5ft high with six side channels, was discovered at York in 1972. There are other examples at

Verulamium, Lincoln and Bath. Connected to the sewers were public lavatories, which in towns were normally part of the public bath complex, the waste water from the baths being used to flush the lavatories. Roman lavatories afforded neither privacy from one's neighbours using the facility nor segregation of the sexes. The best surviving Roman lavatory is the military latrine at Housesteads, though the remains of the public jakes at Wroxeter are still visible. The wooden seats over the channels have, of course, long since perished.

Another essential urban structure was the temple. Once again, most in Britain have perished or vanished under existing towns. Colchester possessed a vast temple of Claudius in true Greco-Roman style with a high podium approached by a flight of steps: only the substructure, impressive enough, remains. This type was, in fact, rare in Britain. More common was the style known as Romano-Celtic with a central shrine surrounded by an ambulatory. The footings of one of the best examples survive at Maiden Castle in Dorset.

The Romans traditionally had a relaxed attitude to religious observance. Provided they did not impede celebration of the state rites on which the *Pax Deorum* and, thus, the well-being and power of Rome depended, or provide a focus for sedition and disturbance, unseemly

Wroxeter, Shropshire, has the best surviving example of Roman public baths in Britain (left). The honeycombed masonry that dominates the site was once the south wall of the palaestra, an exercise yard attached to the baths. Wroxeter, fourth largest Roman town in Brtain, also shows the column stumps of the portico bordering the east side of the forum. Above, Roman amphitheatre at Caerleon, Gwent. It was large enough to seat the 6,000-strong garrison of this legionary headquarters, where the best example of a Roman barrack block can be seen

or immoral practices, both native and imported cults were tolerated. Thus dedications to native deities continue, though, as with the native goddess Sulis and the Roman Minerva at Bath, syncretism tended to occur. With the Romans, too, came first the traders' and soldiers' worship of Mithras and, later, Christianity. The Walbrook Mithraeum in London became famous but is today reduced to the condition of a surburban rock-garden, to use A. J. P. Taylor's not unjust description; that at Carrawburgh on the Wall is a small, simple military shrine. Nearby is the shrine to Coventina, a nymph to whom offerings were thrown into a well. The earliest representation of Christ is a fourth century mosaic from Hinton St Mary, Dorset, now in the British Museum together with other Christian mosaics from Lullingstone and the Water Newton hoard, also from the fourth century, the earliest known collection of church plate from the Roman empire.

Around these great public buildings the streets, paved with local aggregates compacted by use, tended to be laid out in a more or less regular pattern. Houses ranged from simple narrow rectangular buildings stretching back from the street, often with the front part as a shop and living-quarters behind, to elaborate structures with a central court and decorated with mosaics and wall-

paintings. Naturally very few survive, but examples are visible at Canterbury, Verulamium and Caerwent.

Finally, in the course of time, all Roman towns of any size received defences. Three stages can usually be distinguished: an earth mound; the erection of a stone wall in front of the mound; the addition of bastions to the stone wall. Of all Roman town works the city walls, often rebuilt and added to in medieval times, have proved the most durable. Those at Silchester, unusual in that the Roman site did not commend itself for later habitation, and at Caerwent are particularly impressive, but much remains at Rochester, Gloucester, Cirencester, Colchester, St Albans, Caistor St Edmund, Lincoln, Horncastle and London.

The towns, forts and fortresses of Roman Britain were connected by an elaborate network of roads, military in original purpose and built, if possible, in a series of straight stretches. As with towns, so with roads the Roman practice commended itself to later centuries. Thus most of the magnificent road system lies buried under later constructions: Ermine Street, Watling Street, the Fosse Way and so on.

Few stretches of Roman road can now be seen in anything approaching their original state. A section near Holtye in East Sussex retains its metalling of iron slag from the nearby iron works in the Sussex Weald. Traces of the original surface survive also on the three-mile stretch north from Shepton Mallet over Beacon Hill. At Blackpool Bridge in the Forest of Dean a narrow Roman road still has its curbstones, while the remains of the road from Ilkley to Manchester on Blackstone Edge near Rochdale is unique in being not metalled but paved with stone setts.

Perhaps the most impressive remnant of an original Roman road is Wade's Causeway on Wheeldale Moor in

Cold plunge bath in Bath, Somerset, where a sacred tribal spring was developed by the Romans into a spa of great magnificence and re-dedicated to the goddess Minerva. Romans always took a cold plunge after a hot bath to close the pores

Yorkshire. This ran from Whitby to the Roman fort at Malton, but only the foundation slabs now remain. Elsewhere all that survives and is visible of Britain's earliest true road system are the embankments which raised the road surface above the surrounding land to ensure good drainage. No Roman bridge survives intact, but a few abutments and piers may still be seen, notably at Piercebridge, near Scotch Corner, and at Chesters, on Hadrian's Wall, where the north face of the abutment displays a phallus carved for good luck.

Roads and towns – appearances may deceive. All over the Roman empire the most striking monuments relate to military occupation and urban culture. Yet the empire was and remained, to an extent to which we can now hardly imagine, an agricultural enterprise. The typical inhabitant of the Roman world was a peasant engaged in agriculture at little above subsistence level, living in a world of static technology in which manufacture was small-scale, fragmented and local, the population stable and largely immobile, local ties extremely strong. His horizon was bounded by the local fair or market where goods could be exchanged, often by barter. Of those who lived on the land in Roman Britain we know even less than of those who lived in the towns.

The one rural institution which has left major remains is the villa. Today the word is usually applied to a residential building, but in Latin it denoted the whole farm complex, land as well as buildings. In Britain the villa emerged slowly and never supplanted the native type of farmstead, which continued to exist beside it. Few villa buildings are found before the second century, though there does seem to have been a concentration around Verulamium after Boudicca's rebellion. They may, perhaps, represent the country seats of the local native gentry, but lack the later refinements of mosaics and baths. Oddly enough, one of the earliest of all Romano-British villas, built in the last decades of the first century, remained unsurpassed in size and magnificence: Cogidubnus's great palace at Fishbourne, which presumably stood originally at the centre of an estate of comparable size.

As wealth grew in the second century, so more and more farmers replaced their native-style farm-houses with more modern, sophisticated structures, while those who already possessed villas tended to enlarge them. The increased building of large and elaborate town-houses at the same time suggests that the upper classes had begun to move from the country into the towns. The country villas thus may have been the residences of an up-and-coming rural 'middle-class' or of immigrants from Europe, now that conditions in the province were more settled.

The end of the second century was a period of disturbance and upheaval, culminating in an attempted usurpation of the imperial power by the governor, Clodius Albinus, supported, perhaps, by many of the rural gentry. Clodius stripped Britain of troops, crossed to France and was defeated and killed near Lyons by the emperor Septimius Severus. Septimius, together with his son Caracalla, conducted a campaign in north Scotland and died at York on 4 February, AD 211. This may have been the period when most towns received their earth defences and some villas seem to have been abandoned, as at Ditchley and Lullingstone.

The province, however, recovered and the fourth century was the great and golden age of villa building in Britain. These now tended to be large, elaborate and sophisticated structures, decorated with wall-paintings and mosaics and providing all the comforts and amenities, including bath-suites, to be found in the towns. Not that the execution always matched the intention. The Venus from Rudston, now in Hull, like the Wolf and Twins from Aldborough in Leeds City Museum, illustrate the comical results when an owner's desire to display his classical learning and to identify with the dominant power was not matched by the technical skill of a presumably local craftsman. A similar discrepancy between intention and execution in a different medium is the ambitious carving of Venus and two water-nymphs at their ablutions from High Rochester, now in Newcastle. These are all northern examples.

The great majority of villa sites are, in fact, grouped to the south and east of a line drawn from the Severn to the Wash, with an extension northwards through Lincolnshire into the East Riding. A few occur in the Vale of York, the West Midlands and South Wales, but almost none in Devon and Cornwall. In other words, villas were most concentrated in the original Claudian province and in those areas where the agricultural land was best and where access to the road-system and the towns was easiest.

The villa, in its original sense, may have been a

Roman road across the moors at Blackstone Edge, near Rochdale. It ran from Ilkley to Manchester and is unique because it is paved with stone setts. Other roads were metalled

largely self-contained unit, fabricating for itself most of the articles and implements needed. In that it would have conformed to the general pattern of manufacture throughout the Roman world: the predominance of the cottage industry and small workshop production. The primitive nature of land transport which determined this general pattern also, conversely, demanded that some commodities be produced on a larger scale at the source of their raw materials.

For metal, glass and pottery it was easier to transport the refined metal or the finished article. Thus gold was not only mined but also refined at Dolaucothi; lead, important for water-works (the great bath at Bath was originally lined with lead), and silver were cast into ingots at the mines, usually open-cast; copper was similarly mined and processed in Shropshire, Wales and Anglesey, as was tin, in which the Romans were, surprisingly, not much interested, in Cornwall. Iron too, the most common metal in Britain, the most useful and the most difficult to extract, was smelted and prepared for marketing at the mines. Similarly glass, of poor quality suitable for windows or the ancient equivalent of pub glasses, was made near the source of the raw materials, as was pottery, the best known of all Romano-British manufacturing processes.

Much of this production was for local use, but Britain was also connected to a common market that stretched across Europe to Asia Minor. Samian pottery was imported in great quantity from Gaul, and at least one ship loaded with it foundered at the mouth of the Thames. Wine, oil and *garum*, the ubiquitous and revolting fish sauce so essential to all Roman cuisine, came in from the Continent, as did metal work, first from Italy and later from Gaul, including silver-ware of the highest standard like the Mildenhall treasure. Fine glass was imported from the Rhineland. A burial at Holborough in Kent has given up a fragment of damask silk, perhaps from China, while the York sewer has produced a piece of silk woven in the west from Chinese material.

In return Britain exported gold and lead, both imperial monopolies, woollen goods, furs and skins. British oysters, Colchester natives, were certainly sent to Rome – a hazardous undertaking, one would have thought – and Yorkshire jet has been found in the Rhineland. Such trade requires ports, and it was under the Romans that Britain acquired its first proper harbours. Once again, almost all traces of the Roman works have disappeared. The lower courses of a Roman lighthouse (the upper courses are medieval) still stand uniquely at Dover and form the only easily visible remnant of the docks and harbour works of Roman Britain.

Not only docks are demanded by trade, but also a currency. Iron Age Britain had had in its later phases a primitive currency based on gold and silver coins but closely tied to the tribal structure. With the coming of the Romans Britain became part of a common system of currency. Britain itself possessed no mints except those established by the usurper Carausius at London and,

possibly, Colchester, in the third century and closed by Constantine in AD 326. Roman coins circulating in Britain were thus imported from the Continent, mainly to pay the army and the civil administration, through whom the coins passed into general circulation. Money was also brought in by immigrants and settlers and in return for the sale of British goods overseas. Coins in the Roman world were important not merely as items of exchange but also as the only available form of mass communication. What was put on them was of consequence. Britannia makes her first appearance on a Hadrianic issue dated to AD 119–22 and recurs as one of the commonest coins of Antoninus Pius. Imperial victories were not inappropriate for mass propaganda.

The army and the civil administration assured the stability of the whole. The Roman army was, through much of the period of occupation, a fearsomely efficient instrument. It consisted of two quite distinct forces: the legions, nominally of 6,000 men each, recruited originally from men with full Roman citizenship and commanded by a *legatus* of senatorial rank; and the *auxilia*, recruited from non-citizens from the provinces, supplemented by recruits from the areas in which they were stationed, mustered in cohorts if they were infantry or *alae* (wings or squadrons) if cavalry and officered by non-senatorial Roman citizens. It was the *auxilia*, stationed permanently in forts, who were expected to do most of the ordinary fighting and frontier defence. Chesters and Housesteads on the Wall, Hardknott in the Lake District and Caernarvon are the best surviving examples of auxiliary forts. The crack troops were the legions, kept in reserve for serious emergency. The size of the army in Britain naturally varied with time and necessity.

Several legionary fortresses were built and abandoned, but eventually three permanent bases established themselves, Caerleon, Chester and York. Roman forts conformed to a standard pattern. Externally there was, in the earliest examples, a turf or clay rampart with a wooden breastwork and a wall-walk on top and gateways and towers, also of timber. The reconstruction at the Lunt near Baginton gives a vivid, though atypical impression. Later the defences were built of stone, with one or more ditches outside. In each side was a gate and between the gates ran the two main roads of the camp at, more or less, right angles. In the centre stood the headquarters building with a large courtyard in front usually surrounded on three sides by a colonnade and leading to a cross-hall roofed and large enough to accommodate the whole contingent to be addressed by the commanding officer from the raised tribunal at one end. At the back in the centre was the shrine for the regimental standards and the statue of the emperor. The pay-chest was kept under the floor.

The headquarters building was flanked on one side by the commander's house and on the other by two or more granaries. A workshop and hospital are also found. The rest of the fort was taken up by barrack blocks, each

Remains of a fine Roman town house in Colliton Park, Dorchester (top picture). It was built in the fourth century, in an unconventional L-shape, with separate living quarters for servants. One living room was heated by underfloor hypocausts. Bottom picture: caldarium (hot bath house) of the fine bath suite at Chedworth, Gloucestershire, which formed a fourth century addition to a second century villa. Gloucestershire is more thickly scattered with Roman villas than any other part of Britain

designed to hold 80 men and divided into cubicles, with more spacious accommodation at the end for the centurion. If the garrison was a cavalry unit there would also be stables. The clearest impression of a Roman barrack block can be gained from the legionary example at Caerleon.

The permanent legionary fortresses and auxiliary forts by no means exhaust the list of Roman military works. The army on the march, whenever it halted for the night, erected a camp in proper form with a ditch, earth rampart and a timber palisade on top of the rampart. Few of these marching camps are now visible to the eye at ground level except as anonymous humps in the ground, but aerial photography reveals them in astonishing quantity. There are two especially fine examples at Y Pigwn in Powys and Rey Cross in County Durham.

Of all the Roman military works the most extraordinary is Hadrian's Wall, a monument to rival any in the Roman world. It is a complex structure, the building of

which was an undertaking staggering in its magnitude. The Wall itself, running across the Tyne–Solway isthmus, varying in thickness in its final form and changing from stone to turf west of the river Irthing, was only the centre of a complicated series of works. On the north side was a ditch. On the Wall itself was a fortlet at intervals of one Roman mile and between each fortlet two turrets. South of the Wall lay the Vallum, a flat-bottomed ditch with a berm and then a turf mound on either side. This whole earthwork was some 120 feet across and made a formidable barrier marking off the military zone. The reconstructions at Vindolanda (Chesterholm) of a stone turret, a stretch of turf wall and a timber milecastle gateway give a clear impression of what such works may once have looked like. To the rear of the Wall were supporting forts.

Britain shared the later fragmentation of the provinces. At the beginning of the third century it was divided into two; Constantius in 296 divided it into four and a fifth province was carved out by Theodosius in 369. The smallness of the governor's and procurator's staffs was made possible by the regular Roman practice of entrusting administration below the provincial level to the local authorities. The whole Roman empire, it has been truly said, was in essence a vast exercise in local self-government.

Britain made no contribution to Latin secular literature, and Roman writers were interested in this remote province only in the most selective manner. The people of Roman Britain can reach us only through their artefacts and monuments, especially through their tombstones. The most striking revelation of such evidence is the racial diversity produced by Britain's membership of the Roman empire.

Regina, a Catuvellaunian girl from Hertfordshire, married her master Barates. She was an ex-slave, perhaps sold by her parents; he came from Palmyra in Syria. When she died at South Shields, aged 30, he erected an ornate tombstone with an inscription in both Latin and Palmyrene. An even more splendid tombstone from the same place commemorates the freedman Victor, who originated from Mauretania. The fort at South Shields, Arbeia, was in the third century garrisoned by the Fifth Cohort of Gauls, in the fourth by a unit of boatmen from the Tigris. At Burgh by Sands was a unit of Moors, at Housesteads a cohort of Tungrians from Belgium. Examples could be multiplied. Africans, Greeks, Germans, Gauls, Spaniards and men from the Danube and Balkans are all attested in Britain. Conversely units of Britons are found on the Danubian frontier and the first recorded British sailor, Aemilius son of Saenius, was a Devon man, serving with the German fleet on the Rhine and buried at Cologne.

As part of the Roman empire Britain could not escape the effects of the barbarian invasions and the collapse of central control in the second half of the third century. From AD 259 the island was part of a separatist Gallic empire and the south east became increasingly insecure

Floor mosaic of a nymph and satyr on a villa site at Chedworth, Gloucestershire. The fine mosaics here, and at nearby North Leigh, are thought to have been executed by the same craftsman, who was probably based at the major Roman town of Cirencester

because of Saxon raids. In 286 Carausius, commander of the British fleet, declared himself Emperor of Britain and North Gaul. It is from this troubled period that the most spectacular Roman military works, after Hadrian's Wall, come: the forts of the Saxon shore; Brancaster, Burgh Castle, Walton Castle (which fell down the cliff in the 18th century), Bradwell, Reculver, Richborough, Dover, Lympne, Pevensey and Porchester, of which Richborough, Pevensey and Portchester are today the most striking. Similar forts were built in the west and Cardiff Castle, though a modern rebuilding, shows what formidable defences they were.

Britain was restored to the empire by Constantius, who rebuilt Hadrian's Wall, the Pennine forts and legionary fortresses at Chester and York, where he died on 25 July 306 and where his son Constantine was proclaimed emperor. There followed the last period of peace and prosperity, but in AD 367 a great barbarian conspiracy of Picts, Scots and Saxons overwhelmed the island. Theodosius visited Britain to restore the situation, but the western empire was disintegrating and the end for Roman Britain not far off. In 383 Magnus Maximus revolted and withdrew soldiers from Wales and northern Britain to serve his ambitions on the Continent. The end of Hadrian's Wall came in about 400. In 401 more troops were withdrawn to defend Italy. Roman control in Britain collapsed, rebellion and revolt became endemic. In 410 the Britons appealed to the Emperor Honorius. He replied to the *civitates* of Britain that they must provide for their own defence. About 446 a final, desperate plea was made to Rome: 'To Agitius (Aetius), three times consul, come the groans of the Britons . . . the barbarians drive us to the sea, the sea drives us to the barbarians; between the two means of death we are either killed or drowned.'

This time there was no reply. After some four centuries Britain once more stood alone on the edge of the world.

MARITIME TRANSPORT

by Stephen Riley

Britain, surrounded as it is by water and scored by rivers and streams, has a boat and shipbuilding tradition stretching back into the Stone Age and beyond. Log boats capable of carrying heavy goods or being propelled at good speed by 20 or more paddles are known to have been used in sheltered waters almost 3,000 years ago.

Boats made of skin or hide stretched over a wicker framework, forerunners of the coracle still used today, were described by Julius Caesar, who subsequently copied them to enable his men to ford rivers. That skin boats were capable of long and hazardous sea passages is revealed in the tenth century account of St Brendan's voyage across the Atlantic via Iceland, recently successfully retraced by Tim Severin's traditionally-built, hide-covered boat Brendan.

From contemporary accounts the seagoing ships encountered by the Romans around the coast of Britain may well have been broad, flat-bottomed craft with high bow and stern, their oak planks caulked with seaweed and propelled by leather sails rather than oars.

The Vikings subsequently imported their distinctive shipbuilding tradition from Scandinavia. Their graceful double-ended ships had clinker-laid (overlapping) planking fastened to a backbone of keel and ribs, a rudder hung over the stern on the starboard or 'steerboard' side and a large rectangular sail that enabled them to sail reasonably close to windward. Light, seaworthy cargo ships such as these, regularly trading to Iceland, Greenland and the Mediterranean, were particularly suited to navigating well inland up British rivers to load and unload their cargoes. As the Bayeux Tapestry shows, it was in ships of this type that William of Normandy ferried his invading army across the Channel in 1066.

The expansion of seaborne trade in North Europe in the late 12th and early 13th centuries, notably among the Hanseatic merchants, demanded a more efficient cargo vessel. The single-masted cog, deep-draughted and roomy, with its rudder hung on a straight stern post, had far better sailing qualities than its round end, shallow draught predecessors.

The origins of the most revolutionary development in sea transport – the three-masted ship of the early 15th century – are uncertain but its consequences were remarkably far reaching. Combining a broad deep hull with a more complex sail plan resulted in a more manoeuvrable and weatherly ship capable, as Columbus' Santa Maria showed, of making trans-oceanic voyages of discovery.

Fighting at sea had traditionally involved soldiers throwing spears or firing arrows at opposing ships from the deck or high raised 'castles' at bow and stern, but in 1514 the Henry Grâce à Dieu, flagship of Henry VIII, marked the arrival of the purpose-built warship, firing heavier guns through gunports on the upper deck.

The English galleon of the Elizabethan navy, with its superior sailing qualities and improved gun arrangement confirmed itself as the most efficient and successful fighting machine in the Northern world with the defeat of the Spanish Armada in 1588.

Seventeenth century warships steadily improved in handling and firepower. The introduction of the whipstaff, giving the helmsman greater control over steering, and the addition of sails to help turn the ship, significantly improved their tactical manoeuvrability and by the early years of the 18th century had settled in essentials the outline of the major warship for the next 200 years.

The ideal general purpose merchant ship of the 18th century was the North country 'cat', based on the Dutch fluyt, or flyboat. They had wide spacious holds,

8th-century Viking boat

This hypothetical reconstruction represents one of three boats dated to the Bronze Age, c.1500 BC, which were found on the foreshore of the River Humber at North Ferriby, Yorkshire between 1937 and 1963. No nails were used, the oak planks were stitched together with yew withies and the joints made watertight with moss

The Skuldelev Boat is a small Viking cargo ship dated from about AD 1000 discovered in Denmark's Roskilde Fjord in the late 1950s. She was about 13 metres long and was primarily a sailing vessel with provision for seven oars as auxiliary power. Light enough to be hauled overland for short distances and shallow enough to be used in rivers, she may well have crossed the North Sea to Britain

The cat, or bark, c.1750. The bluff bows and almost flat floors, together with its broad cheek 'pink' stern distinguish the cat as a sturdy vessel for bulky cargoes. Carrying capacity and the ability to take the ground were more important than speed in this type of ship, which was developed in the North Sea and the Baltic

Many early steamers were employed as short-sea passenger ferries subsidised by Government mail contracts until marine steam engines could be made more efficient. When the little Irish Sea paddle steamer Sirius became the first vessel to cross the Atlantic under continuous steam power, in 1837, her side lever engines were fed with steam at a pressure of only 5 lb per sq in and consumed 24 tons of coal per day

A dramatic improvement in engine efficiency enabled the compound-engined Agamemnon, in 1866, to steam the 8,500 miles between England and Mauritius without refuelling. She could also carry 2,800 tons of cargo, almost three times that carried by most sailing ships, on her passage out to China

Edge-joined, overlapping planks, known as
clinker-building were a notable feature of the cog, a
flat-bottomed, steep-sided vessel developed in
the 12th century. For about 150 years the cog dominated
the trade routes of Northern Europe and must have
been a familiar sight in British ports, carrying salt fish,
hides, grains, wool and shipbuilding materials

This illustration is based on the drawing
of a kraeck or carrack (c.1470) by a Flemish artist,
which is the most detailed picture known of
a 15th-century three-masted ship. It shows clearly
the carrack's lofty fore and aftercastles and the
additional fore and mizzen sails which, by providing
leverage at bow and stern, helped to make
the ship easier to steer

The iron-built and screw-propelled Great
Britain built in 1843 and now undergoing restoration
in Bristol following her salvage from the Falkland
Islands in 1970, represents a remarkable milestone
in the transition from sailing ships
to power-driven vessels

Despite the inroads of the triple-engined steamer, steel-built,
3,000 ton four-masted barques and full-rigged ships were built in considerable
numbers in the 1890s. Their immensely strong, square section hulls, often over
300 feet long, were cavernous cargo-carriers – guano and nitrate from South
America, jute from Calcutta and grain from California and Australia

**19th-century English
clipper ship**

were cheap to build and maintain, needed small crews and were good cargo-carriers with an adequate turn of speed.

Technical innovation produced steady rather than sweeping changes during the 18th century. In the early years the familiar steering wheel replaced the whipstaff; triangular headsails, such as the jib, were introduced, making warship and merchantman more manoeuvrable and able to sail closer to the wind more safely. The introduction of copper sheathing below the waterline after 1760 was aimed at solving the perennial problem facing wooden ships – that of minimising the effects of the destructive 'ship worm', *teredo navalis*, and trying to minimise marine growth.

During the late 18th and early 19th centuries numerous experimental craft employing steam power and paddle wheels ushered in the industrial revolution at sea. Following the Clyde-built wooden paddle steamer Comet of 1812, the first merchant steamship in Europe, the subsequent early steamers, fitted with low pressure boilers and side lever engines, consumed vast quantities of coal making them suitable only for coastal routes and short sea crossings.

Although Brunel's wooden paddle steamer Great Western had started the first regular steamship service across the Atlantic from Bristol to New York in 1837, it was clear that the wooden hull inherited from the sailing ship was not suited to the vibration and strains exerted by the steam engine and paddle wheels. Brunel's second ship, the Great Britain, built in 1843, incorporated the latest important technical advances. She was built of iron, had a screw propeller instead of paddles and as the first ocean-going, screw-propelled iron steamship was the forerunner of all later steamships. Technical innovation was not confined to the merchant service: no less important was the appearance, in 1860, of the Royal Navy's Warrior. Built of iron and 380 feet long, she was larger, faster and more heavily armed than anything that had gone before. She effectively made all other warships obsolete overnight.

The successful introduction of the compound engine in 1866 – consuming up to 40 per cent less coal by using the same steam in two cylinders rather than one – marked a notable milestone in marine engineering and in conjunction with the opening of the Suez Canal three years later, enabled the steamer seriously to challenge sailing ships on long distance trade routes.

Advances in industrial technology were exploited by steamer and sailing ship alike: composite ships, built of iron and wood, such as the clippers Cutty Sark and Thermopylae, were briefly successful in the profitable China tea trade for which they were built. Iron and later steel sailing ships equipped with all the latest labour-saving devices, continued to compete for cargoes in the bulk-carrying trades until after the turn of the century.

It was the efficient triple expansion engine, fed with high pressure steam from steel boilers, and successfully demonstrated by the s.s. Aberdeen in 1881, that sealed the fate of the sailing ship beyond doubt.

Following the sensation created by the Hon. Charles Parsons' turbine-driven Turbinia at the 1897 Diamond Jubilee Naval Review, by 1907 steam turbines were propelling the record-breaking Cunard liner Mauretania across the North Atlantic at over 27 knots.

THE
DARK AGES

by Peter Sawyer

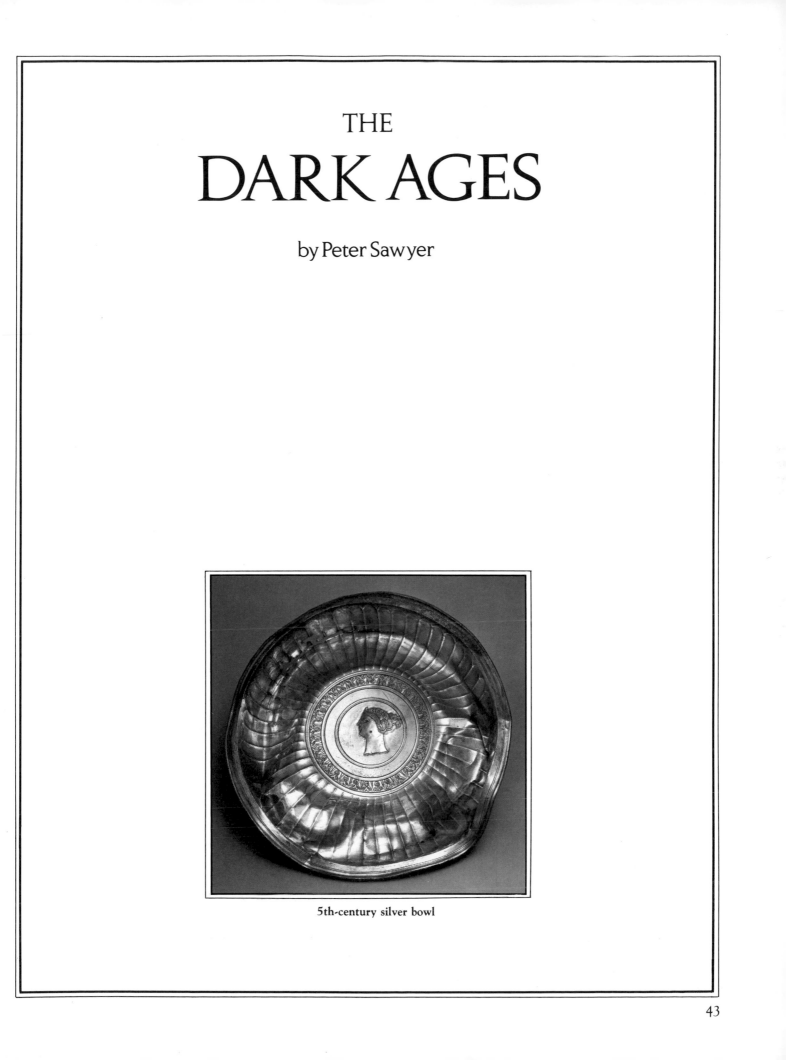

5th-century silver bowl

When, in 410, the Emperor Honorius told the Britons to defend themselves, the way was clear for other forces, less magnificent but more persistent than those of Rome, to reshape the political structure of these islands. The early stages of the process cannot be traced in any detail for our sources are inadequate and in the absence of reliable evidence legends have flourished around such figures as the invaders Hengist and Horsa or the British hero Arthur. It is however clear that by the beginning of the seventh century independent groups of German invaders, variously identified as Angles, Saxons or Jutes, had established themselves in Britain and had begun to create the familiar kingdoms of early English history. That of Kent took its name from a British tribe, but the Saxons, distinguished as West, South and East, gave their names to the kingdoms of Wessex, Sussex and Essex. The East Angles, divided into North and South Folk, were separated by the barrier of the Wash and the Fens from other Anglian tribes who, in the seventh century, were brought together to form the kingdom of the Mercians. North of the Humber a similar process of conquest and absorption was creating Northumbria, and extending it to the Firths of Forth and Solway. To the west, British kingdoms preserved their independence in Devon and Cornwall, in Wales and, in the north-west, Strathclyde. Further north there were Pictish kingdoms and to the west, in what is now Argyll, the Scottish kingdom of Dal Riata had been established in the fifth century by invaders from Ireland.

This pattern of kingdoms was disrupted in the ninth century by the Vikings. These Scandinavian pirates at first raided coastal targets, such as Lindisfarne and Iona, both attacked before 800, but in 865 a much larger force landed in East Anglia intent on conquest. They quickly seized control of East Anglia, and of southern Northumbria, where they created the kingdom of York. Later they took control of eastern Mercia, an area later described as the Five Boroughs; Derby, Nottingham, Leicester, Stamford and Lincoln. Their attempt to conquer Wessex was successfully resisted by Alfred. It was his children, Edward and Æthelfleda, who began the conquest of Danish territory, and the work was continued by Edward's son, Athelstan (924–39) who was even more ambitious and attempted to dominate the Scots. These West Saxon successes naturally provoked opposition and in 937 Athelstan faced an alliance of Scots, Strathclyde Britons and Northumbrians, led by a Viking king from Dublin, Olaf Guthfrithsson. Athelstan's defeat of this formidable array at the battle of Brunanburh was justly celebrated, at least by the West Saxons. The independent spirit of Northumbria was, however, not easily overcome and even after the expulsion and death of the last Scandinavian king of York, Erik Bloodaxe, the Northumbrians continued to be a source of trouble for English kings until after the Norman Conquest.

The consolidation of this English 'Empire' was under-taken by Edgar (959–75), with the enthusiastic support of churchmen who were eager to encourage church reform with royal backing, and by Edgar's son, Ethelred (978–1016). They found it necessary to ensure the neutrality, if not the support, of the Scots by abandoning their claims to Cumbria and to Lothian.

In Scotland itself a similar process of consolidation was taking place under the leadership of the Scottish dynasty of Dalriada. In the ninth century one of these kings, Kenneth mac Alpin, was recognised as king of the Picts, and this claim passed to his heirs. There were however many claimants and it was only in the eleventh century that one branch achieved dominance by violently removing its rivals. The most famous victim was Macbeth, who ruled from 1040–57 and was killed by Malcolm III (1058–93) thus revenging his own father's death at Macbeth's hand.

Ethelred's achievement is overshadowed by the Viking attacks which were resumed on a large scale in his reign. These attacks exposed the weaknesses and internal tensions that were only to be expected in a land that had recently been unified, and the king's reputation has consequently suffered. There is however no concealing the reality of the defeat he suffered and in 1013 the Danish King Svein was recognised as king, and Ethelred driven into exile in Normandy. Svein did not enjoy his victory long, he died in the following year, but his son Cnut was eventually acknowledged as sole King in 1016. For the next 25 years England was ruled by Cnut and his two sons but in 1042 the Old English dynasty was restored in the person of Edward the Confessor, Ethelred's son. When he died childless in 1066 the way was open for another struggle for England and its wealth. The contenders were the Norwegian king, Harald Hardrada, Edward's crowned successor, Harold Godwinson, and William, Duke of Normandy. When William emerged as the victor England had suffered its last conquest.

The history of Britain in the two centuries after the Roman withdrawal is very obscure: our sources are few and their interpretation disputed. It is only in the seventh century that, following the conversion of the English to Christianity, our evidence becomes more abundant and our knowledge, although still limited, more certain – largely thanks to the 'Ecclesiastical History of the English People', completed in 731 by Bede, a monk in the Northumbrian monastery of Jarrow. The early stages in the reshaping of Britain are therefore unclear but there are reasons to think that some semblance of Roman methods of government persisted for a while after 410. There were certainly contacts between Britain and the still-Roman province of Gaul and in 429 Germanus, bishop of Auxerre, came to Britain to deal with an outbreak of heresy. Latin speech survived but coins were neither minted nor imported, the towns

Awe-inspiring royal helmet, from an age that teemed with kings, found in the treasures of the 7th-century Sutton Hoo ship burial, East Anglia, now in the British Museum

decayed and villas were abandoned.

Little by little Britain became more Celtic as it became less Roman, and power passed into the hands of native rulers. These men fought each other, but they also had to contend with invaders who coveted the wealth that was still enjoyed by the former Roman province. The main threat was thought by contemporaries to be the Picts who lived in Caledonia, beyond the Roman Wall; and one British ruler, called Vortigern, recruited some Germans to help the defence of Britain against them. The decision was disastrous, for these warriors, reinforced by others, rebelled, caused widespread disruption and in the end conquered large areas of lowland Britain. Small wonder that Vortigern was execrated by later generations of Britons.

The German invaders who came from the other side of the North Sea were mainly Saxons and Angles, but the Britons followed Roman example and called them all Saxons, a tradition nowadays represented by the Scottish word Sassenach. In time the descendants of the invaders themselves preferred the name Angle, perhaps because of the dominance at that time of Anglian kings, and this preference led to their language being called English, even by the West Saxon king Alfred. By the 11th century their territory was called *Englaland*, the land of the English.

By the year 600 these English invaders had seized control of the Severn estuary and so cut off the Britons of Wales from those living in the south-west, later distinguished as the West Welsh. Some time before 700 another group of English invaders, originally based on the north-east coast, had gained control of Carlisle, thus isolating the Britons of Strathclyde, whose capital long remained at Dumbarton, the fort, or *dun*, of the Britons. The triangular struggle between the Strathclyde Britons, the Northumbrians and the Picts was complicated by the establishment in the fifth century of a Scottish, that is Irish, kingdom of Dál Riata in what is now more or less Argyll. Like the fifth-century English settlements, this proved to be the basis for later expansion and in the ninth century a king of Dál Riata, Kenneth mac Alpin, became king of the Picts as well and so created the more familiar kingdom of the Scots.

Ireland itself had never been conquered by the Romans but it was converted to Christianity in the fifth century and the records preserved by Irish churches provide a precious glimpse of an archaic, Iron Age society with many kings. The Irish churches produced many remarkable memorials, annals and poetry as well as magnificent manuscripts, metalwork and stone carving. Ireland played a key role in the development of Dark Age Britain. Some rulers from other parts of the British Isles sought exile there, some married Irish wives, and

Beowulf's heroes may have caroused here . . . Excavations at Yeavering, near Wooler, revealed a Northumbrian king's palace. The great hall, part of an elaborate complex of timber buildings surrounded by a defensive stockade, was over 80 feet long

Could this have been Camelot? Some legends place it here. Cadbury, Somerset, was certainly a hill fort dating from the Iron Age and refurbished in the late fifth century when a massive gateway and a large timber feasting hall were built

before the English had schools of their own it was a favoured place in which young English converts could study.

In the ninth century the rulers of Britain – Britons, Picts, English, Welsh and Scots – had to face a new enemy, the Vikings: Scandinavian pirates who, thanks to their skill in making and handling sailing ships, had the great advantages of surprise and mobility. Their early attacks were on a small scale and directed against such coastal targets as the island monasteries of Lindisfarne and Iona but by the middle of the century the raiding bands were much larger and their aim was no longer simply plunder and extortion, but permanent conquest and settlement. By the end of the century they controlled Orkney and Shetland, large parts of the Hebrides and the Isle of Man, and they had established bases in Ireland, the most famous being at Dublin. By 880 Scandinavians also ruled large areas of England, from East Anglia to Yorkshire, later known as the Danelaw, and many of the Scandinavian warriors had settled there. These colonists had a remarkable effect on the English language and imported many words, including window, husband,

low, ugly, happy, die, bread and eggs. They have also left their mark on the map of England, with such names as Grimsby, Helperthorpe, Derby, and Wetwang.

The effective resistance to the Viking invaders of England was led by the West Saxons, in particular Alfred (871–99) and his descendants, who not only defeated Scandinavian attempts to conquer Wessex, but also forced the Scandinavian rulers of the Danelaw to accept their authority.

Their kingship was also eventually accepted, sometimes with reluctance, by the English who had escaped Scandinavian domination. The resistance to West Saxon rule was strongest in the north, and some leading Northumbrians, including archbishops of York, were willing to collaborate with Vikings rather than accept the West Saxons as Kings. The Northumbrians long retained an independent spirit, and in the first half of the 10th century from time to time welcomed Scandinavian rulers in defiance of the southern English kings. Even after the expulsion and death of the last Scandinavian King of York, Erik Bloodaxe, in 954, their independent tendencies complicated English politics and William the Conqueror faced the most serious challenge to his rule in the north.

The process of conquest and absorption by southern kings meant, of course, that power was concentrated in the south. That was where English kings had most of their estates, and where they held their councils. When necessary they journeyed north to bring the Northumbrians to heel or to browbeat the Scots, but for most of the time they were content to let the northerners, whether of English, Danish or British descent, largely run their own affairs.

We naturally tend to think of early English history in terms of kings and kingdoms, for our sources are largely concerned with the violent competition between these men for the resources of Britain. The power of a king, British or English, depended in large measure on the loyalty of his companions and that in turn depended on his ability to reward them. It is therefore not surprising that one of the main activities of these rulers was to lead their followers on what can reasonably be described as treasure hunts. A successful king had no difficulty in attracting warriors from far afield. The band commemorated in the sixth-century Welsh poem the 'Gododdin' included men who gathered from many parts of Britain including the lands north of the Firth of Forth, Elmet, Gwynedd and Anglesey.

Early poems commemorate not only great fights but also feasts in which a favoured drink was mead, the Dark Age equivalent of champagne. Under its influence the heroes of the 'Gododdin' behaved in much the same way as those of 'Beowulf' in making proud boasts or promises which it was their ambition to fulfil and 'by earning their mead' win a glorious reputation that would, thanks to the poets, live after them.

Recent archaeological investigations have revealed some of the reality that lay behind such poetic accounts. The excavation of the Northumbrian royal palace of Yeavering, near Wooler, has uncovered a most elaborate complex of buildings including a great hall over 80ft long, with significant parallels in the British complex at Doon Hill, near Dunbar. Other English palaces are known, if not so well investigated, and there are also British strongholds, notably the Iron Age fort of South Cadbury in Somerset which was refortified in the fifth century and occupied for the best part of two centuries.

The treasure that could be accumulated by a seventh-century king is most dramatically displayed in the astonishing riches of the Sutton Hoo ship-burial, now in the British Museum. There are several other notable, if less lavishly furnished, burial mounds, for example at Taplow in Buckinghamshire and at Benty Grange in Derbyshire, that have been found to contain remains of such high quality as to suggest that they were the graves of rulers whose kingdoms appear already to have been absorbed when our written evidence begins.

Politically, seventh-century England was therefore rather like a kaleidoscope with the small provinces or kingdoms being grouped in different ways as the fortune, or fear, of war dictated. In this process some were permanently absorbed by the more successful kingdoms, the largest of which were Northumbria and, south of the Humber, Mercia. Some smaller kingdoms preserved

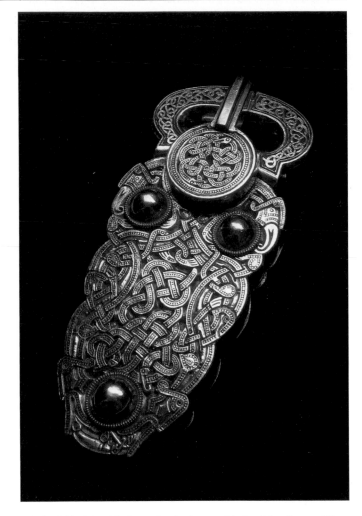

Solid gold belt buckle from Anglo-Saxon ship burial at Sutton Hoo, Suffolk, believed to have adorned the waist of East Anglian king Raedwald. Artistically, it is the finest piece among the ship's treasures, weighs $14\frac{5}{8}$ oz and is over 5 inches long

their identity and a measure of independence despite the efforts of the Mercians, in particular, to subordinate them. One Mercian ruler who made very great efforts to enlarge his hegemony was Offa (757–96) who went so far as to have an East Anglian king executed. Offa also had conflicts with the Welsh but it was in his reign that the boundary of Wales was defined and marked by one of the greatest monuments of the Dark Ages, Offa's Dyke. This bank and ditch ran from the Dee to the Severn estuary, interrupted only where the rivers Severn or Wye made it unnecessary. It was originally furnished with a timber palisade and it must have been a formidable barrier when it was complete. The Dyke is still a remarkable memorial to one of the greatest of early English kings.

Neither the Northumbrians nor the West Saxons had to endure Mercian overlordship for long and it was, in the end, the West Saxons who brought both Mercia and Northumbria permanently under their power. The West Saxons were, in the seventh and eighth centuries, an overlordship like the other kingdoms, but with the remarkable difference that kings appear normally to have

Coin used in Ireland, 11th century. English coins were used as tribute to Viking overlords; the Anglo-Saxon Chronicle reports 200,000lbs. weight of silver paid between 991 and 1018

been unable to pass their power on to a close relative; there was no West Saxon dynasty. Wessex seems, in fact, to have been made up of several kingdoms, some of which probably correspond to modern counties, for example Dorset and Wiltshire, and each of these had one or more royal families. The overlordship over these West Saxon kingdoms, or sub-kingdoms, was never held for long by any one of the constituent dynasties. The West Saxon dynasty to which Alfred belonged was in fact established by his grandfather, Egbert (802–39) who, by defeating the Mercians and extending his authority over Kent, Sussex, Surrey and Essex, laid the foundations on which his successors built.

The greatest of them, Alfred, fully merits his fame. He not only saved Wessex from the Vikings, but he also made skilful use of the resources of kingship to display and strengthen his authority, in laws, on coins, by buildings and by fortifying many towns. He also had a sincere concern for Christianity and made English translations himself of several of the great works of European civilisation; Pope Gregory's 'Pastoral Care', the 'Soliloquies' of St Augustine, and Boethius's 'Consolation of Philosophy'.

Kingdoms not only grew in size, the nature of kingship itself also changed. The power wielded by Offa was very different from that enjoyed by his predecessors in the sixth or even seventh centuries. Early kings could certainly be wealthy and have great prestige, but most of them issued no coins and they had a very limited role in declaring and enforcing the law.

The security of an individual depended not upon the king but on the support of his family or his lord, or both.

Even Alfred had to respect the right of men to pursue their private quarrels by violence. The king's function was originally little more than to be the representative of his people in dealing with both divine and secular powers; his victories and defeats were those of his people.

Early English ideas on the role of kings were shared by the British. Both were affected by the example or experience of Roman power, and the main inheritors of that power in western Europe, the Franks, continued to influence their neighbours across the Channel. Their influence is perhaps seen most clearly in the coinage. The first coins struck by the English, early in the seventh century, were gold shillings, modelled on Frankish coins. By the end of that century English coins still had the same size and weight but they were made of silver. In this the English followed Frankish example as they did at the end of the eighth century when, somewhat belatedly following the lead of Pippin in 755, they began to produce thinner coins with a larger diameter.

English kingship was even more powerfully influenced by the church and this was later symbolised by the royal inauguration rituals that were devised by churchmen. We are fortunate to have the full order of service used at Bath on Whitsunday 973 for the coronation of Edgar. It was a combination of earlier English and Frankish rituals and has been the basis of all English coronations since, including the most recent in 1953, when the anthem 'Zadok the Priest' still accompanied the anointing, but was sung to the music of Handel. The service drew very heavily on the Old Testament, in particular on the Book of Kings, a part of the Bible that describes a society that was in many respects similar to the barbarian world of the time.

By their conversion kings also gained the service of literate men, and the bishops, drawn from noble families, became crucially important agents of royal power. The early bishoprics were in fact created by kings for their kingdoms, and later diocesan boundaries in part reflect the political situation of the seventh century when they were formed. Thus the boundary of the medieval diocese of Worcester followed those of the kingdom of the Hwicce, later absorbed into the kingdom of Mercia.

Very little survives of the first cathedrals – successive rebuildings have destroyed most traces of the earliest structures – but at Hexham, with its crypt, its areas of original flooring and the architectural fragments recovered in 19th-century excavations, it is possible to gain some idea of the scale and quality of the church built before 678. An even better impression of a large seventh-century church is given by the magnificent remains that survive at Brixworth in Northamptonshire, although that was never a cathedral. Conversion re-

Fragments of the 7th-century coffin of St Cuthbert in Durham Cathedral. He died on Farne Island, Northumbria, and was buried on Lindisfarne in 687. Monks brought his body to Durham when Viking raids forced them to abandon Lindisfarne

quired more than cathedrals; kings also granted land on their estates for the establishment of churches from which bishops and their clergy could continue the work.

The first stage may sometimes have been to erect a cross, like that still standing outside the 13th-century church in the Roman fort of Bewcastle, a few miles north of the Roman Wall, but before the end of the seventh century many churches had been built on royal estates. They were in effect the first parish churches. These minsters, as they were called, were centres in which the bishop preached and baptised and they were originally served by members of his household, later by communities of clerks or chaplains. The renders paid to these churches were the spiritual equivalent of the secular dues owed to the king.

Over 300 English churches have clear traces of pre-Conquest fabric, but most of these were built in the century before the Norman Conquest. By then there were few settlements far removed from a church. There were, for example, at that time over 400 churches in Kent, although less than 40 still show traces of pre-Conquest workmanship. Almost all the later parish churches of England existed in 1066, although some had not by then gained parochial status. Some of these 10th- and 11th-century churches replaced earlier buildings, and at Kirkdale in Yorkshire there is an inscription showing that it was rebuilt in the decade before the Norman Conquest. Such rebuildings have left very few early churches standing; but some idea of the character of those built in the earliest days of the English church can be gained at Bradwell-on-Sea in Essex, Bradford-on-Avon in Wiltshire, Wing, near Aylesbury, or in the little church of St John at Escomb in County Durham.

In the conversion period a vitally important role was played by austere and holy men, like Cuthbert and Aidán. When they died their power did not vanish but continued in their mortal remains, which were preserved in shrines served by communities of clerks or monks, very much like the other monastic communities that were founded in large numbers after 650. Kings and laymen were eager to make gifts to such monasteries for the sake of their souls and in the hope of eternal rewards. Some of these communities were very austere, notably Bede's monastery at Jarrow, where excavations around the surviving monastic church have found little sign of the opulence of other houses, like Whitby. Austerity, however, was hardly a necessary virtue and some benefactors must indeed have hoped for magnificence.

The burial places of kings and their close relatives give some indication of where they thought the greatest spiritual power was to be found, and many chose monastic resting places. Ethelbald, the Mercian king who claimed in a charter of 736 to be king of all the South English, was buried at the monastery of Repton, presumably in the mausoleum that now forms the crypt under the church tower.

Monasteries and other churches were natural targets for Viking attack; even the poorest could be a source of

Ruins of a twin-towered Saxon church within the walls of a Roman fort by the sea at Reculver, Kent. Churches like this were natural targets and were often singled out for Viking attack, for even the poorest could be a source of slaves

slaves. A few communities sought safety in flight: St Cuthbert's fled from Lindisfarne successively to Norham on Tweed, Chester-le-Street and finally Durham, where the cathedral church was founded in 998 to house his remains.

Some houses were certainly destroyed but that did not necessarily mean the disappearance of the community. It is, however, likely that some monasteries disappeared because their estates were seized by Viking settlers, who also seem to have driven the bishops of East Anglia, Lindsey and Leicester from their sees. The archbishops of York, on the other hand, did not abandon their post, and many religious communities survived the Viking onslaught.

After the Viking raids there was a growing enthusiasm for monastic reform, with the Benedictine rule as the basis for true observance. It was not until the middle years of the 10th century that these new standards had much influence in England, and that was mainly due to the support given by King Edmund and, even more, by King Edgar. They encouraged the reform of old houses, like Winchester and Worcester, or the foundation of new ones, often on sites of ancient sanctity, like Crowland, Ely and Peterborough. In return for this royal

The Vikings had another, and most positive effect, for some of them had become very wealthy thanks to the plunder and tribute they had extorted from the rulers, the churchmen and the merchants of Frankia and England. When they settled, or perhaps even before, their wealth stimulated a demand for goods that craftsmen were eager to satisfy. Excavations at York and elsewhere have uncovered many objects of wood, leather, antler, bone and metal that were made locally but in Scandinavian styles. The 10th-century expansion of Lincoln, Norwich, York and perhaps Chester must owe much to the wealthy Scandinavians who lived in or near those towns, and the recent excavations at Coppergate in York have shown that the property boundaries along that street were first laid out soon after the Viking conquest. The Scandinavian invaders thus contributed to the wealth of 10th-century England, a wealth that is clearly demonstrated by the voluminous and well controlled English coinage that was, later in the century, produced at some 70 mints under royal control. It was this wealth that attracted a later generation of Vikings whose attacks ended in the Danish conquest of the kingdom.

The reshaping of Britain involved many, often confusing, dynastic changes. Society changed more slowly, but there were in these centuries some major developments in the countryside. In the early period the emphasis seems to have been on self-sufficiency, with large estates providing all the varied resources that were needed by rulers, lords and men. The development of markets and the increased availability of coinage made specialisation possible and by the 11th century taxes, rents and other dues were often rendered in cash.

Some large estates survived, especially those belonging to the king and the larger churches, but in the course of the ninth and 10th centuries many were broken up into smaller units held by men who had, by grant, purchase or usurpation, acquired rights of full ownership over their property. In many ways these landowners resembled the later squirearchy of England; a country gentry living on their estates, patronising the churches they or their ancestors had built, and claiming parochial rights for them, attending the shire court and, when summoned, serving in the army.

Hundreds of such men are named as pre-Conquest tenants in Domesday Book, a survey made in 1086 so that William the Conqueror could discover what rights he had acquired in becoming king of England and what the other landholdings in the country were worth. Its compilation alone is remarkable testimony to the efficiency and potential of English royal government. Perhaps its most surprising revelation is that England was highly urbanised, with some 10 per cent of the population living in towns. It also reveals very clearly the contrast between the north and south. York may have been the second largest city in England, perhaps in Europe, in 1066, but there was no other royal borough north of the Humber. In the absence of an effective royal

patronage the monks offered up prayers for the king and his family, and their houses became key centres of royal influence, a role of particular importance in areas that had no long tradition of loyalty to West Saxon kings.

Other natural targets for Viking attack were the coastal towns and market places that flourished in the eighth century. Some, including London, Lincoln and York, had developed in or alongside old Roman centres but others, such as Ipswich, Southampton and, in Kent, Fordwich and Sarre, had grown to importance under the English. These markets, attended by Continental merchants, were under royal protection and appear originally to have been undefended. The Vikings had no more respect for the peace of kings than they had for the power of saints, and eventually their attacks led to the restoration or strengthening of some Roman defences.

In the 11th century the walls of at least 11 towns had a Roman basis: Canterbury, Chester, Chichester, Colchester, Exeter, Gloucester, Lincoln, London, Rochester, Winchester and York, where a remarkable sequence of wall reconstructions can be seen, including a tower that may have been built before the Viking occupation of the city. Many other centres were fortified by Alfred and his children as defence against Viking attack, and arrangements made for their maintenance and manning by people from the locality. Remains of such defences can be seen in many places, including Wareham, Cricklade and Wallingford.

Full page illustration from an 8th-century Northumbrian commentary on the Psalms of David, possibly made at the monastery of Jarrow. It is now in Durham Cathedral Museum

power of the kind that was being created in the south, Northumbrian society remained archaic. Disputes were resolved in traditional ways, kinsmen and lords were more important than the king and his agents, buying and selling took place in fairs and markets, not in royal boroughs, and, although there were many religious communities in Northumbria, they too were old fashioned; the monastic reformation wrought in the south by royal power did not penetrate so far north. It is, therefore, in Northumbria that we can gain some idea what English society, and royal authority, were like before the West Saxon kings transformed both. It is in the contrast between the north and south that we can perhaps gain the best measure of the achievement of Alfred and his successors, an achievement that had as one of its most significant consequences the creation of a network of royal boroughs as centres of government.

The English paid a high price for their prosperity, for when Edward the Confessor died, childless, in January 1066, there were several contenders for his throne. Harold, son of Godwin, was chosen first but he soon had to face two challenges. Harald, King of Norway, was killed at Stamford Bridge, near York, on 25 September but three weeks later the victorious English king was killed in battle against William, Duke of Normandy, and a new phase in the reshaping of Britain began.

LAND TRANSPORT

by Andrew Nahum

Celtic Britain, as encountered in AD 43 by the armies of Emperor Claudius, already had an extensive system of communications – the ridgeways. In a mere 40 years, though, the Romans had introduced a comprehensive 5,000 mile network of roads. These Roman roads were usually of simple construction, steeply cambered and surfaced with local materials – compacted gravel, flint, or limestone brash.

It is often suggested that road building in the wake of the legions allowed hardware and stores to follow on by cart. This seems unlikely, for the unrelenting directness of the roads imposes gradients that are endurable by marching men, but extremely taxing for draft horses or oxen. Nor was Roman harness particularly efficient, either for traction, or for helping the animal resist the load on the down slope.

The horse was absolutely essential to land transport and remained so into the Victorian age. It served as a mount – the standard method of long distance travel until the coaching era – as a draft animal, but also as a perfectly efficient goods carrier by itself. Packhorses, harnessed in strings, and carrying about two hundredweight each in panniers, formed the basis of overland goods transport and were still the main method in some parts of the country until the 18th century. Packhorses were most economical for light, high value articles, like haberdashery, but they were often the only method for delivering commonplace commodities like coals.

The first works of man to alter this arithmetic were the canals. The ascetic Duke of Bridgewater's Worsley to Salford canal (started in 1759) reduced the price of coal from the Duke's pits by exactly half. Canal pioneer James Brindley, a brilliant self-educated civil engineer, endured ridicule for his proposal to carry the canal over the River Irwell by aqueduct – although more ambitious works already existed on the Continent. Unfortunately his Barton aqueduct was replaced when the Manchester Ship Canal was built, but another by Brindley can be seen on the Trent and Mersey canal, at Stretton, in Staffordshire.

Fired in part by Brindley's achievements, canal building gathered pace until Britain was criss-crossed by a comprehensive network. The huge profits made show how much Britain needed bulk transport as industry expanded. Many companies had a financial history that makes today's high tech stockmarket stars look tame. (In five years to 1835 the Trent and Mersey would have provided a capital return of £12,800 per £1,000 invested – plus a dividend of 75 per cent a year.)

Carriages did not become significant for passenger travel until the mid 18th century. Services were in existence by the 1650s, but the growing wagon traffic cut up the roads so badly that a Lancashire parson wrote 'This travell hath soe indisposed mee, I am resolved never to ride up agayne in ye Coatche'. Coach and road improvement went hand in hand. However even the acclaimed new Telford and Macadam surfaces were rough by modern standards, and it is important although perhaps difficult to realise that the stage coach was a major technological achievement. Wheels, bearings, harness and springs all had to develop to stand the wrenching and straining of continuous long distance service. By 1836, crack coaches like the London to Bristol Mail averaged 10–11 mph. To achieve these speeds was extremely expensive in horses – the 'stages' were shortened to provide fresh teams about every 8 miles.

In their heyday, coaches enjoyed tremendous popular appeal. Richly painted and immaculately turned out, they pandered to the English love of well-staged display. Swaggering in his cape (the many layered 'Benjamin'), the coachman was the aristocrat of the road, and passengers accounted it an honour to sit up on the 'box' beside him (though on occasion, outside passengers died of exposure!) Small wonder

Horseman with a hawk, from a 14th century agricultural calendar

The early 17th-century coach was a relatively crude thing – better suited for nobs to be seen around town in than for undertaking long journeys. The body hung from leather straps which cushioned road shocks, but allowed a swaying motion that was perhaps almost as unpleasant

The wide wheels of the 18th-century stage wagon were imposed by statute in an effort to limit the growing damage that traffic was inflicting on the roads. Historical research has not yet established the relative importance of wagons and pack horses for goods transport, although there are records of regular wagon services over hundreds of miles

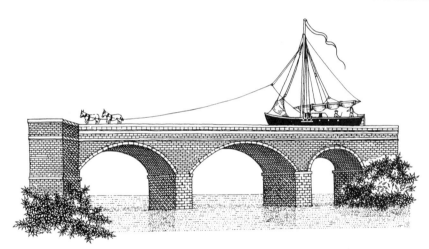

Brindley's 1759 aqueduct over the River Irwell was considered a 'fantastical' solution at the time, although larger aqueducts already existed on the Continent. The new canal cut by half the price of coal from the Duke of Bridgewater's mine

The first compound cylinder traction engine – a Fowler of 1881. Though traction engines were mainly developed for agricultural use, the Road Act of 1878 gave new impetus to the traction engine builders and 'road trains' pulling heavy loads became quite a common sight. Average speed was around 4 mph and the crew was on the road for 2–3 weeks at a time

The sedan chair pre-dates the coach as transport for the wealthy. Human legs could cope with the ruts and alleviate discomfort for passengers in a way that solid wheels could not. Sedan chairs plied for hire in London well into the 18th century

At its height in the 1830s, the long distance coach was a highly evolved machine, as superior to the basic farm cart as a modern Ford is to a Model T. Crack coaches could average 10–11 mph using fresh teams of horses as often as every eight miles

The 'London No. 1' train built in 1838 for the new London–Birmingham railway. Designer Edward Bury built his locomotives on frames of rectangular iron bars, bolted and riveted together. Other engineers used flat plates. Bury believed that a speed of 30 mph was quite enough for both comfort and safety

The 'Safety Bicycle' was the first democratic means of long-distance locomotion. The dramatic 'ordinary', or penny-farthing, had been strictly for the enthusiast who revelled in his skills. In the few years left before the coming of the motor car, cyclists – many of them industrial workers – could enjoy almost perfect peace on British country roads

The Holden was one of Britain's first home-produced motor cycles, devised by Col. H. C. L. Holden in 1895. It featured a four cylinder petrol engine, possibly the first in the world, and was said to be very sweet-running. The frame was derived from a contemporary sporting bicycle

A triumph of Victorian railway engineering: the Olive Mount cutting on George Stephenson's Liverpool to Manchester Railway

that swells often tipped the coachman to let them 'tool' the coach for a stage (the other passengers were seldom keen on this). Some titled enthusiasts even became professionals, like Sir Vincent Cotton, who regularly drove the famous 'Age'. As the coaching age gave way to the railways, there was a nostalgia every bit as poignant as today's for steam trains.

From its opening in 1830, the Liverpool and Manchester Railway, dubbed 'Britain's Great Railway Experiment' was keenly watched. Streams of visitors came to see it, and particularly to see the novel 'travelling engine'. Horse-drawn rail and tram ways had been known for centuries, in collieries and mineral workings, and both the Liverpool and Manchester and the Stockton to Darlington, opened 5 years earlier, relied partly on horse traction. However, Stephenson's 'Rocket', on test in 1829 exceeded anything known before in reliability (70 miles in 6¾ hours) and made it clear that the future lay with the locomotive.

The connection of the Liverpool and Manchester line to Birmingham, and the acclaimed construction of the London to Birmingham link clearly showed what the new commercial axis of the country was. London was now linked to the most progressive industrial areas in Europe.

The heroic age of railway building up to 1850, saw the construction of the major trunk routes radiating from London. The virtuosity of the engineers was not lost on the public – men like Brunel were the superstars of their age, who walked a tightrope at the limit of current technology (and frequently, their backers' purses). Brunel's Box tunnel through the 'Great Oolite' (limestone) near Bath cost double the estimated £6,500,000 and took five years to build. At times, 4,000 navvies worked on the project, using a ton of gunpowder and a ton of candles a day. Once, each year, the rising sun is said to shine through it – on the 9th of April – Brunel's birthday.

By the end of Queen Victoria's reign, railways had achieved an enviable safety record and high speeds – the East Coast Companies reached Edinburgh in 6 hours 18 minutes from London for a special record breaking run in 1895. A huge network of branch lines, some hopelessly speculative, linked rural areas to the main lines and carried the fingers of the rail system into the remotest parts. From the 1850s too, a tramway system had developed in many cities – virtually a railway system reaching to the urban front door.

From about 1870 though, one form of mechanical road transport had been gaining popular appeal – the bicycle. The gentry kept horses, but with a bicycle the town-dwelling artisan could roam over undreamed of distances. The high 'Ordinary' bicycle (or 'Penny Farthing') was fast and potentially dangerous. Its exponents enjoyed their skills and contemporary photographs reveal their pride and sense of panache. In a real way too, they were explorers, rediscovering roads that had lain dormant since the end of the coaching era. Gradients, surfaces, rights of way might all be unknown outside the locality, and the adventurers spread their experiences through the clubs and cycling papers.

During the 1880s manufacturers strove to make lower, more controllable machines, culminating in the famous Rover 'Safety' bicycle. This made cycling an even more democratic pastime, and a few years were left, before another profound transport innovation, the internal combustion engine, completely changed the nature of the road.

THE
NORMANS

by Henry Loyn

Rochester Castle

The Norman Conquest and subsequent settlement was overwhelmingly successful. It brought in its train the introduction of a new French-speaking dynasty and aristocracy. And it put a tremendous concentration of wealth in very few hands among a relatively prosperous agrarian population and a budding urban community.

It has been estimated that at the time of Domesday Book in 1086, as much as a quarter of the total landed wealth of England lay in the hands of only a dozen men, all of them newcomers, mostly Norman, and all closely bound by ties of kinship or interest or both to the royal house. The king and his immediate family held something approaching another quarter, and the Church retained or acquired something between a quarter and a third. The economic consequences of such a concentration of wealth had permanent results, not only in obvious and visible ways such as the building of great castles, cathedrals and abbeys, but also in furthering the moves towards a more complex society. Britain's first borough charters appear in the first generation after the Conquest. An intensification of urban activity at old sites newly dominated, protected and exploited by Norman lords and sheriffs, became a conspicuous feature of the early Norman world. In the countryside manorial lordship, tightened and reinforced by the activities of the new landowners and their servants, flourished under the harsh but effective Norman internal peace.

The Conqueror and his two sons, William Rufus (1087–1100) and Henry I (1100–35), were ferocious but effective rulers with an inbuilt respect for law (at least as it affected others), and a heavy hand with rebellious barons and discontented English. Unfortunately Norman rule broke down on Henry's death in 1135, when the throne was disputed between his daughter Matilda and his nephew, Stephen. The resultant 'unrest' was not ended until 1153, only 12 months before the agreed succession of Matilda's son, Henry of Anjou, Henry II (1154–89), one of the most effective of English medieval kings. He and his sons, Richard I Lionheart (1189–99) and John (1199–1216), ruled a huge continental empire, partly inherited, partly acquired by marriage – not only Normandy, but Anjou, Poitou, Maine, Aquitaine and Gascony.

When much of it was lost to the French by John's disastrous diplomacy and generalship, the monarchy and the aristocracy became locked in a power struggle which began rather than ended with the signing of the Great Charter of English Liberties at Runnymede in 1215. Order and unity were not fully restored until the accession of Edward I Longshanks (1272–1307) who embarked on the conquest of Britain, beginning with Wales and proceeding, less successfully, to Scotland.

The troubles of Stephen's reign and the baronial civil wars of Henry III's reign (1216–72), added to the existing precariousness of rural life in England, and for Wales and Scotland this was also a period of turbulence and growth.

In Wales early Norman successes almost led to complete conquest, but native princes presented their independence in the difficult mountainous terrain of Snowdonia. Great Norman families, Clares and Mortimers, Montgomerys, Bohuns and (later) Marshalls established themselves in Marcher lordships, extending authority deep into central and southern Wales. Pembrokeshire became Normanised and Anglicised, and the line of linguistic division between English and Welsh in the county still ran until recent times roughly along the border drawn by a succession of powerful little Norman castles. The native Welsh rallied, helped by political troubles in England, and the House of Gwynedd built up a strong principality in the course of the 13th century in uneasy feudal relationship to the English kings. Edward I put paid to that, leaving the mark of his energy and authority in great castles such as Harlech, Beaumaris, and Caernarvon.

The Scots had more permanent success in building up their political community in Northern Britain. Scandinavians remained in control of the Northern Isles, Orkney and Shetland, but the Scottish kings from the time of David I (1124–53), helped by a new Anglo-Norman aristocracy, Stewarts (FitzAlans), Balliols, Bruces and Lindsays, gradually brought the mainland under their effective rule. Alexander III's defeats of the Norwegians in the 1260s ensured that the Hebrides became a permanent part of the Scottish realm. The kings had a tangled feudal relationship with the English crown, and succession problems prompted Edward I's intervention, but this phase ended with the military disaster to Edward II at Bannockburn in 1314. But their political independence did not mean that the Scots failed to be subject to the same feudal and social forces as the English, and the great castle at Stirling or the cathedrals at Glasgow and St Andrews testify to the military and religious trends of the age.

Ireland, too, was brought into the British orbit under Henry II (1154–89), when intervention first by Strongbow (Richard de Clare) and his Anglo-Welsh followers from Pembroke was followed by direct royal action. The result was a tangled network of lordship, native Irish and Anglo-Norman, with the interlopers maintaining a precarious control through a network of small castles and their possession of the former Scandinavian ports of Dublin, Waterford and Wexford, and owing a sketchy allegiance to the English king as 'Lord' (not King) of Ireland.

But in the main, the 12th and 13th centuries were a time of growth and permanent achievement in many of the basic fields of human endeavour. In government the Normans inherited much from Anglo-Saxon institutions

The Norman Age encouraged a great flowering of architectural skill, of which Fountains Abbey, Yorkshire, is a haunting example. Cistercian monks founded it in 1132. Its isolated site reflected the Order's original rejection of worldliness, although it soon became one of the richest abbeys in the country

at central and at local level, but inevitably stressed the military and feudal aspects of their rule during the early generations of the settlement. The stages of positive achievement are clearly marked: the legal reforms of Henry II and the origins of a recognisable English Common Law; the resistance of the barons to John and the formulation of the terms of Magna Carta; the rebellion of de Montfort and the summons of knights of the shire and burgesses from towns to central assemblies that culminated in the holding of the so-called 'Model Parliament' by Edward I in 1295.

Local institutions, shire-courts and the courts of hundreds and wapentakes persisted with astonishing continuity from Anglo-Saxon days, and became more and more firmly integrated into the structure of royal government and the community. Royal government itself proved fertile in successful experiment. The Exchequer grew to maturity in the 12th century, and our continuous series of Exchequer records runs from 1155. Law courts, which were to develop into the Court of the King's Bench and the Court of Common Pleas, began to take shape by the end of the century. Our main series of royal governmental records, Close Rolls and Patent Rolls, date from the early 13th century.

A growth in literacy and in legal training accompanied this governmental activity, all part and parcel of a literary and intellectual revival sometimes known as the 12th-century Renaissance. Schooling became more systematic. Oxford traces its origins as a university to 1170, and the beginnings of its continuous college life to the following century. Cambridge was founded a generation later.

Criticism is sometimes levelled at the limited nature and restraint of this renaissance. Theology remained the queen of the sciences and the organised, increasingly authoritative church remained in substantial control. Yet in many fields, technical, mathematical and practical, permanent advance was made, and we are only slowly coming to realise the value of an age that introduced England to the windmill (first reference c. 1170), a better use of water power, improved ploughing techniques, more systematic rotation of crops, improved mining knowledge, superb architectural skill, and better methods of controlling and measuring time.

During these centuries the Western world generally enjoyed a period of increased activity and mobility. England benefited from being a part of the Anglo-Norman world, linked intimately with French politics. No section of the community gained more from this connection than the townsmen, above all the inhabitants of London, which by the late 12th century had grown into a formidable urban community with its own mayor and deep-established rights involving a large de-

Chepstow Castle, appearing to be sculpted out of cliffs dominating the Wye, is probably the oldest stone castle in Britain. It was begun the year after the conquest by William's kinsman, and one of his chief tenants, William Fitz-Osbern

gree of self-government and independent financial authority. London was exceptional in size and vitality, but throughout England urban development was a significant feature of the period.

There are three main paths to a better visual awareness of the world of the Normans and Angevins. Britain, and especially England, is well blessed in recognisable survivals. Then comes the evidence of the archaeologist, growing apace from year to year, not always so easy to apprehend, at times needing the help of the skilled scientist or technician or modern artist to interpret. Finally there is the most fruitful path of all, the evidence preserved by medieval artists in illuminated manuscripts, sculpture, wall-paintings, and brasses that brings us in close touch with the medieval people themselves.

The buildings that have survived give us a picture of some important aspects of medieval life, but caution is needed in assessing the evidence. Buildings do not survive unless use is found for them. In some instances eight or nine centuries of wear and tear, of repair and reconstruction have served to bring our majestic cathedrals or formidable castles to their present condition.

Many of our great English cathedrals preserve their medieval structure substantially intact. A visit to Canterbury or York, to Salisbury, Chester, or Durham is enough to bring home the scale of the effort and of the achievement. Concern with politics or with economics must not obscure the fact that the age had a deeply religious dimension and was prepared to spend much time, money and resource in creating what still rank as among the most powerful and beautiful monuments to religious faith ever constructed in this country.

Many of these great churches date back to the early generations of the Norman Conquest. Concentration of wealth and a desire to find ways of stamping authority symbolically on a community were basic Norman characteristics that could find expression in religious as well as in secular form. Two of these tremendous monuments, Winchester Cathedral and St Albans Abbey, which became a cathedral a bare century ago, can serve well to illustrate this side of the Norman and medieval world, and also to remind us of the constant care and change brought about in successive generations to make the buildings what they are.

Winchester, warm and alive and curiously intimate from the inside, reveals in its exterior a hotchpotch of styles from many and various architectural schools and phases of the Middle Ages. In the heart of the cathedral are the tower and transepts and adjoining bays from the early generations of the Conquest, Norman and solid to

Classic Norman doorway at the Church of St Mary and St David, Kilpeck, Herefordshire (above left). However, there is a touch of the Anglo-Saxon in the figures and monsters carved with brilliant sharpness into the hard local sandstone. The quaintly lugubrious couple clinging to each other so desperately (above right) form a corbel end on the Kilpeck Church. Corbels were a Norman architectural innovation which gave extra strength to the eaves of church roofs and were often exuberantly carved

the core. To the east are the retrochoir and the Lady Chapel in good early 13th-century style, with additions to the Lady Chapel as late as the last years of the 15th century. The west front and massive nave, the longest in any English cathedral, testify to the social attitudes and willingness to spend money, even in one of the more troubled periods of the Middle Ages. The west front was created, characteristically Perpendicular even if rough and unpolished in places, in the 1360s. The majestic nave was the brainchild of William of Wykeham, Bishop of Winchester 1366–1404, and his architect, William Wynford, and was not completed until about 1450, long after the death of its planners.

At St Albans the chronological range is even wider. There is a splendid view of the abbey across the river Ver from the site of the Roman *municipium* of Verulamium. Again, as at Winchester, the contrast between the solid, almost squat Norman tower, transepts, and choir, with the massive nave is overpowering. A closer look reveals still greater complexity. The north side of the nave (invisible from across the Ver) turns out to be as solidly Norman as the central heart of the abbey, its great columns still decorated with magnificent wall paintings. The west bays of the nave are late 12th or early 13th century, the five south bays nearest the nave screen 14th century, rebuilt in somewhat leisurely fashion after their collapse in 1323 (it is said that abbot Richard of Wallingford was more interested in his astronomical clock than in church building). All has been subject to restoration, in parts under the hands of Gilbert Scott and the formidable Lord Grimthorpe in the 19th century. No century from the 11th to the 20th has failed to leave its mark on St Albans, and yet the overall impression, devout and controlled, remains purely medieval, strictly Benedictine.

Smaller churches also serve as living memorials of the Middle Ages. The Normans came to a land already deeply Christian and well endowed with Christian churches. They were content initially to leave well alone, but as settlement persisted and new wealth came, they rebuilt and replaced Saxon churches (some 300 of which still remain Saxon, at least in part). There are many exquisite examples in town and country of 12th-century churches to bear witness to this side of Norman enterprise. Sometimes they were rebuilt and added to later in the Middle Ages, but the 12th century is still visible and preserved in places as diverse as Barfreston in Kent, Iffley in Oxfordshire, Kilpeck in Hereford, Worcester (with its astonishing carvings and grotesques) and Dalmeny, not far from Edinburgh on the Firth of Forth.

With wealth and stability came more rebuilding and additions. Romanesque, with its round arches and solidity, gave way to the pointed arches and soaring heights of Gothic. England produced its varieties of general European types – early English, Decorated, culminating in the later Middle Ages with the elegance and clean lines of Perpendicular. The Norman or Angevin contribution survives to remind us of the colour and inten-

The elaborately carved font of black Tournai marble in Winchester Cathedral, probably dating from mid-12th century. It was a characteristic of the Norman Age to spare no expense or effort in creating the most powerful and beautiful monuments to religious faith. Fortunately for us, much of it survives today

sity of religious experience. In physical reminders of the ecclesiastical life of the Middle Ages England remains among the richest of European sources.

From the secular world also much that was medieval still surrounds us. Far and away the most significant of the survivals are our castles. It is sometimes forgotten how limited in time was the period of castle building in England. Apart from a very few experimental ventures, notably on the Hereford border, during the reign of the Confessor, there were no castles in England before the Conquest. The great age of castle-building came to an end two and a half centuries later with Edward I's tremendous and successful use of the castle to conquer and subdue the Welsh. To the purist the fortifications built in the later Middle Ages bear the characteristics for the most part of fortified manor houses rather than true castles. The function of the castle, it has long been recognised, was much more than military. It was also administrative and governmental, a massive symbol of lordship and superiority, a centre of legal authority which could degenerate into an instrument of tyranny.

There are three main styles of castle architecture to follow. First the imposing and overbearing constructions, normally the work of the king or the very greatest of the tenants-in-chief. The Tower, guarding the eastern approach to London, Colchester, Rochester, and

the heart of Chepstow castle (the great hall put up by Fitz-Osbern before his death in 1071) give us a taste of what is to come. Kenilworth or, in the Welsh context, Caernarvon, Harlech, Caerphilly or Beaumaris (the perfect concentric) provide the flavour of a finished product. Lesser castles are quite as interesting and more plentiful. Mottes and baileys, of the type illustrated in the Bayeux Tapestry, litter the countryside of England, with heavy extensions to Wales and thence to Ireland in the later 12th century. In essential they are mounds of earth, topped by buildings, first in wood and then in stone (the motte), accompanied by an enclosure (the bailey), with further protecting outworks.

There is also a third main line of fortification that has received much attention recently, the small enclosure castle or ringwork. It is surprisingly common, possibly for tenurial reasons, in some areas of Norman settlement, such as parts of Hampshire, Wiltshire, and the Gower peninsula in Wales. Derived from Carolingian designs, the main weight of defence was thrown into the fortified gateway. It sometimes needs the combined help of the archaeologist and an artist to make plain the nature of these fortifications, but they were important in their day, a significant alternative to the familiar pudding-basin motte.

It is a lamentable but inevitable fact that we are better informed about the military and official castles than about domestic architecture. If buildings of the Norman period in this category survive at all it is often as the cellarage of later structures in towns such as Winchester or Canterbury. There are exceptions, of course, and

good stone-built houses, some associated with Jewish financiers, exist in identifiable shape in, for example, Lincoln and Norwich. One good example of a late 12th-century manor house has survived at Boothby Pagnall in Lincolnshire. Not until the later Middle Ages do we begin to enjoy direct contact with domestic buildings in large numbers, usually the homes of substantial men, manorial lords or merchants.

The sheer volume of material that is being slowly and painfully recovered from the medieval past is impressive, encouraging, and at times to the professional historian, a little terrifying. In 1980 alone, for example, from one small area, two coin hoards were uncovered that will in time tell us much. On the hills behind Cardiff a hoard of coins dating from the time of Matilda was discovered, bringing evidence of the existence of a hitherto unknown mint at Swansea. Four or five miles away at the site of the old castle at Rumney, to the east of Cardiff, another hoard was uncovered of the time of Edward I, telling much of the range of enterprise and expertise of that age.

At times a single concentrated excavation can enrich and make more precise the knowledge that already exists in written sources. Recently at St Albans, on the chapter house site, Professor Martin Biddle discovered clear evidence of the building sequence that added to our knowledge of the abbey itself throughout the Middle Ages.

We can also learn a lot from the enterprise of a museum, coupled with archaeology on fruitful sites. The Museum of London, with its interest in finds made within the City and on the Thames foreshore, provides one such example, and the wealth of finds, often of a relatively humble nature – shoes, knives, iron goods, taps and bungs, tailors' shears, pilgrim badges, even a 14th-century bird-cage pot – can add immeasurably to our feeling for a society. From all parts of the country new information appears of monastic sites, farms, mills and kilns, of living quarters and tombs, of cooking pots, seeds and cultivation tools and instruments. From one site alone, at Long Ashton in Avon, over 15,000 sherds of 12th- and 13th-century pottery were recovered in the late 1970s.

Some of our clearest visual images of how people lived in the Middle Ages come from the work of contemporary artists, but the evidence has to be handled with care. Artists in the earlier part of the period, if they illuminated their manuscripts at all, were more inclined to copy from other manuscripts than from life. There are exceptions. The designer of the Bayeux Tapestry, probably an Englishman from Kent, gave what he clearly meant to be representations of, for example, Westminster Abbey and the little manorial church at Bosham. His detailed treatment of costume and armour may well be taken as authentic. Occasionally in formal illumination, or in bizarre pictures within great initial letters, or in sheer doodling in the margin, we are given hints of the appearance, dress and customs of the time. In Matthew

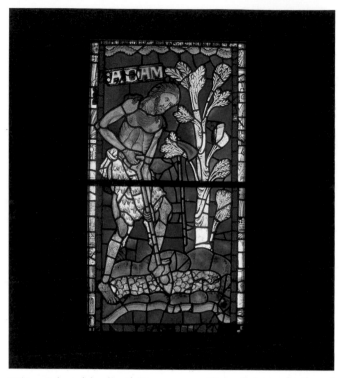

When Adam delved and Eve span . . . One of the sophisticated stained glass panels dating from 1178 in Canterbury Cathedral. Recently restored, they are to be displayed in the west window

Paris, monk of St Albans in the 13th century, England produced one of the most interesting artists and historians of the age. His pictorial representations of incidents he described in his text provide an inexhaustible source of information on battle scenes in the Crusades, royal councils, religious scenes, accounts of martyrdom, architectural details of buildings, heraldic details, and even one magnificent full page illustration of an elephant, based in part at least on his own observation of the elephant presented by St Louis of France to his cousin Henry III.

Effigies in stone in cathedrals and churches bring out the living features of medieval folk. Ivories, fabrics, mosaics and reliquaries prove a fount of knowledge of people, their costumes and style of life. The art of the woodcarver shows us domestic scenes, pastiches from rural or urban life. Above all the art of beautifying books reaches a fine point of perfection.

We finish with an example from Winchester. At some stage in the 12th century and most probably at the order of Henry of Blois, bishop of Winchester 1129–71, a great psalter was prepared. It contains, among many other things, 38 full page miniatures with scenes from the Old Testament and the New. In its richness, vitality and true originality it tells us much of the age. Wall paintings such as those at Kempley and Copford could do for the illiterate what book illuminations could do for those versed in the ways of books. Through what has survived, a mere fragment of the whole, we experience not only the mind of the artist, but the direct reflection of a vibrant, creative age.

THE CHAIR

by Jeffery Daniels

To anyone alive in Britain today, a chair is simply something on which to sit; to a 17th-century French 'précieux', it was a 'commodity of conversation'; to a medieval peasant it was an object of respect, even veneration, and reserved exclusively for the use of the rich and powerful.

In early Christian times, the 'cathedra' was a chair used by a bishop, from which our word 'cathedral' derives, and the phrase 'ex cathedra' means an official pronouncement, made from the chair. The person in charge of a meeting is said to 'take the chair' and all contributions to the discussion are made 'through the chair'.

Chairs were certainly used in Britain in Roman times and samples made of basket work or wicker are recorded on Romano-British sepulchral monuments. However, it should be remembered that when the Romans ate, they reclined on couches, rather than sitting upright. In the Middle Ages long benches or forms were the most common type of seating at table, and only the head of the household and the principal guests would have the use of a chair. They would sit at a top table, raised on a dais, while the rest of the company sat at long tables set at right angles to it. The central chair might be graced with a canopy, thus becoming a 'chair of estate', virtually a throne. The whole household dined together in the hall, which was the social focus of the house, but smaller rooms were used by the head and his family, and it was here that the domestic or household chair developed. Such smaller rooms were often, by the 15th century, lined with wooden panelling, which, when it covered only the lower part of the walls, was known as 'wainscot'. This name was sometimes given to a type of chair which probably evolved from the chest: a back and sides were added, thus producing a massive effect which was to some extent relieved by carved decoration. The 'wainscot chair' remained popular well into the sixteenth century, but the obvious need for a light form of construction led to the emergence of the typical Elizabethan/Jacobean chair, still with a solid back and seat, but raised on turned legs joined by stretchers and with open arms.

The single chair was created by adding a back to a stool, which is why in old inventories such pieces are often referred to as 'back stools'. During the reigns of James I and Charles I these were often covered in rich fabrics but during the Commonwealth and Protectorate, the prevailing taste favoured leather which was more hard wearing as well as less ostentatiously luxurious. Until about 1660, nearly all English furniture was made of oak, but the enormous demand for that wood, which was also needed for shipbuilding and the construction of timber-framed houses, led to the search for alternatives. Fashion, under the leadership of the restored Stuart court, also played its part, and walnut began to replace oak in elegant houses. The influence of foreign designers, especially Daniel Marot, can be seen in the high-backed chairs of the 1690s, usually enriched with carved detail of considerable refinement but sometimes painted and decorated in imitation of Chinese or Japanese lacquer which was being imported in increasing quantities, together with such new luxuries as coffee and tea.

The cabriole leg made its appearance at the turn of the century, while the back of the chair acquired a rounded form: the typical 'Queen Anne' chair, made in walnut, combines these features, together with a solid central back rest known as a 'splat'. The cabriole leg persisted well into the 18th century, often carved on the 'knee' with a mask or stylised leaves and terminating in a claw and ball foot, while the splat was increasingly lightened by pierced decoration, sometimes in chinoiserie or 'gothick' designs.

The influence of the French Rococo can be discerned in much mid-century furniture, especially the chairs designed by the most famous English furniture maker of the period, Thomas Chippendale, who set up his workshop in London in 1735. He

Early 17th-century English armchair, in carved oak with arcaded back and boxed sides

Romano-British wicker chair of the 2nd or 3rd century AD. Chairs have been made of wicker or basket work since at least Roman times and are still produced in this form today, although synthetic fibres are now frequently used

Wainscot, or joyned chair, c. 1525–50. The solidity of such pieces was relieved by carved decoration; the linen-fold design is basically vernacular, but the top panel is decorated in Renaissance style

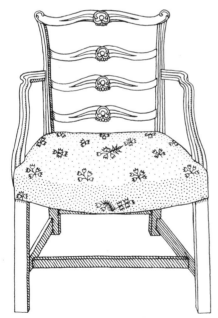

Ladder-back armchair, c. 1755. This mahogany piece, in the style of Thomas Chippendale, combines structural robustness with refinement of decoration in an exemplary way

Country craftsmen have provided chairs like this late 18th-century Windsor armchair since the early years of the 18th century, mainly in and around High Wycombe, Bucks.

Neoclassical chair, c. 1800. Made of beech, japanned and gilded, this elegant drawing room chair derives from ancient Greek prototypes

The panel back on this Elizabethan armchair of c. 1600 is decorated with carving in the form of a lozenge, with fleur de lys ornament, and surmounted by a cresting of stylised foliage and scrolls. The front legs and arm supports are turned

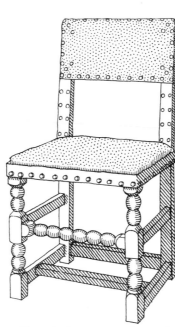

The only decoration on this simple Cromwellian chair of c. 1650 is provided by the ball or knob turning on the legs and stretchers

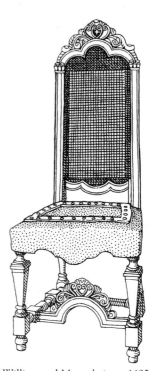

William and Mary chair, c. 1695. Made of walnut, it has a high back decorated with Corinthian capitals and elaborate cresting whose form is echoed by that of the stretcher which links the front legs of 'trumpet' form

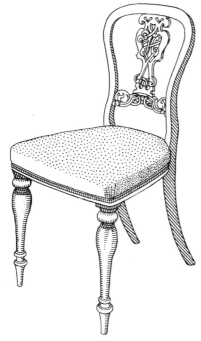

Hindley's of Oxford Street, London, made this Victorian dining chair around 1860. It is a variant of the 'Balloon back' chair so popular in the mid-19th century

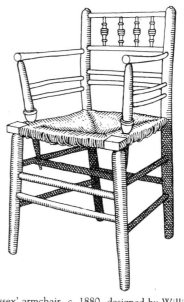

'Sussex' armchair, c. 1880, designed by William Morris and executed in ebonised beech with a rush seat. This was the Aesthetic Movement's answer to High Victorian opulence

A 'novel and useful' article of 1811 – a metamorphic library chair, combining the comfort of an armchair with the practicality of a set of library steps

exploited the possibilities of mahogany, a rich, dark, close-grained wood that rapidly replaced walnut as the most popular material for fashionable furniture. Not all furniture was made in London, however, and country chairs of the 'Windsor' type continued to be made in such woods as beech, elm and yew, with only a minimal acknowledgement to prevailing taste in the form of the ubiquitous cabriole leg, itself going out of fashion as Neoclassicism began to influence architects and their patrons in the 1760s.

The Adam brothers were the leading exponents of the new style, which looked back to Greece as well as Rome for its inspiration, while the publication of the objects excavated from Pompeii and Herculaneum gave it an authentic archaeological flavour which found its most extreme expression in the designs of Thomas Hope. The so-called 'sabre' leg derives from a type of chair frequently depicted on Greek vases, and decorative elements such as lions' masks, the Greek key pattern and the 'anthemion' motif, based on the honeysuckle flower, feature on much furniture of the late 18th and early 19th century. Elegant, fragile drawing room chairs in painted beech are characteristic of the Regency period, but by the 1830s a certain ponderousness makes itself apparent, so that the typical single chair of the William IV period (1830–37) is characterised by a solid horizontal back rest and turned front legs. The round or 'balloon back' chair made its appearance about 1850, usually executed in mahogany and often provided with an upholstered seat that was 'buttoned' to give a quilted effect. The reaction to this over stuffed look, popular with the newly rich manufacturing families, was pioneered by William Morris who looked at vernacular country furniture for his inspiration.

These two trends developed side by side during the Victorian period: the 'Philistines' continued to favour solidly made, heavy looking chairs often decorated with elaborate turning, in the style popularised by Sir Charles Eastlake in his 'Hints on Household Taste', whereas 'artistic' people perched on the 'Rossetti' or 'Sussex' chair designed by Morris. The emergence in Europe of the Art Nouveau style affected Scotland particularly, but the designs of Charles Rennie Mackintosh found a popular echo all over Britain in the 'Quaint' style.

New materials other than wood were tried out: papier mâché, often inlaid with mother of pearl, was used for small occasional chairs and an enterprising manufacturer produced a suite of chairs made of antlers, which has been aptly described as 'the art of making the hideous out of the unsuitable'. At the Great Exhibition of 1851, Michel Thonet, an Austrian, had shown his bentwood chair which rapidly became the norm for shops and tearooms, as well as providing cheap seating in the homes of the less well-to-do on both sides of the Atlantic.

Towards the end of the 19th century there was a revival of the use of oak, and the chairs of the architect-designer C. F. A. Voysey have the unpretentious solidity of medieval furniture as well as looking forward to the functionalism of the 20th century.

THE
PLANTAGENETS

by John Palmer

Painted sedilia, Westminster Abbey

This was a violent age. The period from 1216 to 1485 opened amid the throes of one civil war and closed in the turmoil of another. Kings were seven times driven from their thrones, and five of them were done to death. The aristocracy fared little better. Civil strife or the executioner's axe took its toll of every noble family and of many famous names. Simon de Montfort, Henry 'Hotspur' Percy, and Warwick the Kingmaker all died in battle against their king, along with many others of their class; and 'Butcher' Tiptoft earned that name for his summary executions of fellow peers, before falling to the axe himself in 1471.

Nor was political violence the prerogative of kings and nobles. The Peasants' Revolt in the reign of Richard II, the Lollard rising under Henry V, and Jack Cade's rebellion against Henry VI are reminders that violence was endemic at all levels of society. Civil disorder was compounded by foreign wars of unprecedented scale and duration, while the twin spectres of famine and plague hung like a pall over much of the age.

To all of this, however, the 13th century forms a partial exception. Though punctuated by baronial revolts, the violence was episodic, its social and economic impact slight, and the main political consequence – the emergence of parliament – constructive. Foreign wars, too, were few and brief, and taxation therefore light. Population was everywhere rising, forcing up rents and prices and forcing down the level of wages. Low taxes, rising incomes and falling costs made this the most prosperous of all medieval centuries for the great landowners. No century, in consequence, has left a richer heritage of monumental building.

Kings led the way, the works of Henry III and his son Edward I being unsurpassed by their successors. During their reigns the Tower of London, largely their work, achieved its present appearance; surviving sketches of the Palace of Westminster, and of the Painted Chamber where parliament was often to meet, reveal them to have been patrons of the greatest of the artists of the age. But Henry III's principal monument is Westminster Abbey. Begun in 1245, the abbey is so stamped with the architectural conceptions of the period that later builders have felt compelled to adhere to the style of its founder in completing it. Its chapter house, which was to become the traditional meeting place of the House of Commons in the next century, was declared by contemporaries to be 'incomparable'.

Henry was also a castle builder on a considerable scale, though only minor examples, like Clifford's Tower, now survive. But in this field he was completely outstripped by his son. The great Welsh castles encircling Snowdonia, built to hold down North Wales after its conquest in the wars of 1277 and 1282–3, survive almost intact to proclaim their effectiveness. A monument to the most enduring achievement of Edward's reign, they are also among the greatest examples of medieval military architecture to be seen anywhere in Europe.

Where kings led the aristocracy followed. But their buildings have withstood the test of time less well. Although they were considerable patrons of the new orders of friars, and foremost among the founders of new towns, the urban character of both has militated against their survival. The aristocracy also endowed the majority of the new religious houses of the age, and of these rather more survive, though few as intact as Lacock in Wiltshire, founded by the Countess of Salisbury in 1232. Even their castle building is not easy to disentangle from the work of earlier and later periods, though the castles of the Clares at Caerphilly, of the Bigods at Chepstow, and of the Lancastrians at Kidwelly compare with all but the greatest of Edward I's castles.

But the greatest builders of the 13th century were the ecclesiastical corporations, whose prosperity is overwhelmingly evident in the material remains of the age. Few of our cathedrals or abbeys failed to make substantial additions or alterations to their fabric, and a great many were almost entirely rebuilt. Salisbury is the supreme example. Built on a new site, all but the central tower and spire was raised between 1220 and 1258. No other cathedral belongs so entirely to this century, though Wells and Lincoln very largely do. As for the abbeys, the ruined shells of Fountains, Rievaulx, Tintern and Whitby bear silent witness to the scale of rebuilding by the monastic orders.

The magnificence of these cathedrals and the haunted beauty of many of the ruined abbeys have inspired generations of artists and poets, tending to form our image of the religious life of the period. But they are a misleading guide. Almost without exception, they are the remains of institutions already old and wealthy when the century began. They represent ancient wealth and venerable privilege in an age when poverty and deprivation were the supreme religious virtues.

For this was the century of St Francis. Vowed to poverty and simplicity, the early friars would accept no property, nor even money. They aimed to be 'poorer than the poor and more humble than the humble'. When they first arrived in England in 1224, the Franciscans relied upon charity to take them across the Channel and upon charity to provide their first night's lodging. Tales of inadequate clothing and housing, of meals of black bread, of beer so bitter than even water seemed preferable, all cheerfully told, are the stuff of their early history. It is a chronicle of deprivation and self-denial.

The Franciscans were devoted to poverty with a zeal, and at times a fanaticism, which was not equally shared by the other preaching orders, nor even by all shades of opinion among the Grey Friars themselves. But although there were differences of emphasis, the ideals of poverty and simplicity were common to all, be they

Built when there was a lull in the violence that marked the Age of the Plantagenets, Lincoln Cathedral, finished by the middle of the 13th century, is a definitive example of English gothic architecture, with more elegance than earlier cathedrals

Grey Friars, Black Friars (Dominicans), White Friars (Carmelites), or any other of the many preaching orders to proliferate during the course of the century. The great majority of their friaries were consequently small and poor institutions, ill-equipped to stand the test of time.

Poverty was not the only obstacle to their survival. The friars were overwhelmingly an urban phenomenon. Where the monastic orders had aimed at the perfection of the individual soul, the friars sought to change mankind. The monastic ideal required seclusion from the world; that of the friars, immersion in it. In the social conditions of the 13th century, this meant planting their friaries in the fast-growing towns. All the major towns received friaries, often several of them, during the course of the century. Of the 100 or more houses founded, all but a handful were urban foundations. The occupation of prime urban sites was lethal for them after the Dissolution. Though one or two of their churches survive in towns, the only reasonably intact friaries are atypical plantations in rural areas.

The universities have left even fewer traces. Like the friars, they were largely the creation of the 13th century. Like the friars, they were an urban phenomenon. And like the friars, they were poor (though not from choice). But the scantiness of their material remains is mainly due to other causes. The student of this period was housed and taught in halls, indistinguishable from private houses and as little likely to survive. The university had virtually no 'plant'. Despite its European reputation, it was very nearly invisible even at the end of the century. Although some colleges were founded, and something of Merton survives, the days of the great collegiate establishments lay some way in the future in 1300.

That friars and students should settle in towns is characteristic of the period. The 13th century is the last century of urban expansion before Tudor times. Some 50 new boroughs and towns were planted, and the population of existing towns increased substantially. Of the 100 or so walled towns in medieval England, most built or rebuilt their walls at this time. But little of this is now evident on the ground. The chequerboard pattern of the streets of such towns as Salisbury is an indication of their medieval foundations, and the extent of some others is apparent from the line of their walls, as at York. But not many towns have even this to show. Even the churches – often the best guide to their prosperity – are poorly represented, since little of the urban investment in the friaries now survives. The material remains of the age do scant justice to the importance of its towns.

The first serious check to the boom conditions of the 13th century was produced by the war with Scotland which erupted in 1296. Earlier wars, even the conquest

Peaceful scene with a warlike history: this church at Fotheringhay, Norfolk, is one of the 'war churches' endowed by Plantagenet captains from the spoils of ransom in France. Fotheringhay was founded by Edward III's grandson, Edward of York

Caerphilly, biggest castle in Wales, stands in the middle of an artificial lake. It withstood a siege by the Welsh in 1316. Edward II was besieged here in 1326 by his estranged wife Isabella and her lover, Roger Mortimer, the Marcher lord

of Wales in the 1280s, had been brief and comparatively inexpensive. But the Scottish War of Independence inaugurated almost two centuries of foreign and domestic conflict, soon to be overlaid by famine and plague.

None of this could have been predicted in 1296. It seemed indeed that the resistance of the Scots might prove to be even more short-lived than that of the Welsh before them. It had taken two major campaigns, the execution of their leaders, a prodigious castle-building programme, the exhumation of 'King Arthur' and the theft and destruction of the crown of their 'once and future' king to deprive the Welsh both of their independence and of their cherished hopes of a greater future.

But the 'Hammer of the Scots' subdued his northern enemies in a single campaign in 1296, asserted his overlordship 'as heir to King Arthur', and gave substance to this claim by the removal of the Stone of Scone – on which Scottish kings were traditionally crowned – to Westminster, where it remains to this day to testify to Edward's determination to be master of Britain.

But this initial conquest quickly proved ephemeral. The Stone of Scone was to be Edward's only material

gain from a protracted war which saw the ruin of any realistic prospect of a kingdom of Britain for centuries to come. The main casualty of English ambitions in Scotland, in fact, was the all but entire loss of the lordship of Ireland, denuded of men and money to fight the Scottish war to such an extent that it steadily crumbled away before the Celtic revival of the 14th century.

But all this lay far in the future in 1296. Heavy defeats inflicted on the Scots at Dunbar in that year, and again at Falkirk in 1298, seemed to show that the Scots had neither the resources nor the leaders to defy Edward for any length of time. Yet despite the almost annual invasion of Scotland by the largest English armies raised during the entire Middle Ages, Edward I was finally unable to break the will of the Scots to resist. Under the leadership of such men as William Wallace and Robert the Bruce – probably the only medieval king to be expert in guerrilla warfare – the guile, courage and persistence of the Scots eventually triumphed over the massive resources of the English invaders.

They did so by the use of tactics of self-denial on an almost inhuman scale. Since they could not defeat a competently led English army in a set-piece battle, the Scots melted away into the hills and the forests in the face of each English army, destroying their own lands as they withdrew to deny supplies to the enemy. And since they had neither the financial nor material resources to sustain or to resist protracted sieges, they destroyed themselves every town and castle in their own hands or which they could capture by trickery, treachery or escalade. Even Edinburgh – twice levelled – was not spared. Two famous exceptions highlight the need for such tactics, despite their appalling cost. Attempts to retain Stirling (1314) and Berwick (1333) committed the Scots to pitched battles against invading English armies far superior in numbers and equipment. Only the brilliance of Bruce and the utter incompetence of Edward II saved them on the first occasion. The second cost them all the gains of the previous generation.

The nature of such savage warfare has left its mark on the landscape to this day. Whereas the swift conquest of Wales betrays itself by a ring of noble castles around Snowdonia, the Scottish War of Independence left Lowland Scotland a wasteland of ruined and levelled towns and castles. No major military, or even ecclesiastical building of this period survives, and much of the considerable building of the 12th and 13th centuries also fell victim to the exigencies of national survival. The English – though considerable castle builders in Scotland – contributed their own share to this destruction, principally at the expense of ecclesiastical buildings. In these circumstances it is scarcely surprising that the two principal monuments of the Scottish War of Independence – the Wallace memorial and the 'field' of Bannockburn – are the creations of modern Scottish nationalism.

Having once expelled the English by this grim war of guerrilla attrition, Bruce took the initiative, devastating the northern counties as far south as Yorkshire, with a series of lightning raids which bled the countryside white. But since the small and poorly armed Scottish forces depended entirely for their effectiveness upon the speed and daring of their raids, they were ill-equipped to undertake sieges and would have been foolhardy to try to do so. Their principal victims were therefore the villages, churches and monasteries. Towns and castles were generally by-passed and continued to flourish – militarily speaking – in a devastated countryside. The war which left Lowland Scotland virtually a desert therefore had the apparently paradoxical effect of actually enhancing the architectural inheritance of the northern counties devastated by the same war. Not only did such older centres as Carlisle, Bamburgh, Alnwick and Durham strengthen their existing defences, but new or substantially re-structured castles arose at Bolton-in-Wensleydale, Knaresborough and Warkworth, and at many smaller sites (such as Bywell), even if we exclude the ubiquitous 'peels' of the later part of the war.

Left to themselves, the English might conceivably have worn down the Scots. But there was never any chance that they would be left to themselves. From the outset of the Scottish War of Independence, the kings of France fished for their own profit in the muddied waters, intervening whenever the English appeared to be gaining the upper hand. Pressure, and occasionally war, on

Early English arcading sheltering figures of kings on the west front of Lincoln Cathedral. Lincoln also has two magnificent round windows with original glass – the Dean's Eye, north transept, is 13th century and the Bishop's Eye, south transept, 14th century

two fronts undermined domestic stability. Even the masterful Edward I had to endure a major constitutional crisis, while his inept son, Edward II, lost his throne and his life after a reign of unrelieved failure against the Scots, of which Bannockburn was merely the most spectacular example. His murderer, Mortimer, fared no better, paying with his life for the 'shameful peace' he concluded with Scotland.

Thus, when the youthful and ardent Edward III tore up this peace and resumed the war in 1333, it appeared that the cycle of the past 40 years might well repeat itself. And so, in a certain manner, it did. But Edward III gave the situation a novel twist. Impatient of the pressures from France which were threatening his conquest of Scotland, he decided to reverse his grandfather's priorities and to conquer France first. Scotland, henceforth, was a secondary concern, the affair of the northern barons.

The era of border warfare ensued, a period lasting into the 16th century and characterised by the 'peels', or fortified private houses, to be found in such numbers on both sides of the border. Henceforth the major resources of Plantagenet England were to be devoted to

Charles I stood trial here. Westminster Hall is all that remains of the Plantagenet Palace of Westminster, which burnt down in 1834. It has Britain's finest example of a hammer beam roof. The statues are of kings of England from the reign of Richard II

of 1381, Jack Cade's rebellion of 1450, and the Wars of the Roses all owed their inception to pressures created by the Hundred Years' War.

Political tension was accompanied, and partly created, by enormous financial costs. By the late 13th century, the unpaid feudal armies of earlier centuries had become obsolescent. From the reign of Edward I all ranks henceforth served in the king's pay. The combination of paid service and almost uninterrupted war meant taxation on a scale which had not been seen in western Europe since the fall of the Roman Empire.

War, civil disorder, and heavy and persistent taxation combined to produce significant changes in the balance of social forces, but nothing as significant as the effects produced by the third great catastrophe of the age, the Black Death. Originating in China in the 1330s, the Black Death reached Europe across the wastes of central Asia, devastating the Byzantine Empire in the 1340s before attacking parts of Italy in 1348. By the summer of that year it had arrived in England.

The scale of the catastrophe is almost unimaginable, even in a nuclear age. 'It filled the whole world with terror,' wrote one contemporary, while another believed that 'the whole race of Adam' was about to perish. Within two years half the parish priests in the country were dead. In some villages two out of every three people died. Nationally, something like a third of the population was carried off. Subsequent outbreaks reduced the population even further. The plague of 1361–2 was particularly lethal to children, while that of 1369 was believed to be even more deadly than the first onslaught. By the end of the Middle Ages recurrent outbreaks had reduced the population to little more than half its pre-plague level.

For the landowning classes as a whole this appalling mortality was also an economic catastrophe. With tenants in short supply, rents fell sharply and wages rose, doubling in the course of a century. The enormous contraction in the market for their agricultural products forced prices on a downward spiral which was not to be reversed before Tudor times. High wages, low rents, and lower prices spelt disaster.

But it was a disaster tempered for some, aggravated for others. The Crown, though the greatest landowner, more than made good its declining revenue from land by increasing taxation. The greatest constraint on its ability to build was henceforth the demands of war expenditure. This was already apparent in the reign of Edward I. The great bulk of his expenditure on the Tower, Westminster Palace and the Welsh castles was incurred before the outbreak of the war with Scotland in 1296. His son Edward II, uniformly unsuccessful in war, had few resources for the arts of peace. Typically enough, his main memorial is his own tomb, which he neither commissioned, paid for, nor even occupies! Even his foundation of a friary at King's Langley to enshrine the body of his worthless favourite, Piers Gaveston, was largely paid for by his son, Edward III.

continental adventures. For the remainder of the Middle Ages Edward I's dream of a Britain ruled by his dynasty was all but forgotten. The Hundred Years' War was about to begin.

The opening of the Hundred Years' War in 1337 changed many things but it did not fundamentally alter the domestic pressure of foreign wars. If anything, it increased those pressures. Kings or their ministers continued to receive the shortest of shrifts for failure abroad. Both Richard II, done to death in Pontefract castle in 1400, and Henry VI, murdered in the Tower in 1471, were victims of the war with France.

Their ministers had paid the high price of failure before them. Richard's chancellor and treasurer were dragged from the Tower and executed by a mob in 1381, and Henry's Lord Privy Seal was murdered by angry soldiers in 1450. Some fled the country. Several of Richard's counsellors took this course, including 'old John of Gaunt, time honoured Lancaster', who found safety in Scotland in 1381. But not all were successful. The Duke of Suffolk, who had presided over the final debacle of the war, was intercepted at sea and had his head hacked off with a rusty sword. The Peasants' Revolt

Edward III himself was the very antithesis of his father. Perhaps the greatest of our warrior kings, he was the only king after 1296 to rival the great builders of the 13th century. But Edward made his wars pay for his buildings. It was in the immensely successful years spanned by the battles of Crécy (1346), Poitiers (1356) and Nájera (1367) that most of his major projects were commissioned and executed. Windsor castle – his Versailles – which so perfectly expresses his chivalrous conception of kingship, was begun after Crécy and substantially completed within the next 20 years. Although the most expensive single building raised by any medieval English king, it could have been paid for from the profits of Crécy alone. Indeed, the single ransom of King John of France (£500,000), captured at Poitiers, could have paid twice over for all the building of Edward's 51-year reign.

For most kings, however, the costs of war far exceeded its profits. After the reign of Edward III, only Henry VI and Edward IV have left considerable monuments. Typically enough, Edward IV's great hall at Eltham, and his foundation of St George's Chapel, Windsor, were both the work of the latter part of his reign, when the Hundred Years' War and the Wars of the Roses were rapidly becoming no more than bad memories and when Edward had become the pensioner of the king of France. As for Henry VI's foundations of King's College, Cambridge, and of Eton, these are exceptions which prove the rule. Founded in the 1440s, when the Lancastrian empire in France was crumbling away and when the government was deeper in debt than ever before in its history, they merely demonstrate that Henry VI, the feeblest of our medieval kings, was well accustomed to fiddling while Rome burnt. It was, inevitably, left to his successors to complete his work.

While only the most successful kings gained financially from war, only the most inept or unfortunate of their noble subjects failed to do so. For the Hundred Years' War was a very different affair from the dour struggle against a poor and barren Scotland. France was the richest and most fertile country in Europe. Her very wealth made her the more vulnerable. It was unthinkable that 'the most Christian king' should take to the woods, as his impoverished Scottish cousin had learnt to do in the face of an English invasion. Yet any other course invited disaster. Neither superior wealth nor superior numbers enabled the French to cope with the formidable power of the English longbow. Crécy, Poitiers, Nájera, Agincourt, Cravant, Verneuil, and a score of lesser encounters, testified to its awful effectiveness. For the first and only time in her history, England became the foremost military power in Europe.

It was a situation exploited to the hilt by those who led her armies. War became a business offering immense dividends. Where else was it possible to become a millionaire in the space of an afternoon? The squires who captured King David of Scotland at Neville's Cross and King John of France at Poitiers were instantly wealthy.

An Englishman's home becomes his castle: Sir John Fastolf – the original of Shakespeare's Falstaff – built Caister Castle, Norfolk, on the proceeds of ransoms from prisoners captured in France. He made £16,000 in one afternoon after a battle at Verneuil

In an age when the labourer was worthy of his hire at 2p a day, and when an income of £1,000 a year would sustain an earl, the £16,000 earned on an afternoon at Verneuil by Sir John Fastolf – Shakespeare's rumbustious Falstaff – was a splendid fortune. The Black Prince won more than his spurs at Crécy, and made £20,000 out of just three prisoners taken at Poitiers. On the same day the Earl of Warwick earned £8,000 for the ransom of the Archbishop of Sens – a windfall equal to three times the annual income from his estates in 25 English counties.

A successful battle was the quickest way to riches but not the only one. The plunder of looted or occupied territory could be equally profitable. An entire fleet was needed to transport the spoils of the Crécy campaign back home; and according to contemporaries, the rank and file of whole armies made their fortunes in a single campaign under such leaders as the Black Prince, the Earl of Derby, Sir Robert Knolles and many another. A campaign did not even have to be successful to be profitable. John of Gaunt's abortive attempt to conquer Castile in the 1380s profited him to the tune of £100,000 down and £6,500 a year for the rest of his life, making him one of the richest magnates in Europe. Gains of this kind more than compensated the English aristocracy for their losses elsewhere.

The warrior gentlemen of late medieval England have consequently left traces too numerous to mention. Their tombs, their effigies and their brasses are to be found in churches and chantries up and down the country. The visible signs of their wealth, if less numerous, are even more impressive. Bodiam, Bolton in Yorkshire, Caister, Hurstmonceux, Sudeley and Tattershall, all raised by notably successful captains, represent but a fraction of the castles and manors built from the spoils of the war with France.

They were built, moreover, to standards of luxury unknown to an earlier age, with chimneyed hearths, private apartments, and glazed and decorated windows. In this period, the Englishman's castle became his home. A few earlier examples are known – Stokesay, built by a wool merchant and therefore 'not quite a castle since he was not quite a gentleman' – but the century spanned by the Hundred Years' War with France undoubtedly 'saw the first great flowering of English *domestic* architecture'.

Aristocratic investment in the Church was equally conspicuous and took forms characteristic of the age. Neither the monastic corporations nor the friars any longer represented the dominant religious impulses. They consequently attracted little patronage. Of the mere handful of houses founded, most were small and poor, although the London Charterhouse, built on the site of mass burials of the victims of the Black Death by Sir Walter Mauny, one of Edward III's most dashing captains, was a distinguished exception. But the typical foundation of the period was the chantry or collegiate church, where masses in huge numbers were offered up for the soul of the founder and his family. Like the great castles, the most impressive of these chantries, and of the grander parish churches, were the work of captains and war profiteers. Arundel, Fotheringay, Tattershall and Warwick and others of their kind are the war churches of the late Middle Ages.

The war that enriched the aristocracy served only to deplete even further the shrinking income of the Church. Practically every one of the social, economic, political and religious tendencies of the age had an adverse effect upon the ecclesiastical corporations. As taxpayers, they bore a disproportionately heavy share of war taxation; as churchmen, their benefices were increasingly taxed by the papacy; and as landowners, their revenues slumped badly as a consequence of the Black Death.

These losses might have been sustained without serious damage if the churches had retained their hold upon the religious imagination of the age. But this they manifestly failed to do. In a period when the dominant religious trend favoured an inward-looking, personal piety, the religious orders were increasingly an irrelevance. As Chaucer's portraits reveal, monks and friars were not popularly believed to have much to do

with religion, and nothing at all with piety. In consequence, the 'possessioners' – as the corporations were derogatively known – were not only abused by radical religious movements, such as the Lollards, but were attacked by the gentry in parliament, and selectively plundered by the Crown. For the first time in 500 years, the number of religious establishments declined, foreshadowing their fate in Tudor times.

All this is reflected in the reduced scale and increasingly secular appearance of much of their building. Despite major projects undertaken at Exeter and Ely, at Oxford and Cambridge, there is a perceptible *diminuendo* in building activity, accelerating after the Black Death. The characteristic buildings are the massive monastic gatehouses, the magnificent but liturgically redundant towers which everywhere rose above the abbeys and cathedrals and, above all, the great collegiate establishments of Oxford and Cambridge 'whispering from their towers the last enchantments of the Middle Age'. Such buildings, as one foreign visitor remarked, were 'more like baronial palaces than religious houses'. They are an apt reflection of the religious temper of the Orders.

While the Church groaned under its economic burdens, the peasantry prospered as never before and rarely since. The Black Death has left its mark on the countryside in ruined churches in empty landscapes, and in the bare sites of deserted villages. But for the survivors of this holocaust, the material prosperity purchased by their scarcity value was some small compensation. Their depleted ranks forced rents and prices down and wages and the size of their farms up, while serfdom virtually disappeared.

The consequent 'ease and riches the common folk are of' was widely observed by contemporaries fearful of this novel social power of the peasantry, manifest in its recurrent unrest, in the cataclysm of the Peasants' Revolt, and the spread of egalitarian tendencies:

When Adam delved and Eve span,
Who was then the gentleman?

The 'ease and riches', if not the social pretensions, of the peasantry are writ large on the face of the countryside, in the village churches raised by village communities. No other period can show so rich a heritage. While there are no Perpendicular abbeys and no Perpendicular cathedrals, there are hundreds, possibly even thousands, of Perpendicular parish churches. And although they cluster particularly densely in areas where a nascent rural cloth industry was bringing new forms of wealth to the countryside, no part of the country is entirely without them. Their characteristic towers are testimony to the 'golden age of the English peasantry'.

Townspeople also prospered, though this was a bleak age for towns. Like the great landowners, towns suffered from a shortage of people. Deserted villages had their counterparts in shrunken towns. The records of the day are loud with complaints of urban decay, empty tenements, and corporate poverty. But what was bad for

Another example of the wealth of the church in the Middle Ages: Bede House, Higham Ferrers, Northants., consists of this chapel, a hall, a college and a gatehouse, all founded by Archbishop Chichele in the 1420s and still intact. The house was obliged to provide accommodation for '12 deserving old men and a female attendant.'

towns as corporations was not necessarily bad for townsmen as individuals. Falling food prices were accompanied by a rise in the price of most manufactured goods, a combination beneficial to artisan, manufacturer and merchant alike. Some of the new prosperity of the countryside was inevitably siphoned off into the neighbouring towns. At the end of the Middle Ages the towns accounted for more of the taxable wealth of the country than at the peak of the urban boom two centuries previously.

Individuals were wealthier than ever before. Dick Whittington began his career with little more capital than his cat, but he had become a wealthy man by the time he died in 1423. The de la Poles of Hull rose first to merchant riches and then into the ranks of the aristocracy in the space of two generations in the 14th century, a century which also saw the first marriage of an earl to a merchant's daughter. In the reigns of Richard II and Henry IV, merchants from London and the west country were able to put fleets to sea against the French when the government could not afford to do so.

The typical survivals of the age are therefore the work of individual capitalists or of guilds rather than of urban corporations. No new towns were founded in this period, and the building of town walls had all but ceased by the middle of the 14th century. London was not paved with gold. It is in such buildings as St Mary, Redcliffe, and St Michael's, Coventry, foundations by individual capitalists, in the chantries founded by guilds of merchants and artisans, and in urban churches financed by the bequests of the townspeople, that we can see reflected the prosperity of the century or so after the Black Death.

Despite plague and depopulation, despite foreign war and domestic violence, Englishmen were generally wealthier at the end of the Middle Ages than at any previous time in their history. They were also more English. England, in this age of foreign adventure, acquired much of its insular outlook.

At the beginning of the 13th century England was very much a small part of a wider community. Politically, she was a part – though the most important part – of the Angevin Empire, whose centre lay in France. Her kings were of French descent, and French blood flowed in the veins of the nobility too. Many nobles held lands

Last resting place for an Agincourt hero and his wife: these finely painted alabaster effigies of Lord Bardolph and his wife, Joan, lie in St Mary's Church, Dennington, Suffolk. He died in 1441. It was not until the next century that tombstone fashion changed and monuments to the dead depicted them standing or kneeling

in France, and French was their native language. Their 'Frenchness' was continually reinforced by ties of ownership, marriage and recruitment. Simon de Montfort was a first-generation Englishman, and the favourites of such kings as Henry III and Edward II were typically newcomers from across the Channel. The Scottish border was just as 'open'. Robert the Bruce was an Englishman by descent and an English landowner, as were many other Scottish magnates.

Ecclesiastically, too, England was but a fragment of a larger whole. The Church was never more part of Catholic Europe than in the 13th century, when it was heavily taxed from Rome and increasingly subject to papal supervision. The dominant intellectual and religious movements of the age came from across the Channel, from the schools of Paris, the monks of Cîteaux, or from the friars of St Francis.

But by the end of the Middle Ages all this had changed. The Crown had lost its territories abroad, and the nobility their lands. Scottish nobles no longer held large estates in England, nor Englishmen in Scotland. Frontiers were everywhere more sharply defined. Though Edward IV was the first reigning monarch to take an English wife, the nobility had long since lost the habit of foreign alliances. Even royal favourites had become home-grown by the reign of Richard II.

In all walks of life English had ousted French, even the French of 'the scole of Stratford atte Bowe'. The language of Chaucer and Langland was their inheritance; to speak French had become an accomplishment. Even the religious literature of the age was largely English. 'Wycliffe's bible' was the first complete English translation. Religious movements, too, were indigenous, the mystics and Lollards being English in origin, in language and in sentiment. The 'Church of England' was in name, and very nearly in fact, the product of this period. The stage had been set for the Tudor age.

THE SMALL HOUSE

by Lyndon Cave

The basic shapes of ordinary people's houses and the materials they were made of changed remarkably little over the centuries until the end of the Middle Ages. Only then did factors like new building techniques and changing fashions begin to dictate recognisable architectural styles, each of which lasted successively shorter periods of time. Very few early small houses have survived. They were usually made of perishable materials and almost all of them have vanished, leaving behind few traces of their existence. Unlike fortifications or churches they were not built to last for more than a few generations, so generally the older the building that survives today the more important it was when it was constructed.

The vagaries of the British landscape have until recently dictated what could be used for house-building. Materials had to be locally available, and before techniques for cutting and shaping were developed, the first houses were made of whatever could be picked up from the ground.

Stone, the most durable of materials, was used during the Tribal and Roman periods, and in places like Chysauster in Cornwall and Skara Brae in Orkney the remains of village settlements do survive. The first dwellings were made of small unshaped stones held together with mud, their roofs covered with a layer of grass or heather. Round huts were partly sunk into the ground for protection against the weather. Circular buildings required no skill in shaping corners, but as skills improved huts became larger, rectangular in shape with simple timber roofs supporting the coverings. The Saxons generally used stone and timber only for their larger buildings such as churches. It was not until the Norman period that stone began to be used again for small domestic buildings. The richer merchants built simple two-storey rectangular houses with thatched roofs, later replaced by tiles. A few examples still exist in English cities, perhaps the best known is the Jew's House in Steep Hill, Lincoln.

Clay was also one of the earliest building materials. Known as cob in southern England, it was used from tribal times until this century. The Romans also used clay in the form of unbaked bricks rendering the walls with lime mixed with straw. Remains of such buildings were found during the excavation of a Roman site in Leicester and similar methods were still employed to build cottages in East Anglia up to the 1850s. More commonly, clay was rammed down between wooden shuttering to form a solid wall and then finished with whitewash or in ancient times dried cow-dung. Thick walls, two to four feet wide, and rounded corners are the characteristic signs of clay buildings. One of the largest surviving groups of cob cottages can be seen at Milton Abbas built between 1771 and 1790.

Timber has always been used for house-building in areas where it was plentiful. Before the early medieval period, simple tent-shaped houses were made by leaning rows of posts against each other and securing them at the top. Straw or heather covered the timber. The posts were gradually reduced in number and increased in size, eventually becoming curved 'crucks' which can still be seen exposed in the gabled walls of many old cottages. The first documentary reference to 'crucks' is dated 1225 and there are many subsequent descriptions of their use in buildings, although most surviving examples date from little earlier than the 17th century. No one knows definitely how the curved crucks came to be used or why this particular shape was adopted, but many such houses must have been built, as a 1981 survey recorded 3,000 remaining, either complete or in an altered condition.

The first timber-framed houses, and certainly those from the 15th century onwards, had large vertical uprights spaced closely together with the uprights rarely separated by more than twice the width of the timber, and frequently only the same width apart. Broadly speaking, the larger in size and closer together the vertical

One of Britain's earliest habitations, a hyena den in the Cheddar Gorge, Mendip Hills, which was used as a temporary shelter by bands of hunters between 27000 BC and 8000 BC

A Saxon dwelling reconstructed on the excavated Saxon village site at West Stow in Suffolk. Although the exact construction is conjectural, the details are based on archaeological evidence, the living space being partly sunk into the ground, with timber walls and a roof covered with a rough layer of straw or heather

The Jew's House, Steep Hill, Lincoln, a two storeyed stone building, part of a continuous street frontage. It is a rare example of a merchant's house of the 12th century. In similar houses, entry to the first floor was usually by a door at the upper level, accessible by an external staircase. The arched openings originally had no fixed glazing and the existing sashes are 19th-century additions

A 15th-century timber-framed house from Bromsgrove, dismantled, moved to the Avoncroft Museum of Buildings, Worcester, and there repaired and re-erected. The service end of the house, next to the cross passage marked by the door, is missing. The cross wing contains the two-storeyed hall with the parlour and the upper room known as the solar

A house in the High St, Burford, Oxfordshire which was converted into a chapel in 1849 when the interior was gutted and urns removed from the parapet. Built in 1715 in the Palladian style, it is reputed to have been the work of Christopher Kempster of Burford, who was master mason to Sir Christopher Wren

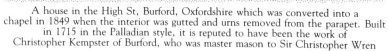

House at Weobley, a good example of a medieval cruck-framed construction. The walls have square timber-framed panels, originally filled with wattle and daub and independent of the curved oak crucks at the ends of the house. The window openings are not original

The house of a prosperous wool merchant, William Grevel, at Chipping Campden, Gloucestershire. He lived until 1401 and built this stone house as part of a continuous street facade, typical of many Cotswold towns. The outstanding feature is the perpendicular bay with its stone mullioned windows. The small windows flanking the bay at ground floor level are later insertions

Little Hall, Lavenham, Suffolk, a 15th-century wool merchant's house. The central part has a hall open to the roof and the jettied cross wing shows timber framing typical of East Anglian houses of that period

Dutch House, Kew, built in 1631 by a Dutch merchant, Samuel Fortrey, is made of brick and one of the earliest examples in England of a building in Flemish bond brick construction rather than the English bond then in common use. Its three gables, with double curved sides, are typical of this style of house and are still called 'Dutch gables' in the eastern and south-eastern counties

Typical Georgian terraced town house, a type familiar in cities and towns all over the country. Their formal symmetry was the result of a series of Acts of Parliament for precautions against fire, which regulated all sorts of details like floor to ceiling heights, proportion of wall to window, and heights of windows

A typical villa of the late Victorian period, found in the suburbs of many cities. Its slate roof, patterned brickwork, arched window heads and 'gothic' doors are standard features of such houses lived in by the professional and business classes of that period

Dutch-style house in Bedford Park, the London suburb designed by Victorian architect Sir Norman Shaw

timbers forming the framing, the older the house.

As joints became more effective, panels could be increased to six or seven feet square. Because of the weak structural nature of these large panels, they were braced at the ends and corners of the building and as houses became larger, the patterns of the bracing became more complicated. Before the final decline of the timber-framed tradition in the 18th century some very large, ornate houses were built in the Welsh Marches, perhaps the most famous being The Feathers Inn at Ludlow. By then the elaborate patterns of timber bracing had long ceased to have any structural use.

Timber houses fell into disfavour for several reasons, including an increasing shortage of wood, the fire risk, as well as popular fashion. There was also a change in structural techniques as whole walls became load-bearing – able to support the roof – rather than the load being taken entirely by the uprights which formed part of the timber frame.

Gradually brick and stone houses appeared in ever increasing numbers – brick especially in the lowlands where clay for making them was easier to find. The Romans had mastered the technique of baking bricks and had used them for important buildings, but this skill had departed with the legions and was not rediscovered here until about the 15th century. Hand-made from local clays, these early bricks were burnt in small kilns, often set up in the corner of the field where the clay was dug and fired with wood. This method produced irregularly shaped bricks of varying colours depending on the type of clay found in the district. At first bricks were laid in a haphazard way, but soon regular courses became desirable and from about 1580–1700 English Bond – the overlap by which bricks are fastened together – was widely used and after 1690 Flemish Bond became popular. By the 19th century cheap factory-made bricks made elaborate bonds and patterned brickwork possible.

Stone houses were common in the rocky areas of western and northern Britain. Until the 18th century they were built of roughly shaped pieces laid as random rubble or in uneven courses, then the manufacture of stone-cutting saws made it possible to cut regularly shaped blocks. This resulted in fine stone-faced houses, complete with carvings, mouldings and cornices, examples of which can be seen in cities like Bath.

Better methods of construction and the invention of new types of roof trusses radically altered the internal layout of houses. By the 17th century the typical English farmhouse built of brick or stone, square in plan with a central staircase opposite the front door, had become a classic of the countryside; and at the same period dormer windows, overhanging and hipped roofs and casement windows became technical possibilities and added to the variety of ordinary houses. Sash windows followed in the 18th century.

After the Great Fire, the Rebuilding Act of 1667, followed by those of 1707 and 1774, controlled the building of houses in London, and similar regulations were soon adopted by the larger provincial towns. These Acts rigidly controlled the height of houses, the floor to ceiling heights of the individual rooms and storeys, the area of external wall in proportion to the windows as well as the size of the windows themselves. Compliance with all these regulations produced what is today called a 'Georgian' house, with a stone or brick front elevation and moulded cornice above a series of standard-sized sash windows. They evolved as a result of obeying the rules which is why such houses resemble each other no matter where they were built. The only stylistic variation in these houses is in the front doors and their surrounds; when they were built the aristocrat, the merchant, the craftsman and the shopkeeper all lived in similar houses, but in different sizes.

During the Regency period the careful symmetry of the Georgian house was forsaken for more 'light hearted' designs, often using inferior materials. Straight lines everywhere gave way to curves, external elevations became curved walls, sash windows were replaced by shallow bow windows, cast iron balconies and all kinds of decorative features.

The Victorian era was an age of brick rather than elegance. Mass-produced, highly coloured brick became common everywhere, even in places where stone was plentiful. Nineteenth-century methods of production were basically those of previous generations, but Victoria's reign was one of invention, and quantities of labour-saving gadgets began to appear. Bathrooms and lavatories, gas lights, solid fuel and gas ovens all became familiar mod. cons. Progress suddenly made great strides away from the world of the simple clay-walled cottage towards the labour-saving house of today.

THE
TUDORS

by Roger Lockyer

Little Moreton Hall

The Tudor age began in a marshy field in Leicestershire on a hot August morning in 1485. The reigning king, the Yorkist Richard III, hearing that the Lancastrian pretender Henry Tudor had landed in Wales and was marching east, gathered an army together and moved into the Midlands to bar Henry's progress. The two armies met just outside Market Bosworth, and the ensuing battle, though brief, was decisive. Richard, fighting bravely, was cut down sword in hand, and his followers fled. As the victors cleared the field they came across the golden circlet that Richard had worn on his helmet and they placed it on the head of their triumphant leader. Henry Tudor was now Henry VII, King of England.

The Tudor dynasty which Henry established lasted over a hundred years and was to leave a glorious name behind it, yet it was always threatened by infecundity in the male line. Henry had only two sons, and the elder of these, Prince Arthur, died during his lifetime. It was his second son, therefore, who succeeded as Henry VIII in 1509. Henry VIII is notorious as the man who broke with the papacy so that he could rid himself of his first wife, Catherine of Aragon, who had provided him only with a daughter, Mary. It was taken for granted that women rulers were too weak to hold a nation in obedience, particularly under a new dynasty; hence Henry's determination to obtain a son.

His second wife, Anne Boleyn, disappointed him by giving birth to a daughter, Elizabeth, and suffered accordingly; but the third, Jane Seymour, presented him with the longed-for heir, Prince Edward, even though she died in the process. However, Edward was still a minor when his father died in 1547, and he reigned, as Edward VI, for a mere six years before illness struck him down. There was no alternative now to a woman ruler, for the only surviving children of Henry VIII were his two daughters. In 1553 Mary became queen, but her sufferings had left her prematurely aged and although she sought happiness and fulfilment in a marriage to her fellow-catholic, Philip of Spain, this proved childless. When she died in 1558 the throne passed therefore to her half-sister Elizabeth, the daughter of Anne Boleyn.

Elizabeth confounded precedent by proving that a woman could be a capable ruler, and at the end of a reign which lasted nearly half a century she had established her place among the greatest of English sovereigns. She never married, however, and at her death in 1603 the Tudor dynasty came to an end after only three generations. Yet Henry VII had prepared the way for her successor. In an attempt to put an end to the incessant conflict between England and the neighbouring kingdom of Scotland he had married his daughter Margaret to James IV, and a hundred years later it was their descendant, James VI, who became James I of England.

Henry himself, despite establishing one of the greatest of English dynasties, was a Welshman – the only Welshman, in fact, to become King of England. Although he was to be buried in Westminster Abbey he had been born at Pembroke Castle, and his father lies to this day in St David's cathedral, near the westernmost tip of Wales. Henry's paternal grandfather was Owen Tudor, a member of an ancient Welsh family who had taken as his second wife no less a person than Queen Catherine, the widow of Henry V. More important from Henry's point of view, however, was the fact that through his mother, Lady Margaret Beaufort, he was descended from John of Gaunt, Duke of Lancaster, the third son of Edward III, and it was as the representative of the royal house of Lancaster that he claimed primacy over the usurping Yorkists.

The struggle between the York and Lancaster factions which is dignified by the name of The Wars of the Roses had been going on for a quarter of a century and there was no good reason why Henry VII's accession should have brought it to a close. Indeed, a mere two years after his victory at Bosworth he was forced to take up arms against a Yorkist challenger, but in a hard-fought and bloody battle at East Stoke, not far from Nottingham, he was again triumphant. The battle of Stoke really marked the end of the Wars of the Roses, for Henry – who had symbolically united the contesting houses by choosing as his wife Elizabeth of York, the daughter of Edward IV – held on to the throne until his death in 1509. But he could never rest secure in his exalted position; the portraits of him, with his hooded, watchful eyes, suggest a man who was deeply distrustful, and with good reason, of all those around him.

It might be thought that his successor, the youthful and ebullient Henry VIII, would have had little occasion for distrust, since the blood of both York and Lancaster ran in his veins. Yet Henry VIII was no less suspicious than his father where potential rivals were concerned. Edward Stafford, Duke of Buckingham, was one of these, since he, like Henry, was descended from Edward III. When the king heard that Buckingham was building himself a great castle at Thornbury in Gloucestershire he had him arrested, charged with treason, and executed. A similar fate befell Margaret Pole, Countess of Salisbury. She was a woman of saintly qualities but she counted Edward III among her ancestors and this made her suspect in Henry's eyes. In the closing years of his reign, when his marital problems combined with religious unrest to create an atmosphere of acute uncertainty, Margaret was brought from her home at Warblington in Hampshire, imprisoned in the Tower, and subsequently executed.

Even Elizabeth was not free from the challenge of pretenders, of whom the most threatening was the Queen of Scots, Mary Stuart. Scotland was an ancient and proud kingdom, as is witnessed by the Scottish regalia displayed in Edinburgh Castle, and her kings

Effigy of England's greatest queen, Elizabeth, on her tomb in Westminster Abbey, where she lies beside her sister, Mary Tudor. The inscription reads: 'Consort both in throne and grave, here rest we two sisters in the hope of one resurrection'

lived in settings of considerable splendour. James IV, for instance, built a princely residence for himself, Holyrood House, at one end of the Royal Mile in the old town of Edinburgh, while his successor, James V, created an exquisite palace within the frowning walls of the castle at Stirling. The Scottish kings were determined to preserve their independence from England, but for this they needed the support of a powerful ally, and the 'auld alliance' with France was the result. There was a heavy price to be paid for this alliance, however, for on the not infrequent occasions when England and France were at war, Scotland was inevitably dragged in. While Henry VIII was occupied in the French war of 1513 James IV attempted an invasion of England, but was defeated and killed at Flodden. Some 30 years later his son did much the same, but his army was routed at Solway Moss and he died shortly after, leaving only a baby girl, Mary, to succeed him.

Henry VIII hoped to unite the two kingdoms through a marriage between his son, Prince Edward, and the young Queen of Scots, but her advisers feared that this would merely be the prelude to Scotland's absorption by England. They therefore packed her off to France and married her to the heir to the French throne. The enmity between the two neighbours might have gone on indefinitely had it not been for the Protestant Reformation. While the French were identified with the cause of Scottish independence they were popular, but from the 1550s onwards, as more and more Scots embraced Protestantism, they came to be hated as the representatives of 'popery'.

If any one man may be said to have brought about the Scottish Reformation it was John Knox (whose house in the Royal Mile is now a museum). In 1559 Knox preached a powerful sermon at St John's Kirk in Perth in which he denounced 'popish idolatry', and this set off a wave of attacks on altars, images, and religious houses throughout Scotland from which the Catholic church never recovered. By the time Mary (now a young widow) returned to her native kingdom in 1560 the Protestants were in control, and although she refused to abandon her own faith she had to promise not to challenge or subvert that of her people. Yet the tension between a Catholic sovereign and a Protestant nation was too great to be resolved, and matters were not helped by Mary's desperate search for affection in her private life.

Scotland is full of reminders of Mary's brief but tragic reign. She was born in the now ruined palace of Linlithgow and crowned at Stirling. At Holyrood she was married to her second husband Lord Darnley – who was, like her, a descendant of Henry VII. This marriage was an affront to Queen Elizabeth, since it seemed to chal-

lenge her right to the English throne, and therefore to the Scottish Protestant lords who looked to Elizabeth for support. Yet it was Mary herself who contrived her own downfall. Quickly tiring of her worthless husband, she turned for comfort to the Earl of Bothwell, an unscrupulous adventurer who removed Darnley from the scene by having him murdered at Kirk o'Field, Edinburgh, in February 1567. Mary, who was widely suspected of complicity, compounded the scandal by marrying Bothwell, and this provoked the rising which led to her enforced abdication, imprisonment in Loch Leven Castle, and eventual flight to England in May 1568. Mary hoped for support from Elizabeth, but she arrived at a time of growing unrest among the Catholics of Northern England, which culminated in open rebellion and the promulgation of a Papal Bull declaring Elizabeth deposed. Mary, as the Catholic claimant to the English throne, was too dangerous to be left at liberty, and her dash for freedom turned out to be the beginning of a long and wearisome captivity. Inevitably she became implicated in plots against Elizabeth's life, and thereby forced the reluctant queen to assent to her execution. Mary went to the block at Fotheringhay Castle in Northamptonshire in February 1587.

While the ruins of Thornbury, Warblington and Fotheringhay testify to the ruthlessness of the Tudors when the preservation of their dynasty was at stake, they are also reminders that the Tudors gave their subjects the inestimable blessing of internal peace. This applied to relations with Scotland as well. Melrose Abbey, in the border country, had been repeatedly sacked by invading English armies, but the last occasion was in 1547, when the Duke of Somerset, acting on behalf of the boy-king Edward VI, attempted to bring the whole of Scotland under permanent English military occupation. The grandiose scheme stretched English resources to breaking point, however, and the invaders had to withdraw. From then on the Scots were left to themselves and the two countries were drawn closer together by the common bond of Protestantism. The ruins of Melrose Abbey are evidence therefore not simply of the abandonment of the Catholic faith in Scotland but of the peace which this brought with it as far as the borders were concerned. Other reminders of the Tudor peace are to be seen in Wales. At Carew Castle in Dyfed, for example, the Elizabethan owner constructed a magnificent hall for himself within the massive medieval walls and filled the tall, defenceless windows so full with glass that it shone like a beacon.

The achievement of internal peace after the disorder that had marked the end of the Middle Ages was not the least of the benefits of Tudor rule, and it was all the more striking in view of the limited resources which the Tudor sovereigns had at their disposal. The Yeomen of the Guard, wearing to this day the livery of Henry VII, were a symbol not of the military might of the Tudor monarchy but of its weakness, for apart from this small bodyguard the Tudors had no standing army. When they

Previous page: Longleat, Wiltshire, shows us how grandly a Tudor courtier could live. First and most classically restrained of the great Elizabethan mansions, it was built by Sir John Thynne, whose descendants live there today. In 1580 it cost £8,016 13s 8¼d

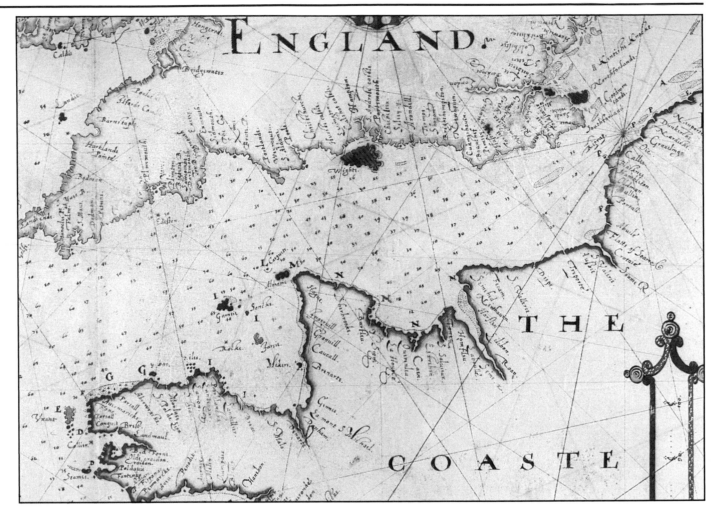

The Elizabethan Age saw great advances in the science of navigation, as adventurers like Drake and Raleigh went 'searching the most opposite corners and quarters of the world.' This chart by Thomas Hood was unusually detailed for its time

needed troops they either had to hire mercenaries – a very expensive undertaking – or call on their greater subjects for assistance. Nor did they have any police force or omnipresent bureaucracy. In fact they depended for the government of their realm upon the co-operation of countless country gentlemen, sometimes serving in an official but unpaid capacity – as Justices of the Peace, for instance – or simply resident in their localities and maintaining the social hierarchy. The Privy Council in London sent out its orders, and twice a year the common law judges rode on assize throughout the whole of England, acting as the Government's watchdogs, but none of this mechanism would have functioned properly without the full-hearted assent of the political nation – that minority of the population which, on account of its privileged position in society, ruled the rest.

There was nothing new about the Tudor system of local government. Indeed, what is remarkable about the Tudors in so many spheres is not what they created or destroyed but what they preserved. Parliament is a case in point. In Europe as a whole the 16th century saw the decline of representative assemblies, since they did not fit easily into the increasingly despotic structure of Renaissance monarchies. This was not the case in England, however. The political nation had learnt its lesson from the Wars of the Roses and preferred co-operation with a strong ruler to confrontation with a weak one. And from the ruler's point of view, so long as Parliament was willing to fulfil its essential functions of making law and voting money to the crown there was good reason for keeping it. The Tudors had no natural affection for Parliaments as such, but Thomas Cromwell persuaded Henry VIII that if these occasional assemblies were carefully managed they could be a source of strength as well as profit to the monarchy, and Elizabeth heard the same message from William Cecil. It was because the Tudors found Parliament useful that they preserved it.

Partnership with the political nation, which became the hallmark of Tudor rule, placed some limits upon the monarch's power. Even the imperious Henry VIII had to accept defeat when he tried to put an end to tax evasion by the propertied classes, for although he had law as well as natural justice on his side he risked inciting rebellion if he pressed his claims too hard. Yet the inherent weaknesses of Tudor monarchy were concealed beneath the surface appearance of wealth and splendour, as demonstrated by the royal palaces that were thickly strewn over southern England. When Henry VII became king

Christ's College, Cambridge, founded in 1505 by Henry VII's mother, Lady Margaret Beaufort, whose coat of arms adorns the elaborately decorated gateway. She also founded St John's College, and her son brought to completion the Chapel of King's College

the quality of the work and described the walls as 'incomparably beautified'.

There was one other palace which the Tudors loved, for it stretched along the river front at Greenwich and looked out on to the bustling life of the Thames, the principal artery for trade to and from London. The old palace of Placentia there was extensively remodelled by Henry VIII, who spent much of his time at Greenwich, since it was conveniently placed for viewing his growing navy. It was there that his eldest daughter, Mary, was born in 1516; and 17 years later Anne Boleyn gave birth there to Elizabeth. Yet the palace at Greenwich, like those at Richmond and Nonsuch, did not long survive the Tudors. Under Charles II it was swept away, to be replaced by the even more palatial buildings of Hawksmoor and Wren.

The surviving Tudor palaces, with one exception, are of minor significance. St James's, although constructed by Henry VIII, was never a principal residence during the Tudor period. As for the old palace at Hatfield, where Elizabeth was staying when she received the news of her accession to the throne, this was the creation of Cardinal Morton, Henry VII's chief minister, and in any case only a fragment of it survives. Even the vast rabbit warren of a palace at Whitehall, which became the seat of government after Henry VIII confiscated it from Wolsey, was totally destroyed by fire in the late 17th century.

The only Tudor palace which, to this day, gives some idea of the magnificence of the monarchy, is Hampton Court. Yet, ironically enough, this was not in origin a royal palace. It was built by Thomas Wolsey, Henry VIII's chief minister, as a monument to his own greatness and that of the Roman Catholic church of which he was a cardinal. Wolsey's low birth, his greed and his ostentation made him hated, yet he was not without his virtues. The Renaissance, and in particular the revival of theology based on the Greek testament and the early fathers, affected Wolsey as it did many of his contemporaries, and he planned a great college at Oxford which should be the fountainhead of the New Learning. Cardinal's College, as it was called, was taken over by the crown after Wolsey's fall and renamed Christ Church, but it is still one of the grandest of all Oxford colleges and preserves not only the memory but also a number of relics of its first founder.

Wolsey was not alone in his concern for the advancement of education. In the early years of the Tudor dynasty Lady Margaret Beaufort founded two new colleges at Cambridge, Christ's and St John's; her son, Henry VII, brought to completion the chapel of King's College, Cambridge (which Henry VI had begun),

he acquired, among many other royal residences, a medieval building at Sheen, in Surrey, and when this was destroyed by fire he rebuilt it on a truly princely scale. The new palace, which he renamed in honour of his Yorkshire earldom of Richmond, covered some 10 acres and was surmounted by a cluster of onion-shaped domes, each with its gilded weather-vane decorated with the royal arms. Richmond became one of the favourite palaces of Elizabeth, and it was here that she spent those last melancholy days of her life when, unable to sleep and unwilling to eat, she lay prostrate as the glory slowly departed from her.

Time has dealt harshly with the royal residences of the Tudor sovereigns, for only the gateway, an insubstantial shadow, remains at Richmond, and there is even less to be seen of Henry VIII's most extravagant and dazzling architectural achievement, the palace of Nonsuch in Surrey. This was Henry's answer to Fontainebleau, and was a bizarre blend of Tudor Gothic with French Renaissance. The overall effect must have been breath-taking, for even the sober Evelyn, who saw the palace in its decline over a century later, expressed his admiration for

The kitchen of Burghley House, near Stamford, Lincs., has a spit big enough to roast a whole ox. William Cecil, Lord Burghley, who was chief minister to Queen Elizabeth, lived here. The painting of a carcass is attributed to Rubens. Skulls at right are from turtles, which were used for soup

Elizabethan houses were designed to impress, and they did so by a lavish use of glass, as in this long gallery at Little Moreton Hall, Cheshire. The gallery was added to this half-timbered black and white manor house in the reign of Queen Elizabeth, is 68 feet long and is on top of the gatehouse

enriching it in the process with heraldic insignia of the new dynasty; while Henry VIII gathered a number of smaller Cambridge institutions into his huge new foundation of Trinity College. The initiative in promoting education was not confined to ecclesiastics and members of the royal family. The first commoner and layman to set up a college was Sir Richard Sutton, co-founder of Brasenose, and his example was followed, later in the century, by Sir Thomas Pope at Trinity, Oxford, and Sir Walter Mildmay, one of Elizabeth's ministers, at Emmanuel, Cambridge. Mildmay was a puritan and intended his college to be a stronghold of evangelical Protestantism. This would hardly have appealed to Wolsey or Lady Margaret Beaufort, but Mildmay shared with them the conviction that the foundation for a good life consisted in a Christian education.

Wolsey fell from power in 1529 because he could not obtain for Henry VIII a papal annulment of the King's marriage to Catherine of Aragon. The frustrated and angry Henry eventually broke away from the papacy, but despite the growing pressure for radical religious change

he held the English church on to conservative lines. Under his son, however, the boy-king Edward VI, the church became avowedly Protestant and a new English prayer-book replaced the Latin mass. This was not to the liking of all Edward's subjects. On Whit Monday 1549 the villagers of Sampford Courtenay in Devonshire stopped their parish priest from using the new book and called for the restoration of 'our old service of matins, mass, evensong and procession in Latin as it was before'. In a few weeks the whole of the West Country was up in arms, and the Government had to call in mercenaries to suppress the rebellion.

A similar protest against religious change, the Pilgrimage of Grace, had come from the north in 1536, and trouble broke out there again in the early years of Elizabeth's reign. While the religious element in all these revolts was genuine enough, they were also protests against the way in which the Tudors were changing England. For Henry VII and his successors consciously and deliberately exalted the dignity and authority of the Crown and asserted their rule over all corners of their realm. They curbed the great magnates; they set up councils at York and Ludlow to control the more distant regions of the north and west; they incorporated Wales into the English administrative system and laid claim to sovereignty over all Ireland. They also resumed a number of franchises (areas of jurisdiction which had been allowed to escape into private or corporate hands) and insisted on the principle that all authority derived from the Crown.

The Roman Catholic church in England was the greatest of all franchises, and by taking it over and turning it, in effect, into a department of state, the Tudors were merely carrying into the ecclesiastical sphere the same principle of unification that dominated their secular policies. They were also struggling to preserve internal peace, which was now threatened not so much by a factious aristocracy as by bitter religious dissension. England was caught up, along with the rest of Christendom, in the religious turmoil that accompanied the Protestant reformation and the Catholic reaction. The intensity of religious passions led to the burning of Protestants under Mary and the persecution of Catholics under Elizabeth. An obelisk at Lewes preserves the memory of 17 of the local Marian martyrs, while the suffering of the Elizabethan Catholics is recalled by priest-holes in country houses such as that at Boscobel, in Shropshire (in which Charles II was later to take refuge, after the battle of Worcester).

Deeply held religious beliefs also led to the destruction of images, including stained glass, which began in Edward VI's reign. The plain windows of many parish churches, with perhaps a few fragments of coloured glass huddled together round the edges, are a silent testimony to the determination of early English Protestants to erase all traces of what they regarded as superstitious idolatry. So are the blank doorways in many a chancel arch that mark where the rood loft once stood, surmounted by the figure of Christ on the cross. Sometimes the rood screen remains, as in the Norfolk church of Attleborough, but more often than not they were swept on to the lumber heap, where they joined such famous medieval relics as the Precious Blood of Hailes and the shrine of St Thomas of Canterbury.

In France, Germany and elsewhere, religious disputes led to civil war. England was saved from this largely through the existence of a national church which was sufficiently broad-based to secure the active or passive adherence of the greater part of the population. To some extent this was a matter of luck, for Henry VIII's attempt to hold the church on to a central course foundered with his death and the pendulum swung violently from uncompromising Protestantism to equally uncompromising Roman Catholicism. It was left to Elizabeth and her advisers to restore the balance by creating a church which, while definitely Protestant, retained as much as possible of the old forms of worship. The foundations for this had been laid by Henry VIII's last Archbishop of Canterbury, Thomas Cranmer, who produced the prayer-books on which the Elizabethan one was modelled. He managed to bridge the liturgical gulf between Catholic and Protestant England in such a way that the new church could draw part at least of its inspiration from the old. The cadences of the prayer book, still to be

The great staircase of Burghley House, with geometrically-patterned plasterwork that was characteristic of Elizabethan interior decor — one of many indications that the influence of the Italian Renaissance was affecting England. Vast sums were spent by courtiers competing with each other to entertain the Queen

heard in some Anglican churches, are a living survival from the Tudor age.

Although the Church of England was meant to be the church to which all English men and women belonged, there were some who rejected it totally, while others sought to effect radical changes in it. Among the latter were the puritan ministers who set up presbyterian cells in places like Dedham in Essex, where they could count on a fair measure of support. While the puritans remained nominal members of the Church of England, a handful of separatists wished to break away from it altogether, as too full of popish superstitions. They were mercilessly harried by Elizabeth's government, as were the Roman Catholics — at least those who refused to make a formal obeisance in the direction of Anglicanism. Many Catholic families suffered irreversible decline because of their constancy to the old faith. Among them were the Treshams of Northamptonshire, whose extraordinary construction called Lyveden New Bield, designed as a symbolic representation of the Passion, is not only a tribute to their courage in the face of adversity but

a reminder that for some people the Tudor age brought disaster.

This was particularly true of the many thousands of monks, nuns, friars and chantry priests who were compelled to give up their entire way of life when the institutions to which they belonged were forcibly dissolved. Henry VIII, having antagonised Catholic Europe by breaking with Rome, needed to strengthen his defences at home. He could not do this without money, however, and the wealth of the monasteries proved an irresistible temptation. Yet while Henry was motivated by greed as well as need, he would hardly have dared attack the monasteries if they had not already lost their hold on public opinion. It was because the political nation was more interested in sharing the monastic spoils than in preserving a system that seemed irrelevant and anachronistic that Henry was able to carry through this coup. The results are to be seen all over England. Some abbeys survived as cathedrals, but the great majority were stripped of anything valuable and then either converted into private houses or left to rot. Over the course of four and a half centuries they have turned into beautiful and romantic ruins, but under the Tudors they were jagged and bleak in their nakedness, frightening symbols of the power of the monarchy when it had public opinion behind it.

The main profiteers from the Dissolution were those who already held property. The biggest and richest monastic estates went, in the main, to Henry's close associates – the Russells, for instance, who were given Tavistock Abbey and its lands, and later Woburn as well. But countless smaller men enriched the King by purchasing confiscated monastic property from him and adding it to their estates. To this day a remarkable number of private houses bear the name of abbey, priory or grange, in witness of their monastic origin. Others, like Syon House, the former home of the Bridgettine nuns, have lost the name but preserve the shape of the monastic cloister under the veneer of later additions and alterations.

While some of the major figures in Tudor England were happy to take a former abbey as their principal residence – as the first Earl of Southampton did at Titchfield in Hampshire – others preferred to build afresh. This was particularly the case in Elizabeth's reign, when powerful courtiers vied with each other by constructing vast palaces in which to entertain the

An unrepentant Catholic, Sir Thomas Tresham, built this triangular folly (above left) at Rushton, Northants, as a symbol of the Holy Trinity. In this age of sectarian strife Sir Thomas was imprisoned several times over a period of 18 years for holding fast to Catholicism. Left: detail of the remarkable painted ceiling in the Room of the Nine Nobles, at Crathes Castle, Grampian, Scotland. Classical and biblical figures and early Christian kings are painted in bold decorative style. Right: big profits from the booming cloth trade paid for this elegant half-timbered house built in 1505 for cloth merchant Thomas Paycocke at Coggeshall, Essex. The town was famous in Tudor times for a cloth known as 'Coggeshall whites'

Queen when she went on progress. The greatest of these was Theobalds in Hertfordshire, built by Elizabeth's chief minister, William Cecil, Lord Burghley. This was so magnificent that when James I came to the throne he took it over for his own use, but today little trace of it remains. Much the same is true of Holdenby in Northamptonshire, which Sir Christopher Hatton built with the aim of eclipsing Theobalds. Holdenby was the Blenheim of its day (though larger than anything Vanbrugh ever built), but nothing is left of it except two arches standing in a garden. However, Cecil's other palace, Burghley House in Northamptonshire, is not only standing but is still the home of the Cecil family. A similar continuity of occupation may be observed at Longleat, in Wiltshire, built by Cecil's friend, Sir John Thynne, whose descendants have lived in it from that day to this.

Elizabethan houses were designed to impress, and they did so by a self-conscious symmetry (one of the many indications that the influence of the Italian Renaissance was affecting England), by a lavish use of glass, and, in some instances at any rate, by a flamboyant roofline. The results are astonishing. To come across Hardwick Hall, set four-square in the Derbyshire countryside, with its immensely tall windows turning it into a great lantern of stone and glass, is still one of the most exciting architectural experiences that England has to offer, and it captures the bravura, amounting at times to arrogance, that was one of the characteristics of the governing class in Tudor England.

This included many men who had made their fortune out of serving the State or out of law, for one result of the long Tudor peace was that disputes were settled in the law courts rather than on the battlefield, and the lawyers grew rich on the proceeds. Commerce was another source of wealth. In the early Tudor period the really big profits came from the cloth trade, as the wool churches of East Anglia and houses such as those of the cloth merchant Thomas Paycocke at Coggeshall in Essex demonstrate. Later in the century the opening up of new markets in northern Europe, the Levant and the Far East brought about a diversification, with rich rewards to the leading entrepreneurs.

Prosperity was not confined to those at the very top of the social scale. Many middling men – small farmers, provincial tradesmen, and master-craftsmen – were also doing well, and in Elizabeth's reign they began rebuilding their houses and making them more comfortable. 'Medieval cottages' of today are more often than not the creation of a thriving Tudor husbandman, and in the same way 'medieval villages' such as Lacock in Wiltshire are really Elizabethan transformations, and this accounts for their look of solid prosperity.

Little remains of Tudor London, yet it was during Elizabeth's reign that the capital city became a magnet for rich and poor from all over England and began swelling at an alarming rate. The lawyers, appropriately enough, have left their mark, for Middle Temple Hall,

though heavily restored, is basically an Elizabethan building. Shakespeare is said to have taken part in a performance of 'Twelfth Night' here, but he would have been more familiar with the suburbs across the river where the theatres, as well as the brothels, were situated. He would have known the church of St Mary Overy (now Southwark Cathedral), where his fellow playwrights Fletcher and Massinger are buried. And in his journeys up and down the river he would frequently have passed Lambeth Palace, the home of the Archbishops of Canterbury. Henry VII's archbishop, Cardinal Morton, built the great entrance tower there, and in its chapel lies Archbishop Matthew Parker, the man who steered the Elizabethan church through its first, difficult decade.

The poor, who flocked to London in increasing numbers during the Tudor period, were driven by despair, for

Aristocratic family life in Tudor times: this charming portrait of Lord and Lady Cobham and their children hangs on the staircase at Longleat, Wiltshire, where the Cobhams were frequently guests of their friends the Thynnes. Family pets shown in the portrait include such exotics as a parrot and a marmoset

European demand for English cloth, turned their estates into vast sheep-runs and evicted their tenants. This was a process that had started well before the battle of Bosworth was fought, but it continued apace under the first Tudor. Its effects are still visible to the trained eye, for isolated churches, such as that at Widford in Oxfordshire, may mark the site of a village eaten up by sheep under the early Tudors. These mute memorials are the only ones the Tudor poor have left, apart from the frequent entries in Quarter Sessions records ordering that 'sturdy beggars' were to be whipped or put in the stocks before being sent on their way.

There was another side to this, of course. The rulers of Tudor England were not insensitive to the suffering of the poor. Indeed it was in their own best interest to relieve it as far as possible, for starving men were a threat to order, and the Tudor peace was always balanced on a knife-edge. The authorities of both church and state put pressure on the wealthier members of society to make some provision for their less fortunate brethren, and many individuals responded by setting up charitable trusts to educate the children of the poor or to provide them with the tools of a trade so that they would be able (or so it was hoped) to pull themselves out of the gutter. And at a national level the Government drew up a comprehensive system of poor relief and wage regulation which, with all its deficiencies, lasted until the early years of the 19th century. The Tudor 'welfare state' was much harsher than the modern version, but it marked a big step forward from earlier assumptions that the Government had little or no role to play in solving social problems.

The Tudor age was full of paradoxes. It was harsh, yet at the same time caring. It was simultaneously emotional and cold-blooded, conservative and radical, deeply religious and profoundly secular. It was obsessed by worldly success, yet acutely aware of the vanity of human ambition. These contrasting attitudes are nowhere better reflected than in the tombs which still adorn (and in some cases obstruct) the naves and chancels of churches and cathedrals throughout the land. The standard type consists of a solid table, not unlike an altar, on which lie lifelike recumbent effigies of the deceased, often richly and even garishly decorated. On the side panels are frequently to be seen their sons and daughters, lovingly carved, whose presence there suggests not only the tightness of family bonds but also a softer attitude towards children than the harsh conditions of their upbringing and education would otherwise imply.

The finest tombs are those of the royal family. Henry VII, the first Tudor, rests in splendour under the fan vaulting of his chapel in Westminster Abbey, and not far away is the noble monument to his granddaughter Elizabeth, the last of the line. The leading commoners of Tudor England are also grandiloquently commemorated, as at Stamford, where William Cecil, Lord Burghley, lies in state, and at Derby, where the tomb of Elizabeth, Countess of Shrewsbury, proudly records the

galloping inflation, from which the rich profited, made their situation ever more desperate. The English population, already increasing in size when Henry VII came to the throne, continued to grow, and by the time of Elizabeth's death there were twice as many people in England as there had been in 1485. Yet the opportunities for employment, in a society that was still mainly agricultural, could not expand at the same rate, and the poor were therefore faced with the grim alternatives of trying to eke out a living at home or taking to the road.

In many cases they were given no choice, for enterprising landowners, anxious to profit from the increasing

Tomb of fitting magnificence for the great Tudor statesman William Cecil, Lord Burghley, in St Martin's Church, Stamford. 'Of all men of genius,' said the chronicler William Camden, 'he was the most a drudge. Of all men of business, the most a genius'

fact that she 'built the houses of Chatsworth, Hardwick and Oldcotes, highly distinguished by their magnificence'.

Tudor tombs should not be taken entirely at face value, however, for those who ordered them to be constructed as an abiding memorial to their greatness were deeply conscious of the truth that worldly success is but transitory and that the ultimate worth of an individual is to be known only in the longer time span of eternity. If any one epitaph may speak for all, and indeed for the Tudor age as a whole, it is that to Sir Thomas Stanley at Tong, in Shropshire, which was reputedly written by Shakespeare:

'Not monumental stone preserves our fame,
Nor sky-aspiring pyramid our name;
The memory of him for whom this stands
Shall outlive marble and defacers' hands.
When all to time's consumption shall be given,
Stanley, for whom this stands, shall stand in heaven.'

WEAPONS

by Dennis Knight

Before the arrival of the Romans the tribal British were skilled in making ornamented weapons in bronze and iron and had developed a technique of fighting from light two-horse chariots that bemused and even routed Caesar's disciplined infantry.

In the 370 years when Britain was a Roman province the people lived under the protection of Rome and little attention was given to weaponry. As a result the Romano-British were quite unable to defend themselves when the legions left. It was then that the Picts attacked from Scotland and a succession of tribes migrated to Britain from the Continent, warring amongst each other and pushing the Britons westwards. The invaders were armed with spear, axe, bow and sword and the latter was the weapon of the noblemen and elite warriors who revelled in individual combat. These swords were badly balanced weapons with which their owners swung and chopped at their opponents, and a well tempered blade that did not break was thought to be endowed with supernatural qualities.

The stirrup, which was not used by Roman cavalry, had come into use by this time and it revolutionised warfare because a horseman could cut, thrust and parry and still keep his balance by moving his weight onto one stirrup or the other. When the Normans arrived they brought new techniques including massed charges by armoured knights with long lances and groups of archers whose discharge of arrows caused havoc among unarmoured opponents.

Throughout the 12th and 13th centuries weapons and armour developed in Britain on similar lines to those on the Continent except for a reluctance to discard ordinary wooden bows for the newly invented cross-bows. Arrows were becoming ineffective against well-made armour and the professional soldiers of Europe had adopted the cross-bow which could propel a short, heavy arrow, called a bolt, at considerable velocity and great accuracy.

Warfare however, was developing into a kind of sport where the actual fighting was done by feudal horsemen and their retainers, supplemented by professional mercenaries who brought their own weapons and would only fight for a commander so long as they received payment. In England a different system prevailed, there being laws whereby a national army could be formed quickly at any time. All men who held land or property had to keep spear, swords and armour according to their wealth and status and were obliged to join the King's ranks at his bidding. They were mostly men who cultivated their own land, hence the term Yeoman of England. In 1252 a law specified that those of modest wealth were required to keep only a bow and arrows and this created an excessive number of archers.

It was Edward I who first used these archers to deadly effect when they sent salvoes of arrows at the Welsh and Scots and then charged before his stricken enemies could recover. With strong-limbed men, well practised to bend the powerful long-bows that were sometimes 6 feet long, it was possible to maintain a fast rate of fire (six arrows a minute) over a range of 300 yards or more. In 1346, Edward III heeded the lessons learned from his grandfather when he took a 16,000 strong army to France and was confronted by a massive Continental army at Crecy. After driving a host of Italian cross-bowmen from the field with salvoes of long arrows, Edward's archers decimated and repulsed charge after charge by mounted knights until in the dreadful slaughter that followed some 15,000 Frenchmen perished for the loss of about 1,000 of Edward's men. From this single victory achieved with the long-bow, the men of Britain had their morale braced to such an extent that it sustained them for another 600 years.

Although regular practice with the bow was compulsory, dexterity with the weapon became a matter of pride and a national leisure pursuit. The exercise alone of bending the bow made weaklings into strong men. At Poitiers, the Black Prince achieved another astounding victory and brought the King of France and his son back to London as honoured prisoners. At Agincourt, Henry V's archers were largely

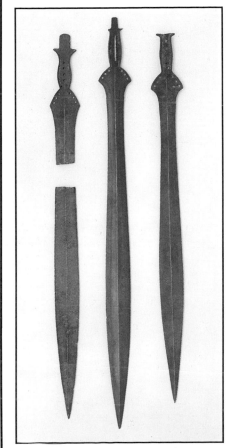

Late Bronze Age swords found in the Thames and now in the Museum of London

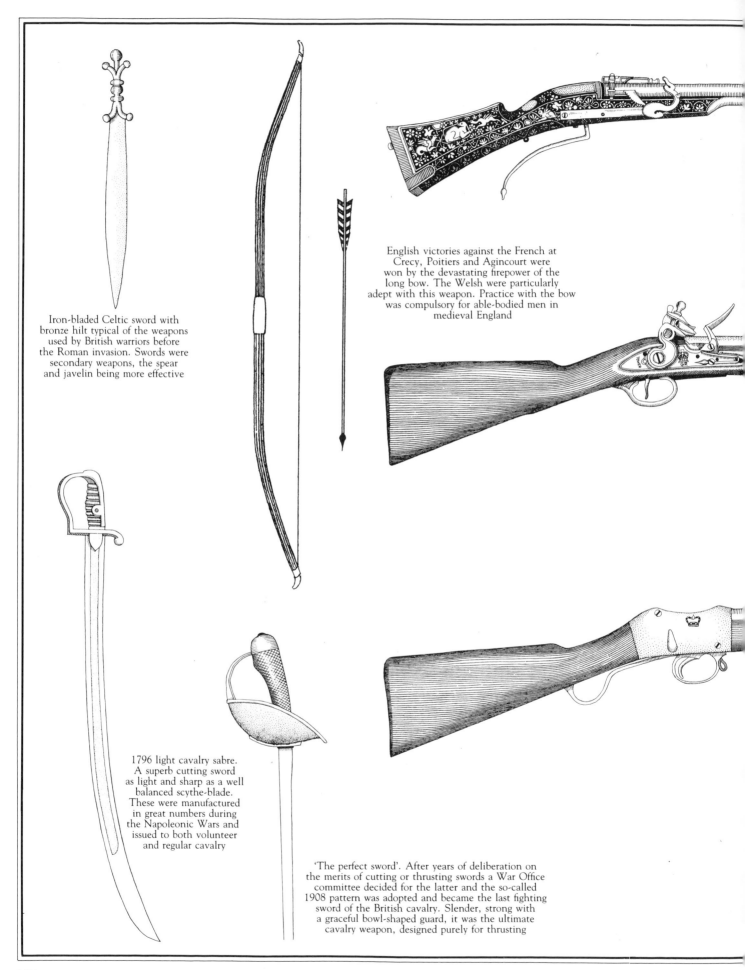

Iron-bladed Celtic sword with
bronze hilt typical of the weapons
used by British warriors before
the Roman invasion. Swords were
secondary weapons, the spear
and javelin being more effective

English victories against the French at
Crecy, Poitiers and Agincourt were
won by the devastating firepower of the
long bow. The Welsh were particularly
adept with this weapon. Practice with the bow
was compulsory for able-bodied men in
medieval England

1796 light cavalry sabre.
A superb cutting sword
as light and sharp as a well
balanced scythe-blade.
These were manufactured
in great numbers during
the Napoleonic Wars and
issued to both volunteer
and regular cavalry

'The perfect sword'. After years of deliberation on
the merits of cutting or thrusting swords a War Office
committee decided for the latter and the so-called
1908 pattern was adopted and became the last fighting
sword of the British cavalry. Slender, strong with
a graceful bowl-shaped guard, it was the ultimate
cavalry weapon, designed purely for thrusting

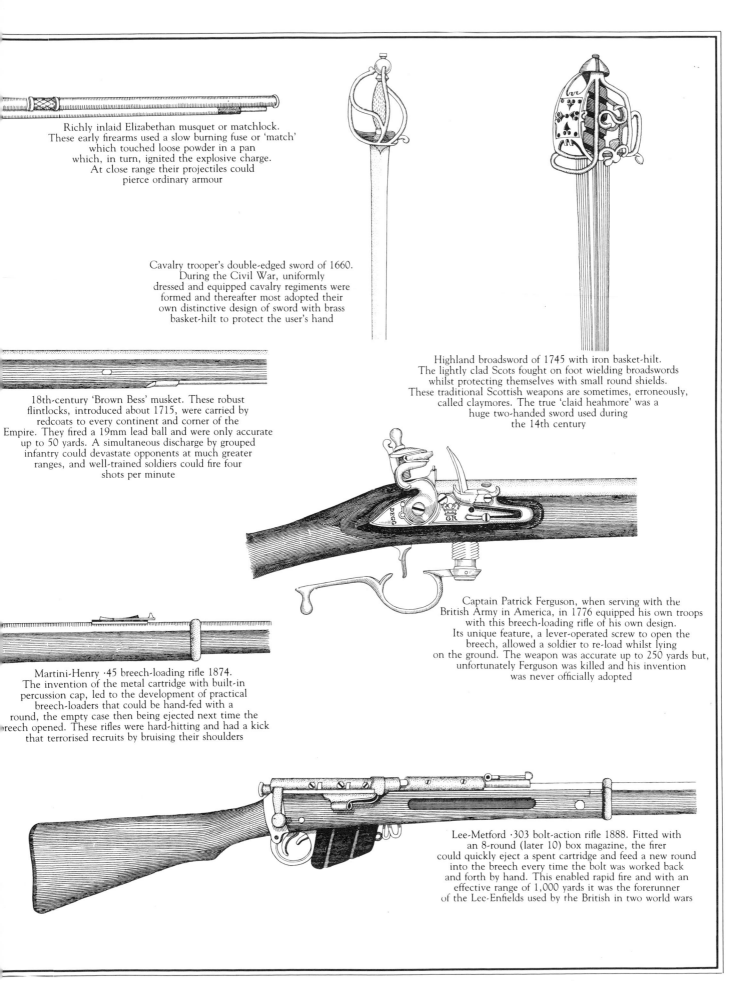

Richly inlaid Elizabethan musquet or matchlock.
These early firearms used a slow burning fuse or 'match'
which touched loose powder in a pan
which, in turn, ignited the explosive charge.
At close range their projectiles could
pierce ordinary armour

Cavalry trooper's double-edged sword of 1660.
During the Civil War, uniformly
dressed and equipped cavalry regiments were
formed and thereafter most adopted their
own distinctive design of sword with brass
basket-hilt to protect the user's hand

Highland broadsword of 1745 with iron basket-hilt.
The lightly clad Scots fought on foot wielding broadswords
whilst protecting themselves with small round shields.
These traditional Scottish weapons are sometimes, erroneously,
called claymores. The true 'claid heahmore' was a
huge two-handed sword used during
the 14th century

18th-century 'Brown Bess' musket. These robust
flintlocks, introduced about 1715, were carried by
redcoats to every continent and corner of the
Empire. They fired a 19mm lead ball and were only accurate
up to 50 yards. A simultaneous discharge by grouped
infantry could devastate opponents at much greater
ranges, and well-trained soldiers could fire four
shots per minute

Captain Patrick Ferguson, when serving with the
British Army in America, in 1776 equipped his own troops
with this breech-loading rifle of his own design.
Its unique feature, a lever-operated screw to open the
breech, allowed a soldier to re-load whilst lying
on the ground. The weapon was accurate up to 250 yards but,
unfortunately Ferguson was killed and his invention
was never officially adopted

Martini-Henry ·45 breech-loading rifle 1874.
The invention of the metal cartridge with built-in
percussion cap, led to the development of practical
breech-loaders that could be hand-fed with a
round, the empty case then being ejected next time the
breech opened. These rifles were hard-hitting and had a kick
that terrorised recruits by bruising their shoulders

Lee-Metford ·303 bolt-action rifle 1888. Fitted with
an 8-round (later 10) box magazine, the firer
could quickly eject a spent cartridge and feed a new round
into the breech every time the bolt was worked back
and forth by hand. This enabled rapid fire and with an
effective range of 1,000 yards it was the forerunner
of the Lee-Enfields used by the British in two world wars

**Soldier of the Napoleonic Wars
– a grenadier of the
West Yorkshire Militia, 1814**

responsible for another shattering victory when 10,000 French were slain for a few hundred British.

However, the era of the bow came to an end during the Renaissance when crude, cumbersome firearms demonstrated a penetrating power that made armour obsolescent, and in 1595 orders were given for the Trained Bands to exchange their bows for calivers and muskets.

During the Civil War new tactics evolved and men were grouped together into regiments and drilled in the use of particular weapons. Musketeers and pikemen formed the infantry, the latter being chiefly needed to protect the musketeers while they were reloading. Cavalrymen were armed with pistols or short muskets, and stiff straight swords. Dragoons were introduced, these being horsemen armed with firearms and sword.

Pikemen became redundant when musketeers started to use bayonets, but the first of these were knives that plug into the musket barrel preventing firing or reloading. This caused a disaster at Killiecrankie when burly Highlanders with broadswords charged infantry who were fumbling as they tried to fit bayonets. Later bayonets alleviated the problem by using a ring-socket fixing. In the early 18th century a stylish and much lighter flint-lock musket was introduced, this being the famous 'Brown Bess' which remained in service for over a hundred years and was still being used by the redcoats who finally defeated Napoleon at Waterloo.

Swords changed little throughout Georgian times, there being two basic types. A slender elegant sword only really suitable for thrusting that was worn by officers and civilian gentlemen, and a straight cavalry broadsword with basket-hilt. By 1780 light cavalry had been created and following the Continental fashion for hussars, were issued with slightly curved cutting swords. Twenty years later, when threatened with invasion from France, thousands of volunteers formed the yeomanry cavalry and were armed with the 1796 Sabre. This superbly balanced cutting sword, also issued to the regular army, became so notorious for inflicting ghastly wounds that the French protested to Wellington about its use. Victoria's reign saw the introduction of a succession of formidable looking sabres that were more decorative than effective. During the Crimean battles the British cavalry became despondent when they could only bruise the Russians through their thick greatcoats. However, at the end of the century a new rapier-like, thrusting sword was designed and this is regarded as the finest cavalry weapon ever made.

When percussion caps supplanted flint-locks in 1842, it was not long before metal cartridges made the breech-loading rifle possible. But it was not until 1874, that British soldiers received a general issue of a new weapon – the .45 Martini-Henry. With this hard hitting breech-loader small bands of steady disciplined troops did prodigious things against enormous odds. However, reloading between shots did take a little time and there were two notable disasters when forces were overwhelmed and annihilated. The bolt-action Lee-Metford with ten .303 rounds in a magazine overcame the reloading problem in 1888 and was basically the same type of weapon used by the British soldier in two World Wars.

THE
STUARTS

by John Kenyon

Fettiplace monument, Swinbrook

Queen Elizabeth's whole reign was dominated by the problem of the succession. The heir presumptive was Mary Queen of Scots, the granddaughter of Henry VIII's sister Margaret, who had married James IV of Scotland. But Mary's loyalty to Roman Catholicism, and her disordered and scandalous private life, gave the Protestant Lords of the Congregation the excuse to depose her in 1567 in favour of her infant son James. Twelve months later she escaped to England, only to be imprisoned again until 1587, when she was finally executed for plotting Elizabeth's overthrow. James VI made the appropriate filial protests, but went no further for fear of jeopardising his own chances. In fact he was now the only viable candidate, though Elizabeth refused to commit herself almost to her last breath. (Subsequently he had his mother's body transferred from Fotheringhay Castle, where she had died, to a sumptuous tomb in Westminster Abbey, and showered honours on the Howard family, who had been her loyal supporters.)

On Elizabeth's death in 1603 James VI & I seemed destined to lead his two kingdoms to even greater glories. He had proved the most able and successful king of Scotland for 300 years, he was a masterly politician, a highly educated and intelligent man and a firm Protestant; and he now had at his disposal the resources of a much wealthier kingdom, with an extremely strong and apparently stable governmental structure.

What went wrong between 1603 and 1642 has been a matter for debate among historians ever since, and the question is still far from settled; but certainly James and his son Charles I were caught up in a train of events which make the 17th century one of the most dynamic periods in the history of England, or for that matter of Scotland and Ireland.

James I's plantation of Scots settlers in Ulster was the first link in a chain which leads directly to the present Troubles in Ireland, and all the other 'troubles' of the past 100 years. It led to the savage rebellion of 1641, the equally savage reconquest by Cromwell in 1649 and 1650, and another rising in support of James II in 1689 which merged into the Patriotic War. Ireland was not subdued until 1692, and the famous siege of Derry in 1689 and King William's victory at the Boyne in 1690 are still meaningful events in Northern Ireland.

As for Scotland, this might well be called the Anglo-Scottish century. The presence of a Scots dynasty on the English throne, the recurrent turbulence of Scotland and her alarming vigour, gave her a disproportionate influence on the affairs of the joint kingdoms.

'United Kingdom' they were not. James I, much to his chagrin, could never persuade the English Parliament to accept anything more than a dynastic union, with common legal citizenship, and when he assumed the title 'King of Great Britain' it was by executive fiat. The Scots were still disliked and despised in England – after all, war between the two nations had been endemic for nearly three centuries – and the favour James showed to his

Scots courtiers and ministers was an important element in his unpopularity. The Scots themselves naturally feared that absentee rule would lead to neglect; James VI returned to Edinburgh only once, in 1617, and his son Charles I only twice, in 1633 and 1641. His visit in 1633 had disastrous repercussions. An attempt to impose the English Prayer Book, only slightly amended, on the Presbyterian Kirk, led the nation to unite against him in the National Covenant of 1638, signed in the Kirk of the Greyfriars in Edinburgh. This was the signal for a rebellion which left the king at the mercy of his opponents in England, and which was not finally suppressed until 1651 (again by Cromwell). Scotland was then put under military rule, which extended even to the Highlands, and forcibly united with England, sending elected members to a redesigned Westminster Parliament.

Meanwhile the Great Rebellion of 1642 had culminated, after two civil wars, in the execution of Charles I in 1649 and the establishment of the only republic in English history. On Cromwell's death in 1658, however, this house of cards began to collapse, and with it the Puritanism which had dominated the war years and the interregnum. Charles II was triumphantly restored to his father's throne in 1660, and his reign, though it had darker undertones, was distinguished for its glamour, frivolity and irresponsibility. The crown could never re-establish the unquestioned political ascendency it had enjoyed under the Tudors; in fact in the continuing tug o'war with Parliament it steadily lost ground; but the king was more emphatically than ever before the leader of fashion and the chief spokesman of polite society.

At the Restoration, Scotland was once more separated from England, and the Presbyterian Church suppressed. Charles II had already been crowned King of Scots at Scone in 1650, 11 years before his coronation in Westminster Abbey, but he showed no disposition to return, though it is significant that in the 1670s he undertook the complete rebuilding of Holyrood House, Edinburgh, to the designs of Sir William Bruce, the Wren of the North, who also rebuilt Drumlanrig Castle, Dumfriesshire, for the Dukes of Queensberry. The new royal palace was used by the future James VII during his exile in Scotland, 1680–83, but he, too, never returned once he ascended the throne; in fact, the next British monarch to cross the Border was George IV, in 1822. But neglect conferred a measure of independence, certainly for the royalist nobility in Scotland, and some of Charles's and James's Scots advisers wielded considerable influence in England – notably John Maitland, Duke of Lauderdale and Earl of Greenwich, who left

Audley End, Essex, was 'too large for a king,' said James I in a cutting reference to the extravagance of Thomas Howard, first Earl of Suffolk, his Lord Treasurer. It was begun in 1605 and was intended to be the largest house in England. This is the Great Hall, a vast unheatable space reminiscent of a medieval castle. The house was designed to accommodate king and court on progress, but was rarely put to use by Stuart kings who, unlike the Tudors, were not keen on leaving London for very long

behind one of the most distinguished of English 17th-century mansions, Ham House, near Richmond.

In fact, such great houses are the most obvious surviving relics of 17th-century Britain. It was an age of intellectual ferment, which saw the dawn of a new science and philosophy with Robert Boyle, Isaac Newton, Thomas Hobbes and John Locke. It was the age of John Milton, John Bunyan, John Dryden and Samuel Pepys. But it is through their books that these men live: their families died out, the houses they lived in disappeared. (Newton is an exception: at Woolsthorpe Manor, near Grantham, his study is preserved as he left it, and a cottage Milton rented still stands at Chalfont St Giles, Bucks).

In painting and sculpture it was a fallow period. What we are left with is an abundance of architecture. The Stuart Age, in fact, is like a mollusc; the living organism inside has died and rotted away, leaving us with a beautiful shell of stone.

It was an age of splendid houses and stupendous mansions. It began with the so-called 'prodigy houses' of James I's favourites. Audley End, in Essex, built by the first Earl of Suffolk, beginning in 1605, was the largest house in England, and intended to be so (it was twice its present size). In 1607 James I admired the first Earl of Salisbury's house at Theobalds (since demolished), and swapped it for the royal manor of Hatfield. Here Salisbury built another splendid mansion, the admiration of England, which stands today as a monument to the endurance of the House of Cecil.

It was an age of splendid, vicious, corrupt and wasteful expenditure by men whose contribution to the national wellbeing was virtually nil. They attempted to ape the great Renaissance aristocracies of Europe without the resources to back them. England was still a small, poor country, living on the faded and unreal splendours of Elizabeth's reign. The psychological harm inflicted by the defeat of the Armada in 1588 was incalculable, because it gave the nation an opinion of its own strength and capabilities which was quite unrealistic, and which was not shared by the rest of Europe. In 1616, with gross over-confidence, England embarked on an overhaul of her staple industry, in woollen goods, whose failure left her at the mercy of slump after slump, and cycle after cycle of inflation, which continued into the 1640s. Yet she still embarked on costly and unproductive foreign wars, with Spain in 1625, France in 1627.

James I knew well enough that much of the money to finance his favourites' prodigy houses was dubiously earned; he remarked that Audley End was too large for a King, though it might do for a Lord Treasurer. In fact, Suffolk was dismissed in 1618, tried for embezzlement and found guilty. The third Earl found Audley End too

Milton fled from the London plague of 1665 to this cottage at Chalfont St Giles, Bucks. Now blind, he finished 'Paradise Lost' here and began 'Paradise Regained', rising each day at four and dictating it to his 14-year-old daughter, Deborah

The Bodleian Library, Oxford, where in 1681, Charles II faced down Parliamentary opponents who were attempting to exclude his Catholic brother, James from the succession. The university was also used for a Parliament by Charles I during the Civil War

expensive to keep up, and sold it to Charles II in 1669 for £50,000. (Typically, Charles never paid the full amount, and William III gave the mansion back to the fifth Earl in 1701.) It is not surprising that Lord Clarendon, seeking in retrospect the causes of the Great Rebellion, should have ascribed it to 'the same natural causes and means which have usually attended kingdoms swollen with long plenty, pride and excess towards some signal mortifications and castigation of heaven'.

Audley End and Hatfield were still Elizabethan in character. Hatfield was built on the 16th-century E-plan; Audley End was an enormous closed H. They were not really fortified, but they affected towers and battlements, their walls were thicker than stability required, and they were afflicted with vast, unheatable great halls reminiscent of medieval castles. They were designed on the assumption that they would have to protect and entertain the perambulating king and his court, a hazard much less frequent after the Restoration. (Charles II never strayed north of Cambridge nor west of Windsor, and on the whole he and his successors, with few exceptions, preferred to sleep in their own houses.)

The breakthrough in architecture came with Inigo Jones, a promising young artist and designer who had served his apprenticeship in the Italy of Palladio. James I engaged him in 1616 to build a mini-mansion for his Queen, Anne of Denmark, at Greenwich. The Queen's House, tiny as it was and is, constituted a revolution in English architecture. It introduced to England the classical ideal, by which a building was considered as a whole, and built to a system of proportion which would not accept any modification or extension without wrecking the overall harmony. Its walls were thin, its windows large, as befitted a new age of carefree security.

In fact, Queen Anne died in 1619, and James took the architect away to work on his new palace at Whitehall. The Queen's House was completed in 1635 for Charles

I's wife, Henrietta Maria of France. At this stage, between the Queen's House and the Thames lay the rambling old palace of Greenwich, much beloved of the Tudor monarchs. The Stuarts scarcely used it, and in 1664 it was torn down to make way for 'King Charles's Block', to the designs of Inigo Jones's pupil and partner, John Webb. Sir Christopher Wren knitted the whole composition together, and established the grand design we see today, at the behest of William III and Queen Mary, who endowed the former palace as a naval hospital. Wren finished it in 1716, in the reign of George I; it was turned over to the Royal Naval College in 1873.

Meanwhile, in 1618, King James had given Inigo Jones a commission to rebuild the Banqueting House at Whitehall, which emerged as the finest Palladian building in England, possibly in Europe. It is, says Pevsner, 'a building of Mediterranean monumentality establishing a new code of order and proportion'. Today it is lost among the huge Victorian office blocks which line this thoroughfare of government, but in the 17th-century prints etched by the exiled Czech artist Wenceslaus Hollar it towers above the rambling, rather sleazy pile of the old Whitehall Palace.

After the Banqueting Hall James I's money ran out; so did his son's. Charles II and James II made a few improvements and additions, but all this was burnt down in the disastrous fire of 1698, which fortunately left the Banqueting Hall intact. The even older Palace of Westminster alongside it, which had been taken over by Parliament and the Courts of Law, was burnt down in 1834. Westminster Hall triumphantly survives, the scene of many famous 17th-century trials, notably that of Charles I himself; but of the boards where Pym and Hampden, Vane and Cromwell trod (not to mention Walpole, Fox, Pitt and Burke) there is no trace.

If we are looking for memories of the 17th-century Parliament, we must look, strangely enough, to Oxford. During the short-lived but violent Oxford Parliament in March 1681, at the end of the Exclusion Crisis, the Commons met in the Convocation House, which survives as the ground floor under the west wing of the Bodleian Library, Selden End. The Lords met in the Geometry School nearby, in the northeast corner of the Schools Quadrangle, first floor. The interior has been much altered to accommodate the Cataloguing Room of the Bodleian, but it was on the steps of this building that Charles II had a famous confrontation with the Whig Earl of Shaftesbury, when he refused to legitimise his bastard son Monmouth and make him heir apparent to the throne.

The Banqueting House in Whitehall, like most of James I's commissions, had to be completed by his son, and it was Charles I who commissioned from Peter Paul Rubens the superb ceiling paintings glorifying Monarchy and celebrating its victory over Ignorance, Discord and Rebellion. (Charles was a noted connoisseur; unfortunately his great collection of Old Masters was sold and dispersed by the republican government after his death.) By a deadly irony Charles walked through these rooms on the afternoon of 30 January 1649 to his execution, which took place on a platform at the level of the first-floor windows.

The usurper Oliver Cromwell founded no dynasty and therefore left few physical memorials behind him. What there are, chiefly personalia of little value in reconstructing his character, are in the Cromwell Museum at Huntingdon, formerly the grammar school where he was educated. (It also educated Samuel Pepys a generation after.) For much of the 19th century, Parliament argued over whether or not to raise a statue to Cromwell. The statue there today was commissioned by the Liberal leader Lord Rosebery for the tercentenary of his birth, in 1899, and paid for out of his own pocket. Even then, the public uproar was such that Rosebery had the statue unveiled by a workman at 7.30 one morning. Otherwise there are singularly few traces of the Civil Wars. The battle sites have been obscured by tree-felling, enclosure and drainage, not to mention the building of new roads.

Cromwell's country has changed more than most. In 1630 the fourth Earl of Bedford, with 13 other 'adventurers', secured a patent from Charles I to drain the wild fens of Cambridgeshire and the Isle of Ely. Between 1634 and 1637 they employed the Dutch engineer Cornelius Vermuyden to cut what is now the Old Bedford River, 70ft wide and 21 miles long on the chord of the arc of the river Ouse from Earith to Denver. It cost £100,000. Charles I then tried to take over the whole project on the grounds that it must be completed in a more effective manner, which did not ease his relations with Bedford and his parliamentary associates, notably John Pym. Once Charles I was executed in 1649 Parliament acknowledged the rights of William, fifth Earl of Bedford, who engaged Vermuyden to cut the New Bedford River, 100ft wide and parallel to the 'old' river; this cost another £300,000, but it was complete by 1651, creating what is still known as the Bedford Level.

It is noticeable that these major engineering works, which created a new landscape over much of Cambridgeshire, Huntingdonshire and west Norfolk, were pushed through during some of the most troubled years of the century. Nor were the Fens the only area of land reclamation. The tactics of two decisive battles, the New Model Army's victory at Langport in 1645, and the Duke of Monmouth's defeat at Sedgemoor in 1685, were both governed by the land drains of Somerset. The Bussex Rhine, where Monmouth came to grief, was a deep drainage ditch, long since filled in.

The Civil Wars took many lives and wrecked more; but they did not involve the whole nation. War was very far from total, and some of the upper classes went on as if nothing had occurred. For instance, when Wilton House near Salisbury was burnt down in 1647 the fourth Earl of Pembroke commissioned his father's old servant Inigo Jones to build another. Jones died in 1652, but it was completed by John Webb the following year. Thus the new Wilton House was built in a span of years which

St Paul's Church, Covent Garden, designed by Inigo Jones in the 1630s as part of a commission from the Earl of Bedford to create a piazza like that of Livorno. Samuel Butler, author of 'The Way of All Flesh', lived nearby and is buried in the churchyard

saw the Second Civil War of 1648, the execution of the King – which Pembroke is reputed to have watched from the windows of his apartments in Whitehall – the creation of a republic, war in Ireland, war in Scotland, and finally the extinction of the republic at the hands of Cromwell. Nevertheless, Wilton was built to the new classical design, with no hint whatsoever of fortification or defence; in fact, with its large windows and thin walls it was one of the first of the great mansions built for an age of grace and peace. The Double Cube Room, with the furniture specially designed for it by William Kent in the 18th century, is one of the great rooms of Europe.

Sir Robert Shirley was another man who ignored the Civil Wars: in 1653 he built a completely new church at Staunton Harold in Leicestershire, though Anglican worship was proscribed. His 'singular praise', according to his memorial tablet, 'is to have done the best things in the worst times, and hoped them in the most calamitous'.

The return of Charles II in 1660 inaugurated one of the greatest periods of English architecture, which was dominated by Sir Christopher Wren. He was Surveyor

This austere little Quaker Meeting House at Chalfont St Peter, Bucks., was built in 1688, following the greater religious toleration that began in the reign of James II. (Cromwell had persecuted the Quakers and put several hundred into prison.) William Penn, Quaker courtier and founder of Pennsylvania, is buried here

of the King's Works from 1669 to 1718, his tenure of office spanning five reigns, two dynasties and a revolution.

Apart from his new buildings at Greenwich for Charles II and William III, Wren also carried out major alterations at Hampton Court and Kensington. The most impressive and probably the least known of his commissions from Charles is the Royal Military Hospital at Chelsea, begun in 1682, though it was not completed until 10 years later. But Charles's chief memorial is really Windsor Castle, for which he conceived a great affection. He was the first English king to live there since the Middle Ages, and the comprehensive alterations and extensions he undertook to the designs of Hugh May, were in progress most of his reign. Unfortunately, later monarchs shared his taste for Windsor, and further improvements in the 18th and 19th centuries have almost entirely buried his work.

Wren's output, over a long career, was prodigious. His first important commission, and in some ways his most attractive, is the Sheldonian Theatre at Oxford (1664–9), with its ingenious ceiling and its general air of dignified frivolity. The variety of his genius is evident when we turn to Cambridge, and the Library of Trinity College (1676–81). But it is with the 52 City churches he built after the Great Fire of 1666, and above all with St Paul's Cathedral, which took 36 years to build (1676–1711), that his name will always be associated. As it neared completion it took on the role of a great temple for the celebration of a new national greatness, as dumpy little Queen Anne rode down in her state coach from Kensington through cheering crowds to offer up solemn *Te Deums* for the victories of her great captains – Vigo, Blenheim, Gibraltar, Ramillies, Oudenarde – and banner after banner floated in the nave.

The chance to rebuild the whole of the City to an ordered scheme was lost after the Fire, perhaps luckily; but the century saw a decided shift westward which altered the axis of the metropolis for good and created the West End.

When James I arrived the City of London still ended for all intents and purposes at Temple Bar. Thence along the Strand to Charing Cross stretched the palaces of great noblemen or prince-bishops – Essex House, Durham House, Somerset House, and so on – facing the river, with long gardens down to the waterfront, their stables abutting on the Strand at the back. North of the Strand was largely open country, with a few small houses occupied by lawyers and other professional men.

Whitehall, Westminster and St James's Palace formed a separate township: Kensington and Chelsea were deep in the country, as was the charming little village of Battersea. William III, who suffered from asthma, and could not abide the City smog, bought Kensington House from the Earl of Nottingham in 1689 as a country retreat.

Under James I Lord Salisbury speculated in property development by building his New Exchange, a smart new shopping centre and office block (as we would call it) between the Strand and the river just west of Temple Bar. In the 1630s the fourth Earl of Bedford took another step westward when he commissioned Inigo Jones to design Covent Garden, fronted to the south by his own mansion, Bedford House, the rest being taken up by a piazza modelled on Livorno. Jones also built a smart new Renaissance church, St Paul's, Covent Garden, which suggests that the number of residents in the area was increasing. In the meanwhile the great Strand palaces were coming down or being converted.

Lord Southampton built a new mansion for himself on his country estate of Bloomsbury. Then came the Civil Wars, but by 1661 he was back, this time as Charles II's Lord Treasurer, and at once began to lay out Southampton Square, later renamed Bloomsbury Square. On his death without male heirs in 1667 his London properties devolved on his daughter Rachel, who carried them by marriage into the family of the Russells, Earls of Bedford, who owned Covent Garden. The fifth Earl, created Duke of Bedford in 1694, continued to develop Bloomsbury, and gave his name to Great Russell Street and Bedford Square.

But in a new climate of wealth, expanding trade and rising land values, the demand for gentlemen's residences near the centre of power was insatiable. Charles II himself encouraged expansion northward as well as westward when he laid out St James's Park and the Mall in 1661–2. His Lord Chancellor, Lord Clarendon, built

Above right: Ham House, Richmond, Surrey, was described by diarist John Evelyn as 'inferior to few of the best villas in Italy itself, the house furnished like a great prince's.' It is one of the few houses of the Stuart period with a completely unchanged interior. Right, the Green Closet, with painted ceiling by Francis Cleyn. Far right, marble-floored hall

Buildings like Sudbury Hall, Derbyshire, are the most obvious surviving relics of an age that built splendid houses and stupendous mansions. This is one of the best surviving 17th-century houses, with painted ceilings, ornate plasterwork, a fine staircase and woodwork by the virtuoso carver Grinling Gibbons

a sumptuous mansion on the road running along the north side of the park, known mysteriously as Piccadilly, and the rush was on. Lord Berkeley built another mansion on what is now Berkeley Street, and laid out Berkeley Square, as well as Charles Street, Hill Street and Bruton Street. At the other end of Piccadilly the Earl of Burlington built Burlington House, which still survives, though in a much altered state. The Earl of St Albans began to develop St James's Street and St James's Square in 1663.

Soho was developed a little later, in the 1680s, by a speculator called Gregory King, who laid out King Square (later Soho Square), and Gregory Street (later shortened to Greek Street). These, of course, were all filled with select gentlemen's residences; the function performed by 20th-century Soho was undertaken by Covent Garden and the New Exchange, which had sunk considerably in status by Charles II's reign. It was also in the 1680s that the former Secretary to the Treasury, Sir George Downing, built Downing Street and Horse Guards Parade, Nos 10 and 11 Downing Street survive

very much as they were built, though of course they have suffered a great deal of internal alteration.

Clarendon House was torn down in 1683 to make way for the development of Albemarle Street and Old Bond Street, and by 1700 the development of Mayfair had reached the line of Bolton Street. There it stopped for the moment; beyond were green fields stretching to Knightsbridge. However, beginning in 1702 John Sheffield, Duke of Buckingham, built Buckingham House across the westward end of the Mall, and by 1761 George III found this just the kind of modest establishment he needed in central London.

This unheralded and remarkably rapid expansion is eloquent of a new confidence and a new dynamism. Expanding trade abroad brought new wealth, land values rose, and the violent political and constitutional changes which ushered in the end of the century gave nobility, gentry and merchants an enhanced political role.

The Stuart kings' continual flirtation with Catholicism proved their undoing. James II (VII of Scotland) actually did what so many of his predecessors had been suspected of doing – he joined the Church of Rome. His brief reign (1685–88) confirmed the worst fears of his enemies and alienated all but a handful of his friends, and he was painlessly deposed in 1689 in favour of his daughter Mary, ruling jointly with her husband William III of Orange. The long wars against France which followed (1689–97, 1702–13) established England as the leading military and financial power in Europe, with London rivalling Paris as a world capital. It had long been a magnet for the upper classes; it was much more so now after the Revolution of 1688, when the institution of annual sessions of parliament lasting all winter obliged most MPs and peers to buy or lease property near Westminster.

But though in these years most of the street system of the modern West End was laid down, very few of the houses first built along those streets survive. Most of the plots were let on 30-year leases, which did not encourage the building of lasting houses; virtually all of them had to be rebuilt in the 18th century, which is why they are now Georgian in design and character.

Why was this? Metropolitan development was an excellent investment; we know that it was an important element in the income of many noblemen, just as important as the income from their broad acres. Did their desire to reap a short-term profit indicate undercapitalisation, or perhaps an underlying lack of confidence in the permanence of the regime, until it was finally stabilised by the succession of the Hanoverians?

Yet it must be said that in the parallel wave of country-house building which followed the Revolution of 1688 the nobility and gentry showed no such caution, and they were now riding on a new wave of prosperity in trade, agriculture and even in government stock; for after the foundation of the Bank of England in 1694 investment in the government was not only a patriotic duty but a source of profit.

Some chose to renovate rather than build anew, but their operations were on a massive scale. For instance, between 1688 and 1715 Charles Seymour, sixth Duke of Somerset, undertook the conversion of his ancestral home, 13th-century Petworth House, into an up-to-date classical mansion. But Sir John Vanbrugh took only three years (1707–10) to modernise the medieval castle of Kimbolton, in Huntingdonshire, for Charles Montagu, fourth Earl of Manchester. Vanbrugh was one of the boldest architects of the age, and his influence was widespread. He had already turned Dalkeith Castle, Midlothian, into Dalkeith Palace, for the Duchess of Buccleuch, and he now had even more ambitious ventures in and at Blenheim and Castle Howard. The wheel came full circle in 1709, when he redesigned Audley End for the fifth Earl of Suffolk, pulling two-thirds of it down in the process.

In an age of wealth and emulation not even the greatest buildings were safe. William Cavendish, fourth Earl of Devonshire, played a prominent role in the Revolution, and was raised to a dukedom in 1694. The Tudor mansion at Chatsworth, which had accommodated Mary Queen of Scots, could not sustain the dignity of a great English nobleman, nor could his other residence, Hardwick Hall, that singular and beautiful

Sheldonian Theatre, Oxford, Sir Christopher Wren's first building, designed when he was still Professor of Astronomy in the 1660s. It was inspired by engravings of theatres in ancient Rome. It began one of the greatest periods of English architecture

Elizabethan creation, 'more window than wall', less than 20 miles away. William Talman, a brilliant though temperamental architect, designed the core of the present Chatsworth House, built between 1686 and 1707.

Nor was it only the titled grandees who were speculating in stone. It was William Lowndes, Secretary to the Treasury from 1695 to 1724, who built Winslow Hall, Buckinghamshire (1699–1702); his architect may even have been the great Wren. Another longstanding civil servant, William Blathwayt, Secretary at War 1684–1704, commissioned Talman to build Dyrham Park in Gloucestershire, with its elaborate formal gardens echoing those at Versailles.

By the end of the century the urge to build transcended party boundaries, too: possession of a stately home had become a status symbol. As Vanbrugh told one of his few recalcitrant clients, John Holles, Duke of Newcastle, who declined to rebuild Welbeck Abbey: 'I believe that if your Grace will please to consider of the intrinsic value of title and blue garters and jewels and great tables and numbers of servants, etc, in a word all those things that distinguish Great Men from small ones, you will confess to me that a good house is at least on a level with the best of them.' So we find Tories, who viewed the Glorious Revolution with marked distaste, as active as their Whig rivals.

Cowick Hall, near Goole, is one of a long string of distinguished houses built during the reigns of William III and Queen Anne for traditionalist Tory squires; in this case Henry Dawnay, second Viscount Downe. It now enjoys an astonishing prominence. Lovingly restored by Croda Chemicals, whose world headquarters it is, it stands, floodlit at night, only a few hundred yards from the M62: a constant reminder to the speeding motorist of a statelier, though equally rapacious age.

But Ireland, ravaged by the Patriotic War (1689–92) and racked by religious persecution, reaped no advantage from the Glorious Revolution. Nor, in the short.

Craigievar Castle, Grampian, a turreted house built between 1600 and 1626 for a rich merchant who fancied himself as the Laird. On the exterior the Scottish tradition of the mansion house with overhanging turrets reaches its apogee

term, did Scotland. In Scotland the religion of James VII had been no more acceptable than in England, and the Revolution saw the final liberation of the Presbyterian Church; but she did not share in the economic boom which enriched her southern neighbour, and she suffered, if only in prestige, by the passing of a distinctively Scottish dynasty. William III, Mary II and Anne, though they were members of the Stuart family (even William), had no connexion with Scotland at all, and the dangers of long-range government from London were spectacularly illustrated by the Massacre of Glencoe in 1692. The exiled Stuarts therefore made a quite illogical but potent appeal to Scottish national sentiment, and under Queen Anne Scotland even threatened to opt out of the Hanoverian Succession, reserving the right to choose another king than George I after her death. This led to the final Union of 1707, put through in circumstances which are controversial to this day. Sporadic Jacobite plots and rebellions, culminating in the '45, were evidence of continuing discontent with the British condominium, and few would have suspected that Scotland was now on the threshold of her golden age.

THE HOUSEHOLD

by Mary Norwak

Domestic equipment has changed remarkably little over the centuries, and has followed an international pattern. Pestles and mortars were used in Babylon in 2500 BC, colanders and frying pans have been found in the ruins of Pompeii, and pastry cutters were part of the kitchen equipment of France in AD 200. Materials and designs for basic cleaning and cooking equipment have scarcely altered in hundreds of years, and our ancestors would be completely familiar with many of them.

The reason is a simple one, for family life started round the fire, and centred on the cooking which took place there. Pots, pans and baking sheets were suspended over the flames, with complete meals of meat, vegetables and puddings being cooked in one large cauldron. Only large houses incorporated beehive-shaped ovens in the fireplace wall, so cottagers took food to the village baker for finishing in his oven. In towns, families hardly needed to cook because public cookshops, bakers and street vendors could supply all their needs.

Large open fires were difficult to control, and limited the range of dishes which could be prepared, but a variety of spits were used in front of the intense heat for roasting meat, poultry, game and fish. The spit, which might be a single rod, or a metal basket, was originally rotated by a boy or a dog, but in the 18th century was controlled by a weighted pulley, or by a paddle-wheel driven by hot air rising up the chimney. By the 19th century, this had developed into a clockwork jack suspended from the mantelshelf and fitted with a rotating hook on which could be hung a small joint more suitable for Victorian families than the previous carcasses.

Cooking was revolutionised at the end of the 18th century by Benjamin Thompson, an Anglo-American commonly known as Count Romford – a politician, philanthropist and inventor. Determined to save fuel costs, he devised an enclosed and insulated stove, soon developed by many manufacturers. The huge old fireplaces were enclosed and kitchen ranges installed, fuelled by coal rather than wood, and including ovens and water-heaters.

As an alternative, gas was tested for cooking in 1812, but was expensive and mainly used for lighting. Although a gas grill was introduced to hotel kitchens in 1824, and Soyer used a gas range at the Reform Club in 1841, the small stove was not introduced into homes until the second half of the century when cheap town gas supplies were provided for lighting. Electricity was considered in 1885, and thought unsuitable for cooking as no flame was visible, but the first electric cooker was demonstrated at the Crystal Palace in 1891, and the first home electric cooker was marketed in 1893.

Eating habits, particularly the hours at which meals are taken, and the names by which they are known, have undergone tremendous changes in the centuries covered by this book. As men began to cultivate crops and develop routines, meals were taken at first light and dusk to leave as much daylight working time as possible. The Romans planted orchards and introduced many vegetables and herbs, spices and dried fruit to vary the standard diet of coarse bread and thin beer, eked out with such flesh and fish as could be trapped. When their empire broke up, the skills of cultivation and fine cooking disappeared, and it was not until 600 years later, when the Normans arrived in 1066, that an interest in the culinary arts was revived and an eating pattern was introduced.

William the Conqueror ate his main meal, or dinner, at 9 a.m., and in the succeeding 900 years, this meal slipped almost 12 hours through the day. At the beginning of the 16th century, Henry VII's England dined at 11 a.m., and 150 years later, Cromwell's England was dining at 1 p.m. As the main meal moved slowly forward, a break-fast was taken on rising, the necessary bread, meat and ale being stored in a livery cupboard overnight.

Medieval winter feast as depicted on an English calendar of the 14th century

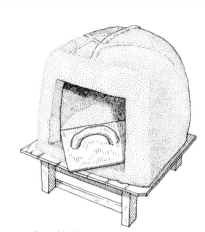

Portable dome-shaped earthenware oven based on a Romano-British design, and still available until the early 20th century. Sometimes known as a 'cloam' oven, it was heated by inserting burning wood, then raking out the ash. The food was then placed inside and the door sealed with wet clay

18th-century bronze skillet, sometimes known as a pipkin or posnet. The pan was designed to stand in the embers of an open fire and the long handle helped to protect the cook from burns. Skillets were used for delicate cookery, such as sauce-making and were the forerunners of today's saucepans

The smoke jack was introduced into England from the Continent in the second half of the 18th century to aid the turning of the spit used for roasting large pieces of meat. A horizontal fan, fitted into the narrowest part of the chimney, rotated in hot air and activated a gear system attached to a power shaft and chains which turned the spit wheels

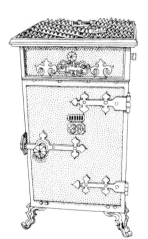

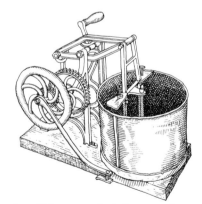

Late 19th-century food chopper and mixer, mainly used for preparing suet and vegetables. Food was placed in a metal container mounted on a wooden stand and then the handle was turned, the metal drum revolved, and a chopping blade, attached to a levered arm, rose and fell

The first gas cooker was designed in the 1830s, but gas was not used as an alternative to coal in the kitchen until the 1870s. These early cast-iron cookers had a large oven and up to four top burners, but were expensive to buy and run. Their widespread use was made possible by a system of hiring cookers and by a pre-payment slot machine in the 1890s which enabled gas to be used in the poorest homes

Refrigerator or ice box produced in 1895. The cabinet had a section in which blocks of ice were placed and the hardwood, zinc-lined box ensured coolness for about 24 hours. Ice had to be replaced daily and was sold door-to-door in horse-drawn carts until 1939. The ice had to be obtained from Norway or North America, and Britain imported half a million tons a year

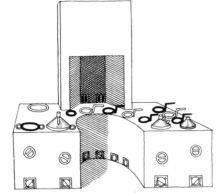

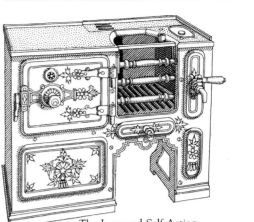

Count Romford's insulated brick cooker designed in 1800.
Each cooking utensil was accurately fitted into its own aperture
and had an insulated cover and projecting handle. Below
each utensil was an individual fire which could be regulated and
refuelled as required, the number of fires
being exactly proportionate to the work being done

The Improved Self-Acting
Cottage Range made by Smith and
Wellstood in 1880. This range could be bricked
into an existing open hearth. It comprised a small
grate and hotplate, side oven and water heater. Many cooks also
suspended pans of food over the grate from old hooks
in the original fireplace

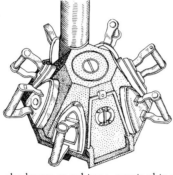

Flat irons, also known as sad irons, remained in use until
the late 1920s when more homes became wired for electricity. At least
two irons were needed so that one could be heated while the
other was in use, and these were placed on the cooking range. In larger
households a special laundry stove kept a quantity of
irons at the correct temperature

19th-century digester, which was an early form of
pressure cooker. A conical weight was fitted inside and the
lid was raised to allow steam to escape when pressure
reached 2–3 lb. This heavy cast-iron pan was mainly used to
extract goodness from bones when making soup

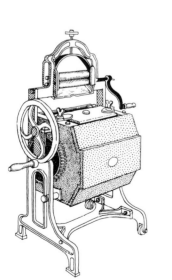

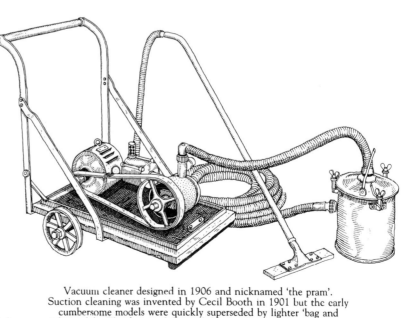

'Vowel Y' washing machine made in 1897 by Thomas
Bradford and very popular in many sizes. The washing was tumbled
by wooden slats when the handle was turned. The mangle
on top was worked by a small handle at the side and pressure
could be adjusted by a wheel mechanism

Vacuum cleaner designed in 1906 and nicknamed 'the pram'.
Suction cleaning was invented by Cecil Booth in 1901 but the early
cumbersome models were quickly superseded by lighter 'bag and
stick' models. The design of the stick has hardly altered to the present
day and some modern models have reverted to the dust canister
shown in this version

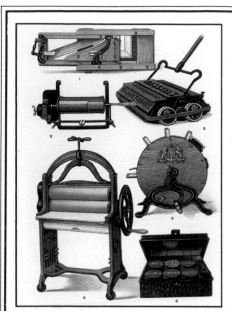

Victorian household equipment,
as endorsed by Mrs Beeton's Book of
Household Management: bread
cutter, coffee roaster, carpet
sweeper, wringer and mangle, knife
cleaner and spice box

It was gradually realised however that the long dinner break in the middle of the day was unsuitable for a cold, dark climate, and Steele (1672–1729) noted that the dinner hour had moved from midday to 3 p.m. in his lifetime, a shift of three hours in some 50 years. Only University and Cathedral circles rigidly maintained the original early hours with dinner at 10 a.m. and supper at 4 p.m. In more worldly society however, hostesses vied with each other to push forward the fashionable hour for the main meal of the day and alter the pattern of living.

By 1780, the day began with an early-morning awakening with tea and paper-thin bread and butter. Then came two or three hours' work before a light breakfast of chocolate and cakes around 10 a.m. In the leisured classes, this was a long, conversational meal, lasting up to three hours, and then serious work was undertaken, or reading, walking and sports indulged in before dinner served at a chosen hour between 3 p.m. and 5 p.m. This again was a long meal, and a dinner invitation would indicate a stay of seven or eight hours, with the main meal being followed by dessert and wine, then coffee which signalled the withdrawal of the ladies while the men continued drinking. They rejoined the ladies for tea and cakes about 8.30 p.m. In a modest house, dinner would appear at 4 p.m. and tea at 7 p.m., but in grander houses, the longer meal would be followed by a supper of cold meats and sweetmeats around 11 p.m., and casual guests would feel free to drop in at that time and might even be offered hot dishes.

As the world of commerce expanded, it became obvious that the day could no longer depend on the two hinges of mid-morning breakfast and mid-afternoon dinner, and a new meal pattern rapidly developed in the 19th century.

As early as the 14th century, 'nunchin' had existed as a snack between meals, and by the 17th century 'lunch' or 'luncheon' was defined as 'such food as one's hand can hold'. It was mainly a snack of coffee and pastries taken in coffee-houses at noon, or an inn meal of cold mutton and sherry. As the gap between breakfast and dinner lengthened, breakfast itself became a more substantial meal with cooked dishes, and men began to leave the house earlier to complete an eight or nine hour working day.

By the middle of the century, business men, or men of leisure who played the newly developing games of golf, cricket and football, enjoyed returning home to a heavy dinner about 8 p.m., and the leisurely dinner/tea/supper evening was telescoped into one meal. This gave a new freedom to women, who now began to enjoy a light sociable midday meal which conferred great prestige on hostesses and guests (the divorce courts also became increasingly busy). The men's coffee houses began to turn into mere cafés for drinks and snacks, while chop-houses, eating-houses and dining-rooms filled the gap with more substantial meals, and at last the recognisable modern day of morning and afternoon was created.

Confusion about the nomenclature of meals abounded, noted by Maria Edgeworth and De Quincey in the 1830s and still continuing. The new meal of lunch was in fact being eaten at the old dinner-hour, and dinner at the former suppertime, while many people still clung to old ways and caused further problems. By 1861, when Mrs. Beeton published her 'Household Management', the meal pattern in all classes had begun to stabilise.

Breakfast was an obligatory and substantial meal, eaten at 8 a.m. and without the former social overtones, and men were at their workplaces by 9 o'clock. City gentlemen might eat lunch (often a mere rock cake or biscuits with sherry), but in general men of all classes ignored this break, indulged in mainly by society ladies. Even in late Victorian times, coffee was served after dinner to the ladies, but when the men arrived they were given tea, a relic of the old tea-and-cakes hospitality.

Tea had actually been introduced to England in 1657, and was drunk in private or in public tea gardens. The tea-party remained after dinner, or as a nursery meal suited to children and delicate digestions, and even at Victoria's accession in 1837, an afternoon snack of tea and thin bread-and-butter was very rare and only intended to bridge the hunger gap for those eminent people who indulged in late and ceremonial dinners. The Duchess of Bedford however moved her sociable after-dinner tea-parties to mid-afternoon, and often served the meal in the garden, but tea never became a sustaining meal, and by the end of the century was used for sociable At Homes for ladies and unattached men, or for greeting weekend guests. Today, only Sunday retains the British meal pattern developed over the centuries with a late and sociable breakfast, dinner in the early afternoon, a break for tea and cake, and a light cold supper.

THE
GEORGIANS

by John Cannon

Door, Bath

When we lived in Bristol a visitor from Denmark, who had driven across southern England from Dover, remarked that it was 'just like driving through a series of parks'. The contrast she was registering was between the landscape she was familiar with in Denmark, based on peasant- and small-holdings, and that created in England in the 18th century by enclosures and 'emparkments'. That pattern is still with us today, though submerged in many places by the growth of the great 19th-century towns and their 20th-century suburbs.

In the middle of the parks, usually behind stout stone walls, stand the surviving houses of Georgian England. In the early years of the 18th century they were often no more than jumped-up farmsteads, sitting in a clutter of barns and sheds and cottages, surrounded by fields. But as the century wore on some were totally rebuilt, others given a face-lift, the squalor removed, pieces of land fenced in to round off corners and add depth and privacy, and the fields drained, planted out and embellished. In shire after shire, the old common lands with their great open fields and vast horizons gave way to private estates.

The fashionable mode of rebuilding was classical, and it is the overwhelming dominance of one architectural style that gives Georgian England so clear a definition for us today. True, in the earlier years, there was a survival of boisterous baroque influence; the middle years of the century saw the tentative emergence of Gothick in its Strawberry Hill variety, and in the 1760s there was even a little Chinese influence, of which Sir William Chambers's pagoda at Kew is the best-known example. But, by and large, the whole century was under the thrall of Greece and Rome.

The classical tradition blends in so well, has become so familiar a part of the English landscape, that it requires an effort of imagination to remember how strange it all is. Eighteenth-century schoolboys spent almost the whole of their time learning the two dead languages, Latin and Greek; Members of Parliament spattered their speeches with Latin quotations and quips; statues of plump Hanoverian kings were decked out in togas as Roman senators. The most famous of Georgian literary assassins wrote under the name of 'Junius', and when he and the printer wanted to insert private codes in the *Public Advertiser* to contact each other, it was agreed to use Latin tags. Never has one civilisation paid such intellectual homage to another.

Nowhere is this more apparent than in the architecture of the period. Whig aristocrats decorated their houses with Corinthian columns, pediments, pilasters, porticos and all the paraphernalia of the classical world. They filled their gardens with urns, nymphs and river-gods and their houses with busts and antiques, some of them genuine, brought back from the Grand Tour to Italy. The virtues of Georgian architecture are the virtues of classicism – restraint, order, harmony,

balance, symmetry – and when it falls into tired cliché, its vices are the corresponding vices of monotony, imitation, repetition and lack of imagination. Georgian buildings are sometimes dull: they are rarely lacking in taste.

Eighteenth-century England also looked to the classical world for political guidance. The Greek historian Polybius had accepted Aristotle's distinction of three types of political regime: monarchy, apt to degenerate into despotism; aristocracy, which could become oligarchy; and democracy, which led through licence into anarchy, and once more to despotism: the Roman Republic's success, he had argued, derived from a mixed constitution, where the parts were in 'exact equilibrium'. It was a formula which the framers of the settlement after the Glorious Revolution of 1688 tried to adapt to their own problem. Power would not be concentrated, but distributed: King and Commons confronted each other, and the aristocracy, by leaning first one way then the other, would provide the essential equilibrium. The result would preserve England from the civil wars and disorders that had been so marked a feature of the 17th century.

By the 1720s it seemed that this indeed might be within reach. Georgian England began to pull herself out of political convulsion, gaining first commercial prosperity, then colonial predominance and, at length, a massive self-confidence. In the Nine Years' War (1688–97) and the War of the Spanish Succession (Marlborough's war, 1701–14) the British intervened in the continental balance against Louis XIV with decisive effect. The Seven Years' War (Pitt's war, 1756–63) saw the French virtually driven out from both India and Canada. The political settlement of 1689 – substituting William and Mary for James II but retaining the Stuart dynasty – was imperilled after 1700 when the death of William, Duke of Gloucester, Anne's only surviving child, forced the English to look to Germany for a new royal family. For some years after 1714, in the light of the English reputation for turbulence and rebellion, it seemed doubtful how long the Hanoverians would remain, but in the 1720s and 1730s the dynasty, amid much carping at 'German politicks', managed to put down roots. The last great Jacobite attempt in 1745, even with the advantage of a charismatic leader, revealed not the regime's vulnerability but its substantial acceptance, at least by the English nation. Meanwhile, colonial wealth began to flow into the country and a steady increase in trade meant, for the fortunate few, luxury on a scale never previously experienced. Even the loss of the American colonies in 1783, believed by many to mark the beginning of the end, was shrugged off with

The south front of Chatsworth, Derbyshire – 'a masterpiece of majestic dignity' – seat of the Dukes of Devonshire. The bridge, by James Paine, was the finishing touch to the landscaping of Capability Brown in the 1750s which transformed a wilderness into the setting the house deserved. Houses on such a scale 'struck awe into the beholder; they breathed authority and stability'

scarcely a tremor and the country moved into a spectacular financial and industrial expansion. The arts of 'management' – that patronage for which the period is famous – together with the cool moderation of the Anglican church and the success of the Union with Scotland in 1707 laid the foundations on which these stupendous achievements rested.

Britain's prestige in the world rose to unprecedented heights. Learned foreigners visited the country to discover the mystery of its remarkable constitution. The native population basked in the most flattering, even fulsome, tributes from Voltaire, Montesquieu and de Lolme to their political acumen. 'Liberty', de Lolme told them, 'had at last disclosed her secret to mankind' and had secured an asylum to herself in their happy island. The natives modestly admitted that they were indeed very fortunate. Though George III and Junius were at daggers drawn in most other respects, they agreed that the constitution was 'the wisest of human institutions'. Whiggism, the prevailing political creed, saw itself essentially as the politics of moderation, steering a careful course between bigoted Toryism on the right and levelling radicalism on the left. It is a political tradition perhaps not quite exhausted.

The connection between the politics and the architecture of the period is not a contrivance of historians. It was well understood at the time. Humphry Repton, the later 18th-century exponent of landscape gardening, drew a direct parallel between the beauty of the great parks and the excellence of the constitution: they had achieved the 'happy medium between the wildness of nature and the stiffness of art, in the same manner as the English constitution is the happy medium between the liberty of savages and the restraint of despotic government'.

It is by no means accidental that, in the settlement after 1688, the critical role in the constitutional balance should have been given to the aristocracy. The Glorious Revolution was largely the work of the nobility and it confirmed their hold on power. Economic conditions favoured the growth of great landed estates; the development of the law of entail helped to protect them against the excesses of spendthrift heirs; increasing wealth flowing from an expanding empire permitted building on a scale never before possible. The 18th century was, above all, the century of the peerage, and it is altogether appropriate to begin our survey at the top. That means Chatsworth and Blenheim, homes of the Cavendishes and the Churchills, Dukes of Devonshire and Marlborough respectively.

Chatsworth was started just before the Glorious Revolution, in 1686, but the Cavendishes backed the right horse and prospered. A dukedom came from the grateful William III in 1694 and the house and gardens grew to fit the dukedom. In the 1750s a Cavendish was prime minister and six of the family sat in the House of Commons between 1754 and 1790. Chatsworth is not a severely classical house: there is a lot of baroque in-

fluence, particularly in the interior decoration. In viewing the exterior, one should disregard the additions to the north, for the alterations made by the sixth Duke in the 19th century spoil the symmetry of the original design. But the south front is a masterpiece of majestic dignity, a statement of true Whiggism. And in the late 1750s, Lancelot 'Capability' Brown was called in to give the house the setting it needed. He grassed over the parterres, dammed the Derwent to give it size, planted out the park, and created a landscape out of what, 50 years before, had been described as a Derbyshire wilderness. James Paine's bridge, finished in 1762, was the final touch the composition needed.

Blenheim is not at all restrained. It was not intended to be. It was a celebration of triumph over the French and its design was correspondingly exuberant. In Sir John Vanbrugh the nation found the ideal architect, florid, enterprising, self-confident, with a splendid streak of vulgarity. It is not a lovable house. But it does impress. Pope summed it up in his extempore couplet:

'Tis very grand and very fine,
But where d'you sleep and where d'you dine?

The palace is redeemed by its setting. It is one of Capability Brown's greatest triumphs. When he was asked to advise in the late 1750s he found the majestic bridge which leads up to the Column of Victory striding across the most absurd little stream, the tiny river

Petworth Park, Sussex, the incomparable achievement of land-scape artist Capability Brown, who enlarged the lake in the 1750s and dotted it with willow-planted islands. Sheep and deer still roam the sweeps of grass and wooded slopes as Brown intended

Glyme. Brown dammed it and created two stupendous lakes on either side which, miraculously, balance the enormous pile of the palace, providing it with a context that can soften and quieten its excesses. Brown's scheme has the genius of total simplicity, and once it was finished, it looked inevitable.

These great houses reflected the aristocratic order of society and its values, but they also helped to perpetuate it. They struck awe into the beholder: they breathed authority and stability. By the correctness of his taste, the owner demonstrated his fitness to rule.

And there were more immediate considerations. Each grand house was the centre of a complex system of patronage and influence, a network which bound hundreds of people to the success of the patron and the continuance of the system. They served as the social and political centres of their part of the shire. The coming-of-age or the marriage of the heir was often the signal for a vast entertainment, involving hundreds of visitors, fed and welcomed according to their rank. By the lavishness of the provision and the condescension of the host, each guest was reminded of his place in the order of things.

The most important neighbours and tenants were

invited to the grand ball; the substantial farmers to the dinner; and thousands of the ordinary country folk to beer and skittles in the park. After a typical election rout, Lady Cork wrote to her husband: 'all my best floors are spoiled by the hobnails of farmers stamping about them; every room is a pig-stye, and the Chinese paper in the drawing-room stinks so abominably of punch and tobacco that it would strike you down to come into it.'

In 1789 when George III recovered from temporary madness, the Marchioness of Buckingham, who had sound political reasons for wishing the monarch res-tored, had the front of Stowe illuminated, roasted an ox entire, and entertained 2,000 people in celebration. At his great and ill-fated house of Cannons in 1722, the Duke of Chandos employed 90 servants, including 16 musicians. Capability Brown was a kind of job-creation scheme in his own right.

Since to impress was of prime importance, it followed that great attention should be paid to entrances and reception rooms. Books on etiquette explained to young men how to make an entrance into company in a dig-nified and correct fashion, neither brashly nor sheepish-ly. Eighteenth-century architects followed suit. Not for them the painful anonymity of modern buildings where the unlucky visitor fumbles at plate-glass doors, hoping to find one that may be open.

The full glory of the Georgian house is only to be seen after that remarkable run of artists – Bridgeman, Kent, Brown and Repton – had developed a landscape which was deliberately designed to provide the perfect setting, house and grounds as a single entity. Until the 1710s or 1720s, the prevailing fashion in gardens remained French, under the influence of André le Nôtre's achievements at Versailles. The manicured parterres, geometrical and formal in layout, with clipped box hedges, crushed gravel paths, abundant fountains, clas-sical statues and elaborate topiary, could be delightful, as the west parterre at Blenheim, reconstituted in the early 20th century, illustrates. But as early as 1710 there were protests against the artificiality of such gardens and moves towards a more natural and flowing landscape.

As French power waned in the later years of Louis XIV's reign and British confidence grew, there seemed less need to imitate French models: horticultural regim-entation might be appropriate to a despotic nation, but British liberties deserved a more expansive and relaxed setting. By mid-century, Capability Brown had got the natural landscape down to its basic ingredients of grass, trees, water and sheep – the landscape of his native Northumberland. Brown, himself of humble stock, was beseeched by proud noblemen to spare them a few hours of his most valuable time to advise them on the capabili-ties of their estates.

Of course, the new landscapes were as artificial and contrived as the old. Trees, as Repton pointed out, do not group themselves naturally on isolated knolls. In-finite pains were taken to construct these careless pastor-al idylls. Vast gangs of labourers sweated to dig lakes,

The Nymph of the Grott is one of the features of the most picturesque of all Georgian gardens, at Stourhead in Wiltshire, designed by an amateur, Henry Hoare. Italy's scenery and the idyllic landscapes of Claude and Poussin inspired him

remove hills, plant trees by the thousand. George III lent Brown a company of soldiers to scoop out the rhododendron dell at Kew Gardens. One innovation in particular symbolises the art that disguises art – the ha-ha, popularised by Bridgeman. Most landscape artists were agreed that sheep and cattle form an essential ingredient in scenery, providing movement and sound in an otherwise static and silent picture. Unfortunately, animals are only too natural. Sheep are very resistant to house-training and their droppings fouled the terrace, while young bullocks at close range were apt to frighten the ladies. The solution was the ha-ha, a sunken ditch, which kept animals at a very proper and pleasing distance, yet was invisible from the house and did not interrupt the sweep of the parkland.

Nor were cattle and sheep the only creatures to be kept at a respectful distance. Many of the grand houses emerged from their medieval squalor with cottages and huts in unsanitary and inelegant proximity. Chatsworth is one of the many places where the old village was pulled down and rebuilt out of sight: there are others at Chippenham in Cambridgeshire, Kedleston, Stowe and

Milton Abbas, Dorset. Superficially, few things could better demonstrate the arrogance of rank and privilege, and there can be little doubt that it helped to separate, physically and socially, the nobility from their tenants. Yet it is a strange charge for the 20th century to bring against the 18th, for it would be hard to devise schemes more conducive to social division than the enormous council housing estates on the edge of great towns, favoured in the 1950s.

Brown's work can still be seen in a large number of places. At Alnwick, he cleared and planted the banks of the river for the Duke of Northumberland, providing a perfect setting for John Adam's bridge, built in 1773, with the Percy lion breathing defiance in the direction of Scotland. At Petworth in Sussex the blend of art and nature is so effortless that it reminds us of Horace Walpole's graceful obituary tribute to Brown: 'Such was the effect of his genius that when he was the happiest man, he will be least remembered.' Petworth Park, with Brown's lake in the foreground and the South Downs in the distance, is incomparable.

But perhaps the finest blend of house and grounds is at Heveningham Hall in Suffolk, built by Sir Robert Taylor for the Vannecks, with the interior decoration left to James Wyatt. It is a more manageable house than Stowe, Castle Howard, Wentworth Woodhouse or Holkham, and the slight wedding-cake opulence is redeemed and purified by the severity of Brown's setting of grass, lake and trees.

Though one thinks first of the great country houses of Georgian England, the urban inheritance is almost as imposing. The early 18th century was a period of prosperity for many provincial towns, and large areas of some towns survive as oases of Georgian elegance. A walk from Saturday market to Tuesday market at King's Lynn takes one past splendid buildings and culminates in perhaps the finest market square in England, presided over by Henry Bell's late 17th-century hostelry, the Duke's Head. Boston, in the same part of the world, was a port of modest affluence in the period and has a number of fine buildings to show for it, and Wisbech can boast in North Brink, by the bank of the river, an outstanding run of Georgian buildings, with pride of place going to Peckover House, built around 1727.

Two of the finest Georgian towns are Stamford and Ludlow. Though it is impossible to decide which is the finer, the attempt itself is a pleasure. If Broad Street, Ludlow, running steeply downhill through the wall-gate, has more houses of real distinction, the suburb of St Martin's at Stamford, from the gates of Burghley Park to the George Hotel, has a remarkable restrained coherence. If the valley of the Teme at Ludlow has the edge in picturesque and spectacular wooded beauty, the Welland at Stamford has its quiet East Anglian water meadows.

The West Country is particularly rich in Georgian town architecture. At Blandford a catastrophic fire in 1731 led to the whole centre of the town being rebuilt

The Georgian model village of identical pairs of thatched cottages at Milton Abbas, Dorset, was created by 'an unmannerly imperious lord' – Viscount Milton – to replace the village he had swept away because it spoilt the view from his house

during the next two decades by the brothers John and William Bastard, leaving a unique Georgian nucleus. Shrewsbury, a very prosperous town for much of the 18th century, has a fine riverside Georgian suburb; the centre of Bewdley is basically Georgian; Worcester, though sorely blighted by planners, retains some excellent classical houses, especially along Foregate Street, running north from the town. In Pershore, the entire length of Bridge Street is Georgian, with few outstanding houses, but a most pleasing overall effect. Upton-on-Severn, only eight miles away, is a kind of pocket-sized Georgian town, where, at the White Lion, Tom Jones and Mrs Waters spent a distinctly disturbed night.

The number of good public buildings which survive from this period reminds us of the importance of local civic life and pride. Though some of the finest guildhalls are 17th century, like that at Abingdon, there are other excellent examples at Wootton Bassett (1700), Brackley (1706), Worcester (1721), Stockton-on-Tees (1736), Dursley (1738), and a fine late one at Bury St Edmunds, built by Robert Adam in the 1770s. Though the mid-century is often scarified for its gross self-indulgence, it was a period of great humanitarian endeavour. Guy's Hospital was founded in 1722, largely on the proceeds from a successful South Seas Bubble speculation; Coram's Foundling Hospital opened its doors

in 1745. Many of the provincial infirmaries and hospitals date from this period. Among the most miraculous Georgian survivals are three provincial theatres – the Theatre Royals of Bath and Bristol, and a tiny playhouse at Richmond in Yorkshire, built in 1788 and beautifully restored in the 1960s.

The Hanoverian Church is celebrated for the attention it paid to its own comforts, and there is scarcely a cathedral close without its share of elegant houses for the prebendaries and canons. Durham, Hereford, Lichfield and Gloucester have fine examples, but pre-eminent is Salisbury, with Mompesson House, built soon after 1701, as the supreme exhibit. Clerical academics were also responsible for a good deal of Georgian building. At Oxford, Gibbs' Radcliffe Camera, finished in 1749, has become the nodal point of the university. Worcester College is completely Georgian, and Queen's nearly so, while other 18th-century buildings include the Clarendon, the Codrington Library, Christchurch Library and Peckwater Quad, the Fellows Building at Magdalen, and the Radcliffe Observatory and Infirmary.

Abraham Darby's furnace at Coalbrookdale, Shropshire, which was the birthplace of the Industrial Revolution. It was Darby's discovery of coke that improved ironmaking in Britain

Eighteenth-century Cambridge is less impressive, but Gibbs brought off a handsome double with Gibbs's Building at King's (1729) and the Senate House, a year later. Peterhouse erected its Master's Lodge in 1701 and its Fellows Building in 1742.

The spas of Georgian England are among the best known features of the period. Their purpose was as much social as curative, though persons were found to testify to the value of the waters. The basic lay-out of Georgian Bath was completed by 1774 when John Wood the Younger finished Royal Crescent. Not much remains of the Hotwells in Bristol, for a time something of a rival to Bath, but there are some pretty houses around Dowry Square, and a charming, if implausible, little colonnade at the foot of the Avon Gorge, started about 1784 but never finished. At the top of the cliff in the 1790s began

Previous page: top left, Stamford Lincs., one of the finest Georgian towns in England, a cool composite of quiet churches and reserved squares sloping down to the River Welland. Bottom left: passage linking streets in Buxton, Derbyshire, a spa town that blossomed in the 1780s with investment by the 5th Duke of Devonshire. Right: decorative balconies on a terrace in Bath, which is still full of exquisitely elegant Georgian buildings

the development of the great Georgian suburb of Clifton, still one of the most agreeable parts of the country in which to live. Buxton, which had had a local reputation since the 17th century, blossomed in the 1780s when the fifth Duke of Devonshire built the Crescent: at one end, now translated into a most splendid library, is the Assembly Room, of cool and striking beauty. Though spa life may appear mannered and artificial, it represented an attempt to eradicate some of the coarseness of the previous century, when gentlefolk relieved themselves in public without ceremony and Pepys complained that he returned from Court with even more lice than he took there.

The only possible rival to Bath as a surviving example of Georgian town planning is Edinburgh New Town. The departure of the parliament to Westminster in 1707 deprived Edinburgh of some of its importance and the development of the New Town was, to a considerable extent, a deliberate attempt to re-assert civic prestige. The old town clung to the spine stretching from the Castle a mile east to Holyrood Palace, its wynds and alleys running down the hills to north and south. The obvious line of expansion to the north was blocked by a precipitous valley where the North Loch, over the years, had degenerated into a noisome and offensive swamp. The first practical step was the building of the North

Bridge, started in 1763 and finished in 1771: at the north end, on a commanding site, Robert Adam began the Register House, a later generation adding the equestrian statue of Wellington. Once this link has been established, the development of the plateau the other side could begin. While the North Bridge was in progress, the Town Council had advertised for a street plan. The competition was won by James Craig, with a somewhat unimaginative rectangular grid, flanked east and west by two squares. The detailed exploitation of the site was left however to individual builders and architects. The most striking feature of Craig's scheme, the absence of houses on the south side of Princes Street, which means that town and country mingle in an almost unique fashion, was not preserved without difficulty. The environmentalists of the 1770s, who included David Hume, were obliged to take legal action to prevent the Town Council permitting further building there, obtaining a ruling from Lord Mansfield in the House of Lords in their favour.

The Georgian period was the high point of road travel before the speed of the railways began to put coaches out of business. The great network of coaching inns can still be traced. A most popular name for taverns was the George, equalling or surpassing the White Hart, the Angel or the Swan. It is a point of some interest and suggests that the Hanoverian dynasty may have been rather more popular than some historians care to admit. Landlords are not usually out of touch with the public mood. It does not, of course, follow that all the Georges are of 18th-century origin. The landlord of the Pilgrim Inn, a magnificent 15th-century hostelry at Glastonbury, perceiving that pilgrims were likely to be in short supply in the age of reason, changed its name to the George. But there are genuine 18th-century Georges at West Wycombe, Portsmouth, Buckden and Grantham. Other early 18th-century inns are the Buckinghamshire Arms at Blickling, and the King's Head at Abingdon and Richmond, Yorkshire; from mid-century date the Green Man at Ashbourne, where Boswell was so handsomely entertained, the Spread Eagle at Thame and the Marlborough Arms at Woodstock; from the later decades are the Angel at Bury St Edmunds, started in 1779, and the Swan at Bedford, built by Henry Holland in 1794. Later Georgian inns include the Fleece in the market square at Thirsk, and the King's Arms at Dorchester where Susan Henchard, after a lapse of 18 years, peered through the window to see her husband, Michael, in the chair at a convivial dinner as the Mayor of Casterbridge.

The speeding-up of road travel, mainly as a result of turnpike trusts, was considerable. In Charles II's reign, the journey from Bristol to London had taken three days, with overnight stops at Marlborough and Reading: by 1775 it could be done in 16 hours, albeit with an early start and a jolting ride. Road surfaces were greatly improved and dozens of new bridges, often of splendid design, opened up the countryside. John Smeaton's

Cromford Mill, Derbyshire, where England's first water-powered spinning machine was invented in 1771 by Richard Arkwright, thus turning textiles from a cottage craft into mass production

bridge across the river Tay at Perth was finished in 1771, rendering superfluous some 30 small ferry boats which had plied their trade since the previous bridge had collapsed in 1621. The Severn was spanned by a whole series of fine classical bridges at Shrewsbury (Gwynne, 1774), Bewdley (Telford, 1798), Worcester (Gwynne, 1780), Tewkesbury (Telford, 1826) and Gloucester (Telford, 1825). John Gwynne was also responsible for Magdalen College bridge at Oxford, built between 1772 and 1782.

The forces that were to undermine this tightly-knit society may also be traced. Growing industrialism, compounded by 20 years of warfare against Revolutionary and Napoleonic France, placed an increasing strain on old institutions, and the years from Waterloo in 1815 to the death of George IV in 1830 were ones of great tension. Greater freedom of travel and movement meant more social mobility and this, in turn, posed problems of government and control. The parish priests and justices of the peace who had kept an eye on their own villages could hardly cope with the challenge of the teeming industrial towns of Sheffield and Leeds, Manchester and Birmingham, none of them even re-

Ironbridge, Shropshire, and its eponymous structure that was the first iron bridge in the world. It leaps the River Severn in a single 100-foot span, cast in the 1770s by Abraham Darby III in the family ironworks at Coalbrookdale

presented in parliament. Large-scale factory production meant, in the long run, the end of the old order. Canals may no longer strike us as very remarkable innovations, yet they did much in the late 18th century to prepare the way for the great leap forward. Two impressive engineering feats that may still be seen are the Bingley five-rise locks on the Leeds and Liverpool canal, opened in 1777, or the 29 consecutive locks on the Kennet and Avon at Devizes, started in 1794.

At Tanfield in County Durham may be seen what has been claimed as the world's first railway bridge, built in 1727 for a horse-worked coal train. The first cotton spinning mill based on water power was built by Sir Richard Arkwright at Cromford near Matlock in 1771, together with cottages for his work force. But the finest of all surviving early industrial sites is at Ironbridge in Shropshire, where the Darby family, great entrepreneurs, developed the iron industry: the bridge itself, erected in 1771, is a masterpiece of sinuous tracery and forms part of a splendid museum complex. Seaton Sluice in Northumberland, two miles from Vanbrugh's gaunt and brooding mansion of Seaton Delaval, is one of the many hopeful harbours of the period: Sir John Delaval had the new cut made in 1761 to improve the facilities begun in the previous century. It did not prosper, but others, like Whitehaven and Milford Haven, lived to make their contribution to the Industrial Revolution.

That the 18th century remained, in many respects, brutal and savage cannot be denied. Most centuries are. The century of Wyatt's Orangery at Heveningham, of Robert Adam's oval staircase at Moccas Court and of the exquisite *chinoiserie* plaster decoration at Claydon House was also the century of Tyburn and Gin Lane, of the press gang, the debtor's prison and the pauper's grave. But, at its best, it possessed a calm and dignified self-confidence that has all but disappeared. If there is a case for privilege, Georgian England puts it at its most persuasive at Beningbrough and West Wycombe, at Studley Royal and Stourhead, and at Sheffield Park.

COSTUME

by Jane Tozer

Textiles rarely survive in any archaeological sense, and we can only speculate about the prehistory of costume. The first clothes in Britain were made of skins prepared with stone tools, stitched with sinews using bone needles. Jewellery was a prized possession to be buried with the dead. We can feel the urgency of the woman who escaped the storm which engulfed Skara Brae, Orkney in *c.* 2500 BC, scattering her beads as she ran.

There are no signs of weaving at Skara Brae, though its people kept sheep. Weaving evolved in settled communities as agriculture developed. Finds of pottery warp-weights, bone combs and beaters show that an upright loom was standard domestic equipment from the Iron Age through the Dark Ages.

Women developed great skill in spinning and weaving; linen would be used for fine clothes and underwear, wool for daily use. Danish bog burials of human sacrifices and criminals have preserved both bodies and clothing by tanning in the wet peat. Female burials yield skin capes, wool tunics, skirts and shawls, and hairnets. Men wore cloth pinned or belted to make kilts, cloaks, tunics and coats, worn with leg bandages and wraparound leather shoes. From the 3rd-2nd century BC we know that Celtic men wore trousers.

Such simple clothes, loom-lengths of bright coloured and patterned cloth, were draped without wasteful cutting. Variations on this theme formed standard British dress to the end of the Dark Ages.

Personal ornaments are found a grave-goods, like the massy gold and bronze torques of chieftains of the Celtic Iron Age. Most significant to the archaeologist are the numerous pins and brooches universally worn as dress fasteners. Their form and decoration are a guide to dating, and the spread of cultural, technological and artistic influences.

After the Roman conquest and colonisation there was a policy of 'Romanisation' which it was hoped would extend to clothing worn by the native Britons. Tacitus describes how Governor Julius Agricola (in office AD 78–84) promoted Roman customs '. . . the toga could be seen everywhere . . .'. This is pure propaganda. The toga was a formal garment, demanding urbane and skilled handling of its impressive drapery. Tunic and cloak were worn every day by Roman townsmen, and for native British in their settlements dress changed little.

Costly linens, even silks, were imported from the East for fine Roman ladies to deck themselves in tunics and shawls. Their hair was elaborately dressed, but in provincial fashion lagging behind Rome. Both sexes lavished care on their bodies. Even frontier soldiery had bath-houses, though life was tough on Hadrian's Wall. A writing tablet found at Vindolanda tells a soldier to await '. . . pairs of socks, two pairs of under-pants (*subligaria*), and two pairs of sandals . . .' sent by some caring person against the climate. They would have been sturdy sandals with studded soles.

A continuous pictorial and literary record of British life begins in the 10th century. Illuminated manuscripts illustrate rich, poor and the clergy. An Anglo-Saxon man would wear a couple of tunics over a linen shirt, with a cloak and hood or cap. His wife donned her two tunics over a linen smock, binding them perhaps with an ornate girdle. Only young girls wore their hair loose or in heavy plaits; a modest matron kept her head covered.

Silk was available to the wealthiest, and to the church. Englishwomen were renowned embroiderers for church and court. The St Cuthbert embroideries in Durham Cathedral were the gift of Queen Aelfflaed (d.916). English hands also worked the Bayeux tapestry, *c.* 1077, our most vivid picture of life and dress.

By the late 14th century styles are changing rapidly enough for us to talk of fashion, and for Chaucer to be using dress details to indicate character. The Wife of Bath wears red stockings and striking headgear; the Squire is embroidered like a flowery meadow. Clothes have a new splendour, using costly Italian velvets and

Medieval peasant's garb for the chill of autumn, as shown in a medieval calendar

A Roman sandal sole. Leather is preserved in waterlogged soil and sites like York and London have yielded large quantities of shoes from the Roman period. A writing tablet found at Vindolanda on Hadrian's Wall tells a soldier to expect a parcel of socks, underpants and 'sandals from Sattua'. Many surviving Roman sandals have nailed soles for harder wear

From the Bayeux Tapestry 1077. In this scene Edward the Confessor receives Harold. As a venerable man the king wears long hair and beard, the more usual English fashion was for shorter hair and most men were clean-shaven. Ceremonial tunics and mantles like the king's are long and might have embroidered or woven borders. Commoners and noblemen dressed for daily activity would wear short tunics, their legs wrapped in bandages. Cloaks were rectangular or semi-circular, fastened with brooches like the king's

From Speed's maps to 'The Theatre of Great Britain' 1611. The citizen wears a furred gown with hanging sleeves, and carries his gloves. His wife wears a frounced farthingale petticoat; her stiffened bodice is unusual in having a straight waist. They both wear ruffs, and large hats (perhaps of felt, or beaver for the very wealthy). Shoes are round toed. Country clothes are simpler and the countrywoman wears a bum roll instead of a farthingale

English woman with rosary c. 1527 by
Hans Holbein. Holbein shows both front and
back of this trained velvet kirtle.
Her sleeves are tight to the elbow, then turned
back to form deep hanging cuffs lined with
fur, her contrasting undersleeves are flashed and tied
with ribbons. The pointed, arched headdress
bordered with jewels, is called an 'English hood',
under it the hair is concealed in silk rolls. Note
the wide, square toes of her shoes

Detail of a scene at the court of Edward IV,
c. 1470–80. These two courtiers wear brightly coloured
clothes. Both long gowns and short jackets with
furred and hanging sleeves were fashionable. Their
long pointed-toed shoes (piped shoes) were
condemned by the church as extravagant.
Examples of them survive
in the Museum of London

Edward Sackville 4th Earl of Dorset attributed
to William Larkin c. 1613. Every part of the doublet
and long trunk hose is covered with embroidery
and metal threads. His collar, starched with fashionable
yellow is edged with needlepoint lace and shows
off a tasselled earring of black silk. A cloak bordered
with embroidery and rosettes is worn over
the arm. Such a costume would be worn only for great
occasions, and might cost upwards of £1,000,
but despite its lavishness, his contemporaries did
not consider him a fop

Lord John and Lord Bernard Stuart by Van Dyck 1638.
The 17 and 15-year-old sons of the king's cousin were both
killed in their early twenties fighting for the Royalists.
Their clothes of soft, rich fabrics are worn with a swagger. Doublets
are high-waisted with many buttons, and are slashed
and left open to reveal white linen shirts. The butterfly leathers
on the boots are for spurs; the boy on the right wears
clogs (overshoes) to protect his boots. Scalloped
lace is used to edge collar and boot-hose. Hair is
long and loose, wigs were not worn

Winter from 'The Four Seasons' by
Wenceslaus Hollar 1643. Winter walks abroad
in a half-mask to protect her complexion.
A hood is drawn up over her linen coif, her
double linen collar is edged with lace.
The velvet gown is worn lifted to protect
it from the dirty streets, and
incidentally to reveal elegant lace-trimmed
petticoat. Hollar enjoyed depicting
fur – here her muff and tippet

From a fan leaf of c. 1714 in the
Gallery of English Costume. The fan depicts
the drawing of a lottery believed to
have taken place in the Mercers' Hall, London,
1714. The fashionable crowd shows men
in loosely fitting long coats, much trimmed
with braid and buttons, wearing full-
bottom wigs. The ladies wear silk mantuas
(robes) draped over petticoats, and
their 'fontange' caps have long lace lappets

Detail of 'The Teaparty' by Richard
Collins 1730. The woman at tea wears
a typical informal dress of
the 1730s. Her bodice is worn open,
the front turned back in stitched-
down pleats, the front opening is filled
by a stomacher. One can see
the hard line caused by the top edge of
her stiff whale-boned stays. The
buckled belt and silk apron are fashionable

Evening dresses 1796 from 'The Gallery of Fashion' by N. Heideloff.
These formal dresses are intended for opera and concerts. Waistlines are
extremely high, just under the bust, and neckline is low.
The long stiffly boned stays of the 18th century have become redundant.
Silks are plain and soft and there is much use of muslins, gauzes
and nets so that dresses resemble classical draperies. High plumed headresses
for formal wear lingered into the 20th century for debutantes

From plates by J. June, mid-18th-century
engraver and illustrator. Collections of small figure
groups were sold to amateur artists to be
copied into their drawings of parks and country houses.
They are livelier than fashion plates, and
show how women's loose 'sack' dresses, jackets and
hooped petticoats looked in movement. Gentlemen wear
loose cloth 'frocks' for day; their waistcoats are
trimmed with metal lace or embroidery

Riding-coat dresses of 1788 and 1794. This style was also
called a great-coat dress, or later in Franglais 'redingote'. It was
fashionable from the mid-1780s and was worn for walking
and riding. The style echoed the elegantly casual country clothes loved
by English men. Such a coat would be of woollen cloth
and like a riding habit it would have been made by a male tailor

From 'le Beau Monde' June 1808.
Kensington Garden dresses. The 'Beau Monde',
published 1806–8, gave equal prominence
to men's dress. For the morning walk the ladies
wear dresses of embroidered India muslin
or net, with a silk tunic, lace tippet, pelisse or
shawl. This is an early depiction of
men's informal 'trowsers', which were originally
a little boy's garment. His coat
is of blue cloth with gilt buttons. The white
neckcloth, inspired by Brummel, is
worn high round the throat

Stone-breakers on the road 1814. From 'Costume of Yorkshire'.
These labourers' trousers are probably of a cotton and linen fabric called fustian.
The cotton handkerchiefs round their necks would have been printed in
Lancashire. Everything from the shapeless felt hat down could have been
bought second hand from a rag fair

Four Englishmen c. 1818 by Richard Dighton. Dighton made full length
drawings of the characters of the day which have an air of caricature. Tom Raikes
(far right) wears a morning dress coat with a velvet-faced, M-notched
collar and trousers. Colonel Arthur Upton (2nd left) wears a frock coat with breeches.
Both have high starched collars and neck cloths. The carrying of
umbrellas and sticks was often ridiculed

'Can't you be quiet' caricature
by H. Heath 1829. A lounger accosts a flirt.
The artist exaggerates fashion, while closely
observing details of dress and behaviour. Note
the girl's tight waist and low neckline, her
beribboned cap and fashionable apron. Her 'gigot'
sleeves have puffs at the shoulder.
The ankle-length skirt is shortened for risqué effect.
The idler's coat is well padded in chest
and shoulders. His trousers are pleated 'cossacks'.
Both sexes admire a narrow waist and foot

Fashions of July 1864 from 'The English Woman's Domestic Magazine'.
French fashion plates were often reproduced in English magazines, sometimes pirated.
Left, a travelling dress with cape in alpaca, a material that tended to crush.
The mauve dress shown in front and side view is called 'The Patti' after the singer.
Thompson's new light weight crinoline was considered necessary for
the new gored shape. Paper models and patterns for these dresses were available:
the mauve dress at six shillings, the travelling cape at three shillings

Evening dress 1893–4.
English tailoring had become world-
renowned for scientific cutting
and skilled handling of cloth. 'A
black tail-coat, waistcoat
and trousers and white tie are the
proper wear and unless
eccentricity is apparent prevail
at the dinner table and at evening
parties,' says 'Complete
Etiquette for Gentlemen' 1880

From 'The Natural History of The Gent'.
Albert Smith 1847. A satire on bad taste and
manners, the drawing shows a 'gent'
in 'large check trousers' and frockcoat,
carrying 'a little stick of no earthly
use, with a horse's silver hoof on top'. He
is annoying a 'pretty girl of modest deportment
. . . after her hard day's toil at a bonnet
shop'. Her silk bonnet, ringlets, dress and
mantle are fashionable and respectable

Fashion for October 1838 from 'La Belle Assemblée'.
Left, a dinner dress of grey Levantine silk worn with a cap of
silk net. Right, a promenade dress of green corded silk with
embroidered, lace-edged flounces worn with a cottage bonnet. The
half-length figure wears a morning visiting dress of
striped and figured silk

From 'The Tailor and Cutter'
August 1888. Dress for Summer. 'The jacket shown
on the lady is of the "Etonian" type
. . . one of the most popular garments of the
year'. It is long-waisted in front, and
short behind. The overskirt with draped
panels is open to reveal a contrasting
underskirt. The young man wears a coat of
vicuna with striped cashmere trousers.
'Young gents' sported loud stripes and checks

From 'Tailor and Cutter' July 1888
'Pleasuring dress'. The tailor's art of cutting and
pressing woollens had reached a peak of
technical skill by the end of Victoria's reign.
Tailormade clothes had a liberating
influence on women's fashion, though this lady
still wears a small bustle ('dress improver').
Boating and bicycling were important leisure
pursuits, and required special clothes like these
'reefer' and 'patrol' jackets, and the bicyclist's 'knickers'

**Elegant Regency couple out
for a stroll. An emphasis
on simplicity and the superb
cutting of cloth was a
feature of men's costume
following the example
set by dandies like Beau
Brummell and Scrope Davies**

brocades, fur linings, fancifully cut borders. Moralists and churchmen condemned such vanity, and sumptuary laws attempted to confine luxury to the court.

Late mediaeval clothing is shaped to the body by cutting and padding to the fashionable silhouette. Tailoring became a craft controlled by men, who also made women's courtly garments. It was the seamstress's job to make underlinen. British woollens, made by craftsman weavers, became a vital export.

In the 16th century dress reached a climax of display. We see in Holbein's portraits of Henry VIII the epitome of masculinity in dress, with padded doublet, codpiece, short, wide-shouldered gown. His sturdy legs might be flattered by knitted stockings now knitting was in wide use. An extravagantly wasteful fashion was to slash sleeves and breeches to ribbons, revealing a contrasting lining. Less rich clothing has been found in the wreck of Henry's flagship the 'Mary Rose'.

A taste for things Spanish meant that male fashions were more subdued in the Elizabethan era; sombre colours and plain shapes prevailed. By contrast, women's silhouette was imposing, the bodice stiffened to a conical shape by whaleboning, the skirt spread wide over a wheel-farthingale or a bum-roll. Bodice, petticoat, gown, ruff and sleeves were separate garments, held together by pins and laces. The only items to survive in quantity are the embroidered accessories worked by ladies themselves, sometimes as gifts.

Nowadays we think of Civil War costume as a political and religious statement: Royalists swaggering in lace-collared doublets, their ladies in decolleté bodices, ringlets and pearls; Puritans in sober colours and plain white linen. This is an over-simplification; some Parliamentarians enjoyed clothes. However it is safe to say that Cromwell discouraged frivolity.

'This day the King begins to put on his Vest . . . being a long Cassocke close to the body. . . . I wish the King may keep it, for it is a very fine and handsome garment.' So Pepys's Diary records the demise of the doublet, on 8 October 1666. The 'persian' vest, a loose coat almost to the knee, became the waistcoat of the 18th century. With coat and breeches it is the ancestor of the three-piece suit.

Silk-weaving reached an artistic and technical peak in the 18th century. Brocades and damasks were made in London at Spitalfields, one famous designer being Anna Maria Garthwaite. Smuggling brought lace and silk from France and Flanders. Widely hooped skirts and loose sack-back robes, worn open over a petticoat, displayed silk to advantage. Silk was so valuable that dresses were made to be refashioned, and clothing of all kinds was an important item in a will. London society indulged in extreme fashions and hairstyles, but the British in general favoured rural informality – ladies in simple gowns and straw hats, men in a comfortable suit of sportsmanlike cut, in good English cloth.

The Industrial Revolution brought cottons on to the market in bulk, and cheaply priced. Late 18th-century fashion is radical in its simplicity. Women's dress emulates the snowy drapery of classical sculpture. Many dresses survive showing an altered waistline, but with the surplus fabric left inside in case high waists failed to catch on.

The influence of Beau Brummell on men's fashion can still be seen today. The style he helped to create depended on understatement; good cut; good materials; absolute cleanliness. Menswear has never recovered its flamboyance, and Victorian dandies like Disraeli had to be content with a bold waist-coat and watch-chain. The end of the 19th century introduced new sorts of sportswear, like the Norfolk jacket and knickerbockers.

Many museums preserve Victorian dresses, and the changes of fashion are well-documented. Etiquette books, magazines and fashion plates help us to understand the conventions of Victorian society. The new middle classes needed to be sure of maintaining the correct appearance, and respectability was the new watchword. Dress for mourning was a particularly rigorous restriction; the life of the needle-woman who made up orders for mourning was poverty-stricken and exhausting.

By the 1880s dress was a subject for reforming zeal. Aesthetes like Oscar Wilde favoured historical styles and adopted precious poses. Others, like Dr Jaeger, demanded looser, healthier clothes and encouraged the wearing of wool. Some reformers even advocated divided skirts and 'Bloomers', and this shocking idea was taken up by a few daring cyclists. By 1900, even the most timid had abandoned many conventions. Though gorgeously dressed in the evening, the New Woman of 1900 wore her smart blouse and tailormade during the day.

THE
VICTORIANS

by Brian Harrison

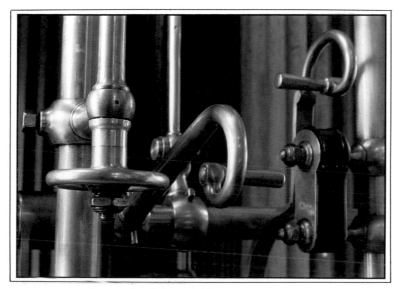

Engine detail, Kew Bridge pumping station

Nineteenth-century Britain may seem stable and secure to us, like a comfortable sofa to relax in and feel safe, but it didn't seem like that at the time. On the contrary, it seemed an alarming century – disrupting settled patterns of life, subverting established authority, hurling its populations into new locations and rupturing long-standing social relationships.

Its impact on the environment can be seen all around us to this day. It was as though some gigantic subterranean monster was gouging through the earth to create new valleys and tunnels and then throwing up the shifted soil at random into unnatural hills and embankments. Slag-heaps sprang up at the pit-head, valleys were flooded with artificial lakes, quarries were torn out of the landscape – all to satisfy industry's inordinate appetite for limestone and minerals, coal and clay, stone, water and slate. Canals were the first major offender.

William Cobbett, the popular journalist and politician who rode round the south of England in the 1820s, grumbled at the very sight of them; they seemed to be robbing an already impoverished countryside of food, without any hope of satisfying the greed of the rapidly-growing towns. These excavations had important consequences even for intellectual life, leading William Smith (the pioneer of British geological mapping) to his discoveries about the earth's stratification; it was while resident engineer to the Somerset Coal Company that he collected the material for his earliest map. The canal builders pioneered many of the engineering techniques later used on the railways. They were still tearing the landscape apart in the 1880s when the Manchester Ship Canal was begun. During its first 15 months of construction, one commentator thought it 'probably safe to say that, never since the world began, has so much been done in so short a time to change the face of Nature over five-and-thirty miles of country'.

Sea and river transport were still integral even to Britain's domestic communications system, and large new docks were carved out to accommodate the ocean-going ships that were exchanging foreign raw-materials for the British manufactured goods which were then in such widespread demand. It was during the 19th century that London acquired its great string of docks – Surrey Commercial, Royal Albert, East India, Royal Victoria – and Bristol its 'floating harbour'. It is the 20th-century decay of these major 19th-century commercial projects – railway sidings, docks, markets and warehouses – that presents us with huge inner-city areas ripe for redevelopment.

Industrialisation seemed a dangerously romantic adventure, and cast the contractor, the builder and the civil engineer in the role of Byronic heroes defying nature and the elements in their quest to impose man's control over his environment. *The Times* saw the Forth Bridge on its opening-day in 1890 as 'the greatest feat of engineering that the world has ever seen', surpassing the Eiffel Tower, and for the journalist T. H. S. Escott the 1880s were 'the era of material triumphs', in which man's conquest of nature gave Englishmen 'a sense of boundless power'. Many of the structures thrown up during this dramatic period still display the unself-conscious beauty that stems from the simplicity of functionalism; engineers did not feel the architect's compulsion towards irrelevant embellishment and embroidery. Man's triumph over nature was sufficiently precarious and recent to demand conspicuous celebration in structures that unblushingly refused to harmonise with their surroundings. Railway-builders took an almost defiant pleasure in confronting and challenging nature's curves and contours, just as architects delighted in bizarre combinations of building materials never before seen in the locality. Lewis Cubitt's 49 brick arches (1849–50) at Digswell in Hertfordshire nowadays stride majestically and uncompromisingly across the landscape.

Yet among the more conservative of contemporary observers, the railway's desecration of the countryside produced an outrage that exceeds even our own motor-way protests in volume. Labour was so cheap that mechanical excavators were not used in railway building till the end of the century; instead, hordes of navvies descended on hitherto quiet localities. Their bad language and rough habits suddenly burst in upon secluded communities and seemed to threaten civilisation itself. By modern standards, a shocking proportion of these men were blown up by explosive or buried alive in their tunnels and embankments – though no doubt the Victorians would be equally shocked at the level of traffic accidents we now tolerate. Yet it was not so much the navvies' casualty rate as their impact on the environment that roused contemporary concern; only 150 years of familiarity with the new structures, together with the softening impact of natural growth, ensure a more tolerant reception for them today.

Industrialisation also transformed the roads, for the new canals, railways and docks required the roads to carry many more goods at the same time as the enclosure of the fields confined the roads within a narrower width. Thus channelled and overloaded, the roads needed to develop a firmer foundation, and J. L. MacAdam obliged with the cheap surface of graded and impacted stones that is now so familiar. By the 1820s Britain had acquired the best network of roads it had seen since the Romans.

Nobody was more struck with these achievements than Karl Marx. His *Communist Manifesto* points out that the bourgeoisie 'during its rule of scarce one hundred years, has created more massive and more colossal productive forces than have all preceding generations

Industrial architects in the Victorian Age often adopted the style of the grand country house, a tall factory chimney being the only giveaway, as in this building, Bliss Mill, Chipping Norton, Oxon. It was built in 1872, equipped with steam-powered machinery for W. Bliss and Son's tweed manufacturing industry

together'; these had resulted in the 'clearing of whole continents for cultivation, canalisation of rivers, whole populations conjured out of the ground'. Almost everything around us – whether we live in north or south, town or country, inland or by the sea – bears the mark of this thrusting, energetic and even brash age.

Yet what is impressive about 19th-century Britain is not just its material achievement, but the fact that it simultaneously generated the humanitarian and even socialist critique of industrialism which has subsequently been used to discredit the Victorians, and which deeply permeates our political outlook to this day. By the 1840s 20,000 people in Manchester were living in cellars and twice as many in Liverpool, while their more prosperous neighbours demurely removed themselves to suburbs and came to regard the slums as unexplored territory. Yet this generated a municipal and socialist gospel which eventually ensured the sweeping away of many slums and shanty towns, so that it would be misleading for us to judge the century solely from the buildings which happen to survive.

Industrialisation may have alarmed Marx, but to others it inspired optimism, as a process that would ensure the moral and material improvement of mankind. The radical working man Henry Vincent in 1847 saw every railway engine as 'a social missionary, bringing nearer together all the nations of the earth, breaking down all the distinctions of community, class, and condition'. There seemed few enough limits to man's ingenuity, if only government and the tax-collector could refrain from stifling the enterprise and energy of the private citizen.

Many 19th-century factories were no doubt squalid structures, housing monotonous and often dangerous processes; yet some employers saw them not as dark, Satanic mills, but as palaces, castles and fortresses rivalling the monuments of classical and feudal civilisation. Look down to the left at Bliss Mill, for instance, as you drive out of Chipping Norton towards Moreton-in-the-Marsh; it is not so much a factory, more a great house set in the midst of a park – with clocktower, inscription and balustraded roofline. Or stand on the ridge above Saltaire, near Bradford, and look down on the model community created in the 1850s by the alpaca manufacturer Sir Titus Salt. His factory chimney resembles an Italian campanile, and an Italianate design percolates down to the houses of his humblest employees.

Salt saw his relationship to them as benevolently feudal, and took care to intersperse their terrace-housing (good by the standards of the day) with improving institutions – chapels, self-help institutes and schools. Even the shrubs and the plants in Saltaire park were labelled with their names and botanical characteristics.

The Forth Bridge, near Edinburgh: 'Greatest feat of engineering that the world has ever seen,' boasted *The Times* on the day that the Prince of Wales opened the bridge in 1890. William Morris, however, damned it as 'the supremest specimen of ugliness'

The Italianate style of this Congregational Church was continued in every building of the town created by alpaca manufacturer Sir Titus Salt for his workforce at Saltaire, Yorkshire – 'wherein the interests of Capital and Labour have been proved to be identical'

educational welfare; yet given the widespread belief that poverty flowed from immorality, and the absence of public welfare, such close supervision of the employee seemed in the interests of all.

In the big cities, commercial buildings grew up whose grandeur rivalled that of the great London clubs on which they were often modelled. Architects paid great attention to facades, and banks and insurance companies felt the need to impress customers with solid structures, elaborate ornamentation and generous internal space. Italianate styles at first seemed best for the purpose, though by mid-century these were giving way to Gothic. The middle classes in the big manufacturing and trading cities of the Midlands and north saw themselves as successors to the Netherlands burgher, the Florentine banker and the Venetian trader in their heyday, and even appropriated their building styles and artistic pretensions. For one of its leading champions, the majestic tower of Leeds town hall in the 1850s was 'a lasting monument of their public spirit, and generous pride in the possession of their municipal privileges'. There were brisk rivalries between adjacent cities – Liverpool and Manchester, Leeds and Bradford, Glasgow and Edinburgh – each competing with its neighbour in the dignity of its civic centre, in the elaboration of its public buildings and in the height of its municipal tower.

Step out of Lime Street station, and you are at once presented with Liverpool's splendid 19th-century civic centre, pillared and porticoed, with equestrian statues of Queen and Prince Consort, with Wellington reared on a high column, and with stately museums, libraries and art galleries enfilading down the hill beside H. L. Elmes's majestic St George's Hall. Corporation Street, begun in 1878, aimed to make Birmingham the metropolis of the Midlands and its leading citizen Joseph Chamberlain forced on his more narrowly commercial committee colleagues a university tower which had no direct educational purpose, but which made the university a landmark for miles around. Alfred Waterhouse's huge town hall in Manchester (now seen at its most dramatic when floodlit at night) is fronted by Albert Square, with its statues of municipal and national statesmen and its miniature Albert Memorial. Seeking continuity between 19th-century Manchester's self-confident present and its relatively obscure past, the town hall clustered busts of local worthies in its arcaded vestibule and adorned its great hall with friezes commemorating major events in the city's history. It is one of the paradoxes of 19th-century Britain that its pride in individual enterprise and effort did not exclude a lavish provision of communal facilities, a vigorous encouragement of community life. Compare Liverpool's 19th-century civic centre with the adjacent and tawdry 20th-century commercial shopping centre, where Liverpudlians are expected to buy their televisions and washing machines before retreating into domestic privacy.

Yet there is paradox within paradox here, for these 19th-century communal facilities aimed at reinforcing

To one contemporary, Saltaire provided 'the most perfect instance wherein the interests of Capital and Labour have been proved to be identical'; when seen on a moonlit night, every window in the mill seemed lit up, and terraces, flights of steps and rows of balustrades receded into the distance in all directions. 'Saltaire by moonlight,' he concluded, 'will rival anything described in the "Arabian Nights".'

The railway companies created entire new communities at places like New Swindon and Crewe, and towards the end of the century enlightened employers – the Cadburys at Bourneville, the Levers at Port Sunlight and the Rowntrees at New Earswick – surrounded their factories with housing of which they had no reason to feel ashamed. In those days, social welfare was channelled to the individual directly from the employer (as now in Japan), with all the benefits to industrial relations which flowed from that. It was underpinned by a poor-law system administered through the community's local hierarchy, and not by any remote and impersonal welfare state. Many 19th-century employers now seem intrusive in their concern for their employees' moral and

The tremendous self-confidence of Victorian city fathers is shown by buildings like Liverpool's magnificent civic centre, St George's Hall. Harvey Lonsdale Elmes won a competition for its design in 1839, but died before it was completed in 1858

an individualist rather than collectivist economic outlook. The imposing statues urged the citizen to imitate not only the famous man who was commemorated, but also the wealthy local philanthropist or councillor whose donation was recorded, not always unobtrusively, on the plinth. For wealthy Victorians, education was no mere classroom affair; their architecture, even their street furniture, aimed at educating the citizen as he went about his daily business. Libraries, museums, mechanics' institutes and art galleries supplied him with the raw-material for personal achievement; street-lamps safeguarded his moral fibre; drinking-fountains brought sobriety within his reach; elaborately ornamented wash-houses and public lavatories captured him for the gospel of hygiene. Informative foundation-stones simultaneously alerted him to the generosity of the rich and imbued him, however poor, with a sense of civic pride. Nowadays the lessons are lost and the statues are ignored, for not only do we question that very concept of the Great Man, and still more the motives of the philanthropist: we have also become sceptical about the ideal of self-improvement, with all its hypocrisies and anxieties, all its strivings, strains and stresses. How many modern Herefordians, hurrying in to change their books at the public library in Broad Street, cast even a glance at the elaborate facade of busts, inscriptions and self-

improving motifs devised for their edification by its architect K. R. Kempson in the 1870s?

Industrialisation dignified the city centre from a rather different direction as well – by speeding up the long-term tendency towards diversifying building types. By mid-century, lifts made it possible to push buildings higher; speaking-tubes and later telephones eased internal communication. Gas and electric light and improved plumbing also made new demands on the architect, but new demands also brought new opportunities. The result was a range of specialised and often striking buildings, now familiar in most city centres, each with its distinctive architectural features, each amplifying the dignity of the town and elevating the dignity of the councillors who ran it: museums, art galleries, exhibition halls, prisons, corn-exchanges, asylums, hospitals, public baths, covered markets, libraries, hotels, barracks, department stores, schools and railway stations. By the end of the century, the huge new asylums housed an average of 2,000 inmates in London and Lancashire, and even a small Victorian market town like Louth in Lincolnshire could boast its Byzantine-Gothic

Even a meat market was built with style. Smithfield still bustles today under the ornate Italianate canopy designed in 1866 by Sir Horace Jones, architect to the City of London

recognisable in their original form, for escalators and the pursuit of mass-custom have destroyed the spacious elegance and exclusiveness of the Marshall and Snelgrove, the Debenham and Freebody that older people can still recall; Harrods alone now dimly stirs the memory. And the supermarket idea has cleared out from Sainsburys and Liptons the crowds of expert sales-assistants and replaced them with young women at cash-registers; most of their labelled and packaged goods are now expected to sell themselves. The huge railway stations which still stand guard near the heart of Britain's cities remind us – with their architectural grandeur and their lists of far-off destinations proudly displayed on walls and canopies – of the glamour and bustle of a long-distance travel that has since been transferred to the international airport. The stations (where they survive at all) were left grey and decaying, oversized and under-equipped for the more limited tasks remaining to them. Like other types of commercial building, the station building itself advertised the wares it sold; the facade was all-important, and splendid many of these were – none more so than Gilbert Scott's St Pancras, with its delicate and colourful richness of ornamentation and romantic skyline.

New types of building were supplemented by new materials and new styles, for improved transport increased the range of building materials available; Oxford's University Museum shows that even the most traditional Mid-Victorian building-styles could employ the iron and glass materials advertised by the Crystal Palace's success in 1851. Wider travel also broadened the architect's range of building styles – from Switzerland to Italy, from Egypt to India he travelled in search of novelty; to modern eyes, the new styles are often applied to incongruously urban and humdrum purposes. For industrialisation disrupted people as well as places. This was a century of rapid population growth, of widespread migration from country to town, of Irish immigration to England and Scotland, and of British emigration to the United States and to the colonies of white settlement. Travel became faster and more frequent for ever wider sections of the community. Overseas visitors steadily increased in number, and British tourists began visiting parts of the country unknown to their ancestors. In Dr Arnold's Rugby, only a third of the boys had seen the sea, and when the novelist Charlotte Brontë first saw the waves at Bridlington in 1839 she seemed 'quite overpowered', according to her companion, and shed tears at the sight. All this was soon to change, as evidenced now by the great mid-century hotels which sprang up not only in London – with its Westminster Palace, its Langham, and its great railway hotels – but in seaside resorts and spas, distinctive with their bulbous mansard roofs and brash elaboration of metalwork and moulding.

Industrialisation produced wealth on such a scale that it gradually filtered down even to the poorest members of the community, and created the Late-Victorian boom in the recreation industry. From mid-century Frederick

market-hall, proudly erected in 1866; with its seven bays of giant girders behind, it was a miniature King's Cross or St Pancras, with market-stalls in place of railway platforms. At the same time, public health considerations concentrated burials into huge cemeteries like Glasgow's necropolis. London's rapidly-expanding population buried itself at Kensal Green, Highgate, Nunhead and Brompton cemeteries, for cremation was rare even at the end of the century, and people sought immortality through the elaborate stone monument.

Perhaps the best-known specialist Victorian building is the elementary school, whose abundance struggled to satisfy the century's thirst for education. Its dark paint, dim corridors, heavy walls and smell of gas mixed with urine from the lavatories haunted the 20th-century Labour leader Herbert Morrison for a lifetime, yet these school buildings greatly improved upon what had gone before. As the sociologist Charles Booth put it, each stood '"like a tall sentinel at his post", keeping watch and ward over the interests of the generation that is to replace our own'.

The great department stores and multiple retailers which also date from this time are nowadays hardly

Pevsner describes the Palm House at Kew as 'one of the boldest pieces of 19th century functionalism in existence.' Dublin engineer Richard Turner designed it. Decimus Burton took the credit

Savage, the manufacturer of agricultural machinery, began designing fairground equipment, and by the 1880s St Giles's Fair in Oxford had acquired its sea-on-land roundabout and its 'trapeze railway'. Here was a popular and unrestrained colourful architecture of enjoyment, with none of the improving austerity of Gothic, none of the stolid solidity of classic styles; it was unashamedly, colourfully and extravagantly baroque, and its styles linger on in the fairgrounds and amusement-arcades which survive.

But if the towns were growing so fast, the countryside could hardly stay unchanged. Cobbett in the 1820s was already grumbling at the large number of commercial travellers he saw; for him, the newly macadamised roads were offensive intrusions catering for alien stock-jobbers whose main concern was to avoid being jolted in the course of their incessant moneymaking travels. The countryside was soon criss-crossed by a network of railway lines which riveted on the rustic mind the triumph of urban over rural values and gradually rendered the countryside merely picturesque. Now that nature was being tamed and domesticated, it could be safely visited, inspected and even ravaged by insensitive urban populations. In later life the author Edmund Gosse nostalgically recalled the Devon rockpools he'd known as a child: 'these rock-basins . . .', he wrote, 'exist no longer, they are all profaned, and emptied, and vulgarised. An army of "collectors" has passed over them, and ravaged every corner of them.'

Notions of picturesqueness quite foreign to the farmer who seeks only profits from the soil could make the fortune of a hotelier in the newly-discovered Lake District, Devon and Cornwall, and in the boom-towns of Southport, Scarborough and Blackpool. Cuthbert Brodrick's aptly-named Grand Hotel in yellow and red brick straddles the Scarborough cliffs – an unblushing witness to the Late-Victorian colonisation of the sea-coast. By the end of the century, the seaside had become studded with pleasure-centres boasting all the trappings of recreation – fairgrounds, piers, parks, boarding-houses and even, at Blackpool, a miniature Eiffel Tower.

The farmer himself complemented this urban transformation of the countryside by espousing an urban commercialism in his efforts to satisfy the town dweller's appetite for food. From the late 18th century onwards, commons were enclosed, estates grew larger, smallholders and commoners left the land for the towns. Huntsmen were now painted in the act of jumping fences – a new excitement rendered the more hazardous towards the end of the 19th century by the advent of barbed wire. Enclosure and clearances had of course been in progress for centuries, but the 19th century reinforced them with science and engineering technique. Fens were drained, dykes were dug, heathland was brought into cultivation, soil was fertilised. Everywhere the forests were being cut down; only during the 20th century did reafforestation and conservation become the vogue. The reclaiming of heathland continued on Exmoor and in Oxfordshire's Wychwood, and in Aberdeenshire it persisted till the end of the century. In East Anglia the remaining meres were drained – the last of the large ones, Whittlesey Mere in Huntingdonshire, vanishing at mid-century. Industrialisation first refined the windmill with spring sail and fantail, and then dispensed with it altogether in favour of the steam pump; there had once been over 700 windmills in the Fenlands, but by 1852 there were only 220.

As refrigeration and improved transport made it possible to import many staple foods from abroad, British farmers – especially those near large towns – began to specialise in the types of cultivation which gave them a major transport advantage, especially in orchards and market gardening. The cut-flower trade grew up in the Scilly Isles towards the end of the century, and market-gardening prospered in the Home Counties, the Mid-West, and near the great industrial centres of the north. The countryside was expected to furnish water as well as food. Liverpool dammed the Vyrnwy Valley and submerged an entire village to supply itself with water; Manchester tunnelled through the hills to convert Thirlmere into its water-tank; and at the end of the century Birmingham created a chain of reservoirs in Wales.

By the end of the 19th century, sharp eyes were beginning to see that the town's recreational, dietary and other needs were destroying the countryside and its wild life. What was left of Epping Forest was opened by the Queen as a public park in 1882, and five years later some M.P.s were able to prevent a railway from being built between Ambleside and Keswick. Before the end of the century, the National Trust had launched itself; a section of cliff at Bournemouth was its first acquisition in 1896, and it obtained part of the Cornish seacoast in the following year. But conservation involved more than just preserving beauty-spots. Darwin had himself recognised that 'plants and animals, most remote in the scale of nature, are bound together by a web of complex relations', and many rural species were now in danger. The legislation protecting animals that had been passed earlier in the century began to move forward from concern with cattle and pets to a preoccupation with wild animals and threatened species, and at the end of the century the first nature-reserves appeared.

But it is time now to move back from discussing the wider environment to discussing buildings, for our concluding theme must be the relationship between 19th-century architecture and politics. How were political

continuity and stability maintained in the midst of all this disruption of people and places? In Ireland, formally united to Great Britain in 1800, the political leadership ultimately failed. Concession after concession came too late to buy off discontent, and in 1886 Gladstone's proposal to introduce home rule for Ireland produced a major disruption of the party system when the Liberal Party split on the issue; even this upheaval could not stave off independence for Southern Ireland in the early 20th century. In Wales and Scotland, though, the pressures for separation were weaker, and political continuity was securely upheld.

There were crises, of course: would the aristocracy be wise enough to moderate discontent by giving votes to the middle class in 1832? or by conceding free trade in corn quickly enough in 1845–6? or by responding to some of the grievances so bitterly voiced by religious groupings outside the established church? Could the vote be safely given to urban working men in 1867 or to agricultural labourers in 1884? and would this effectively incorporate them into the party political framework? The answer to all these questions was yes, but the outcome never seemed certain at the time, and owed much to the shrewd and often courageous political judgment displayed by British statesmen. Their success is com-

The 49 brick arches of the Digswell Viaduct stride majestically and uncompromisingly across a Hertfordshire valley. Lewis Cubitt, an engineer whose bold functionalism created an unselfconscious beauty that did not rely on embroidery, built it between 1849 and 1850

century was a great period for country-house building right up to the agricultural depression of the 1880s. Aristocratic traditionalism flaunts itself in Scarisbrick Hall, remodelled by Pugin in Gothic style for the rich Lancashire landowner Charles Scarisbrick. This is one of the many Victorian houses to revive the great hall with its feudal connotations, and its clock tower provided a prototype for Big Ben. Norman Shaw's Cragside, a miniature Neuschwanstein, illustrates the persisting fascination of the country-house ideal for a later generation – in this case at the behest of armaments manufacturer Sir William Armstrong. To quote Pevsner (that learned, invariably good-humoured and indispensable guide) 'one expects all the time to hear Walkyries ride through the skies over its manifold gables and chimney stacks'. Not content with this, Armstrong later restored the even more romantic Bamburgh Castle in Northumberland.

The country house was complemented by grand aristocratic town mansions, centres of splendid entertainments during the London 'season'; these were not sold off till after the First World War. Aristocratic medievalism could even penetrate the heart of the 19th-century commercial city, surprising the visitor to Carlisle, for instance, with Smirke's two great round assize courtrooms fashioned in 1810–11 out of Henry VIII's fortification towers. Modern visitors emerging from Carlisle's mock-Tudor country-house of a railway station, built a generation later, are taken aback by this dramatic approach to the city centre. Or there is Cardiff's astonishing castle. Forging his way up from Central Station through St Mary Street's bustling banks and shops, the visitor to the city is astonished to find himself confronting a full-scale medieval castle in first-rate condition, lavishly embellished within and without by Lord Bute in the 1870s and 1880s. Its row of towers could have been lifted bodily out of *cinquecento* Milan or Florence, yet there they are, marshalled mysteriously behind the trees in the park to the west, a strange testimony to the dedicated medievalism which could penetrate even a major 19th-century seaport.

Aristocratic ideals were consolidated by the established church, which enjoyed a head-start on all other denominations with its cathedrals, its endowments and its nation-wide network of parish churches and schools. Irishmen might be flooding into the country to set up their catholic churches, nonconformists might assault the privileges of the official religion in a series of radical crusades, but by mid-century the Church of England was vigorously on the counter-attack; it planted its missionstations in the slums and set up the fashionable suburban churches that were then essential to make a middle-class housing estate 'go'. With organisational ingenuity, episcopal energy and a newly-enhanced spiritual life, it was able to embark on a great age of churchbuilding. J. L. Pearson's Truro Cathedral, designed in 1880, can perhaps be allowed to speak for the Anglican's confident defiance of the challenge offered by his Methodist neigh-

memorated by the many statues of political leaders set up in the squares and parks of Victorian cities: Canning, Peel, Palmerston, Disraeli, Gladstone, Salisbury and above all the Queen, who rapidly responded to middleclass demands on the monarchy for hard work and moral leadership. She retained to the end of her life a certain affinity with popular British attitudes in her incomprehension of the Irish, her nervous response to military setbacks, her fondness for animals and her taste for gathering relatives around her in an endless sequence of photographs. The ceremonial role of the modern British monarchy was being gradually elaborated, with a series of royal visits to provincial cities, and with the muchpublicised royal marriages and state openings of parliament which culminated splendidly in the Golden and Diamond Jubilees of 1887 and 1897. The Queen's achievement is commemorated by a host of royal statues all over the country.

Such alert upper-class responsiveness to new situations frustrated those radical middle-class critics of medieval superstition and aristocratic values. The 19th

bours who had earlier won so many local recruits.

In the long term, of course, the whole aristocratic regime was under threat. Looking back wistfully in old age, Willoughby de Broke (born in 1869) said that of all the generations he'd have liked to be born into, that of his grandfather (born in 1810) would have suited him best; times had never been so good for the squirearchy in Warwickshire Vale as between 1850 and 1880, and he would then have reached 70 just before the agricultural depression set in. This undermined the economic foundations of landed estates and established church. The First World War carried off a relatively high proportion of aristocratic sons; the home rule split weakened aristocratic influence over the party of the left, and the advent of the Labour Party destroyed it. In 1908, when H. H. Asquith became Prime Minister, Britain for the first time was led by a statesman who did not own a country estate.

Yet when the Labour Party did eventually come to power, its challenge to the political system produced no greater disruption than the earlier challenge from the radical and nonconformist middle class. This was not simply because the political elite once again responded flexibly to changing events, and took care to initiate new arrivals into well-tried political practices: it was yet another consequence of the pervasiveness of the aristocratic ideal, of the tenacious vision of the Englishman's home as his castle. For the English country house inspired many humbler imitations, inhabited by individualist middle-class and even working-class voters who lacked enthusiasm for socialism of the revolutionary or communal variety.

True, the upper-class flats or 'chambers' were being built in London's Victoria by mid-century, and anyone going to the Proms at the Albert Hall can still see nearby the huge block of flats designed by Norman Shaw, with its Dutch gables and recessed balconies; by the end of the century, blocks of flats were even intruding into several famous London squares. But flats never really caught on during the 19th century except in Scotland, and as early as the late 18th century, professional people had been imitating the aristocracy (and infuriating Cobbett) by lining the roads out of London with suburban villas. With its complement of trees and shrubs, its element of surprise, its interpenetration of house and garden, its all-pervasive privacy, its individuality and even anarchy of styles – the suburb is deeply influenced, however indirectly, by rural and aristocratic ideals. Nowhere is this better seen than in the leafy suburbs of North Oxford, whose rustic doorways lead in from the garden to the high-ceilinged rooms built for the university's

Left: home is the potter, home from his wheel . . . to Bedford Park, London, where in the 1870s Norman Shaw designed a suburb with arts and crafts people in mind. Right: details from magnificent Victorian pub, The Philharmonic, Hope St, Liverpool. Top, main doorway with art nouveau beaten copper and elaborate cut glass. Bottom, stained glass window. Designs were by pupils and teachers at Liverpool School of Art and Architecture

This statue of Queen Victoria greets visitors to the Royal Holloway College, Egham, Surrey, a huge and macabre redbrick building that was one of the early colleges for women

newly-married dons in the 1870s. The ornamental trees in the front gardens during the spring have now matured to present a riot of contrasting colour to the motorist as he approaches the city down the Woodstock and Banbury Roads: a precious 19th-century gift to the twentieth.

A property-owning democracy was continuously recruiting itself in the 19th-century suburb, and by the early 20th century, building society loans were beginning to escalate. In Norman Shaw's Bedford Park, launched in 1876, the suburban estate acquired architectural distinction with its ornamental brickwork, its decorative tiles and its white-painted window-casements. Class contrasts determined both elevation and ground-plan of these Victorian suburban houses; their servants, marshalled in their rigid hierarchies, were normally confined to basement kitchens and sculleries in the daytime and consigned to the attics at night. By the 1870s the suburbs were beginning to provide the Conservative Party with some of its safest seats.

Yet the suburban Conservative exaggerated the threat to social stability posed by the inner city's shrinking working-class populations, for the Conservative Party had outposts even there. Elaborately-glazed public-houses, hung with wrought-iron gaslamps and bright

with music and company, tempted passers-by into the traditionalist intimacy of encrusted and mirrored interiors. Street life was enlivened in the slums by stall-holders and open-air salesmen whose ideal of free competition was scarcely challenged, and who incidentally provided an important source of local entertainment. Victorian cities throbbed with a lively street life – their shops spilling out onto the pavement, their buildings always constructed on a human scale. Then there were all the subtleties of working-class social aspiration. For those in the know, the row upon row of terrace housing, apparently uniform and monotonous to the outside observer, catered for a host of small-scale social gradations. Each street and alley boasted its distinctive social rating, each carved ornament on the facade carried social significance, each parlour-window revealed the subtly differentiated social aspirations of the inhabitants.

The suburban ideal was therefore making converts well below the middle class. Social reformers might set up 'improved' apartment housing for working people, and its austerity reminds us how grim must have been the slum housing which it replaced. But the uniformity and soullessness of the Peabody Building, or even of the municipal housing which began to supersede it by the end of the century, were not at all the aim of significant groups within the working class. On the contrary, respectability seemed to require a move to humbler variants of the middle-class housing estate. As the Early-Victorian temperance reformer Thomas Whittaker wrote in his autobiography, 'the home that had satisfied my wants as a drinker was not in harmony with my self-respect as a teetotaler, and I soon put myself in possession of a house rented at twelve pounds a year'.

The houses that Whittaker and his successors bought or rented for themselves can still be seen in Britain's inner cities – some of them large enough nowadays to attract middle-class colonisation, for large families dictated what are by modern standards relatively large homes well down the social hierarchy. The Artisans and Labourers General Dwellings Company created special estates for the Late-Victorian respectable London working man at Wandsworth, Queen's Park and Wood Green, and took special care to keep the locality in good trim and to reduce the number of pubs.

Tied to the city centre by commuting facilities on train and tram, the Late-Victorian suburb had little need of its own cultural facilities. It was not a fully-fledged community in its own right – except perhaps on Sundays when its recreational needs were met by the Anglican church and the nonconformist chapel, and later perhaps increasingly by the tennis club and the football ground. Walter Besant, the novelist, condemned Late-Victorian South London as 'a city without a municipality, without a centre, without a civic history'. He went on to complain that 'it has no newspapers, magazines or journals; it has no university, it has no colleges, apart from medical; it has no intellectual, artistic, scientific, musical, literary centre'. C. F. G. Masterman, the Liberal politician, a few years later attacked the triviality of outlook and lack of civic responsibility to be found in such places. True, the Late-Victorian London suburb carried forward that specialisation of architectural function which has already been noticed; the suburb was the specialised residential area, distinct from those urban areas designed for commerce, recreation, industry or the professions. It foreshadowed the more fragmented style of urban living that eventually succeeded the tightly-knit, public-spirited Victorian local community. The 20th century could re-create a sense of community only through mass media which were as yet undiscovered.

But this is to anticipate; for most of the 19th century, immediate loyalties were focused on the municipality. These loyalties were concentrated, consolidated, and carried to a higher plane by the symbolism of regional and national government. Grandiose architecture could knit together a precariously-integrated society and could cultivate the loyal sentiments deemed necessary in a dangerous world bedevilled by international rivalry and civil disorder. The design of 19th-century public buildings was employed to emphasise political continuity, national greatness and the majesty of government. So the last and perhaps the best-known way in which the 19th century moulded our world was in creating dignified national governmental buildings that could mobilise support behind established political institutions. This had always been done, of course, with churches and palaces, but the 19th century recognised the need to dignify government – and especially parliamentary and municipal government – in a more general way. Edinburgh, that pinnacle of Britain's 19th-century urban achievement, is a regional capital whose essence is the symbolic. The engineering skills of the age made it possible to link the romanticism of the old city with the classic dignity of the New Town and drain the lake which separated them, yet without destroying the city's major scenic assets. Even the railway was somehow harmonised with the city's distinctive landscape; indeed, when looking down from Princes Street one would hardly guess it was there. Skylines and vistas were enhanced by strategically-placed public buildings and monuments. The Free Church College and the Scott monument lend magic with their spires and pinnacles, the ponderous banks and grand hotels lend solidity with their pillars and towers. Victorian dignitaries look impressively down on Princes Street, where an earnest public spiritedness seems to have survived well into the 20th century – as witness the long row of wooden seats presented to the community by loyal citizens.

Nonetheless 19th-century Edinburgh's symbolism could never be more than purely regional, and it is in London that the century's most energetic pursuit of national symbolism took place. It was first necessary to lend the dignity of a capital city to what the 18th century had left as little more than a collection of urban villages.

Gladstone, Palmerston and Thackeray were members. The Reform Club, Pall Mall, London. It was founded by radicals committed to Parliamentary reform, and designed by Sir Charles Barry

Early in the 19th century, Nash's grand conception for the West End was partially implemented, and public money was later set aside to enlarge Hampstead Heath and create Battersea Park.

The grand town-planning schemes of Paris were not feasible in Britain, and were not then thought desirable; but the French example deeply influenced those who wanted to clear away London's slums in St Giles, or who created Birmingham's Corporation Street. Out to the west, a new complex of cultural buildings was begun in the 1850s, with Kensington's art galleries, museums and concert-hall. The building of London's Embankment during the 1860s – Queen Victoria now presiding at the Blackfriars end – provided a new link between the City and the West End, and gardens studded with statues lined the route. Shaftesbury Avenue and Charing Cross Road resulted from later slum-clearance schemes, and a noble gateway to London was created for river traffic by the Tower Bridge, another engineering marvel in its day.

Within this setting, suitable governmental buildings could be erected. The 19th century rebuilding of clubland in Pall Mall and Piccadilly created a stately home-from-home where aristocrats and politicians could hob-

Oxford University Museum, a gothic structure of iron and glass built in the 1850s when there was a passionate interest in natural history and Darwinism split the country

new Whitehall towards Westminster, now that the clutter of mean shops and houses had been cleared? The century's greatest architectural success of all, the new Palace of Westminster. With its brilliant exploitation of the riverside site, its memorable skyline, and its antique but distinctively English fancy-dress, Barry's new Houses of Parliament presented the nation with a symbol of continuity and dignity in self-government. By these and other symbolic devices, the nation could be held together in difficult times. The British variant of parliamentary government acquired a dignified image at a time when 'the Westminster model' was being exported to many countries overseas. It is a peculiar form of government which has always been under attack, though perhaps rather less so in the Victorian period than in our own day; indeed, its compatibility with opposition and criticism is one of its most valuable features.

The Palace of Westminster, the Natural History Museum, the Albert Memorial and Manchester Town Hall all now benefit from the mid-20th-century change in taste which no longer feels the need to repudiate all things Victorian; all four have been recently revealed in their full beauty by cleaning and restoration. The grimy, weather-streaked Victorian monuments that get the period such a bad name looked very different at the time when they were built, and they are now once more assuming the appearance their creators intended: shining, colourful, adventurous, even exotic. Yet cleaning and restoration are not in themselves sufficient to explain the change in fashion; the explanation is as much psychological as visual. The Victorians are now sufficiently distant in time for us not to feel threatened by them as our fathers and grandfathers were. Besides, we are now less confident than we were even ten years ago that we have solved the many problems they tackled: economic scarcity, political violence and national insecurity. Nor has complete success attended the early 20th century's panacea for grappling with so many social problems – a secularised reliance on 'planning' and on centralised state action. In becoming more critical of ourselves, we have become less eager to accept the Victorians' highly critical assessment of their own achievements, more respectful towards their strenuously serious-minded efforts at solving the unprecedented problems of their day.

nob with writers, administrators and party hacks. The distinguished line of clubs from the Reform to the Travellers and the Athenaeum complements the increasing dignity of nearby Whitehall, whose Victorian additions were made partly under the influence of what Louis Napoleon was doing in the new Louvre. There was no overall long-term plan, nor was the avenue broad or the buildings grandiose – that would hardly have befitted a decentralised nation suspicious of militarism and eager to keep government in its place. Yet here was gradually accumulated a centre of government whose silhouette from the royal parks is memorable – a ceremonial approach from City to Westminster that somehow combined dignity with intimacy in many a procession and public function. The best-known among Whitehall's Victoriana is Norman Shaw's New Scotland Yard, but this was a mere late-comer among the many impressive if unimaginative governmental buildings erected nearby. The contrast between Victorian Whitehall and the concrete desert which the 20th century has created at the other end of Westminster Bridge is disquieting.

And what did the visitor glimpse as he gazed down the

This wallpaper, entitled Blackthorn, was designed in 1892 by William Morris, the man whose influence on interior decor still reaches into middle class homes today. Morris, designer, craftsman, architect, poet and socialist, set out in the 1860s to transform interior design, which he believed to be in a state of 'complete degradation'. He founded a firm which produced wallpaper, stained glass, printed and woven textiles, carpets and furniture

GAZETEER
OF THE AGES

THE
TRIBAL ISLANDS

by Anna Pavord

DWELLINGS

Carn Euny (Cornwall) Stone huts date from 1st c
BC, but splendid fogou (underground passage) built
much earlier when villagers still lived in wooden
houses. Purpose of fogou still in question: storage,
ritual or defence? D of E. Open standard hours summer only. Admission charge. 5m W of Penzance and
N of A30.

Chysauster (Cornwall) Iron Age settlement site
with eight courtyard houses facing central street.
Paved floors, terraced garden plots, best preserved of
all early Cornish settlements. D of E. Open standard
hours and Sun mornings from 9.30 April–Sept.
Admission charge. 2m N of Trevarrack off B3311.

Clickhimin (Shetland) Forerunner of Scottish broch
in form of stone blockhouse, originally made as entrance to massive unfinished fort of 2nd c BC. Walls
up to 20ft thick hide labyrinthine stairways and
passages. Stands on promontory in marshy ground
by A970 out of Lerwick to Gulberwick. D of E.
Open standard hours.

Creswell Crags (Derbyshire) Stone Age hunters
used these limestone caves as shelters from 27000 to
8000BC. Bone needles and fine flint tools found here
together with one of the earliest examples of Stone
Age art in Britain, a horse's head engraved on bone.
14m SE of Sheffield off B6042 from Creswell.

Foales Arrishes (Devon) Bronze Age hut circles up
to 30ft across with prehistoric version of cavity walls
– rubble core inside facings of large stone slabs. Faint
outline of original field boundaries underlies later
medieval strips. Reached from Widdicombe-Haytor
road, SW of Hemsworthy Gate.

Gough's Cave (Somerset) Mendip's natural caves
were occupied by man in paleolithic times. Skeleton
of one of these early hunters displayed in cave
museum together with fox teeth, shells and other
objects found in the grave. Open daily Easter–Sept
10–6, Oct–Easter 10–5. Admission charge. Beside
B3135 through Cheddar Gorge.

Grimspound (Devon) Lonely Dartmoor hut settlement of Bronze Age with massive boundary wall
enclosing a 4-acre pound, 16 huts, two with remains
of porches opening to east. Silent and impressive,
reached by footpath to E of minor road between
Shapley Common and Challacombe Down.

Jarlshof (Shetland) Successive settlements here
swallowed by sandstorms which preserved Bronze
and Iron Age houses, querns and hearths. Later
wheel houses built with stones from fortified tower
(broch). Viking houses as well. Close to Sumburgh
airport. Closed Tues and Wed afternoon. Other
weekdays open 9.30–7, Sun 2–7. Admission charge.

Kent's Cavern (Devon) Intermittent digs over last
150 years have shown that this cave was home to
mammoth, woolly rhinoceros, bear and lion as well
as paleolithic man. Two big chambers and series of
galleries occupied up to 8000BC. Open June–mid
Sept 10–9, mid Sept–Oct 10–6, winter 10–5.
Admission charge. In Ilsham Rd, signposted off Babbacombe Rd, Torquay. Finds in Torquay. Natural
History Society Museum, Babbacombe Rd. Open

Mon–Sat 10–4.45 (closed Sat Oct–March). Admission charge.

Skara Brae (Orkney) Abandoned in a hurry about
2500BC. Inhabitants of this village left behind beads,
ropes of heather, bone pins, mortars and pestles.
Beds and sideboards are built of stone. Open Mon–
Sat 9.30–7, Sun 2–7. Admission charge. Mainland,
7m N of Stromness.

Victoria Cave (Yorkshire) Inhabited during the last
stages of the Ice Age when mesolithic man drove out
the hyenas that had been using it as a den. 1¾m NE of
Settle via A65 and B6479.

MILITARY/DEFENSIVE

Badbury Rings (Dorset) Conspicuous landmark
with topknot of trees crowning Iron Age hill-fort,
three defensive lines of ramparts and ditches snaking
round its base. Last rampart, it seems, thrown up
hurriedly at time of Roman invasion. 3½m NW of
Wimborne Minster, alongside B3082.

Bredon Hill (Worcestershire) Iron Age promontory
fort, protected by natural precipices to the N and W.
Remains of 50 young male skeletons, hacked to
pieces, found by main inner gateway, evidence of a
heroic last stand by the inhabiting tribe. 6m NE of
Tewkesbury, off B4080.

Crickley Hill (Gloucestershire) Neolithic causewayed camp and Iron Age promontory fort, 9 acres in
all, with steep hills falling away on the N and S. 4¼m
S of Cheltenham.

Danebury (Hampshire) Splendid Iron Age hill-fort
restructured about 600BC to provide regular rows of
streets and houses inside two lines of ramparts and
ditches. Excavators have found hoard of 22 iron

Fertility goddess in chalk from Grimes Graves, Norfolk,
in the British Museum

currency bars, roughly the shape and size of a sword
blade. 2¾m NW of Stockbridge between A30 and
A343.

Finavon (Angus) Extraordinary vitrified fort of the
Iron Age. Stone used with timber to build ramparts
was rich in silica. When the fort burnt down, extreme heat melted stone and fused it in solid mass.
Puzzle to archaeologists until classic simulation experiment by Professor Childe in 1937. 4m NE of
Forfar between A94 and B9134.

Ham Hill (Somerset) One of the biggest hill-forts in
Britain, occupied through Iron Age and Roman
times. Defensive ditches cut into richly coloured
Ham Hill stone, two rows increasing to three on
vulnerable north-westerly and south-westerly sides.
S of A3088 from Yeovil.

Hembury (Devon) Bluebells and bracken cover this
Iron Age hill-fort built on top of an earlier neolithic
causewayed camp. Considered one of the most important sites of its kind in the west country. Alongside A373 from Honiton to Cullompton.

Herefordshire Beacon (Herefordshire) Spectacular
view from this Iron Age stronghold of lowlands of
Worcestershire, the Black Mountains and the peaks
of Radnorshire. Reoccupied in medieval times when
motte was built on highest point of hill. Steep climb
up from A449, ¾m SW of Little Malvern.

Maiden Castle (Dorset) Best of all prehistoric hillforts, home of the Durotriges tribe, likened by Hardy
to 'an enormous many-limbed organism of an ante-
diluvian time, lying lifeless and covered with a thin
green cloth'. Labyrinthine entrances at E and W;
magnificent walk about 1½m around inner rampart.
Signposted off Weymouth road SW of Dorchester.
Important finds in Dorchester Museum.

Wandlebury (Cambridgeshire) The craze for landscaping which swept over England's landowners in
the 18th c included this Iron Age hill-fort, where
ramparts and ditches were filled in by enthusiastic
minions creating a classical view for their master,
Lord Godolphin. Nearly 5m S of Cambridge on the
N side of A604.

MONUMENTS/MEMORIALS

Carn Gluze (Cornwall) Bronze Age barrow or burial
mound, with deep pit hacked out of bedrock and
covered by great dome of stones. Excavations more
than 100 years ago discovered ritual offerings of lamb
and pottery. 1m W of St Just.

Duggleby Howe (Yorkshire) Spectacular neolithic
round barrow, probably built before 2500BC. Now
about 20ft high though originally closer to 30ft.
Remains of 53 cremations found here together with
antler tools, a flint knife and long bone pins. 7m SE
of Norton on N side of B1253.

Kit's Coty (Kent) Trapped like some prehistoric
beast behind D of E railings, only three great uprights
and one capstone survive of this neolithic burial
chamber. Famous enough to have detained Pepys on
a journey to Maidstone. 'Certainly it is a thing of
great antiquity,' he wrote in his diary, 'and I am

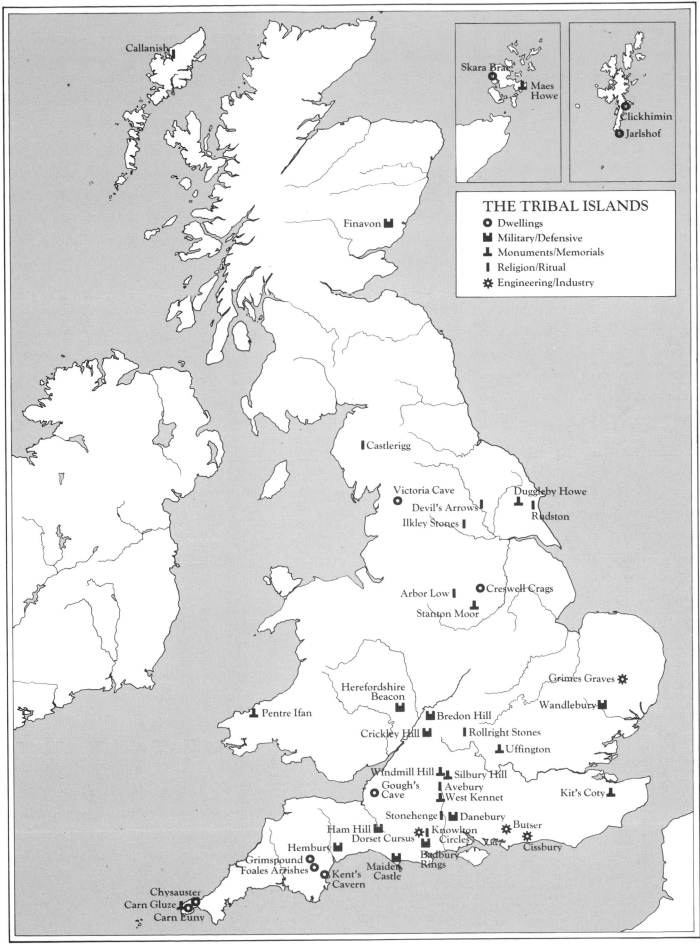

THE TRIBAL ISLANDS

- ○ Dwellings
- ◗ Military/Defensive
- ⊥ Monuments/Memorials
- ▮ Religion/Ritual
- ✿ Engineering/Industry

Callanish

Skara Brae
Maes Howe

Clickhimin
Jarlshof

Finavon

Castlerigg

Victoria Cave
Devil's Arrows
Ilkley Stones

Duggleby Howe
Rudston

Arbor Low Creswell Crags
Stanton Moor

Grimes Graves

Herefordshire Beacon

Wandlebury

Pentre Ifan
Bredon Hill
Crickley Hill
Rollright Stones
Uffington

Windmill Hill Silbury Hill
Gough's Cave Avebury
West Kennet

Kit's Coty

Stonehenge Danebury
Ham Hill Knowlton Circles
Dorset Cursus Butser
Hembury Cissbury
Grimspound Badbury Rings
Foales Arrishes
Chysauster Kent's Cavern Maiden Castle
Carn Gluze
Carn Euny

mightily glad to see it.' 3½m N of Maidstone off A229.

Maes Howe (Orkney) Perfectly constructed stone tomb about 14ft square with buttressed walls and three small side chambers under mound of clay. Most stunning piece of prehistoric building in the country. Raided early 12th c by Viking pirates, who left runic inscriptions recording that they had found treasure. Open Mon–Fri 9.30–7. Admission charge. 9m W of Kirkwall.

Pentre Ifan (Dyfed) On the northern slopes of Mynydd Prescelly, source of Stonehenge's famous bluestones, stands this memorable Bronze Age burial chamber with a massive capstone which seems to float rather than rest over the pointed ends of the three great upright stones. 3m NE of Newport via A487.

Silbury Hill (Wiltshire) The biggest man-made pre-historic mound in Europe, a plum pudding 130ft high with a flat top once used as a cricket pitch. Persistent folklore marks it as burial site, but thorough archaeological investigation has found no clues, and purpose of this gigantic monument still an enigma. Beside the A4 between West Kennet and Beckhampton.

Stanton Moor (Derbyshire) Scene of considerable activity in Bronze Age when more than 70 stone cairns, a number of stone circles and a big menhir were all raised in this place, scattered over several miles. Cremated bones have been found in many of the cairns, undisturbed since 1500BC. 4½m NW of Matlock in area bounded by minor roads to Birch-over, Stanton-in-Peak and Stanton Lees.

Uffington White Horse (Oxfordshire) Sire of all other horse hill-figures, this is the oldest of them all, possibly cut by Atrebates as totemic emblem of their tribes in the Iron Age. Atrebates rule, OK? Long, lean, powerful figure, seen by some as the dragon reputedly slain by St George on nearby Dragon Hill. 6m W of Wantage signposted off B4507.

West Kennet (Wiltshire) One of the biggest long barrows in the country, a great wedge-shaped mound of chalk about 330ft long. Five stone chambers inside contained remains of 46 people, including young children. Probably far more originally, but a Dr Troope of Marlborough came digging here in 1685 and took away bones, 'many bushells, of which I made a noble medicine that relieved many of my distressed neighbours'. Signposted S from A4 close to Silbury Hill.

Windmill Hill (Wiltshire) Classic causewayed camp site, the name of which has been taken to mark the earliest neolithic culture recognised in England. Not a settlement site, nor defensive structure; possibly centre for tribal ceremonies, gatherings, trade. Perfect skeleton of a dog, some kind of fox terrier, found here and displayed in Avebury museum. Windmill Hill is 1½m NW of Avebury.

RELIGION/RITUAL

Arbor Low (Derbyshire) This Bronze Age henge monument lies 1000ft up on the Derbyshire moors, a

Another British Museum treasure – the Snettisham torque, a 50 BC necklace in gold alloy

Celtic bronze mirror found at Desborough, Northants, in British Museum

circular bank of earth with ditch and ring of fallen stones inside. Weatherbeaten, decayed but impressive, its power as a ritual centre possibly explains the presence of many later Bronze Age burial mounds nearby. 5m SW of Bakewell.

Avebury (Wiltshire) Stone circle is centre of amazing complex of prehistoric monuments including Silbury, West Kennet and Windmill Hill. 'This stupendous fabric,' mourned the antiquarian William Stukeley, who visited the monument in 1724, 'has fallen a sacrifice to the wretched ignorance and avarice of a little village unluckily placed within it.' His plan shows *two* great avenues curving from the central circles. Now, only parts of Kennet Avenue remain. Finds displayed in museum on site, open mid-March–mid-Oct 9.30–6.30 daily, mid-Oct–mid-March 9.30–4 daily except Dec–Jan Sundays 2–4. Admission charge.

Callanish (Western Isles) A massive complex of standing stones on the Isle of Lewis, 13 pillars forming a circle and originally approached through a stone avenue 270ft long. Stark, mysterious, remote. 16m W of Stornoway off A858.

Castlerigg (Cumbria) There are 38 great stones in this circle on high land between Keswick and Thirlmere. Inside the circle is a rectangle of 10 stones, the whole inexplicable monument enhanced by magnificent backdrop of Cumbrian mountains. 2m E of Keswick.

Devil's Arrows (Yorkshire) Three monoliths of dark millstone grit, ridged and fluted by the weather, which stand in a straight line running N–S on the outskirts of Boroughbridge. Bronze Age people expended massive energy moving these stones, each taller than three men, from nearest source six miles away. Why? Under whose orders did they work? At Roecliffe to SW of Boroughbridge.

Ilkley Stones (Yorkshire) Collection of elaborately carved stones, some cut with cup and ring markings of the Bronze Age, others with rough swastika shapes. Most accessible is Panorama Stone in gardens opposite St Margaret's Church, Ilkley; most exciting are stones still in position on Rombald's Moor, Addingham High Moor (swastika stone) and Baildon Moor. Ordnance Survey references SE 086472, 132463, 133462, 094470.

Knowlton Circle (Dorset) A neolithic religious centre which has survived rather better than the Christian church placed exorcisingly in its centre. Church (12th c with 15th c tower) now in ruins, 4000-year-old henge circle with ditch and two entrances at NE and SW, still magnificent. 3m SW of Cranborne, parking in Lumber Lane off B3078.

Rollright Stones (Oxfordshire) Stone group, richly swathed in folklore concerning King (Kingstone

monolith), the Whispering Knights (five standing stones) and the King's Men (circle of 70 stones) ossified by witch. Jacquetta Hawkes is sympathetic to such lore: 'The past has left marks deep in the human mind as real as the tangible marks which we search out among our fields and hills.' 4m N of Chipping Norton off A34.

Rudston (Yorkshire) Dwarfing the neat memorials of the village churchyard, this unrepentant monolith stands 25½ft high, the tallest standing stone in Britain. 'By no means destroy the temples of the idols of the English,' said Pope Gregory as St Augustine prepared to convert this island. 'Let holy water be sprinkled over them, let altars be constructed.' Splendid compromise illustrated here at Rudston. 5¼m W of Bridlington on B1253.

Stonehenge (Wiltshire) The one that everybody knows. Anyone who has not been there for some time needs to be braced against shock of new car parks, subway, caff, souvenir shop, lavatories and other razzmatazz. D of E. Open standard hours and Sun from 9.30. Admission charge. 2m W of Amesbury, S of A344.

ENGINEERING/INDUSTRY

Butser Ancient Farm (Hampshire) Reconstruction of Iron Age settlement in Queen Elizabeth Country Park with crops and animals to match. Working replica of pottery kiln and loom in stockaded settlement of thatched huts and animal pens. Open Easter–end Sept 2–5, Sun, Bank Hols 10–6. Closed winter. Admission charge. 4m S of Petersfield on A3.

Cissbury Ring (West Sussex) Iron Age fort with remains of more than 200 neolithic flint mines now mostly reduced to slight depressions on the western end. Some shafts go down 40ft deep, cutting through half a dozen seams of flint. Flint nodules worked loose with deer antler picks and cleared away with shovels of ox shoulder blades. 1½m E of Findon, 3m N of Worthing off A24.

Dorset Cursus (Dorset) Massive engineering feat by neolithic tribes who raised this strange earth monument of parallel banks about 90yds apart which run for a staggering six miles from Thickthorn Down to Bokerley Down. Possibly connected with some cult of the dead, as cursus is aligned with several neigh-

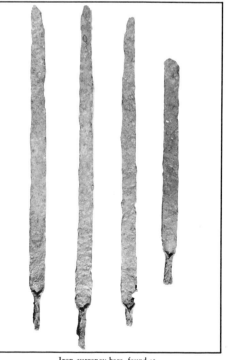

Iron currency bars, found at Winchester, now in British Museum

bouring long barrows. Good stretch can be seen running E and W of B3081 at Bottlebush. W end is 1m NW of Gussage St Michael.

Grimes Graves (Norfolk) Neolithic flint mines, centre of axehead production about 2600BC. Ladder now gives access to typical excavated chamber underground. Touching appeal to pagan fertility gods found in worthless abandoned pit, altar with antler picks, pregnant figure and phallus of chalk, an entreaty for better luck next time. D of E. Open standard hours and Sun morning from 9.30. Admission charge. 7m NW of Thetford, signposted off B1108.

MUSEUMS/ARTEFACTS

Cambridge Museum of Archaeology, Downing St. Chief centre for East Anglian prehistory. Fine iron firedogs and bronze mirror from princely burial and comprehensive collection of local tools and pottery. Open Mon–Fri 2–4, Sat 10–12.30.

Cardiff The National Museum of Wales, Cathays Park. Important collection of early prehistoric material, including new Bronze Age gallery. Open Mon–Sat 10 5, Sun 2.30–5.

Devizes 41 Long St. Particularly rich in material from the neolithic and Bronze Ages, including grave goods from some of the richest prehistoric burials yet discovered: weapons, implements, a bronze dagger, beads of faience and amber. Open Tues–Sat winter 11–1, 2–4, summer 11–1, 2–5. Admission charge adults, children free.

Dorchester Magnificent prehistoric pottery here, representative of the long occupation of Maiden Castle. Bowls with fine beaded rims and a mug, 'pure British Rail' says museum director Roger Peers. Hoard of Bronze Age tinker, unearthed by plough near Lulworth, has broken pots, pans and pieces collected for the melting pot. Evocative collection. Open weekdays 10–5. Admission charge.

Glastonbury Lake Village Museum, The Tribunal, High St. Bronze bowl, dugout canoe and other remains from village which was lived in 2000 years ago. Display of ancient trackways used in 5000BC. Open mid-Oct–mid-March weekdays 9.30–4 Sun 2–4, mid-March–mid-Oct weekdays 9.30–6.30, Sun 2–6.30. Admission charge.

Gloucester City Museum and Art Gallery, Brunswick Rd. Home of the Birdlip grave group, exquisite series of objects found by quarrymen in stone coffin of Celtic princess. Engraved mirror, a silver-gilt brooch worked with design of two beaked heads, a knife handle in the shape of a deer's head, a superb amber necklace. Open Mon–Sat 10–5.

Lewes Barbican House Museum, High St. Fine collection of local quern stones, including three available for grinding your own corn. Reconstruction of typical flint mine with associated artefacts, lamps, picks, shovels. Open Mon–Sat 10–5 throughout year also Sun 2–5 April–Oct. Admission charge.

London British Museum, Great Russell St. Has lion's share of finds, including displays of Man Before Metals and Wessex Culture. Stunning case of gold artefacts, including the famous Snettisham torque and beautiful flat beaten discs called *lunulae*, also worn round the neck. Elegantly simple but sumptuous display of bracelets. Map shows sources of gold. Open Mon–Sat 10–5, Sun 2.30–6.

Salisbury King's House, 65 The Close. Important collection featuring Stonehenge and other prehistoric works of south Wiltshire. In new headquarters, so collection not yet fully displayed. Mon–Sat 10.30–5 also July–Aug Sun 2–5. Admission charge.

Sheffield City Museum, Weston Park. Prime material from the Derbyshire Peak district, including collection of antiquarian Thomas Bateman who 'excavated' busily round here in 19th c. Urns, beakers, stone axes and Bronze Age metalwork. Open Mon–Sat 10–5, Sun 11–5 (open until 8 from June–Aug).

Truro County Museum and Art Gallery, River St. Three splendid *lunulae* here, two found near Padstow and one at St Juillot. Good collection of neolithic stone axes. Open Mon–Sat 9–1, 2–5. Closed Bank Hols and Mon Oct–Easter.

The monolith at Rudston, Yorks, is Britain's largest standing stone, at 25½ft

THE
ROMANS

by Anna Pavord

DWELLINGS

Bignor (Sussex) Successive proud owners tinkered with this house for more than 200 years, changing it from the modest cottage that first stood on the site to the elaborate and elegant show house that it became in 4th c. Famed for mosaics. Latest to be uncovered is corridor, 80ft long. Serene head of Venus with flowers in her hair and cherubs masquerading as gladiators. Open March Tues–Sun 10–5.30, April–May Tues–Sun 10–6.30, June–Oct daily 10–6.30. Admission charge. Small museum on site. 12m NE of Chichester.

Brading (Isle of Wight) Orpheus, Medusa, Perseus, the standard cast of Roman mythological literature cavort in mosaics here, but they are joined by rougher pagan creatures, a man with the head of a cock, griffins. Open April–Sept Mon–Sat 10–5.30, Sun 10.30–5.30. Open winter months by appointment only (Tel 0983 614623). Admission charge. 1½m SW of Brading off A3055.

Chedworth (Gloucestershire) Within easy reach of the Fosse Way, good selling point for Roman estate agents, who surely must have operated in Gloucestershire, more thickly scattered with Roman villas than any other county in Britain. Excellent baths too – both Turkish steamy and Spartan dry. *Nymphaeum*, dedicated to water nymphs built over natural spring. Open March–Oct Tues–Sun and Bank Hols 11–6, Nov–mid-Dec and Feb Wed–Sun 11–4. Admission charge. 3m NW of Fossebridge, off A429, via Yanworth–Withington road.

Din Lligwy (Anglesey) While the Roman nouveaux-riches were showing off with villas and mosaics, indigenous Celts evidently mistrusted such newfangled notions. Spectacular settlement of 4th c looks much like prehistoric forebears – limestone walls enclosing 2 circular and 7 rectangular huts, some with doorsteps and posts. ½m S of Din Lligwy village.

Dorchester (Dorset) Footings of Roman town house (as opposed to villa which was country dwelling) laid out behind County Council offices and library in Colliton park. Roman plumbing most impressive feature. Hut shelters one small mosaic. Open daily, daylight hours. On NW of town.

Fishbourne (W Sussex) Sumptuous palace, possibly the home of Cogidubnus, king of the Atrebates, who had sold out to Romans soon after invasion in AD43. Section open is north wing, corresponding south wing buried somewhere under A27. Interesting attempt to recreate Roman garden along lines established by excavation: lawn, box hedges, lavender, briar rose and espaliered apple trees (juicy Coxes which the Romans never had). Open daily May–Sept 10–6, March, April, Oct 10–5, Nov 10–4, Dec–March Sun only 10–4. Admission charge. Big car park. 1½m W of Chichester on A27.

Great Witcombe (Gloucestershire) Built round three sides of open courtyard, this villa stands in beautiful spot close to Cotswolds. Owner seems to have had trouble with foundations on hillside – series of buttresses built to prevent them settling. Well preserved bath suite with *frigidarium*, *tepidarium* and *caldarium*. Room with central basin and 3 niches has been interpreted as shrine. S of A417.

Lullingstone (Kent) Roman owner of this large villa had to leave in a hurry about AD200 and place later re-occupied by Romano-British family who converted one room into chapel, one of the earliest Christian shrines in country. Chi-Rho monogram (from first two letters of Christ's name) was painted on wall. Original now in British Museum, copy at villa. D of E. Open standard hours and Sun from 9.30 April–Sept, Admission charge. 6m N of Sevenoaks off A225 in Eynsford.

North Leigh (Oxfordshire) Beautifully constructed hypocausts provided heating for this courtyard house which was at its grandest in 4th c. Geometric mosaic in room on W corner has swirling shapes in centre which look like curiously beaked heads. Experts think that Chedworth used the same mosaicist – the fashionable interior designer of his day. D of E. Open April–Sept standard hours. Admission charge. 3m NE of Witney, signposted off A4095.

Tre'r Ceiri (Gwynedd) Steep climb up to hill-fort, refortified and occupied during the Roman times. Outer defences of dry stone walls still 13ft high in places enclosing about 150 huts, shapes and sizes more varied than in earlier Iron Age settlements. Main occupation from AD150–400. 1m SW of Llanaelhaern, approached by footpath signposted off B4417.

Marble head of god Serapis, from Temple of Mithras, now in Museum of London

MILITARY

Antonine Wall (Central Scotland) Best remains are rampart, ditch, fort, beacon platform and military way at Rough Castle. 1m E of Bonnybridge off B816. Good stretch of defensive ditch at Watling Lodge, 1¼m W of Falkirk.

Baginton (Warwickshire) Reconstruction of Roman fort of 1st c, built of turf and timber with ramparts, gateway, unique gyrus (cavalry training area), granary with museum and shop. Original fort raised after Boudicca's uprising in AD60. Occasional happenings with the Ermine St Guard who come to play war games. Guided tours for parties only, phone Coventry 25555. Open May–Sept daily except Mon and Thurs 12–6. Open all week spring and summer Bank Hols, also last two weeks July. Admission charge. 2m S of Coventry off minor road to airport.

Caerleon (Gwent) Wales sullenly pacified by AD78 and this became HQ of Second Augustan Legion from AD74–287. Outstanding amphitheatre, large enough to seat entire garrison of 6,000 men. Competitors' waiting room adjoins the ring. D of E. Open standard hours and Sun from 9.30 April–Sept. Admission charge. 3m NE of Newport on B4596. Museum on main road close to church has excellent display, weapons, sculptures, tombstone inscriptions. Open Mon–Sat May–Sept 9.30–6, Sun 2–6. Closes 5.30 March, April, Oct and at 4 from Nov–Feb.

Caernarfon (Gwynedd) Strategically placed overlooking troublesome Anglesey, first fort built AD78 in rough earth and timber. Rebuilt in stone through succeeding centuries until evacuation AD383. Excellent site museum displays coins, pottery, nails, temple of Mithras from Llanbeblig church. Open May–Sept Mon–Sat 9.30–6, Sun 2–6, March, April, Oct Mon–Sat 9.30–5.30, Sun 2–5, Nov–Feb Mon–Sat 9.30–4 Sun 2–4. ½m outside town on A4085 to Beddgelert.

Chester (Cheshire) Discovering Roman Chester turns into game of hide and seek with walls, hypocausts, parts of fortress and bath houses lurking along Northgate St, Hamilton Place, Bridge St and St John St in dress shops, china shops and other unlikely places. Biggest attraction is amphitheatre, but half is buried under later buildings. Touching shrine here to Nemesis, goddess of fate. *See Museums.*

Hadrian's Wall (Cumbria/Northumberland) Tying a tidy girdle round their empire, Romans built this massive barrier in AD122. It ran for 73 miles from the Tyne to the Solway Firth with a small fort every Roman mile (1,620yds). National Trust owns spectacular section at Housesteads (4m NE of Haltwhistle via B6318) with fort and museum. D of E. Open standard hours and Sun from 9.30 April–Sept. Admission charge. Good sections too at Walltown Crags, Greenhead and at Cawfields. Magnificent site at Chesterholm – Roman Vindolanda – with fort and civilian settlement. *See Museums.*

Hardknott (Cumbria) Difficult to decide which is most stunning: Eskdale to the west, Scafell to the north or this Roman fort with granaries, comman-

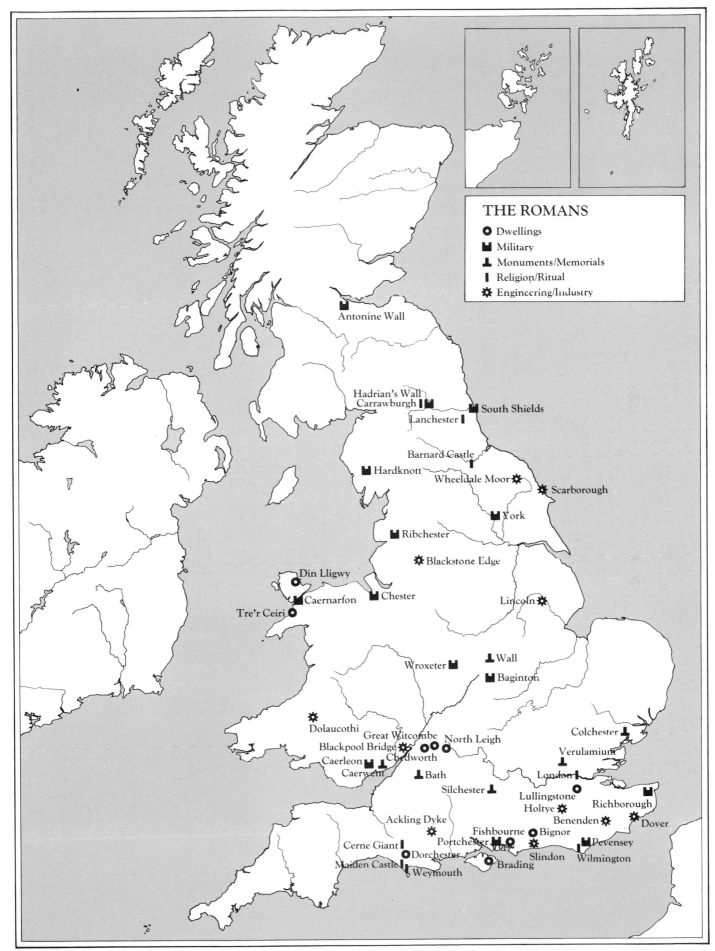

THE ROMANS

- ⊙ Dwellings
- ⌶ Military
- ⟘ Monuments/Memorials
- ❙ Religion/Ritual
- ✻ Engineering/Industry

Antonine Wall

Hadrian's Wall
Carrawburgh
Lanchester
South Shields

Barnard Castle

Hardknott
Wheeldale Moor
Scarborough

York

Ribchester

Blackstone Edge

Din Lligwy

Caernarfon
Chester
Lincoln

Tre'r Ceiri

Wroxeter
Wall
Baginton

Dolaucothi

Great Witcombe
North Leigh
Colchester

Blackpool Bridge
Chedworth
Verulamium

Caerleon
Caerwent
Bath
London

Silchester
Lullingstone
Richborough
Holtye

Ackling Dyke
Benenden
Dover

Cerne Giant
Fishbourne
Bignor

Portchester
Pevensey
Slindon
Wilmington

Dorchester
Brading

Maiden Castle
Weymouth

Granary foundations of Housesteads, finest of forts on Hadrian's Wall, Northumberland

Foundations of barrack block at Caerleon, HQ of Second Augustan Legion

Arbeia, protecting easternmost flank of Hadrian's Wall, and guarding mouth of Tyne. Garrisoned by boatmen from Mesopotamia specially picked to handle the treacherous shoals of the Tyne. First fort refashioned as giant storehouse to back up Severus's Scottish campaign in 3rd c. Excellent museum on site. Baring Street, N of town centre. Open May–Sept Mon–Sat 10–6, Sun 2–5, Oct–April Mon–Fri 10–4, Sat 10–12.

Wroxeter (Shropshire) Fourth largest town of Roman Britain, tribal capital of Cornovii after military occupation by XIV and XX Legions. Lavish public buildings. Old Work is strange honeycombed piece of masonry which dominates site. Was S wall of large exercise hall (*palaestra*) attached to baths? Good site museum. D of E. Open standard hours and Sun from 9.30 April–Sept. Admission charge. 5½m SE of Shrewsbury by B4380.

York (Yorkshire) Military capital and fulcrum of northern fort system. Stretch of original city wall in Museum Gardens on N side of river finishes at Multangular Tower, W corner of old fortress. Patched at top with medieval masonry, the rest as built in 3rd c. *See* Museums.

MONUMENTS/MEMORIALS

Bath (Avon) Large and sumptuous baths, outstanding demonstration of civic elegance. Well designed museum displays detail of Roman life. Agelessly serene head of Minerva, collection of gravestones with touching epitaphs of centurions who died far from home in the service of their Emperor. At Pump Room, Abbey Churchyard. Open daily April–June, Sept–Oct 9–5.30, July–Aug 9–6.30, Nov–March 9–4.30 Sun 11–4.30. Admission charge.

Caerwent (Gwent) Venta Silurum, market place of the Silures tribe. Temple a bit of a disappointment, hemmed in by caravans, but good stretch of wall running along from Coach and Horses pub. You can follow this round through wicket gate and footpath leads up from farm track, over stone stile on left into churchyard. Church sometimes locked, but porch has two fine inscribed stones, one dedicated to a commander called Paulinus and the other to a war god. 5m SW of Chepstow off A48.

Colchester (Essex) First British *colonia*, settlement for retired veteran soldiers, founded here about AD50 and sacked by Boudicca and her wild Iceni followers 10 years later. Superb museum collection at the castle with fine Roman memorials: sphinx holding human head, commemorative statue of Marcus Favonius Facilis in full military rig. Another tombstone shows Longinus, auxiliary cavalryman from Bulgaria. Barbarian writhing underfoot survives intact, while Longinus's face smashed to bits. Chance, or revengeful Iceni work? Vaults of Temple of Claudius deep under castle. Open Oct–March Mon–Fri 10–5, Sat 10–4, April–Sept Mon–Sat 10–5, Sun 2.30–5. Admission charge. Tour of vaults (extra) in July–Aug.

Silchester (Hampshire) Tribal capital of the Atrebates, completely abandoned in 5th c after Romans had gone home; a ghost town, now faintly showing its ribs under the accumulation of centuries of soil. Churchyard has sundial set on Roman pillar and stretch of town wall runs SW from here, facing stones now gone, revealing huge bonding-slabs. Amphitheatre on corner by Wall Lane is overgrown with trees and filled by a sludgy pool. Best finds taken to Reading (*see* Museums) but small museum in rectory garden has photographs and objects from excavation. Open daily 10–dusk. No charge, but donations welcomed. Guide, price 60p. 1m E of Silchester.

Verulamium (Hertfordshire) Important *municipium* (self-governing community) now lying under playing fields of St Albans, but excavations revealed shops, theatre, private houses and streets of prosperous settlement. Museum in St Michael's St has treasures of great beauty, including mosaics and pretty bronze statue of Venus. Fragments of inscription from basilica show name of Agricola, governor in Britain from AD78–85. Open April–Oct Mon–Sat 10–5.30, Sun

dant's house, HQ building, bath houses, all contained within well-preserved wall with corner turrets. 10m W of Ambleside.

Pevensey (Sussex) Castle is Norman, but Romans first fortified this place as bastion in line of Saxon shore forts which they made at end of 3rd c to defend coast against Saxon invaders. Captured AD491 by Aelle of South Saxons who, according to 'Anglo-Saxon Chronicle', wiped out defenders 'and there was not even a single Briton left alive'. D of E. Open standard hours and Sun from 9.30 April–Sept. Admission charge. 5m NE of Eastbourne off A259.

Portchester (Hampshire) Daunting Saxon shore fort with sea meeting walls on the E side. Has 12th c church and castle inside. Wilson in 'A Guide to the Roman Remains in Britain' calls it 'one of the best-preserved and most impressive Roman structures anywhere in Britain.' D of E. Open standard hours and Sun from 9.30 April–Sept. Admission charge. 3m E of Fareham off A27.

Ribchester (Lancashire) River Ribble has swept away much of south-easterly part of fort, but remains of granaries stand in museum grounds. Outstanding collection of inscriptions, carvings and other memorabilia relating to the fort, garrisoned first by a cavalry regiment of Asturians from Spain and later by Sarmatian horsemen from the Danube region. Most famous find is Ribchester helmet of bronze, now in British Museum, replica here. Open Dec–Jan Sat 2–5, Feb–May and Sept–Dec daily except Fri 2–5, May–Sept daily except Fri 2–5.30. Admission charge. 10m NE of Preston on B6245.

Richborough (Kent) Beachhead of Roman invasion in AD43 when Thanet separated from mainland by Wantsum Channel and boats sailed between Richborough and Reculver in the north. Cross-shaped section marks foundation of massive triumphal arch more than 90ft high built to impress the natives. D of E. Open standard hours and Sun from 9.30 April–Sept. Admission charge. 1½m NW of Sandwich off A257.

South Shields (Tyne and Wear) Roman fort of

2–5.30, Nov–March Mon–Sat 10–4, Sun 2–4. Admission charge. Theatre open daily 10–dusk. Admission charge.

Wall (Staffordshire) Monster bath house here alongside solidly constructed building that has been interpreted as a *mansio* or inn, well placed to attract travellers on Watling St close by. Modern road-houses cannot match luxury offered here to the foot-sore: *tepidarium*, *caldarium*, plunge baths for every taste, bed and breakfast all inclusive. D of E. Open standard hours. Admission charge. 2½m S of Lichfield off A5127.

Milestones Roman mile a little shorter than ours. Some of their markers still survive. In the south-west you can see these: **1** S of the A35 1m NE of Dorchester (Dorset) before turning to Stinsford. **2** Tintagel (Cornwall) in S transept of church. **3** Breage (Cornwall) stone dedicated to Posthumus in church. **4** St Hilary (Cornwall) stone dedicated to Emperor Caesar Flavius Valerius Constantinus Pius in S aisle of church. In the north you can see these: **1** By layby on N side of A66 ½m SE of Temple Sowerby (Cumbria). **2** Middleton (Cumbria) in field S of church on W of A683 inscribed MP LIII (53 miles).

RELIGION/RITUAL

Barnard Castle (Durham) Bowes Museum has altar dedicated to Vinotonus, god of hunting, found on wild moorland a few miles S of Roman fort at Bowes. Originally put up by Caesar Frontinus, commander of First Thracian Cohort who garrisoned Bowes AD208. Open Mon–Sat 10–5.30 (Oct, March, April, 10–5, Nov–Feb 10–4) Sun 2–5 (Nov–Feb 2–4). Admission charge.

Carrawburgh (Northumberland) Five temples dedicated to Mithras survive in Britain and this is smallest, able to hold only 12 men. Rigorous cult derived from worship of Persian deity, god of light and truth, but initiates had to go through dreadful ordeals including burial alive. Perhaps that's why it never caught on. Three beautiful altars and remains of torchbearers are replicas – originals at Newcastle (*see* Museums). Spring dedicated to water goddess Coventina (swampy bit 150yds N of temple) out of which 16,000 old coins have been recovered. 2m W of Chesters.

Cerne Giant (Dorset) Rampant Romano-British hill-figure cut into the chalk of steep hillside. He is 180ft tall and suffered badly in the drought when essential parts became dangerously eroded. Bad news for a fertility figure, but D of E have now reseeded him. Best view from A352 on N of village. Pleasant walk from footpath off Abbey St over stone bridge and up steep hillside to Giant.

Lanchester (Durham) Germanic tribe of Suebians, garrisoned at fort here in 3rd c, dedicated an altar to their native goddess, Garmangabis. Now in porch of Church of All Saints, Lanchester. 7m NW of Durham on A691.

London Temple of Mithras discovered in 1954 when building work started at Bucklersbury House, 11 Walbrook. Questions raised in the House, but developers won the day and whole thing moved to present site in Temple Court, 11, Queen Victoria St. Archaeologists remind us that reconstruction has not exactly followed original plan (crazy paving is wrong). Sculptures from original temple in Museum of London (*see* Museums), but replicas in main entrance of Bucklersbury House.

Maiden Castle (Dorset) Romans stormed this great stronghold in AD43 commanded by Vespasian, later to become emperor. Defenders had slings and sling-stones from Chesil Beach – great piles of slingstones survive at strategic points – but Romans fired iron shot from great catapults (*ballistae*). Vertebrae pierced by one of these bolts displayed in Dorchester Museum and remains of hastily buried dead found by E entrance. More than 300 years later, small Romano-Celtic temple built on site, with central shrine and surrounding ambulatory. Pagan tradition flourished alongside Christianity. 2m SW of Dorchester, sign-posted off A354.

Weymouth (Dorset) Small Roman temple on Jor-

Richborough was beachhead of invasion in AD 43, later chief port of Roman Britain

Romano-Celtic temple built inside tribal stronghold of Maiden Castle, Dorset

dan Hill. Rectangular shaft excavated at SE corner held 2 urns, sword and spearhead covered with 16 layers of ash and charcoal, each carefully separated with roofing slabs and each containing one Roman coin and skeleton of single bird. Identified as ravens, crows, starlings and buzzards. Take A353 out of Weymouth and where road turns inland at Overcombe (2m) take footpath on right to Jordan Hill overlooking Bowleaze Cove.

Wilmington (Sussex) Colossal hill figure 240ft tall cut into chalk face of Windover Hill. Possibly Romano-British but dating obscure. Renovated in 1874 by Rev de Ste Croix who first went to check on the Cerne Giant. Jacquetta Hawkes notes 'he had difficulty in overcoming his reluctance to inspect this more virile effigy and it is likely that anyone with such excessive moral delicacy may have enfeebled the drawing of the Wilmington figure.' Interpreted variously as Woden, Mercury or St Paul. 8m NW of Eastbourne then footpath E of Wilmington–Litlington road.

ENGINEERING/INDUSTRY

Ackling Dyke (Dorset) Roman road which originally joined Old Sarum with Badbury Rings. Superb 8m stretch, finishing at Badbury Rings, is right of way. Take Ringwood turning (B3081) off A354 and dyke starts ¼m on right. Forty feet wide sitting on embankment sometimes 6ft above ground.

Benenden (Kent) James Dyer in 'Southern England: An Archaeological Guide' notes Roman ford here which took road running from Rochester through Maidstone south into the weald of Kent. About 11ft wide, it paves way through stream beside Stream Farm on road between Benenden and Iden Green.

Blackpool Bridge (Gloucestershire) Romans mined iron ore in Forest of Dean and this road connected their mine at Ariconium (Weston-under-Penyard) with Caerwent and Caerleon. Only 8ft wide but neatly edged with kerbstones and paved with stone slabs. Take B4431 off A48 west of Blakeney and turn

Fourth century AD silver goblets from fabulous Mildenhall Treasure, in British Museum

right at signpost to Soudley. Roman road on left after railway bridge.

Blackstone Edge (Greater Manchester) Road which climbs on to moors above Littleborough was originally 16ft wide and paved with large stone setts hemmed in by kerbstones. Sunken central channel may have been made by brake-shoes of carts coming *down*, or have been filled with turf to provide foothold for horses struggling *up*. Much grown over but paving best seen at top of hill. Take A58 E from Littleborough and as main road turns N take footpath signposted to E. Road distinguished by light strip of grass going straight up hill.

Dolaucothi (Dyfed) Gold mined here from opencast workings and underground galleries – one 145ft deep – all drained by huge wooden water wheels (fragment in National Museum of Wales, Cardiff). Three aqueducts, longest 7 miles, brought in water to reservoir tank and thence to stepped row of washing tables where ore was cleaned. Turn left south of bridge at Pumpsaint on A482 and left again at crossroads. Mining area on right.

Dover (Kent) Headquarters of Roman fleet in 2nd c. Unique *pharos* (lighthouse) stands about 43ft high with another 20ft of medieval rebuilding on top. Guided Channel shipping with smoke by day, fire by night. Roughly octagonal in shape with windows made of stone and brick, it now survives as tower at W end of church, St Mary in Castro. Close to car park in grounds of Dover Castle.

Holtye (Sussex) Roman B road that branched off from Watling St towards Lewes, possibly made to get iron ore from Ashdown Forest to London. Surfaced with iron slag – unusual. Section preserved by Sussex Archaeological Trust reached by footpath S of A264.

Lincoln (Lincolnshire) Newport Arch at N end of Bailgate is only Roman archway still in use in this country. Originally N gate of city which grew up round fortress founded AD60 for IX Legion. N tower of E gate stands in forecourt of Eastgate Hotel opposite cathedral.

Scarborough (Yorkshire) As Britain threatened by Saxon pirates and barbarians from north, Romans flung up series of signal towers along Yorkshire coast from Huntcliff to Filey, which would warn of impending invasion. Last ditch attempt to retain order was short-lived, towers used only for 30 years. No masonry left here, but plan of site laid out and ditch excavated. E side has fallen into sea. Cliff edge, E of Scarborough Castle.

Slindon (Sussex) Unspoilt section of Stane St, road which ran from Chichester's E gate to London, in 3½ mile stretch from Bignor to Eartham. Made of many layers of rammed chalk and flint, flanked on either side by ditches. National Trust estate, 6m N of Bognor Regis between A285 and A29.

Wheeldale Moor (Yorkshire) Impressive stretch of road here, 1¼ mile remnant of original which joined Malton and Whitby. Foundation slabs, drainage culverts and kerbstones remain, though surface gravel

has long since been washed away. Known as Wade's Causeway. 11m SW of Whitby, then minor roads S of Goathland.

MUSEUMS

Chester Grosvenor Museum, Grosvenor St. Very rich collection of sculptured stones and military remains from II Adiutrix and XX Valeria Victrix who were garrisoned here from AD87. Galleries display a day in the life of your average Roman legionary, together with magnificent tombstones, some of which had been used in medieval rebuilding of city walls. Open Mon–Sat 10–5, Sun 2–5.30.

Chesterholm (Northumberland) Museum on site of Vindolanda has intimate record of life at this fort. Documents written with reed pen on slivers of wood record military provisioning, Celtic beer, vintage wine, fish sauce and pork fat. Also letters: 'I have sent you two pairs of sandals and two pairs of underpants. Greetings to Elpis, Tetricus and all your messmates . . .' Anxious Mum in Rome? Open daily Nov–Feb 10–4, March 10–5, April, Oct 10–5.30, May–June, Sept 10–6, July–Aug 10–6.30.

Cirencester Corinium Museum, Park St. Reconstruction of dining room (*triclinium*) with mosaics of seasons and Actaeon being torn to pieces by his dogs. Simple kitchen with amphorae and raised stone hearth. Intriguing word square puzzle scratched on plaster, possibly Christian acrostic. Open May–Sept Mon–Sat 10–6, Sun 2–6, Oct–April Tues–Sat 10–5, Sun 2–5. Admission charge.

Edinburgh National Museum of Antiquities of Scotland, Queen St. Fine haul here including tools and weapons from Newstead forts with beautiful 1st c cavalry parade helmet. Bridgeness Stone, marking E end of Antonine Wall, also silver from Traprain Law. Open Mon–Sat 10–5, Sun 2–5.

Hull Transport and Archaeology Museum, 36, High St. Mosaic workers flourished on Humberside in 4th c, but native execution not always up to high-flown classical subjects. Splendidly ludicrous Venus mosaic where pot-bellied goddess of love with scrawny arms and wild hair gallivants in front of a nervous merman. Open Mon–Sat 10–5, Sun 2.30–4.30.

Leeds City Museum, Municipal Buildings. Mosaic here from rich Roman house at Aldborough, but mosaicist evidently found subject of Romulus and Remus a bit tricky to handle. Open Tues–Fri 10–5.30, Sat 10–4.

London British Museum, Great Russell St. Has the great treasures, mosaic pavement from Hinton St Mary and Water Newton hoard, both showing Chi-Rho monogram, sign of early Christianity. C of E claimed possession at treasure trove inquiry. Open Mon–Sat 10–5, Sun 2.30–6.

Museum of London, London wall. Has sculptures from Temple of Mithras, Mithras slaying the bull accompanied by his torchbearers. Also domestic paraphernalia, bowls, keys, footwear etc of urban Romans. Open Tues–Sat 10–6, Sun 2–6.

Newcastle Museum of Antiquities, The Quadrangle (University of Newcastle). Many inscriptions from Hadrian's Wall here, giving useful information about who built what and when. Reconstruction of Carrawburgh Mithraeum with original inscriptions and sculptures. Appealingly bizarre native sculpture of Venus, absentmindedly hanging on to bunches of her own hair (found at High Rochester). Open Mon–Sat 10–5.

Reading Museum and Art Gallery, Blagrave St. Main Silchester finds here; iron tools, surgical instruments, scalpels, probes, artery forceps and homely graffiti. 'Clementinus made this box tile.' Another more literary effort quotes opening of Aeneid II 'Conticuere omnes.' Open Mon–Fri, 10–5.30, Sat 10–5.

York Yorkshire Museum, Museum Gardens. Splendid King's Square inscription which dates first stone fortress here to AD107–8 and touching tombstone commemorating Augustinus, his wife and two sons, both of whom died before they were two. Family group carved at the top, all swathed in cloaks. Open Mon–Sat 10–5, Sun 1–5. Admission charge.

Well preserved leather shoe, among many domestic objects in the Museum of London.
Right: mosaic depicting the four seasons, from Roman villa at Chedworth, Glos.

THE
DARK AGES

by Anna Pavord

SETTLEMENTS

Brough of Birsay (Orkney) Norse settlement, once the seat of the Viking earl, Thorfinn, with remains of later 11th c church. Foundations of about a dozen Viking houses with long narrow central hearths. Brough is tidal island connected by causeway at low tide, but cut off at high tide so choose visiting time with care. At N end of mainland 20m NW of Kirkwall: D of E. Open standard hours, but closed Mon in winter and Tues am. Admission charge.

Bygrave (Hertfordshire) Noted by W. G. Hoskins, incomparable interpreter of landscape as 'one of the most interesting survivors' of a primitive self-contained settlement in England. Village stands to W of Icknield Way, 1½m from Baldock. First recorded in Saxon charter of 973, name meaning 'place by ditch'. Essential plan unchanged more than 1,000 years later, though no original buildings survive. Manor house site and church enclosed by moat stand on highest ground, with few cottages strung along street to W.

Dinas Emrys (Gwynedd) Craggy hilltop site in southern Snowdonia, occupied from the early Iron Age through the Roman period and into the Dark Ages. Natural outcrops of rock are linked with ramparts to provide strong defensive structure. Artificial pool source of local legend connected with 5th c British King Vortigern. Tough climb through triple ramparts to approach by original W entrance. More easily attacked from E. 1½m NE of Beddgelert.

Gurness broch (Orkney) Broch, surrounded by rock-cut ditch, is 1st century BC, but longhouse nearby dates from Viking invasion: 'With swords for shuttles. The war-web we weave. Valkyries weaving. The web of victory.' Broch is near Evie, 11m NW of Kirkwall, 1½m N of A966. D of E. Open standard hours. Admission charge.

Singleton (Sussex) Reconstruction of single-storey Anglo-Saxon hut built of flint rubble with thatch and sunken floor, based on original excavation at Hangleton, nr Brighton. Plan of timber hall of same period from Chalton, Hampshire. At Weald and Downland Open Air Museum. Open April–May, Sept–Oct, Tues–Sun, June–Aug daily 11–5. Nov–March Sun only 11–4. Admission charge.

Somerton (Somerset) Boundary bank of large (royal?) Anglo-Saxon estate can still be traced along lane which runs round N and NW sides of Bradley hill, 1½m NW of town. Lane follows rampart of estate boundary before flat lands of Somerton Moor. Similar estate boundary in Devon about 6m NNW of Exeter demarcating monastic estate of Exeter Abbey (ceded by Athelstan about 930) from neighbouring lands of Cada who gave his name to adjoining parishes of Cadbury and Cadeleigh. Boundary runs along sunken lane, Armourwood Lane, W of Thorverton.

Tintagel (Cornwall) Rocky headland of N coast occupied during 5th and 6th c. Foundations of rectangular buildings on promontory first interpreted as monastic cells, but now more widely seen as remains of secular settlement. British Museum has shards of imported red and cream pottery amphorae and jugs which indicate that Tintagel may have been trading post. One of many sites associated with Arthurian legend. ½m NW of Tintagel. D of E. Castle site open standard hours and Sun from 9.30 April–Sept. Admission charge.

West Stow (Suffolk) Reconstruction of village based on excavation of original site occupied between AD400–650. Saxon houses with thatch roofs supported on hazel hurdles built over pits. Modern methods banned in reconstruction work: walls and floors of oak were cut with Saxon tools, axe, adze and auger. No nails. Clay seals the joints. 7½m NW of Bury St Edmunds, via A1101 and minor roads. Open April–Oct, Tues–Sat 2–5, Sun, Bank Hols 11–1 and 2–5. Admission charge. Beautiful pieces from original excavation, combs, tweezers, gaming counters, jewellery, at Moyses Hall Museum, Cornhill, Bury St Edmunds. Open Mon–Sat 10–1, 2–5 (Nov–Feb closes at 4). Admission charge.

York Viking capital of Jorvik, taken over after raids of AD867 and held by invaders until Saxon king Eadred routed last Scandinavian king Erik Bloodaxe from the Danelaw in 954. Excavations at Coppergate over last 5 years have brought to light a staggering quantity of material from this time. Remains of wooden houses, plank built, survive up to 4ft high – others built with walls of woven twigs. Jorvik Viking Centre opens soon underneath modern development at Coppergate. Time tunnel leads visitors back to town as it was 1,000 years ago, thatch on the houses, reeds on the floor. Admission charge. For details telephone York (0904) 32342

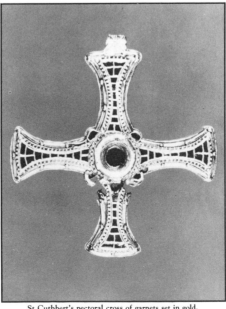

St Cuthbert's pectoral cross of garnets set in gold, Durham Cathedral Museum

MILITARY/DEFENSIVE

Bokerley Dyke (Dorset) Linear earthworks provide some of the most impressive remains of the Dark Ages. This defensive rampart, 6 miles long, first thrown up by Romans across road to Old Sarum, but later dismantled. Subsequently refurbished by indigenous Romano-British to keep Saxons out of Dorset during advances of 5th and 6th c. It served brilliantly for 200 years until Brits forced to retreat to Combs Ditch, second line of defence. Runs close to A354 on Hants/Dorset border, 1¼m SW of Martin Drove End.

Carl Wark (Derbyshire) Hilltop camp of about 2 acres in magnificent position overlooking Derwent valley with strong defences of dour black millstone grit. Masonry still over 6ft high to the W and well built entrance at SW corner. Site protected on all but W side by natural slope. 5m SW of Sheffield, 1¾m E of Hathersage via A625.

Chun Castle (Cornwall) Round Iron Age fort reoccupied in Dark Ages when it had some connection with Cornish tin trade. Large cake of tin slag found during excavation together with complete smelting furnace. Fort walls 6ft high faced with granite blocks. Foundations of circular Iron Age huts have been overlaid with rectangular versions built in 6th c. 1m S of Morvah via B3306.

Devil's Dyke (Cambridgeshire) Built to control Icknield Way, the ridgeway route into E Anglia, a defensive earthwork 7m long and originally about 30ft high from bottom of ditch to top of accompanying bank. Probably raised in 6th c by East Anglians to defend their territory against neighbouring Middle Angles. Runs from Reach in N to Wood Ditton in S, best seen on Newmarket Heath either side of A11.

Liddington Castle (Berkshire) Reoccupied Iron Age hill-fort, possibly site of battle of Mons Badonicus about AD500 when superman Arthur finally thrashed the Anglo-Saxons. Excavation 5 years ago showed that ramparts had been remade for some reason in post-Roman period. Nennius's 'History of the Britons' records: 'The 12th battle was on Badon Hill where 960 men fell in one day at a single onset of Arthur and no-one killed them but he alone and in all the battles he came out victorious.' He was of course writing 600 years after the event. 5m SE of Swindon, just S of M4 at junction 15.

Offa's Dyke (Welsh Border) Longest of all earthworks of this period, running for 80 miles between the Severn and the Dee. Now long distance footpath and subject of excellent HMSO guide for walkers by John Jones (£2.95). Offa emerged as king of Mercia after civil war and murder of Ethelbald. He ruled for nearly 40 years from 757 and probably ordered Dyke's construction between his kingdom and the unruly Welsh the other side. Three week holiday needed to walk entire stretch but good 7 mile section starts at Knighton, where there's also in information centre.

Old Sarum (Wiltshire) Iron Age hill-fort which subsequently became Romano-British village, Saxon town and Norman city with castle and cathedral, an

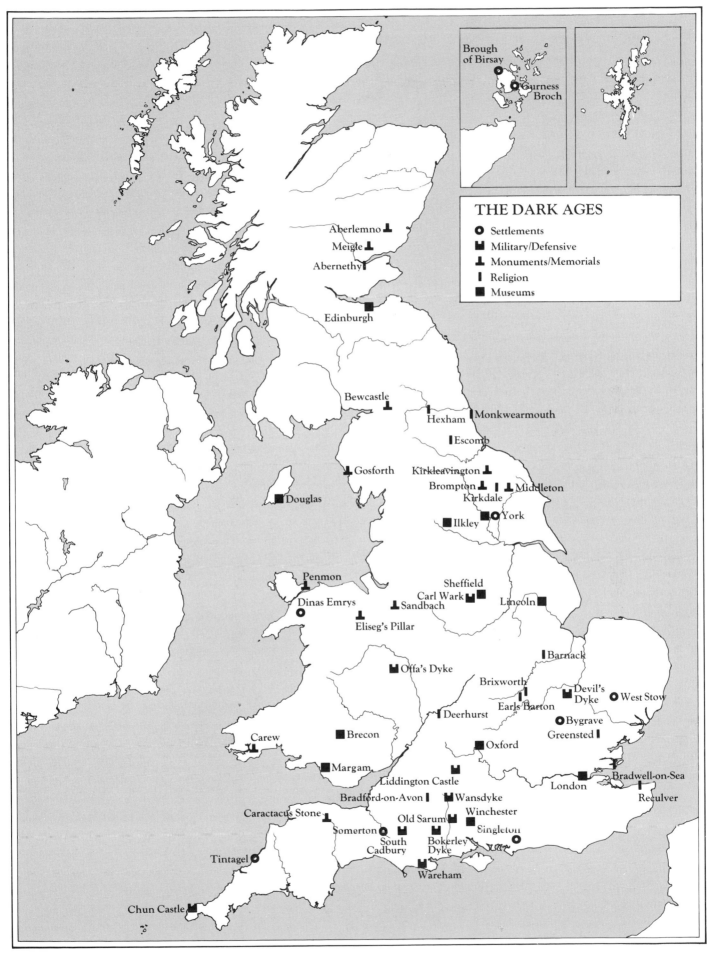

THE DARK AGES

○ Settlements
♜ Military/Defensive
⟘ Monuments/Memorials
▮ Religion
■ Museums

Brough of Birsay
Gurness Broch

Aberlemno
Meigle
Abernethy
Edinburgh

Bewcastle
Hexham
Monkwearmouth
Escomb
Gosforth
Kirkleavington
Douglas
Brompton
Middleton
Kirkdale
Ilkley
York

Penmon
Sheffield
Dinas Emrys
Carl Wark
Sandbach
Lincoln
Eliseg's Pillar

Barnack
Offa's Dyke
Brixworth
Devil's Dyke
West Stow
Earls Barton
Deerhurst
Bygrave
Brecon
Greensted
Carew
Oxford
Margam
Bradwell-on-Sea
Liddington Castle
London
Reculver
Bradford-on-Avon
Wansdyke
Caractacus Stone
Winchester
Old Sarum
Singleton
Somerton
South Cadbury
Bokerley Dyke
Tintagel
Wareham

Chun Castle

173

immensely long period of occupation. Poor old Ethelred moved the Wilton mint here in 1003 when he was being harried by Svein of Denmark. Mint survived though nearby Wilton was sacked. 2m N of Salisbury off A345. D of E. Open standard hours and Sun from 9.30 April to Sept. Admission charge.

South Cadbury (Somerset) Legend places Camelot, seat of King Arthur, at this spot, an isolated hill first fortified in Iron Age times. Topmost rampart refurbished in late 5th–early 6th c with timbers faced in stone. Traces of massive timber gateway at SW end found during excavation, also remains of large timber feasting hall – Arthur's court? Biggest of all contemporary fortified settlements. 5½m SW of Wincanton, ¼m S of South Cadbury village.

Wansdyke (Avon and Wiltshire) Possibly built by Anglo-Saxons of Wessex as defence against their nasty neighbours in the Upper Thames valley after West Saxon king Caewlin's victory over the Brits at Dyrham in 577. In two sections, E half running from Maes Knoll to Bathampton (Avon) and W half from Morgan's Down to Savernake Forest (Wiltshire). Named after pagan god Woden, which tends to confirm that it was built before conversion of Wessex to Christianity in early 7th c. Most impressive sections in W straddling the A361 and continuing along the crest of Marlborough Downs.

Wareham (Dorset) In 9th c Alfred planned network of fortified towns to defend his kingdom against Danes. These 30 'burghs' recorded in document of 914, the 'Burghal Hidage'. Wareham's defences consist of earth bank and deep ditch on three sides. Rivers Piddle and Frome, here only 1m apart, provided defence on N and S sides. Original gridiron pattern of streets survives today. Defences run from W of Castle Mound by River Frome, N up to River Piddle where they follow line of river and after ½m turn back S to Frome. Magnificent early Christian memorials from 7th and 9th c at Church of Lady St Mary, Victorian rebuilding of Saxon original.

MONUMENTS/MEMORIALS

Aberlemno (Tayside) Extraordinary stones carved by Pictish masons between 6th and 8th c. Upright cross slab in kirkyard with vivid battle scene and three stones at Flemington Farm with enigmatic symbols of serpent, disc and other mysteries. One fine early Christian cross with weeping angels. 5m NE of Forfar on B9134.

Bewcastle (Cumbria) Carved in 7th c from single block of stone now about 15ft high (head missing). Three figures on W face, John the Baptist, Christ and a falconer with runic inscriptions between commemorating Alcfrith, son of Oswi. Scrolls of vine fill E side with birds and beasts nibbling at grapes. Pevsner comments: 'There is nothing as perfect of a comparable date in the whole of Europe.' In churchyard of St Cuthbert's, Bewcastle, 10m W of Haltwhistle via A69 and B6318.

Brompton (Yorkshire) Three fine 'hogback' Anglo-Danish tombstones, bow sided and humped. Guardian bears face each other at each end of the tombs, chewing on the interlace that runs along the top ridges. Also Anglo-Danish cross shaft with head. At St Thomas's Church, 1m N of Northallerton.

Caractacus Stone (Somerset) Strange stone about 5ft high isolated on moorland probably set up in 5th c. Writing deciphered only 90 years ago, showing that it is dedicated to *Caraaci nepus*, 'descendant of Caractacus', king of Silures tribe. Excavation has shown that this is not a grave, and the stone's purpose remains mystery. At Spire Cross, beside B3223, 2m SW of Winsford.

Carew (Dyfed) Splendid late Celtic carved cross, best of Pembrokeshire group, showing variety of typical designs, primitive swastika shapes at top and ingenious interlaced designs in lower panels. Bottom-most like an endless maze with no beginning or end. Inscription records that it is 'the cross of Margiteut, son of Etguin' put up about 1033. Close to castle 5m E of Pembroke on A4075.

Eliseg's Pillar (Clwyd) 9th c cross shaft commemorating Eliseg, head of the house of Powys and ancient

Cross 15ft high carved from single stone block, St Cuthbert's, Bewcastle, Cumbria

adversary of Offa of Mercia, written by his great-grandson, Cyngen. Badly beaten up in Civil War and now illegible. Mound on which it stands is said to be burial place of earlier 6th c chieftain. 1½m N of Llangollen by side of A542.

Gosforth (Cumbria) Scenes from Scandinavian mythology decorate tall slender cross in churchyard, round base, turning square on its way up to fine carved head. Odd beasts and fighting men, another man on horseback, but upside down. Also Saxon pieces inside church, two hogback tombstones, one with battle scene. Tiled 'roofs' to tombs, like houses. Cross fragment with snapping dragon. Church of St Mary, 7m SE of Egremont on A595.

Kirkleavington (Yorkshire) Strange Scandinavian figures survive on cross in old Danelaw, man with skirt and helmet and two birds, another man with two animal heads in profile, oddly nightmarish reminders of dark Nordic forebears: 'gone, long gone, fast in grave's grasp while 50 fathers and sons have passed.' Church of St Martin on A19, S of Middlesbrough.

Meigle (Tayside) Small museum with 25 sculpted stones of Celtic Christian times, a splendid collection of Dark Age work. Grotesque animals cavort around Biblical figures in strange mixture of old and new religions. On A94 20m N of Perth. D of E. Open standard hours. Closed Sun. Admission charge.

Middleton (Yorkshire) Small group of elaborate cross shafts done by English sculptors in 10th c for Scandinavian patrons. Finest shows bold Viking warrior with spear, axe, sword and shield, also knife

Perfect small Saxon church, Bradford-on-Avon, Wilts., built about 705 by St Adhelm

hanging from belt. On the reverse writhes big dragon, essential element of Viking mythology: 'the primeval enemy that haunts the dusk: the scaly malicious worm which seeks out funeral mounds.' Church of St Andrew, 2m NW of Pickering on A170.

Penmon (Anglesey) Cool dark nave of St Seiriol's Church has fine Celtic crosses brought in from nearby field and font of AD1000. Footpath leads past silted up priory fishponds to serenity of St Seiriol's cell with spring where he baptised converts in 540. Original church at Penmon raided and burnt by Danes in 971. On E tip of island, N of Beaumaris via B5109.

Sandbach (Cheshire) Two crosses in market place smashed by philistine Puritans and later used in masonry of other buildings. Collected together again and rebuilt in present position in 1816. Sculpted with elaborate religious scenes showing conversion to Christianity of Penda, king of Mercia between 632–654. On A533, N of Stoke-on-Trent.

RELIGION

Abernethy (Tayside) Round towers borrowed from Irish ecclesiastical architecture survive here and at Brechin (Angus), result of Irish infiltration of Pictland sometime in 9th c. On A913 S of Perth. D of E. Normally open standard hours but temporary closure for repairs imminent.

Barnack (Cambridgeshire) Betjeman in 'Collins' Guide to Parish Churches' calls this church of St John the Baptist typical of that inspired architectural hotch-potch which is the English parish church but Saxon core still evident as earliest ingredient in architectural pudding. Superb late Saxon carving of Christ in majesty. 3m E of Stamford in B1448.

Bradford-on-Avon (Wiltshire) Church of St Lawrence was forgotten for centuries until Victorian age when nave was being used as school and chancel as cottage. Clue to its original state was fine carving of two angels hovering with outstretched arms high up above chancel arch. Restoration revealed perfect small Saxon church, probably built by St Adhelm about 705, one of oldest intact buildings in Britain. 8m SE of Bath on A363.

Bradwell-on-Sea (Essex) Church of St Peter's-on-the-Wall built mostly of stone from Roman fort of Othona which stood here at mouth of Blackwater river. Chancel and chapels destroyed, but nave survives, though battered by use as barn when huge openings were made for farm carts. Built by St Cedd c 654, first known church in Essex. Approached by cart track through fields off B1021, 7m NE of Burnham-on-Crouch.

Brixworth (Northamptonshire). All Saints is finest Anglo-Saxon church in the country, mostly original 8th c work, though spire and belfry added 600 years later. Curious underground corridor round apse at E end, possibly passage for pilgrims round shrine. Archaeological game in spotting amount of re-used Roman material in building which was made by monks from mother-house at Peterborough. 7m N of Northampton on A508.

Deerhurst (Gloucestershire) St Mary's Church was scene of historic meeting between Edmund of Wessex and Cnut of Mercia after Edmund's crushing defeat at Battle of Ashington, beginning of 11th c. Two superpowers decided to carve England up between them, but within month of agreement Edmund died (or was murdered) and Cnut, the winner, took all. Triangular headed windows high up on W wall and magnificent intricately scrolled Saxon font. 7m NW of Cheltenham via A38 and B4213.

Earls Barton (Northamptonshire) Church of All Saints was built as refuge as well as for worship when Danes were harrying and hunting. Main door could be sealed off and tower entered by ladder up to first floor door. Church shows several typical features of Anglo-Saxon building: long vertical stones alternating with similar stones set horizontally, strip work panelling on outside imitating timberwork, and belfry opening with central shaft supporting single stone slab as thick as wall. 4m SW of Wellingborough on B573.

Escomb (Durham) Church of St John, a tiny building with tall, narrow interior and small widely-splayed windows, incongruous hangover from Saxon times in blackened former pit village. Bare and simple. Lettered stone from Roman fort at Binchester built into N wall and strange sundial above porch. 2m W of Bishop Auckland off B6282.

Greensted (Essex) Church of St Andrew is oldest surviving example of timber Saxon building. Nave walls made of split oak trunks standing vertically on end. Chancel is 16th c work but nave dates from 850 when timber from Essex forests easier to come by than stone. Setting still well-wooded. 12½m W of Chelmsford off A113.

Hexham (Northumberland) Original church founded by St Wilfrid in 674, a splendid affair with spiral staircases, colonnaded nave and crypt. Wilfrid's biographer, Ennius, said that he had heard of 'no other on a grander scale on this side of the Alps'. Church sacked by Danes in 876 and only crypt remains of original building; rest of 12th and 13th c. Stone 'throne' in abbey may also be Wilfrid's, used for coronation of Northumbrian kings. Later known as Frith Stool and used by fugitives as Sanctuary seat. Abbey is off Market Place in town centre, 20m W of Newcastle off A69.

Kirkdale (Yorkshire) Small Saxon church of St Gregory with remarkable sundial c 1055. Dial designed on octaval system – 24 hrs divided into 8 equal sections – each 3hr period called a tid. Lines marked with cross bar show 6am 9am noon etc. Intermediate lines mark 1½hr. Good Anglo-Saxon carved coffin lids inside church and cross with Crucifixion scene. 4m E of Helmsley off A170.

Monkwearmouth (Tyne and Wear) Church of St Peter with St Cuthbert founded as monastery in 674 by Benedict Biscop on land given by friendly king Ecgfrith of Northumbria. Superbly equipped with books, relics, paintings which Benedict brought back from Rome on 5 separate journeys. W wall of nave and lower stages of tower survive with many fragments of carved stonework preserved inside. Now stands amidst industrial decay of NE Sunderland, via A183.

Reculver (Kent) Ruins of Saxon church stand within walls of crumbling Roman shore fort, half washed away by sea. Church originally a mynster built on ground given in 669 by King Egbert of Kent. 3½m E of Herne Bay off A299.

PEOPLE

Athelstan 'The firm opinion is still current among the English,' wrote William of Malmesbury in the 1130s, 'that no-one more just and learned administered the state.' Most powerful ruler since the Romans' departure had condemned country to centuries of fragmented tribal rule. He revitalised great monastic centre of Malmesbury where he gave the church land and relics and commissioned a holy shrine for St Adhelm. Present remains are later Norman work but battered recumbent effigy on 15th c table tomb is said to represent Athelstan, who was buried here.

St Cuthbert Died in his hermitage on Farne Island in 687, buried at Lindisfarne but later moved by monks when they abandoned Lindisfarne in 875 because of Viking attacks on E coast. Little left of original monastery apart from some inscribed stones. Existing ruins are of priory founded by Durham in 11th c. Saxon remains, sculpture and copy of Lindisfarne gospels in site museum on SW tip of island. D of E. Open standard hours and Sun from 9.30 April–Sept. Admission charge.

Relics eventually found their way after more than 100 years of restless wandering with guardian monks, to Durham Cathedral. Cross of gold and garnet, portable altar of wood and silver, large ivory comb and wooden coffin carved with saints and angels. Most remarkable survivals are rare vestments embroidered with silk presented to shrine by King Athelstan in 934. Museum in cathedral undercroft. Open Mon–Sat 10–4.30, Sun 2–4.30. Admission charge.

MUSEUMS

Brecon Brecknock Museum, Powys, has good collection of early Christian monuments gathered from surrounding villages, also dug-out canoe from lake village at Llangorse. Open Mon–Sat 10–5.

Douglas The Manx Museum, Isle of Man. Important collection representing both Norse settlement of 9th c and earlier tradition of Christian Celts. At Balladoole, Viking boat burial overlay graves of Christian cemetery on same site. Hoards of Viking ornaments and coins. Open Mon–Sat 10–5.

Edinburgh National Museum of Antiquities of Scotland, Queen St. Tools, weapons, bone comb and simple beaker from 7th c lake village at Buston Crannog. Marvellous Pictish sculptures, especially one of bibulous Pict drinking from curly horn cup, his horse looking rather wearied by it all. St Ninian's Isle treasure was buried in 800, perhaps to keep it from Viking raiders: fine Pictish silver work. Open Mon–Sat 10–5, Sun 2–5.

Ilkley Manor House Museum, Castle Yard. Small collection here of cross fragments, one dredged out of River Wharfe close by with fox and grapes in scroll work. Another piece seems to be unfinished, lightly incised with interlace pattern before proper chipping out began. Museum close to All Saints' churchyard where there are three Anglo-Saxon crosses of mid 9th c. Tallest has four evangelists in symbolic form and strange twisting beasts. Museum open Tues–Sun, April–Oct 10–6, Nov–March 10–5

Lincoln City and County Museum, Broadgate. 'Best Anglo-Saxon collection in the country,' says its keeper. 'In quantity if not in quality.' Rich haul from Anglo-Saxon cemetery (1,800 burials) on Loveden Hill: urns, swords, bucket mounts of iron with sheet bronze repoussé work, thin bronze hanging bowl, ceremonial whetstone. Open Mon–Sat 10–5.30, Sun 2.30–5. Admission charge.

London British Museum, Great Russell St. Treasures from the Sutton Hoo ship burial near Woodbridge (Suffolk), possibly that of Redwald, king of East Anglia who died c 624. Impressive helmet made in central Sweden and perfect purse lid enamelled with strange beasts and birds. Unique iron stand, possibly some kind of standard bearer. Beautiful Fuller brooch is 9th c work of silver with black inlay. Franks casket, only 9in long, carved from whalebone in early 8th c. Runic inscriptions surround scenes from Norse mythology. Open Mon–Sat 10–5, Sun 2.30–6.

Margam Abbey Museum has ancient crosses and sculpted stones from Dark Ages. Earliest are 5th–7th c with simple epitaphs, some in Irish ogham script, made up of groups of long and short strokes across base line. Open Sat, Sun, Wed March–Oct 2–5, Nov–Feb 2–4. Admission charge.

Oxford Ashmolean Museum, Beaumont St, has rich haul of goods from Anglo-Saxon cemeteries, gold, jewellery and weapons. Abingdon sword was found in tributary of Thames, iron with fine silver decoration on handle. Also stirrups of iron inlaid with brass wire. Open Mon–Sat 10–4, Sun 2–4.

Sheffield City Museum, Weston Park. Stunning helmet from Benty Grange, unique in design: metal bands originally overlaid with horn strips fixed in criss-cross pattern, surmounted by crest of boar with garnet eyes. Good material from Cow Low, nr Buxton: necklace, pendant, gold pins, rare glass bowl. Open Mon–Sat 10–5, Sun 11–5. (Open until 8 June–Aug).

Winchester City Museum, The Square. Carved ivory plaque of about AD1000, sculpted architectural fragments from old minster. Pottery, brooches, sword from pagan cemeteries at Winnall and Worthy Park. Open April–Sept, Mon–Sat 10–5, Sun 2–5, Oct–March, Tues–Sat 10–5, Sun 2–4. Admission charge.

York Yorkshire Museum, Museum Gardens. Major collection of Viking artefacts from intensive city digs at Coppergate over the last few years. Shoes, skates, pins, scales, amber beads, leather tunics, bowls, locks, fascinating picture of Vikings at home rather than at war. Open Mon–Sat 10–5, Sun 1–5. Admission charge.

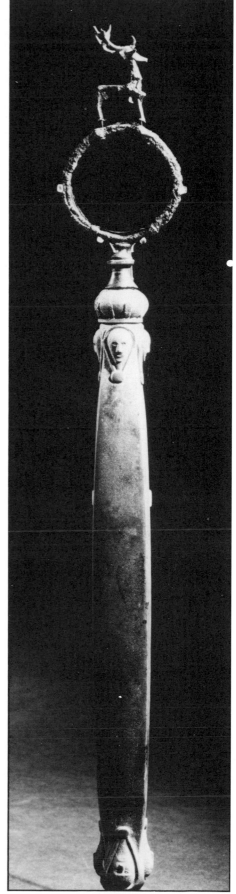

Ceremonial whetstone surmounted by bronze stag from Sutton Hoo Collection, British Museum

THE
NORMANS
by Jessica York

CATHEDRALS/ABBEYS

Castle Acre Priory (Norfolk) Ornateness of W front of ruins gives best idea of style favoured by Cluniac houses in Britain. Cluny in France was one of most powerful religious centres of period. But of its major centres in England, such as Reading, Lewes and Northampton, little beyond the odd capital survives. Open mid-March–mid-October every day 9.30–6.30, winter closes at 4 and on Sun morning. Admission charge. On A1065 N of Thetford.

Durham Cathedral An unforgettable experience – the high point of Norman architecture. Its designer found solution to problems of stone roofing that preoccupied European Romanesque architects. Although this church was built early (1093–1133) it anticipates Gothic in several respects. The ribbed vault, normally associated with Gothic, is an integral part of the Norman design. Complete shift of scale from earlier cathedrals – columns and piers of nave arcade have grown in girth and height, with their bold ornamentation dominate the interior. At the time seemed mainly influential for its use of chevron ornament, which spread from here to become most characteristic form of Norman decoration. At W end of cathedral, the Galilee was built c 1175 – its delicacy delightful contrast to rest of cathedral. Interesting remains of decorative mural painting here, which relate to Durham style of manuscript illumination. The famous bronze sactuary knocker is now in the Cathedral Treasury. Open weekdays 10–4.30, Sun 2–4.30. Admission charge.

Ely Cathedral Founded as a Benedictine abbey. Built late 11th and 12th c, complete nave and transepts give an admirable sense of the scale of Norman building in England. Nave one of finest in the country. Space accentuated by homogeneity of architecture which has alternating scheme of cylindrical and compound piers, with thin shafts rising the full height to restored 19th c painted wood ceiling. Unusual centrally placed W tower used to be flanked by 2 symmetrical transepts, now only one remains. Do not miss marvellously ornate sculpture of the Prior's Door in the S wall. There is also a tomb slab depicting St Michael holding the soul of a bishop like a baby on his knee. (Commemoration of dead in monumental tomb sculptures began in 12th c.)

Fountains Abbey (Yorkshire) Cistercians were the other very powerful religious order who established themselves here. By middle of 12th c Cistercians had 50 abbeys. Isolation of sites reflects their rejection of worldliness, which extended to sculpture, painting, colour, precious materials and bell towers. Nave and transepts mid-12th c. D of E. Open Nov–Feb Mon–Sat 9.30–4, Sun 2–4, March–April, Oct daily, 9.30–5.30, May, Sept daily 9.30–7, June–August daily 9.30–9. Admission charge. Off B6265 W of Ripon, Yorkshire.

Gloucester Cathedral Although this cathedral is a mongrel, with Gothic choir and nave vaulting, its nave is interesting because it embodies a new approach to architecture, which suggests that by 1090 Benedictine monks of W country both here and at Tewkesbury had connections with Burgundy. Instead of Norman idea of thick wall pierced by arcading, nave has continuous series of monumental drum piers. Crypt at Gloucester shows what plan of Norman choir would have been.

Norwich Cathedral Benedictine, begun 1096. Mainly built during the lifetime of first bishop of Norwich, Herbert Losinga – a courtier bishop, whose simony to secure the bishopric was on such a grand scale that it caused public outcry. Similar architectural format to Ely with an even longer nave, but here the apsidal choir with its ambulatory remains. The effect is compromised by exuberant 15th c vaulting and also by Gothic clerestory windows in the choir, rebuilt after the tower fell down.

Peterborough Cathedral The most completely Norman of several cathedrals built in a similar format to St Etienne at Caen in Normandy. Mostly 12th c, with the grand W front and painted wood ceiling of nave – a precious survival, being completed between 1201–18. The rebuilding of the church was undertaken after a disastrous fire gutted the Saxon Benedictine abbey. The tower burnt for 9 days, scattering red hot ashes on the monastery. There are 2 early monumental tomb slabs here, with effigies of 2 abbots.

Romsey Abbey (Hampshire) Benedictine nunnery favoured because Henry I's wife Matilda lived there before her marriage. Sophisticated architecturally – in one bay of nave a giant column rises through 2 storeys with subsidiary arches half way up to support the gallery.

St Albans Cathedral Originally Benedictine abbey. Built in a jumble of different styles, but central sec-

The nave, Durham Cathedral, where Norman architecture can be seen at its finest

tion around tower, crossing, transepts and several bays of nave show architectural style Normans brought with them from France. Built of brick collected from local Roman ruins. At the time it would have been decorated with painting. Examples survive from 12th and 13th c. St Albans was a centre for painting – the 'Albani Psalter' produced here influenced whole school of illumination.

St Andrews Cathedral. A noble ruin, once the biggest church in Scotland. Built between 1161 and 1318. Fire, storms and the iconoclastic followers of John Knox began its decline, which was completed by the townspeople who used its stones as building materials. Now only grand fragments remain including S wall of nave, E and W gables, portions of choir. D of E. Open standard hours.

Southwell Minster Now a cathedral, Southwell was a collegiate church, housing a group of priests called a college of secular canons. Powerful enough in 12th c to own a quarter of Nottinghamshire. Its restored silhouette of 3 towers is closer to original simplicity of early Norman architecture than anywhere else in England. Built in early decades of 12th c. Internally, nave follows entirely different format from other cathedrals. Sense of one row of arcades standing on top of another, gives strong horizontal emphasis. In N transept is lintel carved with St Michael fighting a dragon.

Winchester Cathedral The central core of the great Norman church still survives. It replaced Saxon abbey pulled down in great wave of building which followed the Conquest. In mid-12th c Conqueror's grandson, Henry of Blois, was bishop. He was a splendid patron of arts, encouraging illuminators to come and work at Winchester (*see* Manuscript Illumination, Winchester Bible). The black Tournai marble font probably dates from this time.

PARISH CHURCHES

Barfreston (Kent) S door of church of St Nicholas decorated with delicate reliefs. The backwards bending birds of Barfreston can also be found on Notre-Dame-la-Grande at Poitiers. Off A2 NW of Dover.

Dalmeny (Lothian) St Cuthbert's is best preserved Norman church in Scotland. Built in mid-12th c by Earl Gospatric. Follows 3 apartment plan with apse lower than chancel, nave with new W tower highest part. Only later addition to this plan was a N aisle. Fine carving around S door, including interlaced arches above. May have been influenced by nearby Dunfermline Abbey. Just outside Edinburgh W on A90.

Iffley (Oxfordshire) St Mary is a fine late Norman church. Simple 3 apartment structure originally, but chancel rebuilt in 13th c. Arches under tower splendidly ornamented as are W front and S door. Latter has capitals carved with centaur, Samson and lion and horsemen fighting. W front has signs of zodiac and 2 rows of sinister beakhead ornament. Surprisingly, W front's circular window is 19th c, but there are traces to suggest there was one there in

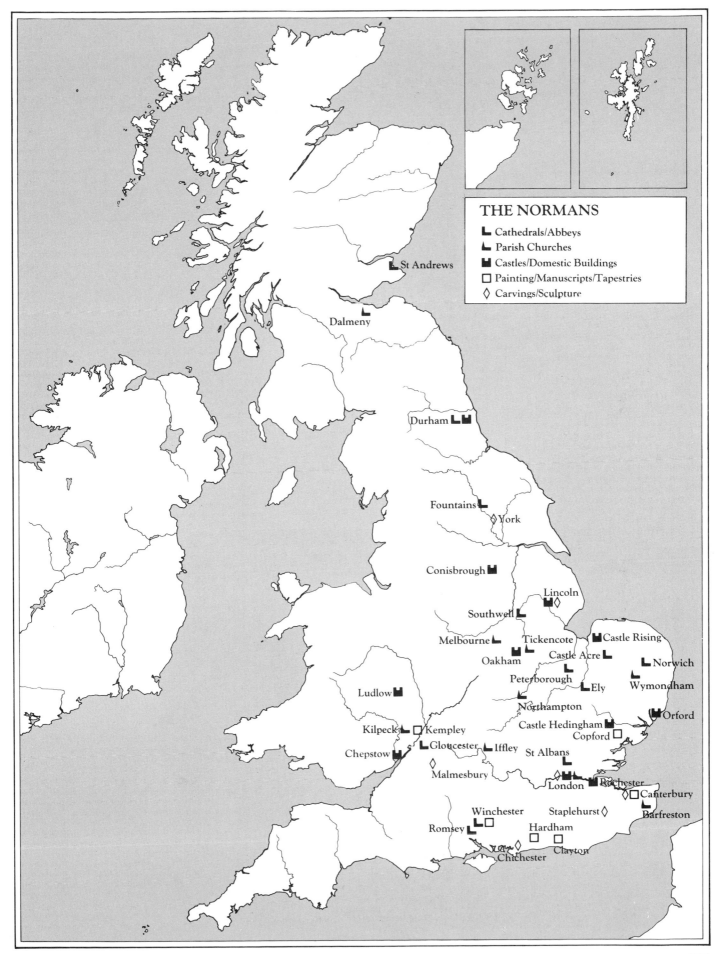

THE NORMANS

⌐ Cathedrals/Abbeys
⌐ Parish Churches
◪ Castles/Domestic Buildings
☐ Painting/Manuscripts/Tapestries
◇ Carvings/Sculpture

St Andrews

Dalmeny

Durham

Fountains
York

Conisbrough

Lincoln

Southwell

Melbourne   Tickencote   Castle Rising

Oakham   Castle Acre   Norwich

Peterborough   Ely   Wymondham

Ludlow

Northampton

Kilpeck   Kempley   Castle Hedingham   Orford

Gloucester   Iffley   Copford

Chepstow   St Albans

Malmesbury   London   Rochester

Winchester   Staplehurst   Canterbury

Romsey   Hardham   Barfreston

Chichester   Clayton

177

Bold carving on the font at St Michael's Church, Castle Frome, Hereford and Worcs.

1170. Just outside Oxford S off A423.

Kilpeck (Hereford and Worcester) SS Mary and David is a lovely little church of 3 apartments – nave, choir and apsidal presbytery with chevroned rib vault. Chevrons are taken up again on chancel arch, but it also has a series of apostles standing one above other. Famous for its sculpture – at its best outside on the S door. Hard local sandstone cut with brilliant sharpness into figures and monsters (*see* Fonts – Herefordshire school). Off A465 SW of Hereford.

London St Bartholomew-the-Great, Smithfield, was founded in 1123 by Henry I's jester for Augustinian canons, who were most widely spread order in England. The large, sombre church that remains is only the choir and transepts of the original priory. This and Worksop Priory are the best surviving examples of the 173 houses the Augustinians had here by 1215.

Melbourne (Derbyshire) SS Michael and Mary is a remarkably grand church, still splendidly complete, for this comparatively small town. Explained by the fact that manor and rectory here were granted to Ethelwold, Bishop of Carlisle, at his inauguration to the newly created see in 1134. Most parish churches are planned as some variation on a sequence of apartments (*see* Iffley and Kilpeck), but at Melbourne you can see the best surviving example of a cruciform plan with aisled nave, a central and 2 W towers, finished *c* 1160. Off A453 S of Derby.

Northampton St Peter's is another church remarkable for its carving. Built on an aisled plan, using the alternating bay common in the cathedrals, but unusual in parish churches. Its proximity to castle perhaps accounts for the ambition of design. Thought to have been built about 1150, before growth of Oxford, when there was a flourishing school of learning in Northampton with famous scholars of science and rhetoric.

Tickencote (Leicestershire) Church of St Peter has massive chancel arch which completely dominates the small church. In chancel mysterious use of a sexpartite rib vault, known elsewhere in this country only in Gothic form at Canterbury, suggests a strong connection with Normandy and a date for the church of around 1160–70. Nave much restored at end of 18th c. On A1 NW of Stamford.

Wymondham (Norfolk) SS Mary and Thomas (dedicated to most famous saint of period Thomas Becket who was murdered 1170). This church was part of a Benedictine abbey. In 15th c parishioners altered clerestory, roof, aisles and added W tower in response to one put up by monks, but there remains fine Norman nave built between 1107 and 1130. On A11 SW of Norwich.

CASTLES/DOMESTIC BUILDINGS

Castle Hedingham (Essex) Private castle probably built by Veres family around 1140. Shows, completely preserved, style of castle building common in first half of c. Four storey, square keep in middle of large bailey is smaller and more elegant version of main idea of Rochester, with ornamental carving surviving on doorways, windows, capitals and fireplaces. Open May–Sept, Tues–Sat 1–5, Bank Hols 11–5. Admission charge. On B1058 SW of Sudbury.

Castle Rising (Norfolk) Gives best idea of a 'forebuilding'. Built to protect entrance and provide extra accommodation, it extends from main body of the keep and is reached by a fine enclosed staircase. Built mid-12th c by William of Albini, who married Henry I's widow. Archaic design from military point of view. Keep rectangular and lower than most – it has 3 storeys. Inside apartments are divided by a crosswall. Castle surrounded by oval earth ringwork, in which are remains of apsidal chapel. There is also a Norman parish church at Castle Rising with good font – one of a series in neighbourhood which were probably produced by same mason's yard. Cats' heads carved on font also decorate stairs at castle. D of E. Open standard hours plus April–Sept Sun from 9.30. Admission charge. 4m NE of King's Lynn off A148.

Chepstow Castle (Gwent) Probably the earliest stone castle in Britain, begun the year after the Conquest by William's relative William fitz Osbern. Narrow site of cliffs between River Wye and ravine meant no room for some usual features of Norman castles like a keep, but its stone hall of standard two storey Norman design. Major additions in 13th c include bailey and twin-towered gatehouse. D of E. Open standard hours plus April–Sept Sun from 9.30. N of town centre.

Conisbrough Castle (Yorkshire) Superb sculptured limestone ashlar keep – cylindrical with 6 wedge shaped buttresses on spreading plinth. Built on a natural hill with curtain wall which also has spreading plinth. Keep's basement houses well and has domed vault. On floors above – carried in thickness of wall – are stairs, fireplaces, lavatories, sinks, an oven, a chapel, cisterns and pigeon roosts. Militarily more advanced than Orford though built very shortly after – buttresses replace vulnerable turret corners. D of E. Open standard hours plus April–Sept Sun from 9.30. Admission charge. On A630 NE of Rotherham.

Durham Castle Much altered and now part of university: still has some very splendid fragments, which indicate it must once have been lavish enough to make a worthy companion to the cathedral. Built for the bishops, whose secular duty it was to raise an army and if necessary command it, especially against the Scots, should the need arise. Chapel's basement belongs to early phase of building at beginning of

Ivory liturgical comb with carved figures, *c.* 1120, in Victoria and Albert Museum

Orford Castle, Suffolk: Henry II's ultimate deterrent, begun 1166, finished seven years later

12th c. It has series of veined columns with crudely carved capitals. These contrast with highly sophisticated geometric carving of doorway to lower hall from second half of century. Open first 3 weeks April, July–Sept Mon, Wed, Sat 2–4, and weekdays 10–12, 2–4.30, other months Mon, Wed, Sat 2–4. Admission charge.

Lincoln Very few domestic buildings survive from period, since it would have been unusual for them to be built in stone or other durable material. The Jew's House is rare example of the town house, built c 1170–80, consisting of 2 rooms, one on each floor. Upper room has fireplace, indicating it was living room, lower one for storage. There is no longstanding evidence to connect house with Jews, although there were Jewish money lenders in Lincoln who could have afforded it, Aaron, for example, who held the cathedral plate and jewels for 7 years as security against a loan, until they were redeemed in 1173. Now a shop.

London The Tower of London's White Tower, so-called because it was white-washed to protect the masonry – stone brought from Caen in Normandy – was probably designed by Gundulf, Bishop of Rochester, who was its chief surveyor and overseer. Prestige building – when completed in 1097 it was probably biggest stone keep in western Europe. Original bailey enclosed by bank and ditch on two sides and Roman city wall on rest. By end of 12th c much money was spent on improving defences – SW Bell Tower and some adjacent curtain walling date from then. White Tower has lost is original entrance. St John's Chapel particularly interesting because it still has original vaulting. Open March–Oct weekdays 9.30–5, Sun 2–5, Nov–Feb weekdays 9.30–4. Admission charge.

Ludlow Castle (Salop) Like Richmond Castle in Yorkshire, which survives almost unaltered, Ludlow is an example of late 11th c plan using curtain walling

Spirited horse and bird from late 11th century manuscript in the Bodleian, Oxford

protected by projecting towers. Original entrance through T-shaped gatehouse was later blocked and new entrance formed. In courtyard is circular nave (chancel destroyed) of castle chapel, probably built about 1130, modelled on Church of the Holy Sepulchre in Jerusalem. Much decorative carving remains on blind arcading, chancel arch and doorway. Castle has later additions due to strategic importance on Welsh border. Open May–Sept daily 10.30–6, Oct–April 10.30–4. Admission charge.

Oakham Castle (Leicestershire) Best surviving example of an aisled hall of type traditional in England. Became popular format for non-military manor house (Westminster Hall is superior version) and influenced design of Oxbridge halls. Doors at E end would have led to buttery, pantry and kitchens, built of less permanent material. Exquisitely carved column capitals with acanthus foliage and corbel figures indicate hall was built late 12th c. Surrounded by earth bank and may have had stone curtain wall and moat, though these could have been added later. Open April–Oct Sun, Mon 2–5.30, Tues–Sat 10–1, 2–5.30, Nov–March same days but closing at 4.

Orford Castle (Suffolk) Experimental polygonal keep (circular inside). Built by Henry II to control Suffolk coast and thwart Earl of Norfolk's ambitions – advanced design seems to have deterred him from attacking it during revolt of 1173. Started 1166, it took 7 years to build and cost £1,400. Keep surrounded by a double ditch, dug after it was built. D of E. Open standard hours plus April–Sept from 9.30. Admission charge. On B1084 on coast NE of Ipswich.

Rochester Castle (Kent) Massive keep 113ft high and 70ft square, has corner towers like Tower of London. Built by Archbishop of Canterbury with Henry I's consent. These square keeps were most vulnerable at their corners, as was shown in 1215 when King John besieged one of rebel barons who had signed Magna Carta here. John's mercenaries were quartered in cathedral. His sappers undermined SW corner of keep, but garrison held out behind internal cross-wall. After 7 weeks, starvation forced them to surrender. D of E. Open standard hours plus Sun April–Sept from 9.30. Admission charge.

PAINTINGS/MANUSCRIPTS/ TAPESTRIES

Canterbury Cathedral St Gabriel's chapel in crypt has Christ in glory on ceiling and another depiction of heavenly Jerusalem. On the walls are scenes from life of Christ and St John. All preserved because chapel was walled up in 1199. In St Anselm's chapel is finest mural painting to survive from the period. Panel roughly 5ft square represents single figure of St Paul and the viper. The strong linear style suggests Byzantine influence and has a marked similarity to painting in the Bury Bible. Well enough preserved to give clear idea of colour composition. Probably mid-12th c.

Clayton (Sussex) Scheme of mural at St John the Baptist church is early version of Last Judgment based on apocalyptic vision of St John. In upper zone of nave you can find death of antichrist, blessed wearing crowns, heavenly Jerusalem, an apocalyptic rider etc. Figures are monumental and very impressive. On A273 N of Brighton.

Copford (Essex) Church of St Michael and All Angels was painted throughout and is now quite heavily restored. Apse vault has Christ in majesty and there is also unusual depiction of raising of Jairus's daughter which is strikingly well-composed. Probably painted towards end of 12th c. Off A12 W of Colchester.

Hardham (Sussex) St Botolph's church was entirely covered in painting, much of which survives. Programme seems to relate to theme of salvation with 'torments of damned' at W end, Christ in majesty on E wall. In between are scenes from infancy and passion of Christ, life of St George, adoration of lamb, labours of months and most memorably of all Adam and Eve, executed in a heavy linear style. Church built 1125, murals probably date from then too. On A29 NE of Bognor Regis.

Kempley (Gloucestershire) St Mary's Church has completely painted chancel. Barrel vault has Christ in majesty with his feet on rainbow, surrounded by symbols of evangelists. On walls row of apostles on each side. Painted in earth colours, predominantly red, yellow and grey. Probably mid-12th c. Off A449 NE of Ross-on-Wye.

Bayeux Tapestry A magnificent strip of embroidery, wool on linen, over 230ft long, telling story of Conquest from Norman point of view. Original still at Bayeux in Normandy – its home since 1070s – but there are replicas here to give you some idea, although being divided up into panels they lose the comic strip, continuous-running-story effect of the original. Reading Museum has one Victorian panel on show and Battle Museum, across the road from the abbey founded by William at the site of the Battle of Hastings, has several large panels. Reading Museum open weekdays 10–5.30, Saturdays 10–5. Battle Museum, open Easter–Sept, 10–1, 2–5, Sun 2.30–5.30. Admission charge.

Manuscript Illumination The most impressive painting to survive from the period is in illuminated manuscripts. As well as elaborate decorative initials, the famous 12th c bibles and psalters often had full-page illustrations of superb quality. They have an intensity in the use of colour that has not been equalled in English painting since. Unfortunately the fragility of these great books means they are difficult to put on show and when they are, you can only see one page. They are usually owned by libraries with minimal facilities for exhibiting them so are only occasionally on view, otherwise only scholars get near them. British Museum always has a display including Shaftesbury Psalter, psalter of Henry of Blois, a bestiary, Bede's 'Life of St Cuthbert'. There are sometimes 12th c manuscripts on show at the Bodleian Library, Oxford, at cathedral libraries, at some Oxford and Cambridge college libraries – notably Corpus Christi College, Cambridge, which owns both the Bury and the Dover Bibles and may occasionally have them on view. British Museum open weekdays 10–6, Sun 2.30–6.

Winchester Bible Bible in Winchester Cathedral library is probably one the monks had made to read aloud at meals. Six different artists worked on it. Apart from 2 'full-page spreads', all the rest of the painting is confined to so-called 'historiated initials' – scenes illustrating the page's text framed in the initial letter. This is different from the earlier bibles

Ivory crozier head with clinging figures, Victoria and Albert Museum

which had full-page narrative scenes, whilst 11th c Norman manuscripts tended to have figures trapped in the foliage of purely decorative initials. Library open weekdays 10.30–12.30, 2.30–4.30. Admission charge.

CARVINGS/SCULPTURE

Canterbury Cathedral Crypt here is 190ft long with marvellous carved capitals on plain columns alternating with plain capitals on carved columns. Carved by several different hands; some unfinished show they must have been worked on in situ. There are animals playing musical instruments – goat and fox on recorder, griffin on harp, Samson fighting the lion and a dog fighting a dragon etc. All done in a vigorous, crisp style, full of movement. Probably early 12th c.

Chichester Cathedral Reliefs of raising of Lazarus and Mary and Martha greeting Christ at gates of Jerusalem. The Chichester reliefs of Caen stone are almost certainly of Norman date though naturally influenced by Saxon art. Interesting as narrative – Christ's relationship to his followers remains very similar in both reliefs, only what is happening on left of slab alters.

Lincoln Cathedral Frieze on W front has series of reliefs of Old Testament scenes and some related to the Last Judgment. They run along top of doors in an otherwise later facade. Remarkable for their storytelling strength – the panel of Dives in story of Dives and Lazarus is particularly good example. There is no mistaking the self-satisfaction of this rich trio.

Malmesbury Abbey (Wiltshire) Outer door of S porch has 8 orders of mouldings running all the way round. Richly carved scrolls and interlacing alternate with 3 orders of medallions with scenes from the Old and New Testaments. Much of this is badly weathered and difficult to make out. Tympanum over inside door has Christ in glory and down sides of porch are rows of 6 seated apostles. The complete way in which this sculptural scheme has been thought out prefigures the great W fronts of gothic cathedrals. On A429 N of Chippenham.

Staplehurst (Kent) Ironwork on S door of All Saints Church is covered with straps of elaborately hammered ironwork decoration, including fish and a dragon. Again difficult to date since it is very similar to Viking and Saxon forms, but church is Norman. Probably late 11th c. On A229 S of Maidstone.

Victoria and Albert Museum Gloucester Candlestick of highly intricate polished bronze is a tour de force of craftsmanship – a tangle of scrolls and stalks into which are entwined figures and animals. Dragons' chins are the feet on which the whole thing

St Cuthbert rebuking crows: page from Bede's Life of St Cuthbert in British Library

stands. Made in 1110. Victoria and Albert also has tiny fragments of an ivory cross with man and winged lion caught in scroll-work, beautifully carved and very similar to candlestick. Among their other early ivories is wedge-shaped relief in ivory of Adoration of Magi, carved with superb precision and detail, and most impressive crozier head crowded with figures but composed with great subtlety – a masterpiece. Enamels, including some similar in figure and drapery style to the Winchester Bible. They are scenes from life of St Paul and may have been used as plaques on an altar frontal. Open Mon–Thur and Sat 10–5.50, Sun 2.30–5.50. Closed Fri.

York Sculpture from St Mary's Abbey in Yorkshire Museum. Column statues of prophets and apostles on an altogether different scale from earlier sculpture – life-size and almost free-standing instead of relief. Extraordinary grace and idealisation of St John figure, particularly, reminds us the Greeks and Romans weren't so far away. Only 4 complete figures and other fragments left from what must have been splendid abbey doorway, heralding beginning of Gothic. Dated about 1200–10. In York Minster library is an interesting relief sculpture in complete contrast. Slab has weathered to be truly expressionist rendering of devils in the flames of hell, Yorkshire Museum open Mon–Sat 10–5, Sun 1–5. Admission charge.

Fonts Like tympana, fonts provide an opportunity for great invention on part of sculptor. A great range from crude village craftsmanship (Hook Norton, Oxfordshire), imported black marble fonts (East Meon, Hampshire), mass produced lead fonts (6 similar in Severn Valley – lead from Mendips). Masons could produce several similar fonts in their yard, instead of working each individually on site.

Great variations also in form and subject. At Holy Trinity, Lenton, in Nottingham is large square font with each side divided into 4 scenes from life of Christ; square font at Burnham Deepdale, Norfolk, has labours of the months. At Southrop, Gloucestershire, the round font has an arcade with figures representing virtues and vices.

Cornish fonts are a more complicated shape – bowl supported on central stem, with 4 narrow columns topped with angel faces and wings making corners. Foliage and serpents in deep relief decorate the bowl (Roche, Cornwall).

Herefordshire school – fonts with vigorous biblical scenes and an edging of platted stone (Eardisley, Hereford and Worcester). St Nicholas at Brighton has a font unlike any other English carving – Last Supper, row of monumental figures with marvellous curly moustaches and beards.

Ivory Chessmen from the Isle of Lewis (Outer Hebrides) Now in British Museum and National Museum of Antiquities of Scotland (67 in London and 11 in Edinburgh). Famous hoard of worried chess-pieces squatting on thrones are dated on appearance to about 1200.

Islanders on Lewis, where they were found hidden on the beach, have a different story – they say they belonged to a sailor who swam ashore in 17th c and then got murdered for them by local shepherd who hid them. Perhaps the sailor really made them all on the long voyage home. British Museum open Mon–Sat 10–6, Sun 2.30–6. Edinburgh National Museum open Mon–Sat 10–5, Sun 2–5.

Tympana Where Georgians put fan-lights above their doors, Normans put carving. Over 200 churches are listed as having Norman tympana. Sometimes they are so basic they look more like graffiti incised into the stone, like the two dragons at Everton, Nottinghamshire. A more sophisticated version of 2 similar beasts at Dinton, Buckinghamshire.

Certain subjects are particularly popular – besides the lamb of God (e.g. Thwing, Yorkshire; Preston, Gloucestershire) and Christ in majesty (Ely – prior's door; Barfreston, Kent; Rowlestone, Hereford and Worcestershire; and Betteshanger, Kent) the most recurrent are various forms of good triumphing over evil – good examples at Stretton Sugwas, Hereford and Worcester; Morton Valance, Gloucestershire; Brinsop, Hereford and Worcester; and Fordington church, Dorchester, Dorset. Often informal and full of invention.

Adoration of the Magi carved in ivory with exquisite precision, Victoria and Albert Museum

THE
PLANTAGENETS

by Jessica York

CATHEDRALS/ABBEYS/
CHURCHES

Bristol Cathedral has 19th c nave by Street, but choir of this Augustinian abbey is very sophisticated and original piece of architecture. There is no clerestory, choir and aisles are same height, but aisles appear lower, because of skeleton arches built to carry thrust from choir vault. Windows, except great E window, concentrated in aisles. Building in progress by 1306.

St Mary Redcliffe, Bristol, is magnificent parish church financed by merchant princes of the city in 14th and 15th c. Lierne vaulting, unusual in parish churches, and design influenced by remodelled Winchester Cathedral. Extraordinary hexagonal N porch, with intricate, almost Moorish, carved doorway.

Burwell (Cambridgeshire) In mid-15th c, ordinary parishioners here could afford to employ the king's architect Reginald Ely to design St Mary's, a handsome church in Perpendicular style. On B1103 NW of Newmarket.

Canterbury Cathedral Choir, earliest English Gothic, is 12th c, the superbly elegant nave is from end of 14th c. Mason in charge of nave was probably Henry Yevele, who created strong vertical emphasis by elongating main arcade at expense of clerestory, concentrating on aisle windows with their Perpendicular tracery for most of the light. (*See* Tombs.)

Chipping Campden (Gloucestershire) St James is a fine example of the Gloucestershire wool churches, with magnificent tower. Concave nave columns a typical feature. Largely rebuilt after 1450, it contains wool-staplers' brasses including one to William Grevel, whose house is still in the town. On B4035 E of Evesham.

Exeter Cathedral Begun by 1280, it took over 80 years to complete, but original conception adhered to. Elaborate W front is covered in rows of saints and kings in niches.

Fotheringhay (Northamptonshire) St Mary and All Saints is one of the war churches founded by Edward III's grandson, Edward of York, 4 years before his death at Agincourt. Only nave with its flying buttresses and octagonal W tower, survive. The chancel was pulled down at the Dissolution. Off A605 SW of Peterborough.

Lincoln Cathedral Considered the definitive English Gothic cathedral. In 1185 earthquake broke back of Norman cathedral, of which there are some remains in imposing W front. St Hugh's Choir has bizarre asymmetrical vaults. Nave more spacious, less massive than earlier cathedrals but with strong horizontal emphasis. Mainly built by mid-13th c.

Long Melford (Suffolk) All round the battlements on outside of Holy Trinity, a fine E Anglian cloth church, are names of the wealthy clothiers who were benefactors in 15th c. (*See* Alabasters) On A134 N of Sudbury. Nearby Lavenham has good later example and many 15th-c houses.

Melrose Abbey (Roxburghshire). There has been a monastery on this site since 7th c, present handsome ruin mostly 15th c. Finest medieval decoration and figure sculpture in Scotland. The heart of Robert Bruce said to be buried here. D of E. Open standard hours. Admission charge. 4m SE of Galashiels on A6091.

Patrington (Yorkshire) St Patrick's was built on profits of Humber wool trade, a grand example of Decorated style, with fine window tracery, sedilia and screen. Mostly early 14th c, spire a century later. On A1033 SE of Hull.

Sherborne Abbey (Dorset) Remodelled with fan vaulting in 2nd half of 15th c. Quarrels between monks and parish had got so bad before this that parish had built separate church on front of abbey, but it was dismantled when they bought abbey at Dissolution. On A30 E of Yeovil.

Wells Cathedral (Somerset) Early English body of church begun in 12th c. Only English W front to come close to French Gothic. Perhaps chief glory is the clusters of vault ribs in the magnificent chapter house, retrochoir and Lady Chapel built in late 13th and 14th c.

Westminster Abbey King and court emerge here as nation's leading patrons drawing masons from all over country and abroad. Mason in charge, Henry of Reyns, probably learnt his trade at Rheims in France. Strong influence of French ideas: apsidal chapels, flying buttresses, tracery of rose windows, height. Much of it built before Henry III's death in 1272, but has been added to since, notably W end of nave towers, and Henry VII's chapel. (*See* Paintings.)

York Minster Starting point for late Gothic design. Lofty and spacious 2 storey design of nave puts much more emphasis on windows (*See* Stained Glass). Tracery echoed in lierne sham vaulting. Mainly 14th c, though transepts are earlier and towers are 15th c.

CASTLES/MANOR HOUSES

Beaumaris Castle (Anglesey) Last of great Welsh castles built for Edward I by James of St George from Savoy. In summer of 1295, 1,800 diggers were at work and by winter most of it was at least 20ft high, but exchequer was running out of money to pay workmen. Over £14,000 had been spent by 1343 and it still was not finished. For defence it had a moat, inner and outer curtain walls and huge gatehouse. However, it was also luxurious with 5 suites of nobles' lodgings and a splendid main hall. D of E. Open standard hours. Admission charge. 4m NE of Menai Bridge on A545.

Caerlaverock Castle (Dumfries) Great triangular-shaped castle, now a roofless ruin, surrounded by a moat, ramparts and ditches. It stands only a few hundred yards away from another slightly earlier rectangular castle. In spite of its impressive defences, which include a huge double-towered gatehouse, it was destroyed and rebuilt twice on the same plan between the end of the 13th c and mid-15th c – Edward I of England was among those who successfully beseiged it. Within the walls is a surprise – the shell of an elegant 17th c classical house, Lord Maxwell's 'Daintie Fabrick'. D of E. Open standard hours. Admission charge. 8m SE of Dumfries off B725.

Caerphilly Castle (Mid-Glamorgan) Built by Edward I's son-in-law, while the king away on Crusade. Took 9 years – finished 1277. It represents a radical advance in castle design – keep is replaced by inner curtain wall with symmetrical towers, surrounded by outer curtain. The whole protected by massive gatehouses. Its water defences are even more remarkable. It stands in middle of large lake, fed by a stream and held in by screen wall dam with sluice gates. One of its towers now leans at a positively Pisan angle. D of E. Open standard hours. Admission charge.

Caister Castle (Norfolk) Built in 1432 by Sir John Fastolf, original of Shakespeare's Falstaff, who in one remarkable afternoon on the battlefield acquired a princely £16,000 ransom money. His castle built of bricks made on site has 100ft slender tower five storeys high, as much to be lived in as defence – but strong enough to withstand French raid in 1458. Style similar to Rhineland castles, but unique in England. The Paston family lived here from 1459–1599 – their famous letters give vivid pictures of upper-class lifestyle at the end of the Middle Ages. Open mid-May–Sept, Sun–Fri 10.30–5. Admission charge. 1½m W of Caister-on-sea off A1064.

Haddon Hall (Derbyshire) A lovely low lying house. Much of it is 16th c, but banqueting hall and

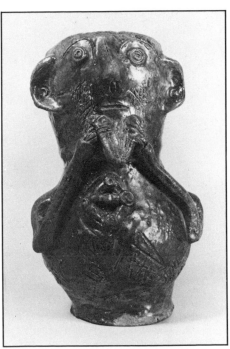

Medieval pottery, like this glazed 13th-century earthenware jug, is in the Museum of London

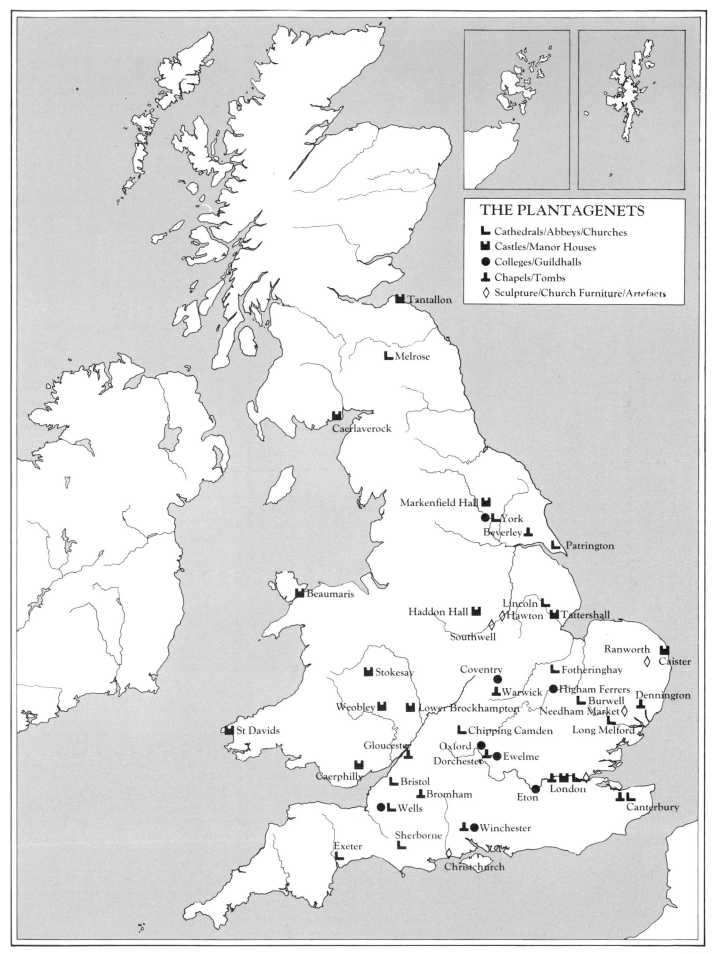

THE PLANTAGENETS

- ⌐ Cathedrals/Abbeys/Churches
- ♙ Castles/Manor Houses
- ● Colleges/Guildhalls
- ⌐ Chapels/Tombs
- ◇ Sculpture/Church Furniture/Artefacts

Tantallon

Melrose

Caerlaverock

Markenfield Hall
York
Beverley
Patrington

Beaumaris

Haddon Hall
Lincoln
Hawton
Tattershall
Southwell

Ranworth
Caister

Stokesay
Coventry
Fotheringhay
Warwick
Higham Ferrers
Weobley
Lower Brockhampton
Burwell
Dennington
Needham Market
St Davids
Chipping Camden
Long Melford

Gloucester
Oxford
Dorchester
Ewelme
Caerphilly
Bristol
London
Bromham
Eton
Canterbury
Wells
Sherborne
Winchester
Exeter
Christchurch

A five-storey brick tower is all that remains of Tattershall Castle, Lincolnshire

kitchen are late 14th c and the chapel is decorated with wonderful 15th c mural paintings of St Christopher wading through swirling water towards banks covered in foliage. Open April–Sept, Tues–Sat 11–6. Admission charge. 2m SE of Bakewell off A6.

Lower Brockhampton House (Hereford and Worcester) Delightful moated, half-timbered house. Hall is late 14th c and little timbered gate house a century later. Nat Trust. Open April–Oct, Wed–Sat, Bank Hols 10–1, 2–6 or by appointment tel Bromyard 2258. Admission charge. 2m E of Bromyard, 11m W of Worcester off A44. Reached by rough narrow road through 1½m of woods and farmland.

Markenfield Hall (Yorkshire) Begun c 1310, this is an L-shaped, moated and fortified manor house, with first-floor hall originally reached by outside stairs. Hall had central hearth but there is solar with fireplace. Gatehouse and other buildings added later. Open May–Sept, Mon 10–12.30, 2.15–5. 3m S of Ripon off A61.

St David's (Dyfed) Ruins give a clear impression of the scale and magnificence of bishop's lodgings, equal to any secular magnate. The palace contains 2 great halls, a chapel and state apartments. Built by Bishop Gower between 1328 and 1347, it has unusual architectural features found in his other build-ings, including polychrome masonry, decorative arcades and ogee arches. D of E. Open standard hours also Sun from 9.30. Admission charge.

Stokesay Castle (Salop) Fortified manor house owned from end of 13th c by a Ludlow wool merchant, who added timber-frame top storey to existing tower, a spacious hall and solar, another tower and curtain wall. Open April–Sept 10–6 (last admission 5.30), closed Tues in July, August, Mon and Tues April, May, June, Sept, March, Oct. Closes at 5 in March and Oct. Closed altogether Nov–Feb. Admission charge. 7m NW of Ludlow off A49.

Tantallon Castle (East Lothian) Stands most dramatically right on the edge of a cliff promontory facing Bass Rock. Built in 14th c of rose-coloured local stone, it was the headquarters of the Douglas family who had huge private armies and twice defied Scottish kings. The castle was unsuccessfully besieged by both James IV and James V and remained impregnable till General Monk captured it during Cromwellian occupation. D of E. Open standard hours. Admission charge. 3m E of North Berwick off A198.

Tattershall Castle (Lincolnshire) Great 5-storey brick tower (its turrets originally had French style conical roofs) is all that remains of once formidable defences. Built by Lord Cromwell, Henry VI's treasurer and one of country's richest men, a profiteer in the French wars. He also rebuilt the old parish church as a collegiate church next to the castle. D of E. Open standard hours. Admission charge. 9m SW of Horncastle on A153.

Weobley (Hereford and Worcester) Has an uncommonly large number of 14th and 15th c timber-framed houses, some very obviously supported by massive curved cruck beams. On B4230 NW of Hereford.

Westminster Hall This magnificent hall is all that remains of the royal palace that burnt down in 1834. Its reconstruction began in 1393 with Henry Yevele and William Wynford as master masons. Hugh Herland was carpenter of the handsome hammer-beam roof. The statues of kings are from the reign of Richard II. Check opening times, tel 219 4272.

CHAPELS/TOMBS

Beverley Minster (Yorkshire) Wonderful canopy over the Percy Tomb, which has no effigy, but is thought to be for one of the mid-14th c ladies of the powerful Percy family. Canopy is beautifully proportioned and encrusted with sculpted foliage and figures, topped with seated Christ and angels on pinnacles. An enclosed spiral staircase joins canopy to screen behind high altar.

Bromham (Wiltshire) The Baynton aisle is a good example of a Perpendicular chantry chapel built on to the parish church by the local landlord, Lord Amand. Chapel, dedicated to Our Lady, is large and very ornate with a fine painted wood ceiling. Off A342 NW of Devizes.

Canterbury Cathedral Tombs of the Black Prince and Henry IV have 2 contrasting royal effigies. The plain tomb of the Black Prince, who died in 1376, has a fine bronze figure of the ideal slim-hipped warrior, as he requested in his will – 'an image shall be placed in memory of us all armed in steel for battle'. With the tomb of Henry IV, who died 1413, there is a remarkable combination of characterisation and regal imagery, which makes you assume this alabaster must be a portrait. Both prince and king endowed charities here too to celebrate mass 'daily forever'.

Dennington (Suffolk) Chantry chapels on a more modest scale can be found in many parish churches. Here at St Mary's the end of the aisle has been screened off with a splendid wooden parclose screen, complete with loft. In centre of chapel free-standing tomb with fine alabaster effigies of Lord Bardolph, who fought at the battle of Agincourt, and his wife Joan. He died in 1441. At Dennington there is also carving on the bench-ends of similar period which included a fabulous Skiapod lying on his back shading himself with his huge webbed feet. On A1120 W of Yoxford.

Dorchester (Oxfordshire) Here is the famous curvaceous knight about to draw his sword. This unusually animated effigy was probably carved c 1310. There is a much more resigned knight at Warkworth, Northamptonshire, carved in a fine white stone allowing the sculptor to show the detail of his elaborate belt, the lacing of his tunic and his walrus moustache. A much more romantic canopied wall tomb at Reepham, Norfolk, is of about the same date – 1350. But here Sir Roger de Kerdeston lies on a bed of sculpted stones and he used to have a painted scene of hunters in a wood behind him. Dorchester on A423 SE of Oxford; Warkworth off A422 E of Banbury; Reepham on B1145 NW of Norwich.

Gloucester Cathedral After fall of Mortimer in 1330, wooden figure originally placed on Edward II's coffin replaced by alabaster effigy of superb quality. Christ-like figure and elaborate canopy overhead turned tomb into shrine, which became object of pilgrimage in atonement for king's murder despite fact that it may not contain his body. Edward II is probably buried in Lombardy. Abbey became so rich with pilgrims' offerings that choir was remodelled and cloisters built in sumptuous Perpendicular style.

Warwick The Beauchamp chapel at St Mary is a parish church chantry chapel of great aristocratic

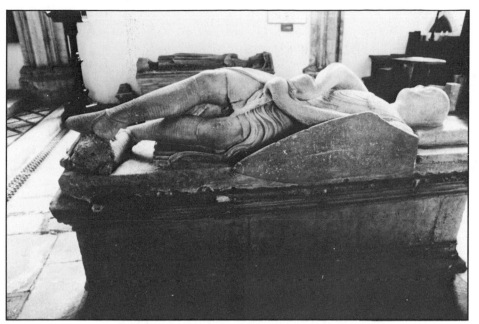

An unusually animated effigy of a 14th-century knight in the church at Dorchester, Oxon

luxury, built here in accordance with will of Richard Beauchamp, Earl of Warwick, and consecrated in 1475. Documentation survives, so we know it cost the fabulous sum, then, of £2,481 4s 7½d. In centre of chapel is his tomb, with figures of weepers and angels in niches round base. On top is effigy in gilt bronze of earl resplendent in armour he once wore to defeat all comers in 3 day tournament. Surprisingly, it is probably not a portrait – his will refers simply to figure of a man and then details the armour. Off this spacious chapel is another tiny fan-vaulted one.

Winchester Cathedral The elegant chantry chapel of William of Wykeham was built into an arch of nave the bishop remodelled before his death in 1404. At the feet of his effigy in the chapel, are the figures of the 3 chantry priests he endowed to celebrate masses for his soul. Most cathedrals have several of these chantry chapels – there are 8 others at Winchester, all for churchmen, although they were often for aristocrats too. They were a mark of conspicuous wealth.

Brasses First known to have been used in 1208, 13th-c brasses were mainly of churchmen. By 14th c all ranks, below the princely, were being commemorated by them – it is estimated more than 100,000 were laid down. The floor of the chancel in St Mary Magdalen's Church, Cobham, Kent, is completely covered with them. By 15th c fashion was on the wane. People were represented as types, not individuals. Good example of knight at Chartham, Kent, is brass of Sir Robert de Septvans who died 1306. By mid-14th c there were brasses to fishmongers and inscriptions in English (Brightwell Baldwin, Oxfordshire). Aristocrats had moved into 3 dimensional alabaster. Wealthy merchants in King's Lynn were importing handsome brasses from the Hanseatic port of Lubeck (Adam de Walsoken 1349, Robert Braunche 1364, in St Margaret's)

Queen Eleanor's Crosses When Queen Eleanor of Castile died at Harby in Nottinghamshire in 1290, Edward I decided to copy what had been done for St Louis in France and set up crosses at each place where the funeral cortege stopped on way to Westminster. Of the 12 crosses only 3 survive – the best preserved at Geddington, Northamptonshire. Others at Hardingstone, Northamptonshire, and heavily restored at Waltham, Essex. The Westminster Abbey tomb has a splendidly elegant bronze effigy of the queen, completely idealised, by William Torel. Candles were kept continually burning on it for 250 years until Reformation extinguished them.

COLLEGES/GUILDHALLS

Coventry St Mary's Hall is an example of the splendid buildings often erected when local guilds representing various trades banded together. Here cloth and wool traders, dyers, iron-founders and glaziers were all united by 1369. They began to build present hall in 1394 and it was finished 20 years later. It has a fine ceiling decorated with musical angels. The carving on the elaborate 15th c guild chair includes elephants and the castle of Coventry. Guild got so powerful that merchants from other areas were members, the rolls include not only Dick Whittington, 2 Italians, several women, but also knights, ecclesiastics, nobles, 2 dukes and Henry IV. Open mid-April–Sept, Mon–Sat 10–5.30, Sun 12 5.

Eton College (Berkshire) Henry VI visited Winchester College when planning his own twin foundations of Eton and King's College, Cambridge, in 1441. Original foundation was like that of Higham Ferrers and had equal number of 'poor and needy scholars' and 'poor and infirm bedesmen', but soon the idea of almshouses was dropped in favour of 70 scholars. Much of the building had been done by the time of Henry's deposition in 1461. (*See* Painting for chapel murals.) Open daily 2–5. Admission charge. Guided tours 2.15, 3.30.

Ewelme (Oxfordshire) In 1437 Duke of Suffolk and his wife Alice, Chaucer's granddaughter, were granted royal licence to build a hospital for 12 poor men and 2 priests – one to be master, the other 'a well-disposed man apt and able to teach and inform children in the faculty of grammar' in the free school. School and almshouses stand near church. Almshouses built round quad are some of earliest brick buildings in Oxfordshire. They would have had thatched roofs originally. School much altered. In church is fine tomb for Alice, who died 1477, but none for the duke. Exiled over 25 years earlier for corruption, he was murdered at sea. On B4009 NE of Wallingford.

Higham Ferrers (Northamptonshire) The bede house hall, chapel and college gatehouse built by Archbishop Chichele in 1420s are all still there, as well as a very grand parish church with its high spire. The college originally housed 8 chantry priests, 4 clerks and 6 choristers, the bede house 12 old men and a female attendant. On A6 N of Rushden.

Oxford There was lecturing in Oxford from early 12th c, but earliest hostel there for students who were not members of a religious order was probably Merton, 1262. In early 14th c Oriel first to be called 'college of scholars'. At Oxford 4 more colleges founded by end of century and 7 in Cambridge. Bits and pieces are left of the earliest college buildings, but at New College largely built between 1379 and 1386, William of Wykeham's grandiose plan brings together all the ingredients of a college for first time. Chapel, hall, library, treasury, warden's lodgings and a range of chambers were all included in a quadrangle entered by a tower gateway. Aim to transform 'poor and indigent scholars' to 'men of great learning' to counteract 'the fewness of the clergy, arising from pestilence, wars and other miseries'. Open term-time weekdays 2–5, Sat, Sun 12–6, vacations daily 11–6.

Winchester College William of Wykeham's twin foundation with New College, was set up in 1382 to prepare boys for Oxford. College originally endowed for 70 scholars, one warden, 10 fellows, 3 chaplains, 16 choristers, a master and an usher. The school room they used, known as the 7th chamber, is still there. Open April–Sept, Mon–Sat 10–6, Sun 2–6, closes at 4 in winter. Admission free, but charge for guided tour.

Wells (Somerset) A rare piece of medieval town planning, Vicars Close is street of 26 houses built

Oxford's earliest college, Merton, founded as a non-religious hostel in 1262

*A fine glazed pitcher with geometric design
in the Museum of London*

to provide identical lodgings, with gardens, for 40 vicars. No 22 is closest to the original design. These vicars from the cathedral were incorporated into a college with a hostel full of chantry priests. Although they lived as a community they were not subject to a definite rule, as monks were.

York Guild which built grand timber-framed hall in Fossgate became Merchant Adventurers in 16th c. Before that they were merchants and mercers who had absorbed a 14th c religious guild. Two-naved hall with open timber roofs, is built on brick undercroft, which contains a chapel. Open April–Oct, Mon–Sat 10–4.30, Nov–March, Mon–Sat 10–3. Admission charge.

BUILDINGS/FARMS/BRIDGES

Barns Bradford-on-Avon, Wiltshire, has a splendid stone barn over 160ft long. Built by Abbess of Shaftesbury in 14th c to hold produce of Barton Farm. Abbey Barn, Glastonbury, Somerset, is a smaller barn of early 14th c built as storehouse for the home manor of Glastonbury Abbey. (Now houses Somerset Rural Life Museum.) Bradford Barn can be visited any time. Glastonbury open April–Oct, Mon–Fri 10–5, Sat, Sun, 2–6.30. Admission charge.
Bridges Monmouth has one of few remaining fortified bridges in Britain. Its tower was equipped with portcullis and machicolations from which missiles could be dropped on enemies attacking the gate. Wakefield, Yorkshire, bridge has chapel built on it *c* 1360. Almost entirely rebuilt in 1848 by Gilbert Scott (its facade was removed to front a boat-house at Kettelthorpe Hall). It was endowed as a chantry by Duke of York in 1398. Crowland, Lincolnshire, has a curious triangular bridge spanning three streams. This bridge with stone figure of Christ was built in late 14th c, but there is a mention of a similar one here in 943. Maud Heath's Causeway, Kellaways, Wiltshire, is not a bridge but a raised path, built with the life savings of Maud Heath who died in 1474. The causeway stretched for 4m from Wick Hill to Chippenham replacing her muddy route to market.
Deserted Village Wharram Percy, Yorkshire, probably the clearest example of a deserted village. People finally left in 2nd half of 15th c for combination of reasons including plague and growth of sheep farming. 7½m SE of Malton (B1248 and SW on minor road at Wharram le Street).
Dovecote Standing mysteriously isolated in a field near the church at Sibthorpe, Nottinghamshire, is imposing, plain building with conical roof. Has nesting-places for 1,260 birds. Medieval equivalent of battery farming.

Monks' Kitchens Glastonbury Abbey, Somerset, has intact 14th c kitchen with sequence of diminishing octagonal roofs, covering single central chimney – outlet for the 4 fireplaces inside. Handsome detached building. Open 9.30–7.30. Admission charge. Durham also has complete kitchen from 14th c, with 4 fireplaces, a kiln for smoking bacon and beautifully intricate vault and octagon for light and ventilation. Standing separate to keep food smells away from church, it is connected to frater by covered passage. Open Mon–Fri 10–1, 2–5, Sat in term 9.30–12.30.
Open Field System Laxton, Nottinghamshire, has the only surviving traces of the open field system by which all medieval villages organised their farming. 4m E of Ollerton off A6075.
Prison Hexham, Northumberland, has a plain rectangular building dating from 1330–2 originally built as a prison and used as such till 19th c. Now houses tourist information centre and Museum of Border Life. Open July–Sept, Tues–Fri, 10–1, 2–5, Sat, Sun 2–5.

SCULPTURE/CHURCH FURNITURE/ARTEFACTS

Christchurch (Dorset) The Tree of Jesse showing the long royal ancestry of Christ was a popular subject in this feudal period. In this sculpted version – probably mid-14th c – recumbent Jesse is flanked by Solomon and David at the harp, with a very endearing nativity scene above. Most of the important figures were made of wood plated with silver, so they have long since vanished.
Hawton (Nottinghamshire) Easter sepulchres were the equivalent of Christmas cribs. They were often temporary wood structures covered in embroidery, but at All Saints, Hawton, there is a permanent stone sepulchre in the chancel, shaped like a wall tomb with a tomb-chest and triple arcade above it. It is elaborately decorated with carving similar to the pulpit at Southwell and was done at about the same time. Just outside Newark to SW.
London The Museum of London has a range of medieval objects on show including kitchenware and pottery, weapons like the daggers all men in London carried, leather shoes with long pointed toes, 14th c copper lanterns, a child's cradle, lead badges from various pilgrimage centres and lead crosses from a mass plague grave. Open Tues–Sat 10–6, Sun 2–6, closed Mon.
Needham Market (Suffolk) The nave roof at St John's is a timber roof of great virtuosity, built at the very end of the period with money from the bishop of Ely. From the hammer beams, which end in a flight of angels, posts rise the full height of the roof and meet massive but delicately carved beams which cross the nave. On A45 NW of Ipswich.
Ranworth (Norfolk) Fine example of painted rood screen from mid-15th c. A figure of a saint against a

*Another Museum of London artefact – tile from
St Stephen's Chapel, Westminster*

brilliantly coloured background decorates each panel. Ranworth is off B1140 NE of Norwich.
Southwell Minster (Nottinghamshire) 'Early English' chapter house, built about 1290, with no central column which makes it light and spacious. Its glory is the carving round the doorway and growing out of the capitals of leaves – oak, hawthorn, vine, ivy, hop – in such deep relief that they have room to curve and intertwine, as though on the tree. The decorative carving of Southwell's stone pulpitum or screen, done about 40 years later, is equally good. On A612 W of Newark.
Alabasters During 14th and 15th c a thriving trade was developed in alabaster carving. Quarried in Derbyshire and Staffordshire, it was carved mainly around Nottingham. Alabaster was widely used for tomb effigies, but the main trade and export was relief panels. They were enriched with painting and gilding. Early panel of Adoration of Magi at Long Melford, retable and other panels, some with colour intact in Victoria and Albert Museum, free standing figures and others in Nottingham Castle Museum. Open April–Sept daily 10–5.45, Oct–Mar 10–4.45. (For V and A see *Opus Anglicanum*.)
Choir stalls, bench-ends and misericords Choir stalls in Chester Cathedral like a forest of spires, are fine example of obsessively elaborate architectural decoration of period – here carved in wood around 1380. Good parochial wood carving on bench ends and screens at Winthorpe and Addlethorpe N of Skegness, Lincolnshire, and at Fressingfield, Suffolk. It is on misericords – the little ledges to lean against under tip-up choir seats – that wood carvers seemed to have the most freedom. There are many lovely examples – Worcester Cathedral has a late 14th c set which includes a fully and fashionably dressed Adam and Eve delving and spinning.
Fonts Orford, Suffolk, and Fritton, Norfolk, have 2 East Anglian fonts of a common regional type, probably produced in workshop and sent all over the area. Both are octagonal with panels filled by single large figure – symbols of the evangelists, angels etc. Both have lions round the base – at Orford they are unbelievably smug-looking, and alternate with little savage men with large clubs and a discreet length of beard. At Fritton the lions seem to have gone over the top and have manic grins and staring eyes. Orford on B1084 E of Woodbridge, Fritton 6m N of Harleston.
Gittern The British Museum has the rare example of a medieval musical instrument. This one is a kind of guitar, elaborately carved along its sides with foliage, animals and huntsmen and was probably made around 1290–1330.
Tiles and bathrooms Chertsey Abbey was most important producer of tiles in 13th c. There are some good individual examples decorated with scenes from Tristan and Iseult in British Museum. The most extensive laid floor is at Westminster Abbey chapter house. Medieval people were not all as unwashed as you might have thought. Edward I had leopard-shaped bath taps, Edward III had running hot and cold water in his bathroom and Richard II had a tiled bathroom in Shene Palace.

PAINTINGS/EMBROIDERY/ STAINED-GLASS

Abingdon (Berkshire) In N aisle of St Helen's Church is an unusual painted ceiling decorated at top with interlocking lozenge patterns and down the sides with a series of long thin panels each painted with a full-length figure from the Jesse Tree. Painted in full range of colour including gold by a least 2 craftsmen, who were granted indulgences by Pope Boniface IX for working on it in 1391.
Ashwell (Hertfordshire) Many old churches have graffiti drawings and remarks, but they are often very difficult to date. On N wall of the tower of St Mary Church are a whole series of remarks and a drawing of a large church which Pevsner takes to be old St Pauls. The inscriptions in Latin commemorate the arrival of the plague in 1349. In another inscription one craftsman says what he thinks of another – 'The

corners are not properly joined. I spit on them.' 5m E of Royston off A505.

Eton College (Berkshire) Wonderful series of monochrome paintings on N and S walls of chapel show links with the Renaissance, in its northern (Flemish) form at least. Dated 1479–88 painted by 2 men – Gilbert and William Baker – the scenes depict miracles of the Virgin interspersed with figures in architectural niches painted to look like sculpture, with a strong sense of spacial illusion specially on the N wall.

Great Malvern (Hereford and Worcester) Priory Church has enough glass surviving to offer a survey of developments in English glass design through 15th c – it ranges from 1430 to 1501, by which time a strong influence of Flemish glass from Bruges can be seen. At St Peter Mancroft, Norwich, glass of 3 different periods has been collected from various windows of church and brought together in E window.

Longthorpe (Cambridgeshire) In tower of late 13th c house, secular paintings rare for period – subjects include ages of man, labours of months, beautifully drawn birds and animals. D of E. Open mid-Oct–mid-March, Mon–Sat 9.30–4, Sun 2–4, mid-March–mid-Oct Mon–Sat 9.30–6.30, Sun 2–6.30. Nr Peterborough.

Norwich Cathedral has a series of panel paintings dating from 1380 onwards, of scenes mainly from the passion of Christ, richly coloured against tooled gilt backgrounds. At Christchurch Mansion, Ipswich (open weekdays 10–5, Sun 2.30–4.30), and at Fitzwilliam Museum, Cambridge (open Tues–Sat 10–5, Sun 2.15–5), there are related panels.

Thornham Parva (Suffolk) Retable here is almost the only surviving panel painting, besides sedilia figures at Westminster, painted in early years of 14th c. It consists of 9 panels with central crucifixion, flanked by Peter and Paul and other saints under arches, which are ornamentally carved and gilded. Off A140 S of Diss.

Westminster Abbey In S ambulatory of the abbey is the retable – a panel 11ft long and 3ft high divided into 5 sections framed with arches and colonnettes. The frame was originally covered with imitation mosaic of coloured glass similar to the Italian Cosmati work on the tomb of Henry III nearby. What remains of the superb style of the painting shows Italian influence too, combined with slender elegance of French and English court style. Probably painted end of 13th c. There are also sedilia figure paintings in the choir and fragments of apocalypse in the chapter house. On S side of nave is fine portrait panel of Richard II enthroned, from end of 14th c.

York By far the richest collection of 14th c glass survives at York Minster. The rigid formal designs of medallions of earlier glass, has here given way to long panels with single figures under architectural canopies in the Peter de Dene window of N aisle and in great W hall, dated c 1310 and 1338 respectively. By the time John Thornton of Coventry designed the E wall of the choir in 1405–8 even this repetitive formal structure had gone for the ambitious apocalypse theme of this window.

Opus Anglicanum In the Victoria and Albert Museum. English ecclesiastical embroidery was famous throughout the 13th c, reaching its best in the last quarter. It was exported all over Europe. Vatican inventory of 1295 mentions *Opus Anglicanum* 113 times. Royal accounts record name of one needlewoman – Mabel of Bury St Edmunds. Probably most of the work was done by the many small and under-endowed nunneries. Little of the embroidery survives in England, but V and A has the Clare Chasuble, the Syon Cope, the Steeple Aston Cope on loan, the Butler Bowden Cope and several other pieces. Open Mon–Thurs, Sat 10–5.50, Sun 2.30–5.50, closed Fri.

Wilton Diptych The most famous painting to survive from the period is in the National Gallery. It represents Richard II as a young man being presented by his patron saints to the Virgin and child and her 11 attendant angels, each of whom wears his personal livery badge of a white hart. The 2 panels still have their original frames. Their exquisite workmanship supports Richard's reputation as an art patron. Open weekdays 10–6, Sun 2–6.

One of many 13th-century brasses depicting members of the Cobham family in St Mary Magdalene Church, Cobham, Kent

187

THE
TUDORS

by Pamela Brown

PALACES/HOUSES

Burghley House (Cambridgeshire) Built 1574–89, the smaller of William Cecil, Lord Burghley's 2 great houses – the more palatial Theobalds now lost. More solid and conventional than Longleat, Wollaton, Doddington, etc which contemporary chronicler William Harrison thought 'like cut paper-work'. Nevertheless roofscape is fantastic jumble of cupolas, chimneys, steeples and balustrades. Interior much redecorated. Several portraits. Open April–early Oct Mon–Sat 11–5, Sun 2–5. Admission charge. 1m SE of Stamford.

Hampton Court Palace Started 1515 by Thomas Wolsey, site carefully chosen for its 'extraordinary salubrity'. Built around sequence of courtyards, it already had 1,000 rooms and 3 miles of lead plumbing when Wolsey gave it to Henry VIII, 1529, in last-ditch attempt to stave off his downfall. Henry enlarged it further still, but only parts to escape Wren's subsequent rebuilding are Great Hall (being restored), Chapel Royal, Haunted Gallery (together with ghost of Catherine Howard) and Great Watching Chamber.

Wolsey's Closet with chequerwork ceiling of badges and Tudor roses and wall panels representing Passion of Christ, best conjures up original strong colours and lavish decoration. On the outside – Roman medallions by Giovanni de Maiano were Wolsey's idea, Henry embellished the Anne Boleyn Gateway during her short reign, and in 1540 installed Nicholas Oursian's famous clock, from which you could even calculate high water at London Bridge.

Tudor kitchens are of suitable dimensions for gargantuan feasts prepared there. Tennis doesn't seem to have kept Henry's weight down – court here built c. 1530, rules of the game often demonstrated now by new generation of 'real tennis' enthusiasts.

D of E. Open May–Sept, Mon–Sat 9.30–6, March, April, Oct 9.30–5, Nov–Feb 9.30–4, Sun May–Sept 11–6, March, April, Oct 2–5, Nov–Feb 2–4. On A308. Also reached by river from Westminster, Richmond and Kingston.

Hardwick Hall (Derbyshire) Started 1591 by indomitable 70-year-old Bess of Hardwick, using proceeds from her 4 marriages. Designed by Robert Smythson, with a good deal of interference from Bess: most splendid and least altered of all Elizabethan houses. Using extraordinary amount of glass and initials flamboyantly silhouetted against skyline she 'cast forth her beames of stately and curious workmanship into every quarter of the country'. Many good portraits, some exquisite furniture and embroidery (see Needlework). Nat Trust. Open April–Oct Wed, Thurs, Sat, Sun 1–5.30 or sunset if earlier. Admission charge. Off A617 between Chesterfield and Mansfield.

Hatfield House (Hertfordshire) Only one wing remains of Old Palace where Elizabeth I spent her girlhood, because Robert Cecil used rest of bricks to build new house he started 1607. House has 2 splendid symbolic portraits of Elizabeth – eyes and ears covering her dress in one suggest she saw and heard everything that happened in the kingdom; the ermine on her sleeve in other is symbol of purity and virginity. You can also see her gloves, silk stockings (believed to be the first pair worn in England) and garden hat – perhaps a bit too summery-looking to be the one she tossed in the air on hearing of her accession here in November 1558. House open daily late March–mid-Oct except Mon and Good Fri, weekdays 12–5, Sun 2–5.30, Bank Hols 11–5. Admission charge. Elizabethan banquets held regularly in Old Palace – for details tel Hatfield 62055.

Holyroodhouse (Edinburgh) Became a Scottish royal palace in 15th c, most of building reconstructed by Charles II, but NW tower early 16th c with many associations with Mary Queen of Scots. Her apartments are on second floor – here Rizzio her secretary was murdered before her eyes in 1566. In her bedroom are two panels she embroidered while imprisoned in England. One shows mouse with fat ginger cat – herself and Elizabeth perhaps. Check opening times tel Edinburgh 556 7371. Admission charge.

Layer Marney Tower (Essex) Most dramatic of early Tudor buildings. 80ft high gatehouse (similar to Oxburgh), intended to impress rather than defend, was showpiece for new terracotta Renaissance decoration. Started 1520 by Henry, Lord Marney, Captain of the Bodyguard to Henry VII and VIII, his death 1523, followed by that of his son 2 years later, brought building to an end. Nearby church of diapered brick, also built by Lord Marney as part of the grand design. His effigy lies inside under great terracotta canopy, his son alongside. House open April–Sept Thur and Sun 2–6, also Tues during July–Aug

Portrait of Arabella Stuart, cousin of James I, as a child, Hardwick Hall, Derbyshire

2–6, Bank Hol weekends 11–6. Admission charge. 3m from Tiptree off B1022.

Little Moreton Hall (Cheshire) Black and white exterior exuberantly covered with trefoils, quatrefoils and stripes looks like 'giant's game of noughts and crosses', says John Betjeman, while its 'noisy gaggle of polygonal bays' disguises fact that it was 150 years in the building. Windows filled with elaborate geometric shapes show same fertile inventiveness. Great Hall, c 1480, is oldest part of the house. Biblical frieze (taboo in churches but popular in houses) has recently been uncovered in parlour above *trompe l'oeil* panelling. Nat Trust. Open March–Oct Sat, Sun 2–6, April–Sept daily except Tues, Good Fri 2–6. Admission charge. SW of Congleton.

Longleat (Wiltshire) First to be built and most classical and restrained of the great Elizabethan mansions which Sir John Summerson has christened 'prodigy' houses. Flat symmetrical facade is given shade and light by carefully spaced bay windows, first used in old Somerset House. Built 1572–80 by Sir John Thynne to flaunt his dubiously acquired wealth – he did a brief stretch for embezzlement – around core of earlier house of 1554 that burnt down. Eccentric chimney pots perhaps date from this time.

Inside, only Great Hall has survived. Several Tudor portraits dotted around, and on main staircase, enchanting picture of meal-time with the Cobhams, their 6 children accompanied by extraordinary assortment of exotic pets. Open Easter–end Sept daily 10–6, remainder of year daily 10–4. Admission charge. Nr Warminster, between Bath and Salisbury on A362.

Loseley Park (Surrey) Elizabethan mansion surrounded by even more famous herd of Jersey cattle. Built 1562 by one of Queen's advisers, Sir William More, and still the home of his descendants. Hall panelling came from Henry VIII's Nonsuch Palace and it has many good paintings and some remarkable pieces of furniture. Open June–Sept Wed, Thur, Fri, Sat 2–5. Admission charge. Between Guildford and Godalming off A3100.

Mary Queen of Scots House (Roxburgh) Finest Scottish example of fortified 16th c town house – imposing, turretted stone building. Queen Mary stayed here in 1566 on her way to meet Bothwell – lots of touching mementos on show including her death mask, order of execution, her watch and one of her very small shoes. Check opening hours, tel Jedburgh 3331. Admission charge. Queen St, Jedburgh.

Parham Park (Sussex) Grey stone manor house built 1577 by Sir Thomas Palmer, who sailed with Drake to Cadiz. Double-cube great hall, lit by tremendously tall mullioned windows, has splendid Renaissance oak screen and collection of 16th c portraits. Open Easter Sun to first Sun in Oct, Sun, Wed, Thur and Bank Hols 2–5.30. Admission charge. 4m S of Pulborough on A283.

Paycocke's (Essex) House completed about 1505 for the Paycockes, rich Coggeshall clothiers – Tudor cloth town famed for its 'Coggeshall Whites'. Fine half-timbered building, carving around gateway and on frieze along bottom of first floor, has great naive

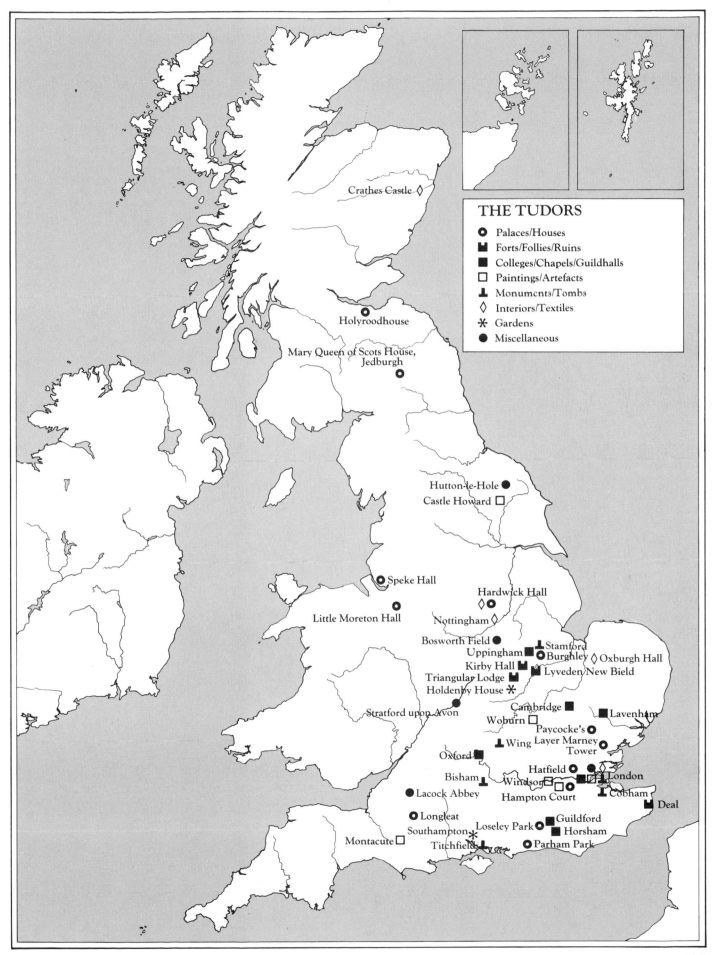

THE TUDORS

- ◉ Palaces/Houses
- ♙ Forts/Follies/Ruins
- ■ Colleges/Chapels/Guildhalls
- □ Paintings/Artefacts
- ⊥ Monuments/Tombs
- ◇ Interiors/Textiles
- ✳ Gardens
- ● Miscellaneous

Crathes Castle ◇

Holyroodhouse ◉

Mary Queen of Scots House, Jedburgh ◉

Hutton-le-Hole ●
Castle Howard □

Speke Hall ◉

Hardwick Hall
◇ ◉

Little Moreton Hall ◉

Nottingham ◇

Bosworth Field ●

Uppingham ■ Stamford ⊥
Kirby Hall ■ Burghley ◉ ◇ Oxburgh Hall
Triangular Lodge ■ Lyveden New Bield ■
Holdenby House ● ✳

Stratford upon Avon ● Cambridge ■ Lavenham ■
Woburn □ Paycocke's ◉
Wing ⊥ Layer Marney Tower ◉
Oxford ■
Bisham ♙ Hatfield ◉
Windsor ◇ London ⊥
Lacock Abbey ● Hampton Court Cobham ⊥
Longleat ◉ Deal ♙
Southampton Guildford ■
Loseley Park ◉ Horsham ■
Montacute □ Titchfield ✳ Parham Park ◉

189

Trinity College, Cambridge, founded by Henry VIII, 1546, using money appropriated from monasteries

charm. Nat Trust. Open April–end Sept Wed, Thur, Sun and Bank Hols 2–5.30. Admission charge. West St, Coggeshall, nr Braintree.

Speke Hall (Merseyside) Striking black and white half-timbered manor house built 1490–1612. Richly decorated interior with plenty of carved panelling; intertwining fruit and flowers drip from stucco ceiling in Great Parlour. Catholic owners the Norris family had several Priest Holes hidden alongside the chimney stacks. Nat Trust/Merseyside County Council. Open all year Mon–Sat 10–5, April–Sept Sun 2–7, Oct–March Sun 2–5. Admission charge. Off A581 8m from Liverpool.

FORTS/FOLLIES/RUINS

Deal Castle (Kent) One of chain of coastal forts built by Henry VIII after break with Rome, when joint invasion by France and Spain to re-establish Pope's authority seemed inevitable. First artillery fortifications to be built in England – coldly efficient and lacking medieval romance – Deal is fine example of new style in castle building: semi-circular bastions and tiers of gun emplacements cluster around central tower like a squat rose. D of E. Open standard hours, also Sun morning in summer. Admission charge. Other good examples at Walmer, Kent; Portland, Dorset; St Mawes, Cornwall.

Kirby Hall (Northamptonshire) Half-ruined, half-preserved mansion started 1570 for Sir Humphrey Stafford and 'modernised' 1640 by Inigo Jones. Classical motifs used in profusion on front of house and Parisian-style pilasters in courtyard unknown elsewhere in England. 'An amazing mixture of bucolic simplicity and high sophistication,' says Sir John Summerson. Glorious place on a sunny day. D of E. Open standard hours. Admission charge. Off A427 near Gretton.

Lyveden New Bield (Northamptonshire) Elizabethan eccentric and recusant Sir Thomas Tresham's unrepentant proclamation of his Catholic faith, built in shape of a cross symbolising the Passion, now stands lonely and compelling in middle of a field. He spent 18 of last 25 years of his life in and out of prison and died before it was completed. Nat Trust. Open any reasonable hour. Off A427 4m SW Oundle.

Triangular Lodge (Northamptonshire) Another of Sir Thomas Tresham's enigmatic buildings, and perfect example of Elizabethan love of symbolism and conceit. This one is a play on the figure 3 symbolising the Trinity: 3-sided, 3 gables on each side, windows like trefoils. D of E. Open standard hours. Admission charge. Rushton 3m NW of Kettering.

COLLEGES/CHAPELS/GUILDHALLS

Cambridge Christ's College was founded 1505 by Henry VII's mother Lady Margaret Beaufort. Most of original buildings now hidden behind 18th c refacing, but gateway still remains – her coat of arms supported by 'yales', deer-like creatures which could move their horns one at a time.

Gonville and Caius College: John Kaye, physician to Edward VI, Mary and Elizabeth, added many buildings to Gonville Hall along with latinised version of his name, and introduced revolutionary medical school of kind he had attended at Padua (one of its early products, William Harvey, discovered circulation of the blood). Kaye is said to have designed college's 3 gates – Humility (now moved to master's garden), Virtue and Honour – to symbolise 3 stages of academic advancement.

King's College Chapel contains under one glorious fan-vaulted roof some of finest examples of 16th c craftsmanship. Completed 1508–15, stained glass windows were partly inspired by Raphael's cartoons, screen and stalls exquisitely carved.

St John's College was also founded by Lady Margaret Beaufort in 1511 on site of St John's Hospital. Except for conspicuous Victorian Gothic chapel, First Court has been restored to give the most authentic impression of Tudor Cambridge. Hall has fine linenfold panelling and hammerbeam roof.

Trinity College was founded 1546 by Henry VIII in attempt to outdo his grandmother by merging Michaelhouse and King's Hall. Money appropriated from monasteries was used to build imposing Great Gate, while Henry's daughter made pragmatic use of their timber to add the chapel roof.

Guildford (Surrey) Royal Grammar School was founded 1509 by grocer Robert Beckingham and given charter by Edward VI 1552. Original headmaster's house, ushers' gallery, school room and great room (living quarters) still in use – witticisms of earlier pupils scored in the oak panelling. Headmaster's study contains chained library – first books given to school 1575 include one printed by Caxton's suitably named successor, Wynkyn de Worde. Visitors by prior written arrangement only.

Horsham (Sussex) Christ's Hospital is one of King Edward VI's foundations, 1552. The school moved out of London early this century, but preserves its Tudor school uniform – long blue coats, clerical bands, breeches and yellow stockings still worn today by the boys – originally a reminder that they were recipients of public charity.

Lavenham (Suffolk) The Guildhall is one of many Tudor buildings still surviving in Lavenham, important centre of the mighty wool trade. Built 1528–9, not long before trade went into sharp decline, by guild of Corpus Christi who also used it until their dissolution for religious feasts and ceremonies. In 1555 during Marian persecutions, Rector of Hadleigh was imprisoned here before being burnt at the stake on Aldham Common, where his grave can still be seen. Now houses local museum. Nat Trust. Open daily March–end Nov 10.30–12.30 and 2–5.30, closed Good Fri and Fri in March and Nov. Admission charge.

London Middle Temple Hall was built 1562–70 – much of the work by Robert Smythson – and restored

Plaster relief of peasants in hall at Montacute House, Somerset

after 2nd World War bomb damage. Members of the Inn still lunch under darkened hammerbeam roof and it has spectacular Elizabethan screen. Usually open 10.30–12 and 3.30–4.30, but often closed for Inn functions and during vacations unless porter is on duty.

The chapel of King Henry VII, Westminster Abbey, was started by Henry in 1503 – his tomb its centrepiece. Magnificent fan-vaulted ceiling probably the work of brothers Robert and William Vertue. Open Mon–Fri 9.20–4, Sat 9.20–2, 3.45–5. Admission charge but free Wed 6–8. (See Monuments/Tombs.)

Oxford Brasenose College was founded jointly 1509 by Bishop of Lincoln and lawyer Sir Richard Sutton. Gate Tower was built 1512 and Old Quad, apart from addition of 3rd storey, is little altered.

Christ Church was founded 1525 on a grand plan by Wolsey in unwise bid, as at Hampton Court, to outdo everybody else. Tom Quad nearly finished by time of his downfall, but it was Wren who finally completed it, 1681, and put the top on Tom Tower.

Uppingham (Leicestershire) Uppingham School was founded 1584 by Archdeacon Johnson during Tudor education boom. Considerably added to since first 60 pupils, but still retains all its original honeyed stone buildings with mullioned windows including first headmaster's house, dormitories and Hall (art room for last 50 years). For a visit, write first.

PAINTINGS/ARTEFACTS

Castle Howard (Yorkshire) Has one of few Holbeins which might be an original of Henry VIII. Also one of Thomas Howard, 3rd Duke of Norfolk, who missed being executed only because Henry died earlier that morning. Open Easter–end Oct 11.30–5 daily. Admission charge. Near York off A64.

Hampton Court Palace Appropriate setting for Treviso's strange grisaille – 'Stoning of the Pope' – from Henry's collection of anti-Papal allegories. Other pictures include 'Field of Cloth of Gold', showing kind of fantastic architecture put up for royal junketings, and copy (original destroyed) of Holbein's dynastic portrait of Henry VII and VIII and wives Elizabeth of York and Jane Seymour. (See Palaces.)

Montacute House (Somerset) In delightful Elizabethan house, marvellous exhibition of 16th (and early 17th c) portraits on loan from National Portrait Gallery, displayed in chronological order in 172ft Long Gallery. Includes some beautiful Holbeins – especially one of Thomas More, Henry VIII at his least lovable, a world-weary Burghley, icon-like images of Elizabeth and some of her courtiers dressed to kill. Nat Trust. Open April–end Oct daily except Tues 12.30–6. Admission charge. A3088 4m W of Yeovil.

Museum of London Dazzling collection of Elizabethan jewels in the Cheapside Hoard – thought to have been hidden by a goldsmith during outbreak of plague, 1603. Some of the fashionable hat-badges and buttons, drops for the hair etc, use exotic gems and may be foreign imports, but the long gold chains enamelled with roses and daisies are probably of English manufacture. Several fine antique cameos – one of Elizabeth. Open Tues–Sat 10–6, Sun 2–6, closed Mon and some Bank Hols.

National Portrait Gallery Has largest collection with one gallery devoted to faces of Tudor monarchs, politicians, humanists, martyrs, sea-dogs, poets and playwrights. Includes Rowland Lockey's genealogical painting of Sir Thomas More and family based on original by Holbein; superb Holbein cartoon and archetypal image of Henry VIII – working drawing for Whitehall Palace fresco; memorial picture of Sir Henry Unton illustrating his life from cradle to grave; and Cobham portrait of Elizabeth, probably last to depict her realistically. Extremely conscious of her looks, she seldom sat for painters when older, and vast number of portraits were copied one from another so that her face became stylised mask, clothes and jewels full of symbolism. Also several miniatures, wood engravings etc. Open Mon–Fri

Mercator's terrestrial globe, 1541, in National Maritime Museum

10–5, Sat 10–6, Sun 2–6, closed some Bank Hols.

Ranger's House 2 or 3 Tudor portraits including a resplendent Sir Jerome Bowes in gold embroidered 'canions' (breeches) covered with leaves of English trees, which he probably wore as ambassador to Moscow in 1583. Open daily 10–5, Nov–Jan closes at 4. Chesterfield Walk, Blackheath, London SE10.

Tate Gallery Small collection of some half-dozen lively looking but less well-known 16th c personalities. Portrait of Elizabeth attributed to Nicholas Hilliard illustrates style where sitters were painted in bright even light, without shadows. Also late Elizabethan (or early Jacobean) look-alikes in the 'Cholmondeley Sisters' side by side in bed having given birth to equally matching babies. Open Mon–Sat 10–6, Sun 2–6, closed some Bank Hols.

Victoria and Albert Museum Finest collection of miniatures includes 'Young Man Among Roses', best known work by Nicholas Hilliard, founder of the British school and its most brilliant exponent. Influenced by Holbein's later work he developed flat, linear style – Elizabethan hallmark. Also several by his pupil Isaac Oliver. Painted in watercolour on vellum, mounted on card (sometimes a playing card) miniatures were often declarations of love, pledges of devotion, their messages hidden in fashionable and elaborate symbolism – 'the deliberately created language of an "in-set"', says Roy Strong in museum

Marquetry games table in Hardwick Hall, Derbyshire

pamphlet on the subject (30p). Open Mon–Thur and Sat 10–5.50, Sun 2.30–5.50, closed Fri and some Bank Hols.

Windsor Castle (Berkshire) Changing display in Drawings Gallery selected from their superb collection of 85 Holbeins realistically brings to life the great personalities at court of Henry VIII. Also several paintings by Holbein in the King's Closet, State Apartments. Open Oct–Feb Mon–Sat 10.30–3, March–Oct Mon–Sat 10.30–5, Sun 1.30–5. Castle subject to closure at short notice worth checking, tel Windsor 68286. Admission charge.

Woburn Abbey (Bedfordshire) Among many Tudor family and royal portraits, has famous Armada portrait of Elizabeth, one hand resting on a terrestrial globe, the Spanish fleet wrecked behind her. Open daily Feb–Easter, Nov 1–4.45, Easter–Oct Mon–Sat 11–5.45, Sun 11–6.15. Admission charge.

MONUMENTS/TOMBS

Bisham (Berkshire) Alabaster effigies carved 1556 of brothers Sir Philip and Sir Thomas Hoby lying side by side, heads propped on arms, cross-legged Sir Thomas the more nonchalant of the two. ½m S of Marlowe.

Cobham (Kent) Effigy of George Brook, 9th Lord Cobham (d. 1558) rests on Renaissance tomb-chest decorated with colonnade of Ionic pillars, his children kneeling devotedly in the arches in between. 4m SE of Gravesend.

Stamford (Lincolnshire) In St Martin's Church William Cecil, Lord Burghley, (d 1598) lies in magnificent tomb with elaborate arched and carved canopy. 12 m NW of Peterborough.

Titchfield (Hampshire) Handsome tripartite monument c 1594 to Thomas and Henry Wriothesley, first and 2nd Earls of Southampton, and first Countess. Effigies lie on triple dais, corners flanked by 4 elegant obelisks, like an upside-down table. Erected by 3rd Earl, Shakespeare's patron. 3m W of Fareham.

Westminster Abbey Henry VII's beautiful marble tomb with gilded figures, heralded Tudor Renaissance. Designed 1512–18, at a cost of about £1,500 by Italian sculptor Pietro Torrigiani (famed for having punched fellow pupil Michelangelo on the nose) – classical motifs and graceful cherubs and saints replace earlier static, elongated Gothic figures. Elizabeth (d 1603) lies nearby between black marble pillars and golden lions in a very dignified and dramatic tomb designed by Maximilian Colt. (See Chapels.)

Wing (Buckinghamshire) Classical tomb of Sir Robert Dormer, 1552, looks 100 years before its time. Small sarcophagus decorated with garlands and ox-skulls under elegantly pillared canopy, is remarkable for superb carving and purity of line. 3m SW of Leighton Buzzard.

INTERIORS/FURNITURE

Crathes Castle (Grampian) Built 1553–96 with most remarkable painted ceilings – classical and biblical figures and early Christian kings adorn beams in Room of the 9 Nobles, and some lively lady musicians in the 9 Muses Room – suitably mind-improving inscriptions on the joists in between. Nat Trust for Scotland. Open May–Sept Mon–Sat 11–6, Sun 2–6. Admission charge. Near Banchory on A93.

Museum of London Tudor Gallery's assortment of 16th c table and household wares includes watering pot used to lay dust and freshen rushes on the floor; above and below stairs table settings with prettily decorated roundels – sweetmeat platters with a witticism on other side to raise a laugh at end of the meal – and some nice cutlery – forks were thought highly effeminate and only used for sweets. (For opening times see Paintings/Artefacts.)

Victoria and Albert Museum Has best collection of the few pieces of Tudor furniture that survive. 10ft 7in extravaganza, 'Great Bed of Ware', was made about 1590, one theory suggests as a sort of advertis-

'The Virtues' – appliquéd wall hangings in Hardwick Hall

ing gimmick for the White Hart at Ware. Its fame must have spread rapidly – by 1601 Toby Belch talks of it in 'Twelfth Night'. Canopy and columns carved within an inch of their lives, window-like inlaid panels in headboard depict fantastic architecture put up for Elizabethan pageants. A room in itself when the curtains were drawn.

Henry VIII's Writing Box c 1525 is well-preserved and vivid example of Tudor colours and patterns. Nonsuch Chest shows new method of cabinet-making probably introduced from Germany which used perspective inlays to make furniture look like castles and palaces. Often copied during 19th c anti-quarian craze. Elizabeth's charming spinet reflects the more refined taste in music, while England's earliest surviving harpsichord is rather solidly deco-rated with plenty of much-favoured Elizabethan strapwork. (For opening times see Paintings/Arte-facts.)

NEEDLEWORK

Museum of London Has a few pieces of costume, mainly knitted or leather, preserved by mud and discovered in archaeological digs. Includes some shoes, stockings, 'pinked' leather jerkin and cap with droopy earflaps of kind worn by young Tudor wags. Walter Raleigh-style embroidered cloak, domed hat and a few pairs of long-fingered gloves from the splendid Spence collection – date c 1600. (For open-ing times see Paintings/Artefacts.)

Nottingham Museum of Costume and Textiles Has Middleton Collection containing several late Eliza-bethan embroidered coifs, collars, bodices, plus one or 2 pieces of geometric lace work. Collection came from nearby Wollaton Hall, built 1580-88 by Robert Smythson and the only one of his buildings to be remembered on his tomb. (Hall now houses natural history museum.) Open all year daily 10-5.

Oxburgh Hall (Norfolk) Enchanting house built 1482 has 3 of the famous green velvet Oxburgh wall hangings – fragmented 4th at V and A. Medallions of engaging beasts, plants, emblems embroidered

together by Mary Queen of Scots and Bess of Hard-wick perhaps in a rather chilly atmosphere since Bess's conviction that her husband the Earl of Shrewsbury was having an affair with his royal pris-oner destroyed her marriage. Nat Trust. Open April–mid-Oct Mon–Wed, Sat, Sun 2-6. Admis-sion charge. Stoke Ferry Road, 7m SW Swaffham.

Hardwick Hall (Derbyshire) Marvellous collection includes two remarkable appliquéd wall-hangings – the Heroine and Virtue panels – showing imagina-tive use of fabrics to give perspective. Made 1570-75 under supervision of professional broiderer employed by Bess as in most other great households. (For open-ing times see Palaces/Houses.)

Victoria and Albert Museum Has one of earliest of few pieces of costume to survive – 1539 boy's embroi-dered shirt – plus a few later ornate caps and gloves.

Late 16th-century kid gloves with embroidered cuffs, Museum of London
Right: Henry VII chapel, Westminster Abbey

Fine collection of domestic needlework – Bradford table carpet, numerous cushions (much needed for the hard seats), earliest dated sampler by Jane Bos-tocke 1598 – shows range and skill of Elizabethan stitchery, themes and patterns often taken from her-bals, bestiaries and books of symbols and devices. Several examples of much-loved 'black work' – black stitches on white fabric, and 'slip work' – motifs embroidered on canvas, cut out and applied to richer fabrics. (For opening times see Paintings/Artefacts.)

GARDENS

Holdenby House Gardens (Northamptonshire) Small replica of original garden reconstructed, in part of grounds, around remains of Sir Christopher Hatton's ruined palace. Designed by Rosemary Verey using only plants available in 1580s. Open April–Sept Sun and Bank Hols 2-6 also Thurs June–Aug 2-6. Admission charge. 7m NW of Northampton off A428 and A50.

Southampton Tudor Garden is tiny but completely authentic 16th c 'living garden museum' established at city's Tudor House Museum. Central knot design with arbour, 'herber' (pergola), heraldic poles with gilded beasts and painted rails. Open Tues–Sat 11-5, Sun 2-5.

MISCELLANEOUS

Bosworth Field (Leicestershire) Battle trail uses information boards to illustrate the fight, and at Battlefield Centre there are replicas of shields, armour, flags, plus models of the battle and slide and film shows. Centre open Easter–end Oct Mon–Sat 2-5.30, Sun and Bank Hols 1-6. Admission charge. Near Market Bosworth signposted from A444, A447, A5 and B585.

Hutton-le-Hole (Yorkshire) Ryedale Folk Museum has a rare Elizabethan glass kiln discovered locally and reconstructed in Folk Park. Type of furnace introduced into Britain by Huguenot glaziers. Pro-bably in use 1572-1600. Open April–Oct daily 11-6. Admission charge.

Lacock Abbey (Wiltshire) Has one of earliest sur-viving brew-houses, installed when Sir William Sharington acquired Abbey in 1539 and hardly changed since. Many large households made their own ale and beer – the brewster traditionally a woman. In use until 18th c. Nat Trust. Open April–Oct daily except Tues 2-6. Admission charge. Nr Chippenham off A35.

Stratford upon Avon Birthplace Trust look after host of buildings connected with Shakespeare and his many relatives: birthplace, Henley Street, with small museum; his mother, Mary Arden's Tudor farmhouse at Wilmcote 4m outside; Anne Hath-away's picture postcard cottage near Shottery; and New Place, Shakespeare's retirement home. Adjoin-ing knot garden is authentic 16th c design but with modern planting, though Elizabethans might well have loved gaudy petunias had they been around. Also one of more fascinating places – Hall's Croft, Old Town, home of Shakespeare's daughter and hus-band Dr John Hall with dispensary kitted out in style of Elizabethan consulting room c 1600.

Shakespeare's Birthplace, Anne Hathaway's Cot-tage open April–Oct weekdays 9-7, Sun 10-6, Nov–March weekdays 9-4.30, Sun 1.30-4.30. Admission charge. Mary Arden's house, Hall's Croft, New Place, open April–Oct weekdays 9-6, Sun 2-6, Nov–March weekdays 9-12.45 and 2-4, closed Sun. Admission charge.

Tower of London Was on the Tudor tourist route, in between beheadings, when it had menagerie of wild animals and museum with crown jewels, furniture, armour etc. Tudor Gallery in White Tower still includes armour made for Henry VIII including grotesque horned helmet – present from Emperor Maximilian I. Open March–Oct weekdays 9.30-5, Sun 2-5, Nov–Feb weekdays 9.30-4. Admission charge.

THE
STUARTS

by Oenone Holland

HOUSES/CASTLES

Ashdown House (Oxfordshire) Designed c 1665, probably by William Winde. A Dutch-style house of unexpected height isolated in flat countryside. An 'adorable doll's house' (Pevsner). A tall testimony of Lord Craven's love for Charles I's sister, the Winter Queen, for whom it is said he built the house as a refuge from the plague. She died without seeing it – of the plague. The grand staircase is hung with portraits of the queen and her circle. Nat Trust. Hall, stairway and roof open May–Sept, Wed, first and 3rd Sat of each month 2–6. Admission charge. 3½m N of Lambourn on W side of B4000.

Audley End House (Essex) Built 1603 for Thomas Howard, Earl of Suffolk, renovated 1721 by Vanbrugh for 5th Earl. House was used as a royal palace after the restoration. Great Hall shows a confrontation between two styles. A massive elaborate oak screen carved 1605 faces a simple classical stone screen attributed to Vanbrugh in 18th c. Open April–Sept Thurs–Sat, Bank Hol Mon 1–6.30. Admission charge. 1m W of Saffron Walden.

Blenheim Palace (Oxfordshire) Vanbrugh's massive baroque palace built to commemorate Marlborough's Blenheim victory of 1704. Carving by Gibbons. Hawksmoor designed ceiling in Green Writing Room. Splendid tapestries and murals by Laguerre. Late 17th-c porcelain from China and Japan. Park and lake 18th c one of Capability Browns's most successful projects. Open mid-March–Oct, daily 11.30–5. Admission charge. 8m N of Oxford off A34.

Blickling Hall (Norfolk) Built 1616–27 for Sir Henry Hobart, Lord Chief Justice, by architect Robert Lyminge. Retains many heavy 16th c features: roof line of turrets, gables and chimneys. A few details of new classical style – tower with pediments over windows. Splendid Jacobean ceiling in Long Gallery. Open April–mid-Oct Tues, Wed, Thur, Sat, Sun and Bank Hols 2–6, May–Sept from 11 but closed 12.30–1.30. Admission charge. 1½m NW of Aylsham on N side of B1354.

Burton Agnes Hall (Yorkshire) A Jacobean mansion built 1601–10 by Robert Smythson. Owner Sir Henry Griffith chose sturdy Elizabethan style owing nothing to Renaissance. Soaring chimneys, unexpected bow windows. Elaborately carved staircase and stone screen in hall. Carving of Dance of Death above fireplace. House once haunted by ghost of Sir Henry's murdered daughter, her skull is built into the Walls. Unlikely but effective setting for collection of modern French paintings belonging to present owner. Fine brick gatehouse with arms of James I. Open April–Oct Mon–Fri 1.45–5, Sun 1.45–6. Admission charge. 6m SW of Bridlington off A166.

Craigievar Castle (Grampian) Romantic and isolated, tall turreted castle of pink Aberdeen granite. Built between 1600 and 1626 for William Forbes, a rich Aberdeen merchant nicknamed 'Baltic Willie', it has survived unscathed by either the Civil War or Victorian restorers. Interior contains much fine plasterwork, especially grand royal coat of arms of United Kingdom over fireplace in the great hall which pro-

claims the laird's role as tenant-in-chief, direct representative of the king's authority in his own lands. Nat Trust for Scotland. Open May–Sept, Sat–Thurs 2–6. Admission charge. 6m S of Alford on A980.

Drumlanrig Castle (Dumfriesshire) Not a fortified castle, a stately home built to impress. Shaped like a hollow square, tall and imposing with corner turrets, forests of chimneys, classical detailing. Built between 1679–91 for William Douglas, 1st Duke of Queensberry – horrified by having spent so much on it, he slept only one night there after it was completed. The interior has fine contemporary objets d'art, including cabinet from Versailles, good Rembrandt, silver chandelier weighing over 9 stone. Open Easter, May, June Mon, Thurs, Sat 12.30–5, Sun 2–5 July, Aug Mon–Thurs, Sat 11–5, Sun 2–6. Admission charge. 18m N of Dumfries off A76.

Hatfield House (Hertfordshire) Rebuilt 1607–12 by Robert Lyminge for Robert Cecil. Contains exquisite carved staircase with dog gates and carving on newel post of naturalist John Tradescant Sr who laid out the garden. Tons of bulbs and plants were brought to Hatfield from abroad. Open March–Oct Tues–Sat 12–5, Sun 2–5.30, Bank Hols 11–5. Admission charge. Off A1000 in Old Hatfield.

London The Queen's House at Greenwich built 1616–37 as quiet retreat for James I's Queen. First important design by Inigo Jones – began architectural revolution. No turrets, level skyline, nothing heavy or overblown as at Audley End, built the same decade. 'Best 3-bedroomed house in England'. The galleried hall most impressive with black and white marble floor reflecting design of painted ceiling. Spiral staircase with wrought iron balusters set against white walls has pure cool classical look. Open Summer Tues–Sat 10–6, Sun 2–5.30, Winter Tues–Sat 10–5, Sun 2–5.

Oliver Cromwell's death mask
in the Museum of London

Springhill (Co. Londonderry) Simple 17th c manor house with roughcast walls and slate roof built by Ulster settler Colonel William Conyngham in settlement of his marriage contract of 1680 which stipulated that he should provide 'a convenient house of lime and stone, two stories high' for his bride. Large costume collection housed in old laundry and cottage kitchen set up in the courtyard. Conyngham family furniture and pictures still in the house. Nat Trust. Open April–end Sept daily except Fri 2–6. Admission charge. 1m from Moneymore on B18.

Sudbury Hall (Derbyshire) Built 1665–1700 for Vernon family. Best unchanged 17th c great house. Outside, attractive brick pattern and mixture of Jacobean and Restoration features. Inside, richly decorated ornate plasterwork in Long Gallery. Probably last long gallery to be built. Exquisite Grinling Gibbons carving. Pine staircase with carved panels by Pierce who painted Wilton House ceiling and worked on Wren's churches. Paintings by Laguerre. Nat Trust. Open April–Oct Wed–Sun and Bank Hols 1–5.30. Admission charge. 6m E of Uttoxeter off A50.

Wilton House (Wiltshire) The Palladian rebuilding of Wilton House c 1632–57 contains theatrical and ornate elements. Inigo Jones with nephew and pupil John Webb designed the Double Cube Room (length twice its breadth) for Van Dyck portraits. Unaltered since 1653. Amazing ceiling with *trompe l'oeil* effect. Lelys, Rubenses, good walnut furniture c 1670. 'Charles I did love Wilton above all places and came thither every summer' (Aubrey). Open April–Oct Tues–Sat, Bank Hol 11–6, Sun 1–6. Admission charge. 2½m W of Salisbury.

CHURCHES

Chalfont St Peter (Buckinghamshire) Quaker Meeting House built 1688. Austere, humble interior with deal dadoes. Partition between caretaker's house and meeting room can be removed for extra space. Seats of the elders slightly raised, with panelling behind rising too with balustrade in front. Some eminent Quakers in graveyard: William Penn, founder of Pennsylvania, and Thomas Ellwood, who read to blind Milton.

Edinburgh Greyfriars Church, simple rather Italianate looking building, east end dates from 1620, with lots of Covenanting connections. The National Covenant was signed here in 1638 and the graveyard is full of Covenanters' tombs. Many other Scots notables buried here: Sir George Mackenzie, 'The Bluidy Advocate', Duncan Forbes of Culloden, William Robertson the historian etc. After the Battle of Bothwell Brig in 1679, when the Covenanting army was finally destroyed by royal troops, 1,000 prisoners shackled together were confined in the churchyard for 5 months.

Ingestre (Staffordshire) St Mary's built 1676, attributed to Wren: he was friendly with local squire who paid for original private chapel. Very elaborate country church with black and white marble paved floor

Craigievar Castle 🏰

THE STUARTS
🏰 Houses/Castles
⌐ Churches
◼ Colleges/Buildings
✳ Gardens
⚖ Monuments
◇ Interiors
☐ Paintings/Artefacts
✿ Engineering/Science

Falkland ◇

Edinburgh ⌐

◼ Drumlanrig Castle

✳ Levens Hall

◼ Burton Agnes Hall

Bramham Park ✳

Liverpool ✿   ☐ Manchester

Stoke-on-Trent ☐   ☐ Chatsworth

Sudbury 🏰   ✿ Woolsthorpe
Ingestre ⌐   Manor   🏰 Blickling Hall

◇ Powis Castle   ✳
                    Moseley Old Hall

⚖ Stowe Nine
   Churches

Elmley Castle ⚖   ☐ ◼ Cambridge

Willen ⌐   ✿ Colchester
            Audley End 🏰
Blenheim 🏰   ✿ Ivinghoe
       ✳ Oxford   Hatfield 🏰 ◇ London
Abingdon ◼   ⚖ Bisham   ☐ ✳
Lydiard Tregoze ⚖   Chalfont St Peter ◇ ⌐
Ashdown House 🏰   Ham House ◇
            Hampton Court   The Queen's House,
Wey Navigation Canal ✿ ✳   ◇ Knole   Greenwich
Wilton 🏰   Wotton House
       ☐ Montacute   ☐ Petworth   ⚖ Ashburnham

Kilmington ⌐

195

Urban church in rural setting – St Mary Magdalene, Willen, Bucks., finished 1680

fashionable after 1660. Fine plaster ceiling encrusted with fruit and flowers; oak screen with king's arms. W doorway has Tuscan columns, pediments with shields and garlands above; beautiful stucco reredos. Full of monuments. 4m E of Stafford.

Kilmington (Devon) Loughwood Meeting House built 1653. Very simple thatched church, used till 1833. Inside unaltered, early 18th c scrubbed wooden floor, pews with doors and retiring rooms for discussion between morning and evening services. Nat Trust. Open all year. 4m W of Axminster.

London St Paul's Cathedral, built 1676–1711. Wren made 3 plans for the cathedral – the 3rd was accepted. His son laid the last stone. Wren was first to be buried here. A black marble slab commemorates him in Latin: 'Reader, if you seek a monument look around you.' From golden ball on top of the classical dome is a view of all the spires of his city churches. Choir stalls and organ cases by Grinling Gibbons, wrought iron gates to aisles by Tijou, who made Hampton Court gates.

St James, Piccadilly, built 1676–84. Designed by Wren to accommodate new London suburb. Most capacious church Wren thought possible without becoming 'Romanish'. White marble font sculpted by Grinling Gibbons showing tree of life. Organ case and wooden reredos also by him: of these, Evelyn said, 'None anywhere in the world more handsomely adorned.'

St Paul's Church, Covent Garden. Designed by Inigo Jones 1631–8 for 4th Earl of Bedford who wanted expenses kept low. 'The handsomest barn in England.' First Renaissance parish church – simple and well-proportioned with colonnaded Tuscan portico facing the Earl's piazza – London's first square. Sir Peter Lely, portrait painter of Stuarts, is buried there – also Grinling Gibbons.

St Stephen Walbrook, Mansion House, built 1672–9 and most praised of 52 city churches designed by Wren. The dome foreshadows St Paul's. Remarkable steeple, planned to pierce skyline as were all his

city steeples. Plain and pale green windows dazzle with light. Beautiful Corinthian columns. The pulpit, visible from all points, has twisted Renaissance balusters, is carved with fruit, flowers and angel heads. Constantly changing vistas. Steps to W entrance show slope to the brook which once flowed there.

Willen (Buckinghamshire) St Mary Magdalene built 1679–80. Designed by Robert Hooke for one-time headmaster of Westminster School, Dr Busby. A countryside setting for a city church. Fine stucco panelling and ceiling. Original pews and candle holders. Scrolls on panel frames and organ case. 2m NE of Milton Keynes centre.

MONUMENTS

Ashburnham (Sussex) Contrast in St Peter's Church between stiff Jacobean monument to John Ashburnham, 2 wives with children 1671, and baroque one to Sir William Ashburnham and wife (d 1675) by John Bushnall: this shows a dramatic and emotional scene with Lady Ashburnham semi-reclining as putto swoops to deliver a wreath. Her husband with outstretched hands kneels in anguished entreaty, as if to stay her death. 4m W of Battle off A2027.

Bisham (Berkshire) All Saints has large alabaster monument of the Hoby family. Lady Elizabeth Hoby (d 1609) kneels in widow's weeds under a canopy. Behind her a procession of children in clearly depicted costumes with splendid ruffs. Lady Margaret Hoby (d 1605) is unusual – a red heart high on an obelisk with 4 life-like swans. 2m S of Marlowe.

Elmley Castle (Hereford and Worcester) Monument to Sir William Savage, wife and son Giles c. 1631. Each recumbent figure is depicted differently. William Savage has hands together in prayer as in older monuments. Giles, more classically, has one

hand on breast and one on sword hilt. Wife holds a baby clutching a ball. 3m SE of Pershore off A44.

London Westminster Abbey has monument to George Villiers, Duke of Buckingham (d 1628), favourite of both James I and Charles I – effigy is by Le Sueur, whose equestrian statue of Charles I is in Whitehall. Also colourful effigy of Princess Sophia, daughter of James I (d 1603 3 days old) by Maximilian Colt who also did monument of Elizabeth I nearby. The baby lies in alabaster cradle with embroidered cover: 'Sophia, a royal rosebud untimely plucked by death'. Sir Francis Vere, Elizabethan soldier (d 1609), has unusual monument – 4 knights kneeling on one leg support slab carrying his armour: beneath lies effigy of Sir Francis himself. Clear features and classical grandeur. There are fine examples of semi-reclining effigies introduced in the 17th c – including Thomas Thynn (d 1682) by Quellin. Below his effigy a relief depicts scene of his murder in Pall Mall by assassins under instructions from a count who fancied his wife. Nicholas Stone's monument to Sir Francis Hollis (d 1622) was first to show Englishmen in Roman garb.

St Paul's Cathedral has strange effigy of poet-dean John Donne (d 1631) wrapped in his shroud, carved by Nicholas Stone. It survived the fire in Old St Paul's and was re-erected in Wren's cathedral.

Lydiard Tregoze (Wiltshire) St Mary the Virgin has a fine collection of monuments including Sir John St John and 2 wives 1634. One wife holds a child, the other a book. Sir Giles Mompesson and wife 1633: seated opposite each other, they seem to be in melancholy conversation. He, in armour, looking up from book, she leaning head on right hand while on her lap her left hand holds a skull. 'The Golden Cavalier', Edward St John 1645, stands undaunted in gilt armour beneath a canopy held open by 2 boys. 4m W of Swindon.

Stowe Nine Churches (Northamptonshire) Monument to Elizabeth, Lady Carey (d 1620) in Church of St Michael. Portrait carved by Nicholas Stone in her lifetime. Relaxed and natural pose with one hand resting on breast. Exquisite detail of her dress and of the embroidered cushion on which she rests shows trend towards realism in 17th c monuments. 7m NW of Towcester.

Monument to poet John Donne in St Paul's Cathedral where he was Dean

The Savage family monument in Elmley Castle Church, Hereford and Worcester

COLLEGES/BUILDINGS

Abingdon (Oxfordshire) Town Hall is impressive free standing building c 1677. Built and probably designed by Kempster, who had worked for Wren on city churches. Kempster provided stone for his Renaissance building from his own quarry in Burford. It is topped by a cupola with arched open market place below and court room above holding some 17th c regalia including tankards and maces. Much-travelled Celia Fiennes called it the finest town hall in England. D of E. Open daily 2–5. Admission charge.

Cambridge Trinity College Library was designed by Wren in 1676 for his friend, Isaac Barrow, geometrician and Master of the college. The plan was to complete Nevile Court 'according to the manner of the ancients'. On the outside are statues by Cibber and the inside has good light from windows, plenty of shelf room and 'celles' for individual study. Wren employed Gibbons to carve decorative limewood panelling and some busts. The library contains Isaac Newton's private library and the manuscripts of Milton's shorter poems with corrections.

London The Banqueting House in Whitehall was built 1619–23 for James I for ceremonial occasions and masques, many by Ben Jonson with scenery by Inigo Jones. Last masque was in 1637 when Rubens's ceiling paintings were installed and Charles I feared torches might damage masterpiece. The theme of the paintings was the divine right of kings. Ironically from this room Charles I walked to his execution, and William of Orange and Mary accepted terms for their reign laid down by Parliament. Open weekdays 10–5, Sun 2–5. Admission charge.

The Royal Hospital, Chelsea, still fulfils function intended by Wren when he designed it c 1681. Charles II required a hospital and retirement home for aged and infirm veterans. It opened in 1692 and was later described by Thomas Carlyle as 'quiet and dignified, and the work of a gentleman'. There is a statue of Charles II in Roman toga by Gibbons in the grounds. Wren's own medical interests extended to studies with microscopes and plans for injections into the blood. He also 'cured his lady of the thrush by hanging a bag of live bog lice about her neck' (Hooke). Grounds open daily 10 sunset, chapel and dining room 10–12, 2–4.

Oxford Museum of the History of Science is a fine example of English Renaissance building opened in 1683, the oldest purpose-built museum in England. Originally built to house the fascinating 'natural curiosities' collected by John Tradescant and his son. Now houses collection of scientific instruments – astrolabes, early mathematical instruments, timepieces and microscopes. Open Mon–Fri 10.30–1, 2.30–4.

The Sheldonian Theatre was Wren's first architectural work 1663–9, designed while still professor of astronomy. Wren was inspired by engravings of Roman open air theatre. The ceiling is a great engineering feat. It is painted by Robert Streeter to give impression of opening to the sky where triumphant figures of the arts soar above a figure of malice. Open (except during performances) Mon–Sat 10–12.45, 2–4.45, closes 3.45 in winter. Admission charge.

GARDENS

Bramham Park (Yorkshire) Layout is hardly changed since its completion c 1700. It escaped Capability Brown's attacks, unlike Chatsworth. Fine avenues with tall clipped hedges, formal lakes and ponds. Le Nôtre style garden, temples and obelisks typical of late 17th c. Open Easter–Sept Tues, Wed, Thur, Sun and Bank Hols 1.15–5.30. Admission charge. 4m S of Wetherby on A1.

Levens Hall (Cumbria) Laid out by Guillaume Beaumont, pupil of le Nôtre in 1690. Gardens planned to surprise rather than impress with long beech avenue at right angle to entrance, fantastic shapes of tight packed topiary garden – hats, birds, umbrellas. Fashion for topiary began in 17th c. Some original plantings. Garden open daily Easter Sun to Oct. Admission charge. 5m S of Kendal on A6.

London Chelsea Physic Garden was founded by and for Worshipful Society of Apothecaries in 1673 for educational and scientific purposes. Covers 4 acres with 5,000 species of plants laid out not to allure but to instruct on family relationships. Apply for tickets for open days by sending sae to Clerk of Trustees, City Parochial Foundation, 10 Fleet St, London EC4.

Moseley Old Hall (West Midlands) Small timber manor house of 1600. House much altered, but contains bed Charles II slept in when he escaped after battle of Worcester 1651 – he was disguised, curls cropped, face smeared in walnut juice. House contains secret chamber where he hid during search. Garden is a reconstruction of 1640s design using plants available then. Knot garden, walk of trellised vines and clematis, nut walk. Nat Trust. Open

April–Oct, Wed, Thurs, Sat, Sun, Bank Hol Mons, 2–6, March, Nov, Wed, Sun 2–6. Admission charge. 4m NE of Wolverhampton off A460.

Oxford Botanic Garden is the oldest British botanical garden, laid out in 1621 by Earl of Danby for the study of medicinal herbs. Has 3 gateways carved by Stone with statues of Charles I and II. Bobarts (father and son) exchanged plants and seeds with Tradescants. Younger Bobart probably raised London plane tree – also brought Oxford ragwort to England from Etna. One yew remains of Bobart's yew avenue. Many of 1,600 plants listed in 1640s still grown today. Open weekdays 8.30–5, Sun 10–12, 2–6. Closes 4.30 on winter Sundays.

Wotton House (Surrey) Evelyn family seat. Diarist John Evelyn born here 1620. Landscaped gardens laid out by him for his brother from 1643. The terraced mound and temple remains. Mulberry trees, tulip tree (originally a Tradescant import), many interesting shrubs. Evelyn was regarded as arbiter of taste by the court and his books popularised gardening among gentry. To view send sae to College Secretary, Fire Service Staff College, Wotton House, Abinger Common, Dorking.

INTERIORS

Falkland (Fife) Remarkable reconstructed room in small remaining part of Scottish monarchs' 16th c palace. King's bedchamber contains baroque golden bed of Brahan. Nat Trust for Scotland. Open April–Oct weekdays 10–6, Sun 2–6. Admission charge.

Ham House (London) Built 1610 but alterations of 1670s create the rich impression of Lauderdales' country house. Inside the rooms are small by Elizabethan standards but packed with luxurious 17th c decorations acquired by the rapacious Duke and Duchess – an adjustable armchair, Japanese lacquer cabinets, chairs covered in silk and velvet, rich carpets. John Evelyn compared Ham to the 'best villas in Italy itself'. Notable staircase with carved panels showing military trophies. Collection of miniatures and portraits showing stars of Charles II's court in unchanged surroundings. Nat Trust. Open April–

Entrance to Oxford's Botanic Gardens, the oldest in Britain, laid out in 1621

197

Sept Tues–Sun and Bank Hols 2–6, Oct–March 12–4. Admission charge. 1m S of Richmond.

Hampton Court Palace In 1689 William and Mary commissioned the extension of the Tudor palace originally built for Cardinal Wolsey. Wren, with talented team of Gibbons, Hawksmoor, Cibber, Tijou and sometimes truculent Talman, created a small Versailles. New apartments built round Fountain Court. Behind grandiose facades, much rich classical detail: tapestries, paintings and sumptuous furniture. D of E. Open April–Sept weekdays 9.30–6, Sun 11–6. Oct–March weekdays 9.30–5, Sun 2–5. Admission charge.

Knole (Kent) A vast mansion enlarged by Sackville family 1604. Unique collection of Jacobean and Caroline furniture. Chairs upholstered in velvet and brocade. Charles I's billiard table and Knole settee. Silver room has elaborate gold and silver threaded bed topped with ostrich plumes. Gilt toilet set of Charles II. Fine 17th c tapestries, needlework. Nat Trust. Open April–Sept Wed, Sat and Bank Hols 11–5, Sun 2–5, Oct–Nov Wed–Sat 11–4, Sun 2–4. Admission charge. Sevenoaks, E of A225.

Powis Castle (Powys) Bought by Herbert family in 1587. Contains splendid state bedroom with acanthus mouldings prepared for Charles II. The bed is placed behind ornate balustrade, French style, for receiving morning visitors. Red and white upholstery of sofa, chairs and stools matches drapes of grand 4-poster. Good silver toilet set of 1700. Nat Trust. Open mid-April–Sept Wed–Sun 2–6, Bank Hols 11.30–6. Admission charge. 1m SW of Welshpool off A483.

PAINTINGS/ARTEFACTS

Cambridge Fitzwilliam Museum has great quantity of 17th c slipware and Delftware including 'Toft' dishes. Toft brothers of Staffordshire started to make more highly decorated slipware in 1670s. Large dish depicts Charles II hiding in oak tree. Ravenscraft glass with early seals. Embroidered caps and stomachers. Embroidered picture of lady, perhaps Catherine of Braganza. Also many 17th c coins and medals. Open Tues–Sat, lower galleries 10–2, upper galleries 2–5, Sun all galleries 2.15–5.

Chatsworth (Derbyshire) Contains fine decorative paintings by Thornhill (Sabine Room). Also good Lelys. Excellent examples of Mortlake tapestries 1635–45. Open April–Oct daily 11.30–4.30. Admission charge. Nr Bakewell.

London Museum of London has some Toft ware and Delft pieces: Charles II coronation mugs, large platters decorated with paintings of William and Mary, puzzle jugs, bottles marked sack and claret, beer bottles, clay pipes. Lantern clocks of the period and a 'squirt', used to put out fires in 1660s. There is Oliver

Portrait of Elizabeth, Princess Royal, by Van Honthorst, at Ashdown House, Oxon.

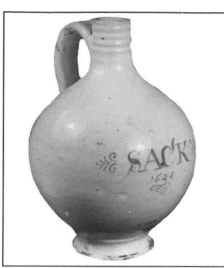

Jug for sack – popular drink of the period – in tin-glazed earthenware, Museum of London

Cromwell's death mask, Charles I's execution shirt and chessmen said to have belonged to Pepys. Open Tues–Sat 10–6, Sun 2–6.

Galleries 54 and 56 of Victoria and Albert Museum display furniture and artefacts of the 17th c. Embroidered bed hangings exotically oriental, influenced by East India Company imports. Notable silverware: candle cup for hot punch and earliest teapot – cylindrical like coffee pot. Among ceramics, posset pot for warm curdled milk and ale and decorated dishes showing Dutch influence. Magnificent jewel casket, silver dressing case with scissors, combs etc. Extensive glassware and fashionable japanned cabinets. Miniatures by Oliver and Cooper show contemporary dress. Open Mon–Thur, Sat 10–5.50, Sun 2.30–5.50.

National Portrait Gallery has contemporary portraits of kings, courtiers and Cromwell. An uncomfortable looking James I by Mytens. Van Dyck's charming '5 eldest children of Charles I'. Lely's somewhat affected Nell Gwyn dressed as innocent shepherdess, a contrast to his painting of her nude at Chiddingford Castle, Kent. Gallery of important creative men of 17th c: Ben Jonson, Marvell, Hobbes, Locke, Evelyn, Bunyan, Milton, Harvey, Boyle and Pepys, who holds a song he'd set to music and wrote of sitting, 'I do almost break my neck looking over my shoulders to make the posture.' Open Mon–Fri 10–5, Sat 10–6, Sun 2–6.

Ranger's House, Blackheath, is a brick villa house of 1688 with fine collection of full length Elizabethan and Jacobean portraits particularly notable for costume and accessories. Portraits by William Larkin, last great exponent of the Elizabethan style, Richard Sackville, Earl of Dorset in 1613 and the 'Redlynch long gallery set' of splendid court ladies. Paintings of Charles II, James II, their wives and mistresses by Lely and more sober paintings by Kneller. Open Feb–Oct, daily 10–5, Nov–Jan 10–4.

Manchester Gallery of English Costume, Platt Hall. Very few suits and dresses have survived (there is one 1660 dress of silver tissue in Bath Museum of Costume) but the Filmer collection, on loan here shows variety of richly embroidered garments and some plainer linen and lace accessories. Women's and men's hats, gloves and handkerchieves and a girl's linen bib and tucker of mid-17th c. Check opening hours, tel Manchester 224 5217.

Montacute House (Somerset) Fine collection of Jacobean portraits on permanent loan from National Portrait Gallery including poet Francis Quarles by painter William Dobson, who used classical busts and friezes in background to illustrate character of sitter. Open April–Oct Mon, Wed, Thur, Fri, Sat, Sun 12.30–6. Admission charge. 3½m W of Yeovil on A3088.

Petworth House (Sussex) Fine rooms matched by art collection. Among Van Dycks, many portraits of Percy family: Henry Percy the 'wizard' earl, scientist

who was imprisoned in Tower for his cousin's part in Gunpowder Plot. On view is his globe given by Raleigh. Algernon, 10th Earl of Northumberland, mediator in civil war, who was entrusted with Charles I's children, painted by Van Dyck. Paintings of Sir Robert Shirley and wife in oriental costume. Kneller's portrait of Newton may be viewed on Tues only. Also contains a fine Tompion long case clock 1700 in original walnut case. Nat Trust. Open April–Oct Wed, Thurs, Sat, Sun, Bank Hols 2–6. Extra rooms open Tues (not after Bank Hols). Admission charge. 5½m E of Midhurst.

Stoke-on-Trent (Staffordshire) City Museum and Art Gallery has greatest collection of Staffordshire slipware. Toft items – one with CR and royal coat of arms. Plate of 1670s depicts Catherine of Braganza. Spice boxes, eggstands and harvest jugs. Clear contrast between dark Cromwellian pots and Restoration explosion of colour from France and tulipomania from Holland. Open weekdays 10.30–5, Wed 10.30–8.

ENGINEERING/SCIENCE

Colchester (Essex) Bourne Mill is a charming late Elizabethan building probably used as a fishing lodge by Sir Thomas Lucas. Mullioned windows, huge end gables with exotic chimneys and obelisks. Gerard in his 'Herball' noted the interesting marsh plants he acquired during a visit to the Bourne ponds. Dutch refugees took over from Lucas when he was in trouble during the Civil Wars. They turned it into a cloth mill for weaving and bleaching. Much of the machinery is still in working order. The huge 26ft water wheel is inside the building. Nat Trust. Open April–Sept Wed, Sat, Sun, and Bank Hols 2–6. Admission charge. 1m S of Colchester off B1025.

Ivinghoe (Buckinghamshire) Pitstone Windmill is the oldest windmill in England, timbers dated 1627. A picturesque post mill worked until 1902 when storm damaged sails. Now restored and 2 sets of millstones for corn grinding are still in place. Nat Trust. Open May–Sept Sun and Bank Hols 2.30–6. Admission charge. 3½m NE of Tring off B488.

Liverpool In Time Gallery of Merseyside County Museum a collection of about 40 watches, clocks and sundials of 17th c. Open weekdays 10–5, Sun 2–5.

London Navigation room of National Maritime Museum at Greenwich has compasses, dividers, graphometers, sea charts and chronometers by John Harrison. Terrestrial globe of 1647 shows Australia as 'Incognita'. Neptune Hall houses splendid barge given by William III to Mary. Along gallery to Queen's House containing oldest collection of model ships, built to scale by 17th c designers.

Old Royal Observatory, Greenwich, was founded 1675 for first Astronomer Royal, John Flamsteed, 'in order to the finding out of the longitude of places for perfecting navigation and astronomy.' Designed 'a little for pompe' by Christopher Wren, who chose the site. Flamsteed's degree clock on view, other year clocks by Tompion are replicas of those in British Museum and Holkham Hall. Models of 17th c sextants, quadrants, telescopes. Open Tues–Sat 10–6 (10–5 in winter), Sun 2–5.30.

The Science Museum has a selection of clocks. Sandglasses – like egg timers – to time sermons. Lantern clocks of first half of century and pendulum clocks of second half. One splendid pedestal clock of 1695 shows time of day, date, zodiac, phase of moon, high tide at London Bridge. Typical Tompion 8-day clock and many watches by Quare, Jackson Taylor. Open Mon–Sat 10–6, Sun 2.30–6.

Wey Navigation Canal Sir Richard Weston (1591–1652) builder of Sutton Place and agricultural reformer, introduced the principle of the canal lock. Wey navigation canal completed to his designs in 1653 to transport timber and corn through a series of 10 locks. Travellers on canal nowadays pass through unspoilt scenery where once 50 water mills worked. Extends 15m from Guildford to Thames. No navigation dusk to dawn. Guided boat trips from Guildford to Godalming, April–Sept. Tel Guildford 504494.

Woolsthorpe Manor (Lincolnshire) A small farmhouse, Newton's birthplace, where he returned after Cambridge, 'in the prime of my life for invention.' Little Newtonia left. Furniture is contemporary on loan from V and A. An experiment is set up in his study modelled on his work on prisms. Replicas of telescope, letters. Interesting drawing by young Newton of church and postmill. Outside is probable descendant of famous apple tree. Nat Trust. Open April–Oct Mon, Wed, Fri, Sun, 11–12.30, 2–6. Admission charge. 7m S of Grantham.

MISCELLANEOUS

Burford (Oxfordshire) In 1649 Cromwell imprisoned 340 mutinous soldiers for 3 days and nights in Church of St John the Baptist. They were protesting about low pay and the prospect of being sent to Ireland. 3 leaders were shot. Scratched into lead lining of the font is 'Anthony Sedley, 1649, prisoner,' 16m W of Oxford off A40.

Cambridge The Pepys Library in Magdalene College bears the date 1724, referring to the date when Pepys's 3,000 books were placed in his old college according to his will. These are housed in his own book cases; there is also his desk. As a student in 1651, he called himself a 'cheerful Roundhead' and was admonished for being 'scandalously' drunk – a practice he continued after the Restoration when he returned to drink the King's health. Open mid-Jan–mid-March, Oct–Dec Mon–Sat 2.30–3.30, April–Aug Mon–Sat 11.30–12.30, 2.30–3.30.

Chalfont St Giles (Buckinghamshire) Small half-timbered cottage where blind Milton fled from the city when plague raged in 1665. There are portraits, busts and Milton's study where he is alleged to have finished 'Paradise Lost'. He lived here with his 3rd wife and youngest daughter. Open Feb–Oct Tues–Sat 10–1, 2–6, Sun 2–6. Admission charge. 3m N of Gerrards Cross off A413 in village.

Edinburgh Gladstone's Land, best preserved example of old Edinburgh tenement house, 6 storeys high from arcaded entrance to gabled roof – 17th c version of a block of luxury flats. Built in 1620 for Thomas Gladstone, rich merchant ancestor of British P.M. He probably lived on third floor, 4 other apartments housed a knight, a guild officer, a minister and a merchant. Interior decorated with painted walls and ceilings. Nat Trust for Scotland. Open April–Oct, Mon–Sat 10–5, Sun 2–5, Nov–mid-Dec, Sat 10–4.30, Sun 2–4.30. Admission charge. 483 Lawnmarket.

Eyam (Derbyshire) When plague broke out in 1665, Rector Mompesson encouraged villagers to isolate themselves to prevent disease spreading elsewhere. A year later 262 of 350 inhabitants had died of plague. Drama of place revealed by graves – one woman lost husband and 6 children within week. Row of plague cottages (outside only), trading places where vinegar soaked coins were left in exchange for food, museum containing documents: inventories of victims' goods, wills etc. Museum open by appointment. Tel Hope Valley 31030. 12½m NW of Chesterfield.

Huntingdon (Cambridgeshire) Small museum recently established in Cromwell's old school. Contains portraits of Cromwell family and friends, including Lely picture of Cromwell. Among selection of Cromwell relics on show: the hat he wore when dissolving Parliament, his gloves, riding boots, spurs and walking stick. There's his Soldier's Pocket Bible for spiritual needs and splendid pomade chest for temporal work on warts and all. Open Tues–Fri 11–1, 2–5, Sat 11–1, 2–4, Sun 2–4.

London The new Jewel House at the Tower of London has crown jewels fashioned for Charles II's coronation 1661 after destruction of previous ones during Commonwealth. Elsewhere, arms, clocks, ceramics and grim shrew's bridle like a death mask. Open March–Oct weekdays 9.30–5, Sun 2–5, Nov–Feb 9.30–4, closed Sun. Admission charge.

The Geffrye Museum houses John Evelyn's 'closet of curiosities' recreated from inventory of 1702 with his ebony cabinet of 1652 specially made for him in Paris. Open Tues–Sat and Bank Hols 10–5, Sun 2–5.

The Venetian Ambassador's Room at Knole, Kent, a mansion full of fine Stuart furniture

THE
GEORGIANS

by Sarah Howell

PARKS/GARDENS/TEMPLES

Blenheim (Oxfordshire) Sir John Vanbrugh's austere park transformed by Capability Brown in 1760s. As well as creating the lakes, he planted thousands of trees, and swept away the formal gardens near the palace (new ones laid out in 19th and early 20th c). Park open daily 9–5. Palace mid-March–Oct daily 11.30–5. Admission charge.

Castle Howard (Yorkshire) Grounds as grand and dramatic as Vanbrugh's splendid house. He also designed the beautiful Temple of the 4 Winds which looks out over a river valley with a bizarre, overgrown bridge towards Hawksmoor's huge mausoleum. 'It would tempt one to be buried alive,' said Horace Walpole. Whole park a triumphantly successful attempt to create an ideal landscape. Open Good Friday–Oct daily 11–5, house 11.30–5. Admission charge. 15m NE of York off A64.

Heveningham Hall (Suffolk) House recently changed hands and should have re-opened, grounds alone, worth visiting. The view of the N front from the road, column after column reflected in the water of Capability Brown's lake, is a cliché but comes off magnificently. Brown also contributed a 'crinkle-crankle' brick wall for the kitchen garden and James Wyatt added 1791 an orangery of cool beauty. Tel Ubbeston 355 for opening times. 4m SW of Halesworth on B1117.

Petworth Park (Sussex) Capability Brown's naturalistic manner at its finest – simple and seemingly inevitable. He enlarged the lake in 1750s and dotted it with islands planted with willows. Great sweep of grass, deer, sheep, wooded slopes – all little changed from time Turner painted it. His pictures of the park are in the mostly 17th c house. Nat Trust. Park open all year 9–sunset. House open April–Oct Tues–Thur, Sat and Bank Hols (closed following Tues) 2–6. Admission charge.

Rousham (Oxfordshire) Most complete surviving garden designed by William Kent. Planned to make a series of framed pictures linked by woodland walks. Kent punctuated it with classical temples, an arcade overlooking the river, fountains and cascades. Begun 1730s, it contains many features that were to become essential motifs of garden-designers later in the century including an early ha-ha, the 'serpentine rill' – forerunner of many winding streams and paths – and the 'eye-catcher', a fake ruin on a hill to add interest to a vista. Garden open April–Sept daily 10–6. Admission charge. House (17th c) open April–Sept Wed, Sun and Bank Hols 10–6. Admission charge. 12m N of Oxford off A423.

Stourhead (Wiltshire) Dreamlike garden designed 1740s by an amateur, Henry Hoare, inspired by his travels in Italy and the paintings of Claude and Poussin. Lakes, streams, sweeping hills, temples and a grotto where a nymph lies asleep make up a series of haunting pictures. House Palladian with good 18th c furniture. Nat Trust. Garden open all year daily 8–7. Admission charge. House open April, Sept, Oct Mon, Wed, Sat, Sun, May–Aug every day except Fri 2–6 or dusk if earlier. Admission charge. 3m NW of Mere off B3092.

Stowe (Buckinghamshire) Gardens of Stowe School evolved between 1713 and 1775, getting gradually less formal. Aim throughout to create scene of 'more than mortal magnificence'. Almost all the best Georgian garden designers contributed to it including Vanbrugh, Bridgeman, Kent, Gibbs and Capability Brown, who began his career as an undergardener here. Crowded with over 30 garden buildings and temples. Grounds and garden buildings open during school Easter and summer holidays, daily 1–6. Tel Buckingham 3164. Admission charge. 3m N of Buckingham.

HOUSES

A la Ronde (Devon) Odd, 16-sided house with cone-shaped roof and diamond windows. Built 1790s by 2 women, it's endearingly feminine, a complete contrast to the pompous masculinity of many Georgian country houses. Inside, the cousins Jane and Mary Parminter filled it with examples of fashionable female crafts – featherwork friezes, shell collections, seaweed pictures, cut paper work. All slightly moth-eaten, but enchanting. Open April–Oct daily 10–6. Admission charge. 2m N of Exmouth on A376.

Castle Coole (Co. Fermanagh) James Wyatt's austere masterpiece in Portland stone stripped of all superfluous ornament, a central block with tall temple columns flanked by low wings on either side. Wyatt's plan for the four principal rooms was based on a 6ft module – each measures 36'×24'×18'.

Toby jug in lead-glazed earthenware, c. 1780,
Victoria and Albert Museum

Severity softened by elegant oval saloon looking out to the NW with splendid plasterwork by Joseph Rose, Adam's plasterer at Syon and Kenwood. By June 1795, the 1st Earl of Belmore had spent £53,971. 11s. 2¾d on his house, at a time when labourers could be hired for a shilling a day: bills were still coming in for the elaborate chimney pieces that dominate the chief rooms. Nat Trust. Open April–end Sept daily except Fri 2–6. Admission charge. 1½m SE of Enniskillen on A4.

Castle Ward (Co. Down) Built in the 1760s for Benjamin Ward and his wife, Lady Anne, who were evidently unable to agree what sort of house they wanted. Benjamin's front facing SW was an exercise in the restrained Palladian manner. His wife's front facing NE was spiky gothic, with boudoir, saloon and morning room in the same style. Contemporary comments were tart. Mrs Delaney, visiting in 1762 found that 'He wants taste and . . . his wife is so whimsical that I doubt her judgement.' On the shores of Strangford Lough with formal garden, temple, stable yard with theatre and Victorian laundry. Nat Trust. Open April–end Sept daily except Fri 2–6. Admission charge. Nr. Strangford village on A25.

Chiswick House In 1725, Lord Burlington, much impressed by Palladio's architecture during his Grand Tour visit to Italy, designed this symmetrical temple to the arts based on the Villa Capra at Vicenza. It was used for entertaining and for displaying his collection of pictures. Mundane activities like eating and sleeping took place in a now vanished big house nearby. Whole conception – central dome, grand staircases and porticos back and front – was Burlington's, but William Kent helped him with detailing of interior and garden, which like house itself helped to start a new fashion. D of E. Open daily March, April, Oct 9.30–5.30, May–Sept 9.30–7, Nov–Feb 9.30–4. (Oct–March closed Mon, Tues.) Admission charge.

Holkham Hall (Norfolk) Designed by Kent for the Earl of Leicester in 1730s. Facade, built of dun-coloured brick, austere, almost forbidding, but entrance hall with alabaster Corinthian columns is splendidly grand in the ancient Roman manner. 'Like a bath-house of the utmost magnificence,' wrote Arthur Young. Fine, solemnly classical long library and sculpture gallery. Open June, Sept Mon, Thurs 2–5, July–August Mon, Wed, Thurs, Bank Hols 11.30–5, June–Sept, Sun 2–5. 2m W of Wells off A149.

Kedleston Hall (Derbyshire) Robert Adam was the 3rd architect to work on the rebuilding of Kedleston for the Curzons. James Paine had already designed the conventionally classical front when in 1760 Adam eased him out of the job with his usual ruthlessness. Garden side of the house is Adam's – an original and graceful composition with dome, sweeping staircase, columns topped with statues. He also designed the beautiful interior. Marble hall and pink alabaster columns have a chill perfection, the tall, domed saloon equally elegant. Open last Sun April–last Sun Sept Sun and Bank Hols 2–6. Admission charge. 4½m NW of Derby.

Mellerstain (Berwickshire) Begun by William Adam in 1720s and finished by his son Robert in 1770s. The exterior is perhaps a little simple but the

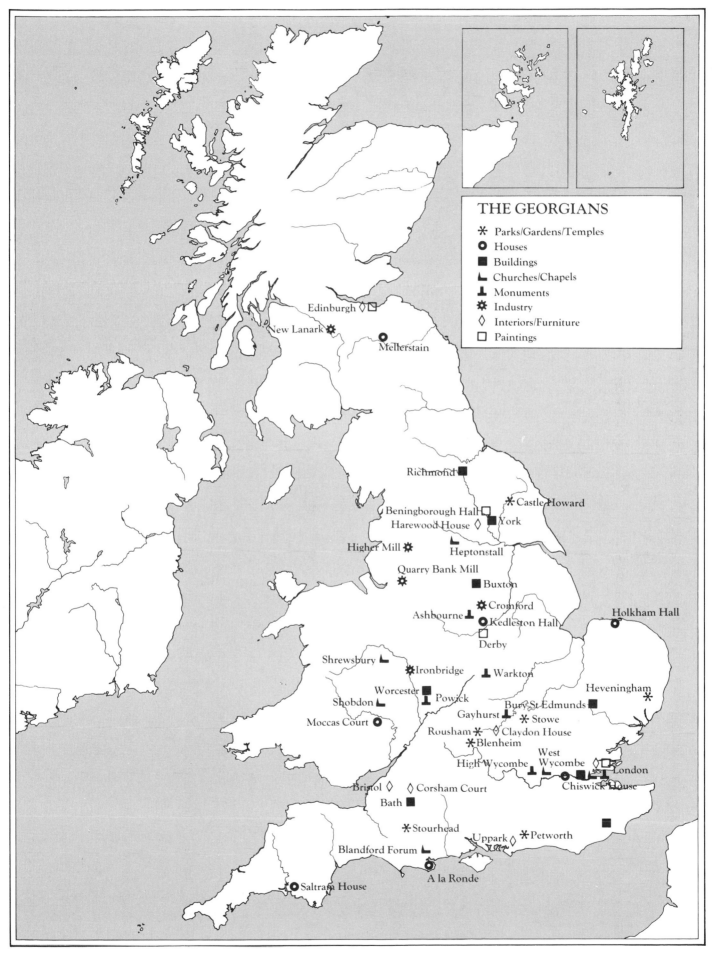

THE GEORGIANS

✳ Parks/Gardens/Temples
◉ Houses
◼ Buildings
∟ Churches/Chapels
⊥ Monuments
✾ Industry
◇ Interiors/Furniture
▢ Paintings

Edinburgh ◇ ▢
New Lanark ✾
Mellerstain ◉

Richmond ◼
✳ Castle Howard
Beningborough Hall ▢
Harewood House ◇ ◼ York
Higher Mill ✾   ∟ Heptonstall
Quarry Bank Mill ✾
◼ Buxton
✾ Cromford
Ashbourne ⊥ ◉ Kedleston Hall   Holkham Hall ◉
▢ Derby
Shrewsbury ∟
✾ Ironbridge   ⊥ Warkton
Worcester ◼   Heveningham ◼   ✳
Shobdon ∟ ⊥ Powick   Bury St Edmunds ◼
Gayhurst ⊥ ✳ Stowe
Moccas Court ◉   Rousham ✳ ◇ Claydon House
✳ Blenheim
High Wycombe West   London ▢
⊥ Wycombe ◉ ◼▢
Bristol ◇ ◇ Corsham Court   Chiswick House
Bath ◼
✳ Stourhead   ✳ Petworth
Uppark ◇
Blandford Forum ∟
A la Ronde ◉
Saltram House ◉

201

Family group in silhouette, a fashionable Georgian technique for likenesses

interior contains some of Robert Adam's finest work, particularly the library, the small drawing room and the music room. Open May–Sept Sun–Fri 1.30–5.50. Admission charge. 7m NW of Kelso off A6089.

Moccas Court (Hereford and Worcester) Handsome, tall house built of bright red brick, startling in its green setting. Interior Adam-inspired, the round drawing-room overlooking the River Wye is decorated with cut-out paper collage in the Pompeian manner – a room for summer use only: fires were never allowed as smoke would damage the delicate paper. Open April–Aug, Oct Thur 2–6. Admission charge. 13m W of Hereford off B4352.

Saltram House (Devon) Outside plain and seaside with painted rendered brickwork. Inside an interesting mixture of 2 of the 18th c's most appealing styles. In 1740s Lady Catherine Parker, a flamboyant and forceful woman, commissioned and probably herself designed rococo decoration and stucco ceilings. The hall, small sitting-rooms and bedrooms – charming with Chinese wallpaper and elaborate chinoiserie frames to looking-glasses and pictures – reflect her taste. Her son employed Robert Adam to design the saloon, one of his loveliest rooms, with specially woven carpet and Chippendale chairs, and the dining-room. Good Georgian pictures, pottery and porcelain. Nat Trust. Open April–Oct Tues–Sun and Bank Hols 12.30–6. Admission charge. 2m W of Plymouth off A38.

BUILDINGS

Bath Overlooking the Roman bath in pleasing golden building near the Abbey, Pump Room designed 1780s when town already almost past its prime. Statue and portrait of inimitable Beau Nash, social dictator and Master of Ceremonies, still presides. He looks prepared to inflict crushing snubs. Here, as long as they kept his rules, duchesses, invalids, rakes and social climbers drank the cloudy, rather nasty waters. Today tea and coffee served in grand room with tall arched windows. Open daily 9–6. Admission charge.

Bury St Edmunds (Suffolk) Market Cross designed in 1770s by Adam as columned market hall with theatre above. Upper floor now an art gallery. Open Tues–Sat 10.30–4.30. Admission charge.

Buxton (Derbyshire) Assembly Room in John Carr's fine crescent built for 5th Duke of Devonshire in 1780s, now the public reference library. In spite of its new use still evocative and elegant with its origin-

al chandeliers, Corinthian pilasters and painted ceiling. Open Mon–Fri 10–7, Sat 9.30–12.

London In 1740 Thomas Coram, an irascible sea-captain, horrified by the sight of babies left to die on dung-heaps, set up Thomas Coram Foundation for Children. Aristocrats, artists and musicians, inspired by the new spirit of philanthropy, donated some splendid treasures to the Foundling Hospital. Original building pulled down 1930s, but old Court Room with rococo ceiling, staircase and Foundlings' Picture Gallery incorporated into new one. Contains some of the best Hogarths, including his vivid portrait of Coram, works by Reynolds, Gainsborough, West etc. Handel presented keyboard of his organ and score of 'Messiah'. Most touching relics, trinkets – cheap necklaces, rings, medallions etc – mothers left with their babies. Open Mon–Fri 10–4, closed Bank Hols.

Richmond (Yorkshire) Georgian theatre is almost the oldest playhouse in Britain – Theatre Royal, Bristol, though much altered, is a little older – and best preserved 18th c public theatre in whole of Europe. Opened by actor-manager Samuel Butler 1788. Very charming interior with boxes, seats for only 200, some original scenery. Also museum. Open May–Sept daily 2.30–5, Sat and Bank Hols 10–1. Admission charge.

Worcester Guild Hall is a grand brick town hall built 1720s. Facade decorated with statues of Stuart kings and queens and elaborately carved pediment. Assembly room on upper floor. Open when not in use Mon–Fri 9.30–5.30, closed Bank Hols.

York Lord Burlington, who owned estates in Yorkshire, designed distinguished interior of the Assembly Rooms with marble Corinthian columns. 'Festive, but nobly restrained,' says Pevsner. Now it is used for meetings, lectures, even – the earl must be turning in his grave – model railway exhibitions. Open when not in use during office hours on weekdays – ask for caretaker.

CHURCHES/CHAPELS

Blandford Forum (Dorset) St Peter and St Paul built 1730s by John and William Bastard, who also designed much of rest of town after fire destroyed the original. Outside stone columns and tall tower topped by a cupola, inside good box-pews and a minstrels' gallery supported on fluted wooden columns.

Heptonstall (Yorkshire) Dour little octagonal stone chapel in village above Hebden Bridge. Built 1764 for old-established weaving community, which in

last part of century became booming mill town: John Wesley preached here and it's the oldest continually used chapel to survive. Pleasing interior with columns and balcony. 1m NW of Hebden Bridge off A 646.

London St-Martin-in-the-Fields, James Gibbs's masterpiece, by far finest building in Trafalgar Square. Built 1720s, exterior has imposing portico with Corinthian columns and royal coat of arms, steeple inspired by Wren. Inside elaborate plasterwork and woodwork and more Corinthian columns. The grandest post-Wren London church.

Shobdon (Hereford and Worcester) St John the Evangelist, lovely rococo gothic confection built as an estate church for Viscount Bateman in 1750s by unknown architect. His great house has vanished and the little church stands alone on the side of hill. Its wedding-cake interior with ogee arches and elaborate pews has much light-hearted charm. 12m SW of Ludlow off B 4362.

Shrewsbury (Shropshire) St Chad, an elegant rotunda in fine position overlooking river. Inside cast iron columns, simple pews, Regency monuments. Designed by George Steuart 1790.

West Wycombe (Buckinghamshire) St Laurence, most secular, if not most cynical of Georgian churches. 'A temple built aloft in air, that serves for show and not for prayer.' Medieval shell on hill-top was altered for notorious Sir Francis Dashwood, dilettante MP, owner of nearby West Wycombe Park and founder of Hell Fire Club. Tower is topped by golden ball big enough to have seats inside – a bizarre drinking spot for John Wilkes and his Hell Fire Club cronies. Interior has marble floor and rich carvings. Near church mausoleum and at foot of hill caves that must have made damp and chilly setting for legendary orgies. 2m NW of High Wycombe off A40.

MONUMENTS

Ashbourne (Derbyshire) Penelope Boothby (d 1793) by Thomas Banks. Very touching, but unsentimental carving of little barefoot girl lying asleep – Queen Charlotte wept when she saw it. Inscriptions in 4 languages – English one reads: 'She was in form and intellect most exquisite. The unfortunate parents ventured their all on this frail Bark and the

Georgian formality: precisely detailed monument to Sir Nathan Wright and son in church at Gayhurst, Bucks

wreck was total.' 13m NW of Derby.

Gayhurst (Buckinghamshire) Sir Nathan Wright (d 1728) and his son. Very realistic bewigged gentlemen – precisely detailed costume down to the peculiar way they buttoned their coats. 'Grandest and most successful of its type in England,' says Pevsner. Set in almost unchanged Georgian church. 3m NW of Newport Pagnell.

High Wycombe (Buckinghamshire) Earl of Shelburne (d 1754) by Peter Scheemakers – fine, crowded classical group – everyone in togas including women and children.

London St Paul's. Has Dr Johnson grumbling in a toga, and its crypt and side aisles are full of scantily dressed heroes striking classical attitudes.

Westminster Abbey. Look out for Handel by Roubiliac – wigless but impressive in fur-lined coat, surrounded by musical instruments. General William Hargrave rising melodramatically from his tomb and David Garrick hurling aside stone curtains. Any number of politicians and soldiers disguised as Roman senators.

Powick (Worcestershire) Mary Russell (d 1786) by Thomas Scheemakers. Mourning muse reclines on a sarcophagus carved charmingly with a mother teaching a little girl music. 3m SW of Worcester.

Warkton (Northamptonshire) Rococo monuments to Duke and Duchess of Montagu by Roubiliac, 1750s, and striking one to another duchess, 1770s, gesticulating classical figures set in elegant alcove designed by Robert Adam. 2m NE of Kettering.

INDUSTRY

Cromford (Derbyshire) Richard Arkwright invented the water-powered spinning machine and in 1771 set up his first mill here on banks of a brook flowing into the River Derwent. Now a trout farm, but handsome red-brick Masson Mill with its Georgian central block and Venetian windows still spins cotton. Cromford still a working town – rather run down now – not an industrial museum. None of the buildings open to the public, but whole place with its hilly setting, canal and workers' cottages very evocative. In North St a line of cottages Arkwright built for his work-force that have big attics for use as framework knitting-rooms. 2m S of Matlock on A6.

Higher Mill Museum (Lancashire) Late 18th c waterpowered fulling mill where heavy woollen materials were finished. First floor contains important collection of early textile machinery, Hargreaves's Jenny and several original machines from Arkwright's mill at Cromford including a water twist frame. Open March–Nov Mon–Fri 2–5 also July–Sept Sat. Admission charge. Machinery collection on upper floor only shown to prebooked parties up to 20. Plans to open next door mill soon. Tel Rossendale 226459. 1m S of Haslingden on B6235.

Ironbridge Gorge Museum (Shropshire) The Industrial Revolution could not have happened without the series of innovations in the manufacture and use of iron that took place in Coalbrookdale in the 18th c. Now the whole area of several sq m has become a unique industrial museum complex. Among the Georgian relics are the Iron Bridge itself – the first in the world, an elegant single span – and Abraham Darby's old blast furnace where iron was first smelted with coke in 1709 and where the bridge itself was cast. Open daily 10–6 (10–5 in winter when clocks go back). Admission charge. Telford, off junction 12 M6.

New Lanark (Strathclyde) Founded by Richard Arkwright and David Dale in 1785 and managed for 30 years by Robert Owen. The intention was to create a complete working community, with good houses, schools and shops near the cotton mills. The mill buildings beside the Clyde were originally waterpowered, terraces of solid sandstone houses line the hillside – among them is The New Institution where adult and child workers were educated. Owen's approach to town-planning had a great effect, particularly on the later Chartists. 1m S of Lanark off A73.

Quarry Bank Mill (Cheshire) Samuel Gregg built

The Palladian symmetry of Chiswick House, London, built by Lord Burlington

this well-proportioned cotton-spinning mill with classical detailing in 1784. An early example of a paternalistic industrialist, he paid his employees low wages but provided them with pleasant surroundings, purpose-built cottages, school, chapel, farm for fresh food. Apprentices, mostly pauper children, lived in specially built Apprentice House – their working hours were from 6am–7pm. Nat Trust. Check opening hours, tel Wilmslow 527468. Admission charge. 1m N of Wilmslow A34 and B5166.

INTERIORS/FURNITURE

Bristol Sugar merchant's rather austere 1790s house in Great George St. Good re-creation of prosperous middle-class interior. Furniture includes fine harpsichord and collector's cabinet of 1740s. Built-in cold plunge bath for fashionable daily dips to stimulate the system. Open Mon–Sat 10–5.

Claydon House (Buckinghamshire) Series of enchanting rococo rooms. Their exuberant plasterwork designed by local virtuoso craftsman, Luke Lightfoot. Delightful Chinese room with pagodas, bells, Chinamen taking tea, high point of mid-century English taste for chinoiserie. Nat Trust. Open April–Oct Sat–Wed 2–6 or sunset. Bank Hols 12.30–6. Admission charge. 3½m SW of Winslow.

Corsham Court (Wiltshire) Here Capability Brown turned interior designer. His picture gallery with bold plasterwork ceiling is still hung symmetrically from floor to ceiling in the Georgian manner. Paintings typical Grand Tour collection – mostly Italian.

Rustic chairs for outdoor use in arbours and garden temples, Victoria and Albert Museum

A great age for painting: 'The Reapers' by George Stubbs, in the Tate Gallery

Open mid-Jan–May, Oct–mid-Dec, Wed, Thurs, Sat, Sun, Bank Hol Mon 2–4, June–Sept same days 2–6. Admission charge.

Edinburgh In Charlotte Sq, masterpiece of Georgian town-planning designed by Adam, 1790s. No 7, one of plainer houses, recently furnished very sympathetically in style of that period. Some good Scottish furniture, original colour schemes and interesting period pieces like portable lavatory and domestic medicine chest. Nat Trust for Scotland. Open April–Oct Mon–Sat 10–5, Nov–mid-Dec Sat 10–4.30, Sun 2–4.30. Admission charge.

Harewood House (Yorkshire) First great house decorated by Robert Adam. Everything most meticulously composed – fine plasterwork and furniture designed for house by Thomas Chippendale (born in nearby Otley). Some extraordinary touches like his *trompe l'oeil* wooden curtain-swags in the gallery. Check opening hours, tel Harewood 886225. Admission charge.

London Victoria and Albert Museum. Splendid examples of furniture throughout period from George I's lacquer cabinet to George IV's royal bath-tub. Reconstructed rooms include almost whole of Music Room from Norfolk House, Duke of Beaufort's gorgeous chinoiserie bedroom, Glass Drawing-room from Northumberland House, all sparkly pink and green vulgarity, and a little Strawberry Hill Gothic

room from Lee Priory. Open Mon–Thur, Sat and some Bank Hols 10–5.50, Sun 2.30–5.50.

Dennis Severs's House. Unique, slightly dotty but most successful evocation of the past in a tumble-down area of Spitalfields. Dennis Severs, a young American, gives a 2-hour tour of his 18th c home, candlelit one-man show, total theatre with sound effects, authentic smells – vivid commentary about several generations of imaginary silk-weaving family. Magical conjuring up Georgian atmosphere, expensive but well worth it. 18 Folgate St, E1.

Osterley Park. Adam again – demonstrating his remarkable versatility. Rooms and furniture in different styles from pure neo-classical hall to florid rococo Tapestry Room. Etruscan Room with painted walls and furniture inspired by discovery of Pompeii, curious and attractive. Many of Adam's original designs for decoration and furniture on view. Nat Trust. Open April–Sept Tues–Sat and some Bank Hols 2–6, Oct–March 12–4. Tel 01–727 3039. N of A4 near Osterley station.

Uppark (Sussex) Lovely late 17th c house mostly decorated and furnished in 1750s. Saloon has fragile white and gold colour scheme, original ivory silk festoon curtains and pelmets, English gilt wooden chairs in Louis XV style. Charming fully furnished and lived-in 1730s dolls' house. Nat Trust. Open April–Sept Thur, Sun and Bank Hols 2–5.30, Wed 2–5. Admission charge. 5m SE of Petersfield off B2146.

PAINTINGS

Beningbrough Hall (Yorkshire) In early 18th c baroque house, many Georgian portraits from National Portrait Gallery including series of Kit-Kat Club – Whig writers and politicians – by Kneller. Also excellent exhibition 'The Portrait and the Country House', including all sorts of background information and social history. Nat Trust. Open April–Oct Tues–Thurs, Sat, Sun 12–6. Admission charge. 3m W of Shipton on A19.

Derby City Art Gallery best place to see the work of Joseph Wright of Derby including his dramatic scientific and industrial scenes like 'Arkwright's Mill by Moonlight' and 'A Philosopher Lecturing on the Orrery'. (*See* Pottery/Porcelain.) Open Tues–Fri 10–6, Sat 10–5.

Edinburgh Scottish artists Raeburn and Ramsay can be seen at their best in National Gallery of Scotland – look out for Ramsay's lovely portrait of his 2nd wife, plus Reynolds, Gainsborough, etc. Open Mon–Sat 10–5, Sun 2–5.

London Tate Gallery has a room full of Hogarths, beautiful Stubbses including his 'Reapers' and 'Haymakers', Zoffany, Romney, Joseph Wright etc, well represented, plus all the great watercolourists including Rowlandson. Good Reynoldses and Gainsboroughs, but even better examples of their work in National Gallery. The National Portrait Gallery also has fine examples of most of the big names. Tate open weekdays 10–6, Sun 2–6.

The Iveagh Bequest, at Kenwood House, Hampstead, includes some splendid English 18th c paintings including one of Gainsborough's masterpieces 'Countess Howe' – also good Adam rooms. Open April–Sept daily 10–7, Oct–March 10–5 or dusk.

Foyers of the National Theatre now permanently house Somerset Maugham's collection of Georgian theatrical paintings – some good pictures by Zoffany including Garrick in drag, also less well-known specialists in painting theatrical scenes like Samuel de Wilde. Open Mon–Sat 10am–11pm

POTTERY/PORCELAIN

Barlaston (Staffordshire) Josiah Wedgwood founded his famous pottery in 1759 – today in the factory next door to the Wedgwood Museum they are still producing some of his designs like the elegant Black Basalt teaset. He employed artists of the calibre of Flaxman and Stubbs – their plaques, portrait medallions etc on view. Also great variety of Georgian products from replicas of the Portland Vase to shoe buckles. Demonstrations of traditional and modern techniques. Open Mon–Fri 9–5. Admission charge. No children under 5. Off A34 5m S of Stoke-on-Trent.

Derby City Art Gallery holds biggest and best collection of Derby porcelain. Factory's most important period from 1785–1800 when it was run by William Duesbury, who also for a time owned the Chelsea factory. Firm concentrated on tableware finely decorated with landscapes, seascapes and charmingly painted naturalistic flowers, also figures and groups inspired by Sèvres. (*See* Paintings.)

London Victoria and Albert Museum Holds largest and most representative collection of English 18th c pottery and porcelain in the world. Open Mon–Thur, Sat and some Bank Hols 10–5.50, Sun 2.30–5.50.

Stoke-on-Trent City Museum and Art Gallery holds one of the best ceramic collections well displayed in recently opened museum. Literally thousands of Georgian teapots, everyday household crockery, many charming, rather primitive saltglazed stoneware figures and groups produced by local potteries early in century. Open Mon, Tues, Thur–Sat 10.30–5, Wed 10.30–8.

Worcester Dyson Perrins Museum specialises in

Chelsea porcelain group, 'The Music Lesson', 1760s, in the Victoria and Albert Museum

Patriotic engraved glasses with air-twist stems characteristic of the period

Worcester, longest lived of English porcelain factories. Nice early chinoiserie pieces on show plus the Chinese porcelain that inspired them, also lots of blue and white and transfer-printed tableware – Worcester pioneered this process. Open April–Sept Mon–Sat, Oct–March Mon–Fri 10–1, 2–5.

PEOPLE

William Cowper's House Cowper, afflicted by periods of dark depression, lived here from 1767–1786. His pet hares gambolled every evening on the Turkey carpet in the hall, he wrote 'John Gilpin' and hymns like 'God Moves in a Mysterious Way' in the parlour. At the bottom of the garden stands his evocative little summer-house 'no bigger than a sedan chair' which he called his boudoir or 'sulking room'. House open 10–12, 2–5. Admission charge. Orchard Side, Olney, Buckinghamshire.

Horace Walpole's House Strawberry Hill is now a Roman Catholic College of Higher Education. In the 1750s Horace Walpole – prime-minister's son, aesthete, wit and writer of gothic romances – transformed an ordinary suburban villa into a mock-medieval romantic fantasy. Battlements and buttresses, interior a riot of spiky arches, suits of armour, patterning, elaborate fretwork. Walpole gave gothic a new social status, and Strawberry Hill still communicates his pioneering excitement. College organises occasional guided tours, must book well in advance, worth waiting for. Tel or write Principal's Secretary, St Mary's College, Strawberry Hill, Twickenham. Tel 01-829 0051.

John Wesley's House Modest house next to his chapel. He lived here from 1778 till his death in 1791. Study contains his hat, umbrella, preaching bands, silver-buckled shoes. Off the bedroom where he died is his prayer room, the 'powerhouse of Methodism'. Each morning at 4am he waited here for God's commands for the day. Open Mon–Sat 10–4, Sun by appointment. Admission charge. Tel 01-253 2262. City Road, London.

William Wilberforce's House Wilberforce was born in this handsome house in 1759. Vivid relics of his long campaign against slavery – branding irons, shackles, whips, bills of sale and the model slave ship he showed to the House of Commons. A disconcerting wax effigy of the great campaigner sits in his favourite Chippendale armchair. Open Mon–Sat 10–5, Sun 2.30–4.30. 25 High St, Hull.

COSTUME

Bath Georgian items in Museum of Costume include interesting accessories – shoes, nightcaps, fans etc – bizarre 1750s court dresses too wide for any but the most palatial doors. Open April–Oct Mon–Sat 9.30–6, Sun 10–6, Nov–March Mon–Sat 10–5, Sun 11–5. Admission charge.

Manchester Gallery of English Costume in Platt Hall has scholarly and comprehensive collection of complete garments – specialises in dress of well-to-do middle classes from mid-18th c onwards. Check opening hours, tel Manchester 224 5217.

MUSICAL INSTRUMENTS

London Fenton House in Hampstead has a fine collection of harpsichords, clavichords etc. Often played by musicians at weekends. Also good Georgian porcelain. Nat Trust. Open Feb, March, Nov Sat, Sun 2–5, April–Oct, Sat, Mon–Wed 11–5, Sun 2–5. Admission charge.

Finchcocks (Kent) In early Georgian house, musician Richard Burnett's collection of early keyboard instruments. Musical demonstrations on all open days, also evening recitals. Open Easter–July, Sept Sun, Bank Hols, Aug Wed–Sun 2–6 Tel Goudhurst 211702. Admission charge. 2m SE of Goudhurst off A262.

A shooting party idealised for a 1760s wallpaper design, Victoria and Albert Museum

THE
VICTORIANS

by Pamela Brown and Sarah Howell

CASTLES/HOUSES

Castell Coch (South Glamorgan) Much used by television thriller directors to stand in for Dornford Yates's Bavarian castles or SS hideouts. But exterior, though dramatic, is never stagey – beautifully simple and direct – 3 round towers with cone-shaped roofs, a curving courtyard, an entrance with drawbridge and portcullis. It was William Burges's 2nd masterpiece for his great patron the Marquess of Bute (see Interiors – Cardiff Castle). Less wildly exuberant than Cardiff, but still full of charming details – the vaulted ceiling of the drawing-room with gold ribs and painted birds and butterflies, Lady Bute's round bedroom with castle-shaped washstand. Open mid-March–mid-Oct daily 9.30–6.30, mid-Oct–mid-March Mon–Sat 9.30–4, Sun 2–4. Admission charge. 6m N of Cardiff.

Carlton Towers (Yorkshire) Northern home of the Dukes of Norfolk was transformed in 1870s by E. W. Pugin from a subdued 17th c house into a top-heavy monstrosity weighed down by towers and turrets. After Pugin – son of the more famous A. W. Pugin – died in his 40s, unbalanced and bankrupt, the interior was taken over by another Catholic architect, J. F. Bentley, who was later to design Westminster Cathedral. He adopted a medieval manner and meticulously designed everything himself from furniture and curtains to towel-rails and pokers. The Venetian drawing-room is especially successful. Open Easter, May–Sept Sat–Mon, Wed 1–5. Admission charge. 1½m N of Snaith on A1041.

Cragside (Northumberland) Built between 1864–95 in a seemingly impossible position on the side of a cliff for millionaire armaments manufacturer Sir William Armstrong. His architect, Norman Shaw, was skilful enough to turn all the difficulties of the site to dramatic effect with striking changes of level, half-timbering, gargoyles, twisted chimneys. Fittingly for the home of a successful inventor, it was equipped with all sorts of pioneering gadgets. First house in the world lit by electricity generated by water power and had hydraulic lifts. Inside Morris stained glass, oriental pottery, minor Pre-Raphaelite paintings, huge Italianate fireplaces. Nat Trust. Open mid-April–Sept Tues–Sun and Bank Hols 1–6, Oct Wed, Sat, Sun 2–5. Admission charge. ½m E of Rothbury.

Osborne House (Isle of Wight) Queen Victoria's seaside retreat, designed by Albert with the help of Thomas Cubitt 1840s. Deliberately a house, not a palace – 'a place of one's own, quiet and retired'. The private apartments shut up undisturbed for 50 years after Victoria's death – touchingly modest, crammed with family portraits and mementoes. State rooms downstairs almost as evocative and much more exotic, especially the Durbar room where Indian plaster-work runs riot. Osborne became one of the most influential and well-known houses in the country – scaled-down versions of it crop up all over the place as town halls, stations and hotels. D of E. Open Easter–June, Sept–mid-Oct Mon–Sat 11–5, July, Aug Mon–Sat 10–5. Admission charge.

Scarisbrick Hall (Lancashire) In the dull, flat countryside near Southport the spindly tower and pointed roofs of Scarisbrick Hall look as unlikely as a mirage. Built for the landowner and antiquarian recluse, Charles Scarisbrick 1837 by A. W. Pugin, it reflects both the owner's and the architect's passion for the medieval. The great Hall with its carved fireplaces is, says Mark Girouard, 'The most assured and splendid piece of work to be produced to date by the Gothic revival in England.' Now a boarding school. May be visited by appointment only, preferably weekdays during school holidays. Write to The Principal, Scarisbrick Hall School, Scarisbrick, Lancashire. Tel Scarisbrick 880200.

Somerleyton Hall (Suffolk) A huge and heady mixture of Elizabethan, French and Italian details, yellow stone, scarlet brick, oak panelling, stuffed polar bears and stained glass. The garden with sweeping terraces, rose-beds, a yew maze, must have made a perfect setting for the croquet and confidences of summer house parties. Designed in 1840s by John Thomas, sculptor and mason who worked on the Houses of Parliament – for Sir Morton Peto, a railway magnate. After he lost his fortune in 1860s, the hall was bought by another hugely successful businessman determined to turn himself into a country gentleman – Frank Crossley, millionaire, MP and 3rd generation Halifax carpet manufacturer. Open mid-April–June, Sept–early October Sun, Thur and Bank Hols, July, Aug Tues–Thurs, Sun and Bank Hols 2–6. Admission charge. 5m NW of Lowestoft off B1074.

The Red House (Kent) William Morris and Philip Webb became great friends when as young men they worked together in the office of the architect George Edmund Street. When Morris got engaged to the beautiful Janey, he and Webb designed this simple, romantic country house for them set in the apple orchards of Kent. Now surrounded by suburbia – but with steeply pitched roofs, dormer windows, tall chimneys, still has an informal, comfortable charm. In 1860s it looked original and eccentric – only schools and the occasional vicarage had been built in this picturesque style. Inside though much of the Pre-Raphaelite decoration has gone – a communal effort by Morris and his friends – there are still fine hooded brick fireplaces, built-in Gothic sideboard, miniature minstrels' gallery. View by appointment only, 3 weeks' notice if possible. Write to Mr and Mrs E Hollamby, The Red House, Red House Lane, Bexleyheath, Kent.

Waddesdon Manor (Buckinghamshire) The Rothschilds were grand enough to be undeterred by the fact that by 1870s the French chateaux style was beginning to seem 'nouveau riche' in fashionable circles. Their enormous castle is Francophile in every detail. Both house and formal garden were designed by Frenchmen. Outside a jumble of ideas borrowed from the banks of the Loire, inside filled with fine, mostly 18th c French furniture and pictures. Nat Trust. Open late March–Oct, Wed–Sun 2–6 (connoisseurs' days when extra rooms shown. Tel Aylesbury 665211). Admission charge, children under 12 not admitted. 6m NW of Aylesbury on A41.

CHURCHES

Cheadle (Staffordshire) St Giles commissioned by pious millionaire Lord Shrewsbury. A. W. Pugin 1841 set out to design 'the perfect parish church of the time of Edward I'. No expense was spared. Its immensely tall spire dominates the town. Interior is lavishly decorated, sizzling with colour, pattern and gilding from floor to ceiling. 8m E of Stoke-on-Trent.

Glasgow United Presbyterian Church in St Vincent St now Free Church of Scotland. 19th c Scottish Presbyterian churches were much grander than nonconformist ones in England and Wales and throughout century were still often built in the classical style. This is a particularly imposing one, designed 1860s by Alexander 'Greek' Thomson, who was responsible for many of Glasgow's heavy neo-classical offices and streets. Temple front is set a whole storey above street level. With its strange tower and forbidding square-headed windows it looks more like a pompous municipal building than a church.

London All Saints, Margaret St, built on a cramped site in central London – the most ecstatic and original of Victorian churches. William Butterfield designed it 1850 for the Camden Society faction of the High Church Oxford Movement. Outside red and black banded brickwork and a tall graceful spire, inside an Aladdin's cave of colour and pattern and extraordinary sense of scale. Geometry of arches gives feeling of tension and excitement. Ruskin

Cragside, Northumberland, designed by Norman Shaw for armaments manufacturer Sir William Armstrong

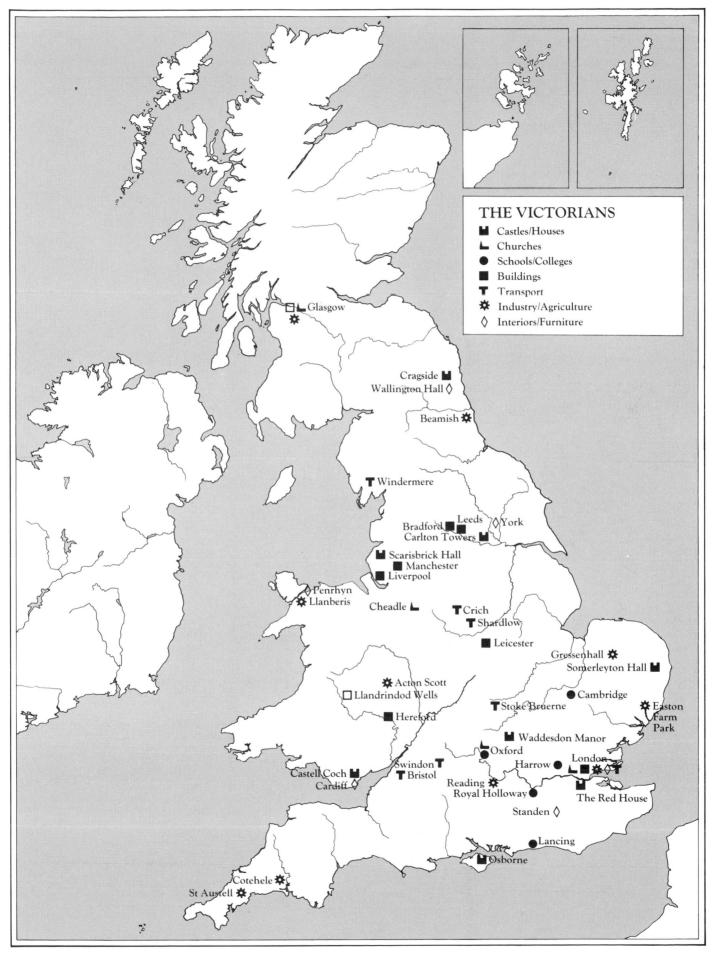

THE VICTORIANS

- ◧ Castles/Houses
- ∟ Churches
- ● Schools/Colleges
- ■ Buildings
- ⊤ Transport
- ✲ Industry/Agriculture
- ◊ Interiors/Furniture

Glasgow

Cragside
Wallington Hall ◊

Beamish ✲

⊤ Windermere

Leeds
Bradford ◊ York
Carlton Towers

Scarisbrick Hall
Manchester
Liverpool

Penrhyn
Llanberis ✲   Cheadle ∟   ⊤ Crich
                                        ⊤ Shardlow

                              ■ Leicester

                                        Gressenhall ✲
                                        Somerleyton Hall ■

                    ✲ Acton Scott
            □ Llandrindod Wells   ● Cambridge
                              ⊤ Stoke Bruerne   ✲ Easton
            ■ Hereford   Farm
                                                            Park
                                        ■ Waddesdon Manor
                              ∟ Oxford
            Swindon ⊤   Harrow ●   London
Castell Coch ◧ ⊤ Bristol   ✲◊⊤
Cardiff ◊   Reading ✲
                      Royal Holloway ●   The Red House

                              Standen ◊

                                        ● Lancing
                    ◧ Osborne

        Cotehele ✲
St Austell ✲

207

admired it – 'having done this, we may do anything' – it made Gerard Manley Hopkins want to shout, and Sir John Summerson compares it to 'a saint in fetters'. Sunday services, still packed every week and heavy with incense and ritual, keep alive Victorian High Anglicanism.

Holy Trinity, Sloane St, Arts and Crafts church of 1880s full of interesting craftsman-made details – beaten bronze panels on choir stalls, wrought iron light fittings inspired by leaf forms, charming carved putti. Whole spacious interior with window completely filling end wall has feeling of light and sophistication.

Westminster Cathedral: by 1890s Gothic no longer seemed the only fitting inspiration for ecclesiastical buildings. J. F. Bentley was commissioned by Cardinal Vaughan 1894 to design a new Roman Catholic cathedral and travelled in Italy in search of inspiration. The result is a huge orange and white Byzantine building with tall campanile and lots of domes, striped like the churches of Florence and Siena, but with garish brick and stone instead of marble. Interior is cavernous, impressive and very dark – the sparkling mosaics with which Bentley wanted to cover the walls have never been finished. **Oxford** George Edmund Street designed St Philip and St James in the new spirit of 'muscular Christianity' 1859. A heavy stone building with a chunky spire and inside squat columns, wide nave, no elaborate detailing. Everywhere a feeling of directness and masculinity, just right for future empire-builders and hearty married dons.

SCHOOLS/COLLEGES

Harrow School, whose buildings make up most of the village of Harrow-on-the-Hill, is an anthology of Victorian architectural styles. Chapel and equally Gothic Vaughan Library were designed by George Gilbert Scott 1850s, Burges's New Speech Room with 13th c exterior and plan based on ancient Greek theatres is an original, interesting building and the Butler Museum of the 1880s is a good example of the late-19th c popular 'Queen Anne' style. They are interspersed with gaunt, Gothic boarding-houses and the boys themselves in their flat boaters and cut-away coats add the final Victorian touch.
Keble College (Oxford) In 1833 a sermon by John Keble sparked off the High Church Oxford Movement which split Anglicans into warring factions. When he died in 1866 an Oxford college was founded in his memory for the children of clergymen. William Butterfield's building symbolises all the intensity of the movement. Instead of traditional stone, he chose bright red brick with clashing bands and checks of yellow and white. It is asymmetrical, original and emphatic in every detail. Inside the chapel feels awesomely tall and grand. Butterfield himself designed pulpit, lectern and ironwork – contains one of the most famous Victorian paintings, Holman Hunt's 'Light of the World'.
Lancing College In many Victorian public schools the size and splendour of the chapel symbolised the importance that schoolmasters hoped religion would have in their pupils' lives. Here the huge chapel in the Early Decorated style completely overshadows the pleasing Early Victorian Gothic school buildings. Begun 1868, it has only recently been finished – stone quarried locally by several generations of family of Sussex masons. 4m NE of Worthing.
Newnham College (Cambridge) Suitable setting for Tennyson's imaginary 'sweet girl graduates with their golden hair'. Domesticated, rambling buildings at Cambridge designed 1874–1910 by Basil Champneys in the 'Queen Anne' style. Effect informal and charming – red brick, lots of bay windows, white paintwork – nice, relaxed contrast to the rival women's college Girton, whose tight-lipped Gothic buildings – set miles away from all the dangerous men's colleges – tried unsuccessfully to emulate their severe style.
Royal Holloway College Spectacular, bizarre building, 1879–87, an early college for women founded by Thomas Holloway who had made a fortune from

selling patent pills and had also built a slightly less demented lunatic asylum nearby. His college at Egham, Surrey, is an enormous spikey red brick pile with elaborate gatehouses, 2 huge courtyards, scores of cone-shaped turrets and pointed cupolas and forests of chimneys. Picture gallery has very fine collection of Victorian paintings, especially social realists including Frith's 'Railway Station' and tearjerkers by Millais, Landseer etc. Gallery open mid-July–Sept Tues, Wed 2–5. Admission charge.

BUILDINGS

Bradford Wool Exchange, built in the 1860s, a soaring Venetian Gothic building designed by Lockwood and Mawson, architects of Saltaire. Outside it has arcades with Victorian worthies in the spandrels, 2-colour stonework topped by a heavy parapet, pinnacled turrets and clock-tower with spire. Inside the Great Hall has tall marble columns, Gothic tracery and a double hammerbeam roof. Members of Bradford Wool Exchange still use the hall on Mon and Thur, but other days you can see inside. There are markets there on Tues and Sat.
Hereford Library financed by Sir James Rankin in 1870s. The building's elaborate polychrome facade is decorated with a complex scheme of sculpture which includes coats of arms, symbolic figures, signs of the zodiac and fantastic animals, all calculated to 'appeal to the popular mind'. Open Tues–Sat 9.30–4.
Leeds Town hall is a massive square building completely encircled by giant Corinthian columns and pilasters, made more imposing and less classical by the clock tower rising on another Corinthian colonnade above the main entrance. The tower helps to mask the high roof of the Great Hall, which is the main feature of the interior, with its tunnel vault, double columns and elaborate organ. It is reached through a high entrance hall with statues of Victoria and Albert. Town hall built between 1853–8 and designed by Cuthbert Brodrick who was also the architect of Leeds Corn Exchange and the Grand Hotel, Scarborough. Visits by arrangement with the town hall manager. Tel 462352.
Leicester The Secular Hall is not strictly a public building, but this unique hall is in a category of its

own. It was designed by Larner Sugden for the Leicester Secular Society and built by 1881. It caused a scandal because the terracotta busts among the Renaissance motifs of the facade included Jesus on a par with Voltaire, Tom Paine, Robert Owen and Socrates. The Secularists chose them because they stood 'in a general way for wholesome criticism, for revolt against priestly pretensions, and for endeavours after a happier social environment.' Mrs Besant, Bradlaugh and Holyoake came to the hall's opening and later William Morris, Hyndman and Bernard Shaw lectured at their Sunday meetings, which still continue in the members' club room and retain the policy of an open platform. To see round the hall and club room contact The Secular Society, 75 Humberstone Gate, Leicester.
London Houses of Parliament: after Westminster Palace burnt down in the dramatic fire, Charles Barry won the competition to design a Gothic or Elizabethan replacement. His assistant was A. W. Pugin, who designed the decorative detailing both outside and in. His work is at its most magnificent in the House of Lords. The foundation stone was laid 1840, but the building process was fraught with problems for Barry and both he and Pugin died before it was completed in 1867. Prince Albert suggested the new building should give artists public patronage, the Fine Arts Commission ran competitions and monumental frescoes by prizewinners Maclise, Watts, Cope, Horsley, Armitage and Dycce can be found throughout the corridors and in the House of Lords. Tel 219 4272

Law Courts: 12 leading architects took part in the Law Courts competition in 1866. All their entries were Gothic, including a towering picturesque design by Burges. The turreted, asymmetrical facade that now dominates the Strand was designed by G. E. Street and built 1874–82. Inside, from the great vaulted hall open to public, sequences of corridors and staircases lead to the courts.

Smithfield Market: on the site of the old cattle market in London, but from 1852 the animals on the hoof were driven into the Caledonian Market, behind King's Cross. Only the Caledonian clock tower remains, but the meat and poultry market at Smithfield is still operating in the Italianate market hall that was built for it in 1866. Many of the finest 19th c market halls have now sadly been pulled

The municipal grandeur of Leeds Town Hall, designed by Cuthbert Brodrick in the 1850s

down, or the markets moved elsewhere. Architect was Sir Horace Jones.

Liverpool At the centre of Liverpool's handsome series of civic buildings stands St George's Hall, like an expanded temple, on its plateau. Designed by H. L. Elmes and built 1841–56, it is the culmination of British neo-classicism. It contains the richly coloured Great Hall, flanked by 2 law courts (originally courts and concert hall were to be 2 separate buildings, but Elmes won both competitions). In an apse at one end is the elegant Concert Room, with its bulbous balcony supported on caryatids, designed by C. R. Cockerell. He completed the building after Elmes died of consumption. Hall open to visitors for a few days each summer in August or early Sept, tel Liverpool 7093752.

Manchester Alfred Waterhouse won the competition for Manchester's town hall largely because of his ability to plan within the difficult triangular site. The site also caused problems in elevation, but Waterhouse's picturesque use of Gothic allowed him to soften the sharp corners with oriel windows and odd angles. Inside he linked 2 staircases of different sizes, so you can look through their arches from one to the other. The Great Hall, which occupies the centre of the triangle, has a hammerbeam roof and frescoes by Ford Madox Brown of Manchester's historic and scientific progress. Free tours Mon–Fri 10am and 2.30pm.

TRANSPORT

Bristol Brunel's city, with suspension bridge 1831, train sheds at Temple Meads station 1840 and SS Great Britain 1843 showing 3 completely different aspects of an engineering genius. Bridge only finished after Brunel's death in 1859. Train sheds are fake Tudor, frontage altered, but interior with mock hammerbeam roof reasonably intact and used as car park. Great Britain salvaged from Falkland Islands more than 10 years ago and towed back to original berth on Avon. Restoration still in progress. Open Easter–Oct daily 10–6, Oct–Easter 10–5. Admission charge.

Crich (Derbyshire) Vintage trams run on rebuilt section of George Stephenson's narrow gauge line linking quarry with lime kilns at Abergate. Cast iron Victorian tram shelter comes from Birmingham, its stained glass panels from Matlock, iron gates from Marylebone, tram stop sign and pillar from Liverpool, gas lamps from Oldham. Open Easter–Sept Mon–Thurs 10–4.30, Sat, Sun 10.30–5.30. Admission charge (includes tram ride). 6m SE of Matlock.

Glasgow Museum of Transport appropriately housed in city's old tramway depot with Corporation horse drawn tram No 543 c 1895 still in its original home. Oldest surviving pedal cycle in world is solid contraption 1839 with heavy slatted guard to prevent tailcoats catching in the wheel. Elegant Royal Mail coach of same period would provide less bumpy ride. Open Mon–Sat 10–5, Sun 2–5.

London Midland Railway's temple to steam built at St Pancras, grandest of all London termini. Work began 1866 with spectacular single span roof, 689ft long, designed by R. M. Ordish and Midland's engineer, William Barlow. Structural proportions determined by size of Burton's beer barrels lucratively stored in vaults under platforms. Gothic hotel, now offices, with fantastic roofs and pinnacles is work of

Backyards in Swindon, Wilts., purpose-built Victorian railway town

Plaque depicting broad gauge locomotive, Swindon Station, Wilts.

Sir Gilbert Scott who felt that it was 'possibly too good for its purpose', but he didn't want to waste all the homework he'd put in on his rejected design for the Foreign Office.

Shardlow (Derbyshire) Inland port with cottages and warehouses of Midland brick which cluster round junction of Trent and Mersey Canal with Trent Navigation, Grand Union and Derby canals. Pretty semi-circular fanlights in some warehouses. Pleasant walk along towpath from Derwent Mouth to Wilne Lane Bridge, round the wharf and lock. Cast iron milepost and other remnants of solid Victorian work, though much is 18th c. Warehouse straddling canal arm has exhibition 'The Canal Story'. Open April–Oct daily 9–5.30, Nov–March 9.30–3.30. Admission charge. W of A6 leaving M1 at junction 24.

Stoke Bruerne (Northamptonshire) Developed in wake of Grand Union Canal, which serves as village street; granary houses Waterways Museum. Narrow boat Sunny Valley is painted with traditional roses and castles designs and crammed with decorated ware. Open Easter–Oct daily 10–6, Oct–Easter Tues–Sun 10–4. Admission charge. 7m S of Northampton, between M1 (junction 15) and A5. ½m N of village along towpath is Blisworth tunnel, 3,075yds of dank darkness, the longest canal tunnel still in existence, now being restored, will reopen soon. Hired teams of 'leggers' lying flat on projecting boards used to walk the boat through.

Swindon (Wiltshire) New town built for GWR 1840s by Wyatt, architect of Paddington station. Model estate had 300 cottages for railway employees (accommodation allocated according to job status), school, church and Mechanics Institute. Streets named after stations on GWR line: Exeter, Taunton, Bathampton. Cottage at 34 Farringdon Rd decorated and furnished in late Victorian style, harmonium and potted palm. Railway Museum next door is housed in The Barracks, provided by all-embracing company as lodging house for unattached males. Marvellous posters, prints, handbills, 19th c track equipment and gleaming replica of 1837 locomotive North Star. Check opening times of both museums, tel Swindon 26161. Admission charge.

Windermere (Cumbria) Elegant collection of early steamboats with gently raked funnels and long, slim hulls. Earliest is c 1850 Dolly, reckoned to be oldest mechanically powered boat in the world, recovered from lake bottom in 1962. Steam yacht Esperance, built 1869, is Captain Flint's houseboat in Arthur Ransome's classic 'Swallows and Amazons'. Built for Furness industrialist H. W. Schneider, who used it as ferry to his private train at Lakeside while butler served breakfast in panelled saloon. Open Easter–Oct Mon–Sat 10–5, Sun 2–5. Admission charge.

Stations Whimsical echoes of 100 architectural styles still quixotically survive under drably unifying motifs of BR design. Stowmarket in Suffolk is gabled in Dutch fashion, with front that has hints of Jacobean and octagonal towers punctuating the wings. Opened 1849. Timbered Gothic is the style on the Bletchley-Bedford line, at Woburn Sands and Fenny Stratford. Trains still stop, but the stations are now houses. Classical restraint at Wadhurst and other stations on the South Eastern Railway, splendid cast iron foliage and pillars at Great Malvern. By 1870s standardisation of designs gradually replaced anarchy. North Rd Station, Darlington, gaunt classical, is now museum with original fine ironwork and fittings. Open Easter–Sept Mon–Sat 10–5 Sun 11–4, Oct–Easter Mon–Sat 10–3. Admission charge.

Tom Norton Collection of Old Cycles and Tricycles (Powys) Some 20 assorted velocipedes, penny farthings and 'safety' cycles dating from 1867, collected by early cyclist and racer Tom Norton. His son inherited his enthusiasm along with 1911 garage, The Automobile Palace, and the eccentric machines are now suspended from its lofty ceiling. Detailed booklet serves as a guide. Open Mon–Fri 8–6, Sat 8–1. Llandrindod Wells.

INDUSTRY/AGRICULTURE

Acton Scott Farm (Shropshire) Small farm worked with help of 3 Shire horses and techniques of the late Victorians. Original machinery and old breeds of cattle, sheep, pigs and poultry. Work depends on weather and season: ploughing, sowing, shearing, threshing. Dairymaid produces butter (for sale), farrier works on Mondays. Craft demonstrations every weekend. Check opening hours, tel Marshbrook 306. Admission charge. Off A49 5m S of Church Stretton.

Templeton's Carpet Factory, Glasgow – industrial fantasy at its grandest

engines used to pump up London's water supply from the Thames for over 100 years. Engines work all day. 90in Cornish beam engine, 1846 – largest working in the world – in operation 12.30–1, 3.30–4. Open Sat, Sun and Bank Hols 11–5. Admission charge. Green Dragon Lane, Brentford, Middlesex.

Llanberis (Gwynedd) North Wales Quarrying Museum housed in old engineering department of quarry. Built like a fort in mid-19th c by Indian Army engineers who seem to have forgotten that they had left the Empire behind. Twin towers of massive slate slabs before backdrop of terraced workings of Dinorwic quarry. Blacksmith and slate splitters at work, displays of Victorian quarrying techniques. Open Easter–Sept daily 9.30–6.30. Admission charge.

Reading (Berkshire) Museum of English Rural Life holds huge collection of material, harvesting and winnowing machines, the country's biggest gathering of farm waggons (each area had its own style) and a new exhibition in the Ransome Hall devoted to ploughs. Horse gear set up in natural surroundings but no room here for practical demonstrations. Open Tues–Fri 10–4.30 Sat 10–1, 2–4.30.

St Austell (Cornwall) Tin mining and the china clay industry provide most dramatic relics of Cornwall's industrial past. Wheal Martin, frozen into 1880s, is typical 19th c clay works, giant 35ft iron water wheel powers slurry pumps which feed clay-laden water into refining and settling pits. Open April–Oct daily 10–5. Admission charge. 2m N of St Austell on A391.

Spectacular ruins of tin mining industry at Botallack, with engine house of 1858. Machine at Levant Mine is 1840 Harvey of Hayle Cornish beam engine. Exposed position on cliff between St Just and Pendeen. 1m N of St Just on B3306.

INTERIORS/FURNITURE

Cardiff Castle Between 1865 and 1881 the Marquess of Bute used his wealth from Cardiff's development as a coal port, to transform the ancient castle. His architect was William Burges, described in Rossetti's limerick as: 'a babyish party . . . Who from infancy hardly emerges'. Together they created a fabulous brightly-coloured world inside the castle, combining medieval romanticism in the Banqueting Hall, Library and Chaucer Room, Moorish influences in the Arab Room and Roof Garden, with Victorian luxuries like Smoking Rooms, Marble Bathrooms and Fairytale Nursery. Outside the castle's silhouette sprouted towers and turrets and the 'Animal Wall' which still delights passing citizens who share Burges's mental age. Open May–Sept daily 10–6, March, April, Oct daily 10–5, Nov–Feb daily 10–4, conducted tours till hour before closing. Admission charge.

London Linley Sambourne's House, 18 Stafford Terrace, Kensington, is a rare survival, still decorated and arranged as it was in 1870s when Linley Sambourne, *Punch* cartoonist and illustrator, began married life here. To us the house may seem cluttered, a miniature greenhouse full of plants on the half landing, pictures by Sambourne and his friends hung 3 deep in the drawing room. Light furniture, oriental ceramics and rugs became popular in 1870s with emerging artistic and professional middle class reacting against heavy upholstery and antimacassars. Open by appointment only Wed 10–4 Sun 2–5.

Leighton House, Holland Park Rd, is one of a colony of large houses built for successful artists and their patrons around Holland Park – Burges, Frith and the Ionideses lived nearby. In Lord Leighton's house, the Arab Hall is a truly exotic combination of brilliant Moorish tiles brought from Cairo and Damascus, with ceramics by De Morgan and mosaic friezes by Walter Crane. Collection of High Victorian paintings, work by Alma-Tadema, Millais, Burne-Jones and Watts as well as Leighton himself. Open Mon–Sat 11–5. Children under 16 must be accompanied by an adult.

Victoria and Albert Museum has a cross-section of Victorian furniture on show. Examples of High Victorian taste include inlaid papier mâché chairs,

Beamish (Co. Durham) Buildings from Cleveland, Durham, Northumberland and Tyne and Wear gathered in 200-acre North of England Open Air Museum site, furnished and working in period style. Rowley Station 1867 has perfect booking office and ladies waiting room. Complete town being rebuilt with aged, but functioning, fish and chip shop. Victorian bandstand from Gateshead (brass band concerts Sun pm). Complete row of pit cottages 1860 from Hetton-le-Hole, No 1 furnished as colliery office, No 2 lushly claustrophobic in 1890s style. Home Farm has Cleveland Bay horses, Durham Shorthorn cattle and Saddleback pigs. Open April–Sept daily 10–6, Oct–March Tues–Sun 10–5. Admission charge. 5m NW of Chester-le-Street off A693.

Cotehele (Cornwall) Near 14th c house is 19th c agricultural complex of watermill, cider house, wheelwright's shop, blacksmith's forge and saddlery, all meticulously restored by Nat Trust, which owns whole property. Cider house powered by donkey wheel, overshot water wheel drives 2 pairs of stones in the mill. Forge was used recently for repair work on old Tamar barge, Shamrock, now moored at Victorian quay, also rescued and reinstated with lime kilns and warehouse. Open April–Oct every day 11–6. Admission charge. 8m SW of Tavistock.

Easton Farm Park (Suffolk) Original buildings of model farm built for Duke of Hamilton 1870. Splendid dairy with cooling centre fountain, rustic floral tiles made by Maw and Co, marble shelves and stained glass windows. Early breeds of longhorn cattle, Jacob, Soay and St Kilda sheep. Complete fitted laundry of 1892, loose boxes, harness rooms, stallion yard (with stallion). Open Easter–Sept daily 10.30–6. Admission charge. 9m E of Woodbridge.

Glasgow Old Templeton carpet factory, Glasgow Green, is surprising eruption of Turkish exotic in fairly grim northern surroundings. Facade swirls with all manner of arches, roundels, zig-zags and columns, borrowed from Romanesque, Gothic and the architect's most fevered dreams. Coloured bricks, tiles, mosaic in buffs, orange and emerald green. Bought by Scottish Development Agency who are restructuring interior to provide small industrial workshops.

Gressenhall (Norfolk) Norfolk Rural Life Museum – the perfect props department for 'Lark Rise': harvesting tools with sickles, rakes, costrel of beer and frail plaited basket for dinner in the fields. Emphasis on use rather than static display. Open mid-May–mid-Sept Tues–Sat, 10–5, Sun 2–5.30. Admission charge. 3m N of East Dereham.

Kew Bridge Pumping Station Houses monster beam

ornate pianos, classics from the Great Exhibition like the chairs with portraits of Victoria and Albert. Against these can be set a range of furniture by Morris and his associates and elegant designs from 1870s onwards by Godwin, Voysey, Ashbee etc.

Morris's Green Dining Room, unlike most of the period rooms in the V and A, was part of the original museum, designed by William Morris and Philip Webb as the Directors' Dining Room from 1866. The Gambles Room, close to the Green Dining Room is the original refreshment room designed by James Gambles in 1868 – lined with elaborate ceramics made by Minton's. Open Mon–Thur, Sat 10–6, Sun 2–6.

Penrhyn Castle (Gwynedd) This pseudo-Norman castle was built 1830s by Thomas Hopper for the Pennant family out of their profits from local slate mining. Where there were precedents to go on, as in the Keep, Hopper's imitation Norman was faithfully copied, but the demands of 19th c luxury forced him into flamboyant adaptations like the heavy wood arches in the library and the elaborate interlaced arches of the Grand Staircase. The State Bedroom has a Norman 4-poster, and the slate bed, which literally weighs a ton, is flanked by Norman pedestal cupboards. Nat Trust. Open April–Oct daily 2–5, end May–end Sept daily 11–5, and Bank Hol weekends 11–5. Admission charge. 1m E of Bangor at junction of A5 and A55.

Standen (Sussex) Built by Philip Webb in 1890s, this is one of the few remaining interiors to show the summery atmosphere of fashionable late-Victorian houses, with painted panelling, wallpaper, fabrics and furniture by Morris and Company, metal and brass furnishings by Benson and ceramics by De Morgan. Nat Trust. Open April–Oct Wed, Thur, Sat 2–5.30. Admission charge. 1½m S of E Grinstead, signposted from B2110.

Wallington Hall (Northumberland) 17th c mansion owned by Trevelyan family, who in mid-19th c made it a haven for poets, painters and scientists. Ruskin suggested roofing in the central courtyard and John Dobson, the architect of Newcastle station, was employed to turn it into a picture gallery. William Bell Scott painted a series of murals of the history of Northumberland, including his famous 'Iron and Coal', one of the few attempts by a Victorian artist to represent industrialisation. Nat Trust. Open April–Sept Mon, Wed–Sun 1–6, Oct Wed, Sat, Sun 2–5. Admission charge. 12m W of Morpeth on B6343.

York Dr Kirk, the Castle Museum's founder, 'mocked-up' several rooms as he remembered them from his childhood, with objects he had collected. There is a well-to-do middle-class drawing room, a Dales cottage room and a late 19th c farmhouse

Leighton House, Kensington – replica of a Moorish palace and home of artist Lord Leighton

kitchen. The famous Victorian street in the museum contains shop windows for a wine merchant, sweet shop, clock makers and apothecary and a cobbler's and candlemaker's workshop. Open April–Sept weekdays 9.30–6, Sun 10–6, Oct–March weekdays 9.30–4.30, Sun 10–4.30. Admission charge.

Queen Victoria's Railway Carriage is in the National Railway Museum at York. She used to make her regular trips between Windsor and Balmoral in this lavishly appointed carriage, upholstered from floor to ceiling. It was built in Wolverton in 1869. The museum has a number of other carriages showing difference between 1st and 3rd class travel. Open weekdays 10–6, Sun 2.30–6.

ART GALLERIES/MUSEUMS

Beckenham (Kent) The Bethlem Royal Hospital has a small collection of about a dozen works by Richard Dadd, of varying obsessiveness and quality. These were done while Dadd was a patient at the hospital, shortly after he had stabbed his father to death. Open by appointment only. Contact Ms Audridge, Bethlem Royal Hospital, Monks Orchard Rd, Beckenham, Kent. Tel 01–777 6611.

Bedford Cecil Higgins Art Gallery in a late-Victorian house has rooms laid out with furniture and objects from the Handley-Read Collection of Victorian and Edwardian decorative arts, to evoke the atmosphere of a home of the period. Fine collection of watercolours and drawings includes work by Cox, Dadd, Palmer, Ruskin, Linnell, Lear, Wilkie, Whistler, Hunt and Millais. Open Tues–Fri 12.30–5, Sat 11–5, Sun 2–5. Admission charge, children free.

Birmingham City Museum and Art Gallery houses a good collection of Pre-Raphaelites including Millais's 'Blind Girl', and Ford Madox Brown's 'Last of England', as well as work by Burne-Jones, Egg's 'Travelling Companions' and representative work by artists spanning the whole period. Open weekdays 10–5.30, Sun 2–5.30.

Bournemouth Russell-Cotes Art Gallery and Museum, an Italianate villa built on the cliffs for Sir Merton Russell-Cotes in 1894, contains mementoes of his world travel – miniature versions of the Taj Mahal, Chinese temples, pyramids, Henry Irving Collection, watercolours and paintings by Rossetti, Frith, Etty, Landseer and much more. Open weekdays 10.30–5. Admission charge.

Guildford (Surrey) Compton-Watts Gallery in a leafy part of Surrey where artist G. F. Watts used to

Dinorwic Quarry, Llanberis, Wales – slate quarry designed as Indian hill fort

Top: 'Sweetness and light' furniture in the drawing room at Standen, Sussex, designed by William Morris and Co.
Above: Papier mache sofa decorated with mother of pearl, in Victoria and Albert

live. Mrs Watts built this gallery specially to house her husband's painting and sculpture. She and her pupils also built his mortuary chapel nearby. They even made the bricks and decorated the whole of the interior with richly coloured symbolic figures and foliage. Open Wed–Sat 11–1, 2–6, Mon, Tues, Fri, Sun 2–6 (Oct–March closes at 4).

Hull Ferens Art Gallery has a large and fascinating collection of Humberside marine painting – memorial portraits of vessels returning from long voyages, whalers in the Arctic etc, painted by self-taught artists like John Ward, Binks, Redmore and Settle, who started life as ship painters. Open Mon–Sat 10–5, Sun 2.30–4.30.

Liverpool Walker Art Gallery collection includes famous Victorian history paintings like Yeames's 'When did you last see your father?', Maclise's 'Death of Nelson', as well as Brett's 'Stonebreaker', Millais's 'Lorenzo and Isabella' and many others. Open Mon–Sat 10–5, Sun 2–5.

Manchester City Art Gallery contains some of the most famous paintings of the period – Holman Hunt's 'Hireling Shepherd', Ford Madox Brown's 'Work', Millais's 'Autumn Leaves', sketches of Hunt's 'Light of the World' and 'Lady of Shallot'. Also interesting work by Etty, Wilkie, Landseer, Collison, Hughes, Windus and others. The mill girls in Eyre Crowe's painting of 'The Dinner Hour, Wigan' act as a reminder of the Manchester which Engels described. Open Mon–Sat 10–6.

Oxford Pitt Rivers Museum has wonderful early anthropological collection still laid out according to General Pitt Rivers' ideas of the evolution of cultural forms, including the development of firearms with which his collection began, development and diversification of different types of musical instruments through different societies. Collection given to the university 1883 on condition a museum was built to house it. This was built behind the University Museum, which is itself a splendid 1850s Gothic iron and glass structure. Its stone facade is decorated with naturalistically carved animals and plants appropriate to its natural history collection. University Museum open Mon–Sat 2–5, Pitt Rivers 2–4.

Port Sunlight (Merseyside) In the middle of the model village Lord Leverhulme built for his employees, is the neo-classical gallery to house his collection. He started buying paintings in the 1880s and 90s to be used as advertisements, like Frith's 'New Frock', for Sunlight Soap. Later they were used as promotional gifts. Millais, Lord Leighton and Waterhouse were favourites and there are also famous paintings like Hunt's 'Scapegoat' here. Open Mon–Sat 10–5, Sun 2–5.

Tate Gallery Famous collection includes some of the most interesting early Pre-Raphaelite paintings, including Millais's 'Christ in the House of his Parents' and 'Ophelia', Hunt's 'Straying Sheep', several Rossettis, Wallis's 'Death of Chatterton', Dyce's 'Pegwell Bay', Dadd's 'Fairy Feller's Master Stroke', epic John Martins, Whistlers. Open Mon–Sat 10–6, Sun 2–6.

Wolverhampton Central Art Gallery collection includes Victorian genre paintings by 'The Cranbrook School'. These are closely observed scenes of anecdotes from everyday life – children playing, the vicar visiting, which show in detail the domestic conditions of the rural poor. Open Mon–Sat 10–6.

LEISURE

Fairs You can still ride in an elaborate 19th c gondola on a splendid switchback roundabout at the Thursford Collection, nr Fakenham, Norfolk. It was built by Savage of King's Lynn, pioneer designer of steam-driven fairground machines. The steam organ in its centre still churns out turn-of-the-century hits. Open Easter–Oct daily 2–5.30, Nov–Easter, Sun 2–5.30 Admission charge.

Lady Bangor's Fairground Collection, Wookey Hole, Somerset, has a Victorian spinner shaped like a sea-monster, a rococo bioscope front – 19th c forerunner of the cinema – and lots of high-spirited gallopers. Open April–Sept daily 10–6, Oct–Mar

10–4.30. Admission charge. Includes caves and other attractions.

Pubs Many splendid Victorian pubs survive fairly unscathed especially in big cities. London ones worth seeking out include The Salisbury, St Martin's Lane – 1890s pub with lots of sparkling engraved glass, bronze nymphs as lamp stands, lots of mahogany and red plush. The Prince Alfred, Formosa St, Maida Vale – an 1860s building with iron columns, small bars, lovely curving windows. The Tottenham, Oxford St – mirrors painted with fruit and flowers, imitation tapestries of seductive ladies. The Tabard, Bath Rd, Turnham Green – designed by Norman Shaw, first 'improved public house' with De Morgan tiles, snug settles, everything cosy and artistic for the residents of this suburb for aesthetes, Bedford Park.

Liverpool has two particularly exotic pubs. The Philharmonic, Hope St – probably the grandest in England, decorated in 1890s by teachers from nearby School of Art and Architecture, rich with tiles, art nouveau carving, marble, brass counters. The Vine, Lime St, is almost as posh with chandeliers, oil paintings, lots of mahogany. Edinburgh's pride is The Café Royal, West Register St, with stained glass of sportsmen, mahogany panelling, Doulton tile pictures, marble bar tops. The Nat Trust has taken over and refurbished the best pub in Belfast, The Crown Liquor Saloon, Great Victoria St – tiles everywhere, pineapple columns, carvings, fine lettering, seats like box pews for serious drinking.

The Seaside Brighton, not surprisingly best place for piers, though sadly future of dilapidated West Pier – put up in 1860s and one of most elegant and earliest surviving in country – still in doubt. Palace Pier with its silvery domes, echoing Brighton Pavilion, and curly ironwork is a delight. At its far end is Vintage Penny Arcade with fine collection of turn-of-the-century 'What the Butler Saw' machines, still working. Open daily 10–pier closing time. Admission charge. Brighton Museum and Art Gallery has an excellent display on the development of the town as queen of English seaside resorts in the 19th c including elaborate model of first real seaside pier in the country, the Chain Pier of 1823. Open Tues–Sat 10–5.45, Sun 2–5.

Blackpool best place for lots of lavish, 'no expense spared' Victorian resort buildings. The tower was put up in 1894, 5 years after the Eiffel Tower, but the canny Northerners made theirs quite a bit shorter and didn't waste the space at the bottom. Its permanent circus ring, one of first, lavishly decorated 'like a Moroccan sultan's palace', hydraulic machinery could fill it with 60,000gal of water in 5 minutes for 'magnificent water pantomimes'. Tower ballroom with gilt plaster ceiling restored to original opulent glory. Admission charge, tel Blackpool 25252.

Top: late Victorian doll's house from Bethnal Green Museum, London. Above: Armies of tin Empire-builders like these were imported from Germany

3 piers – the ultimate Victorian seaside status symbol: best North Pier with nice 19th c ironwork and pavilions.

Toys Bethnal Green Museum, London, has an excellent collection of Victorian toys and games including rocking-horses, automata, juvenile theatres, Punch and Judy puppets, jigsaws, dolls, spinning-tops and doll's houses. Open Mon–Thur, Sat 10–6, Sun 2.30–6.

The Museum of Childhood, Edinburgh, for late Victorian toys and games including an especially grand doll's house of 1880s and some evocative improvised toys made by slum children from clothes pegs, bones and rags. Open June–Sept Mon–Sat 10–6, Oct–May 10–5. Admission charge.

PEOPLE

Brontë Parsonage Museum Most of parsonage is similar to the Brontë original; the later part of the house contains a manuscript collection of the sisters' books. In the nursery are drawings scratched on the plasterwork by the young Brontës and their miniature 'Angrian' stories in tiny writing. Mr Brontë's study has the long white neckerchief the stern pastor wore wrapped round and round his neck. In the dining room is the sofa on which Emily died. Outside are Branwell's pub, the graveyard and the moors. Open weekdays 11–5.30 (4.30 in winter), Sun 2–5.30 (4.30 in winter). Closed last 3 weeks of year. Admission charge. Haworth 4m SW of Keighley off A6033.

Carlyle's House Thomas and Jane Carlyle rented the 'at once excellent and cheap' house in 1834. 'Here we spent our 2 and 30 years of hard battle against Fate', until first Jane and then Thomas died in their Chelsea house. It remains decorated in their taste much as they left it. Thomas's well-known hat hangs in the hall by the garden door; Jane's screen pasted with engravings, prints and cut out celebrities stands in the drawing-room. Tait's paintings depict the interior as it was when Ruskin, Browning, Dickens, Leigh Hunt, Darwin and other visitors came to listen to the great man. The top of the house has Thomas's carefully planned, sound-proofed (it wasn't!) study where he worked on 'Frederick the Great' and 'The French Revolution' – only one sheet remains of his original manuscript, the rest was used to light a fire when in the care of John Stuart Mill. Carlyle painfully rewrote the whole volume. Nat Trust. Open April–Oct Wed–Sat 11–dusk, Sun 2–dusk and Bank Hols. Admission charge. 24 Cheyne Row, Chelsea.

Darwin's House Darwin bought Down House in

'The Awakening Conscience' by William Holman Hunt shows a 'fallen woman' at home

One of Britain's greatest Victorian pubs, the Cafe Royal, Edinburgh. Right, the iron and glass splendour of the Palm House, Kew Gardens

Downe in 1842 for his growing family and to work in seclusion away from London. He died there in 1882 having written 'On the Origin of the Species by means of Natural Selection' in his 'capital study'. This is furnished as in his day with his microscope, books and enclosure with chamber pot and washstand to avoid time wasting trips elsewhere in the house. His life preserver and notebooks are here as reminders of the Beagle voyage. Personal relics like snuff jars and hats and notes on his health, diet plans and garden plant lists. Surrounding countryside hardly altered since Darwin's time. Open all year except Christmas and February Tues–Thur, Sat, Sun 1–6. Admission charge. 5½m S of Bromley off A233.

Dickens's House Charles Dickens lived at 48 Doughty Street, London WC1 from 1837–40. The births of 2 of his children here are recorded by him in the family bible. Mary, his sister-in-law and inspiration for his idealised heroines, died in the house, a portrait hangs in her bedroom. There's a desk he used on reading tours and a desk he worked at when he was a lawyer's clerk. Among the first editions and manuscripts ('Pickwick Papers', 'Oliver Twist' and 'Nicholas Nickleby' were written in Doughty Street), there's the earliest surviving letter by 13-year-old Dickens containing quite terrible puns. Open weekdays 10–5 (closed Bank Hols). Admission charge.

Disraeli's Hughenden Manor Disraeli bought Hughenden in 1848 and lived there, when he could escape London commitments, until 1881 – and was buried in Hughenden Church graveyard. He and Countess Beaconsfield set about creating a Gothic 'Romance', adding battlements to the house, peacocks to the terrace and a 'German forest' to the grounds. His 'gallery of friendship' includes portraits of Wellington, Byron, George Smythe (one of the creators of the Young England Party and the model for the hero of Disraeli's novel, 'Coningsby') and the impeccable d'Orsay. His study remains unaltered: the black rimmed letter paper he always used after his wife's death is on his desk. Nat Trust. Open March–Nov Sat, Sun 2–5, Wed–Sat 2–6, Sun and Bank Hols 12.30–sunset. Admission charge. 1½m N of High Wycombe off A4128.

Michael Faraday's Laboratory and Museum Faraday's magnetic laboratory in the Royal Institution, Albemarle St, London, is a reconstruction of the room where he performed his amazingly varied experiments. The instruments and apparatus he used are labelled and explained with the clarity he believed so important and which made his lectures at the Royal Institution so popular. Outstanding example of self-help, Faraday was an apprentice bookbinder until a lecture by Humphry Davy spurred him on to becoming a great theorist and pioneer of electrical engineering. The first dynamo, transformer and electrical motor are displayed. There are specimens of the optical glass he made, connected with his work on lighthouses, and examples of steel alloys he produced from his furnace. Open Tues, Thur 1–4. Admission charge.

Fox Talbot Museum of Photography William Henry Fox Talbot, 'the Caxton of sunprinting', inventor of the photographic negative (an improvement on Daguerrotypes which could not be multiplied) did most of his pioneering work at Lacock Abbey, his family home. The museum, in a barn, displays his early cameras, calotypes and photographs of his family and local workers, often using Lacock Abbey as background. It contain's Talbot's 'The Pencil of Nature', the first book to have photographic illustrations, and many letters to fellow members of the Royal Society. Talbot's wide range of interests is evident from his microscopes and Egyptian tablets: he was one of the few able to decipher Cuneiform writing. Nat Trust. Open March–Oct daily 11–6. Admission charge. 3m S of Chippenham off A350.

David Livingstone Centre The cotton factory where young David worked has disappeared but the tenements erected for its employees, where he was born, still stand. The Livingstone home, just one room, contains the furniture which surrounded him during his harsh Scottish boyhood and a spinning wheel, a clothes beetle and bible. Elsewhere in the building, displays trace his life from cotton spinner to dedicated African missionary and Victorian hero. There are relics of his journeys: notebooks, dispatch box, surgical instruments and the red jacket he was presumably wearing when *New York Herald* correspondent Stanley found him. Open Mon–Sat 10–6, Sun 2–6. Admission charge. Blantyre 3m NW of Hamilton off A724.

Ruskin's House Ruskin bought Brantwood in 1871 for its views over Coniston Lake. He died here in 1900 and is buried in Coniston churchyard. The grounds were laid out by him with viewing points, shrubs and cypresses brought from Italy. Out-houses contain his boat, his bathchair and a specially made double brougham, a leisurely form of transport he preferred to railway. Inside, paintings by Collingwood, Severn, Burne-Jones and an abundance of Ruskin's own watercolours and architectural drawings. Open Good Fri–end Oct Sun–Fri 11–5.30. Admission charge. SW of Ambleside off B5285.

MISCELLANEOUS

Kew Gardens Contains two great examples of Victorian confidence and enterprise. The Palm House designed by Decimus Burton 7 years before Paxton's Crystal Palace – beautiful sweeping curves of iron and glass to house a jungle of tropical plants. 'One of the boldest pieces of 19th c functionalism in existence,' says Pevsner.

Nearby is Marianne North Gallery in pokey little building on Kew Rd side of gardens. Interior an exhilarating surprise – walls completely covered with a patchwork of over 800 bold flower paintings and landscapes, the lifework of one intrepid lady traveller, amateur botanist and artist, Marianne North. In 1880s she had this museum specially built to house them – it's a vivid period piece and reminder of the drive and independence of some Victorian women. Admission charge to gardens.

Cemeteries Bradford City fathers and wool magnates built their extravagant memorials on dramatic 25-acre site overlooking city. Darkened and decaying Egyptian mausoleums and fancy Gothic pinnacles now eerily submerged in ivy and undergrowth, but Undercliffe Cemetery was once a popular place with Bradford people to take the air and stroll among the 'sleepers'. Founded 1854 by local consortium.

Kensal Green Cemetery, London, was the first of the great London cemeteries, opened 1832. Creeper-clad tombs of baronets, Bengal army generals and manufacturers of patent remedies all a bit dishevelled now. Gothic crockets and finials sprout in profusion from the grandest, which line avenue to porticoed church – the occasional sphinx lurking in the privet bushes. Open Mon–Sat 9–6, Sun 2–6.

Costume V and A's costume court should reopen this year, otherwise the Gallery of English Costume at Platt Hall, Manchester, has the best Victorian collection in the country. Current display of chic travelling clothes includes glimpse inside early railway carriage and Rational cycling gear – divided skirt and lighting-up times printed inside hat. Among more unusual items – specially constructed breast-feeding dress c 1860, croquet outfit c 1865, greenery-yallery Aesthetic dresses of the 1870s, and 1880s tennis dress. Also new display of Fanny Jarvis's neatly labelled underwear and nightwear. Check opening times, tel Manchester 224 5217.

Paisley Museum and Art Galleries houses fine collection of paisley shawls – fashionable way of counteracting chilly evenings and low necklines. East India Co introduced them end 18th c, Paisley started production 1805. All the rage in 1840s, but gradually moved downmarket until 1870s when they wouldn't go over the bustle and became a workaday garment. Open all year Mon–Sat 10–5.

Street Furniture The combination of civic pride and social conscience which burgeoned in the 19th c found material expression in many odd ways: drinking fountains, horse troughs, benches, monumental clocks, palatial lavatories and elegant street lighting. Foundries, supremely confident in their skill with iron, turned out hundreds of designs for footscrapers, coal covers, valve and hydrant signs.

The temperance movement was the instigator of the great flood of fountains that were put up in public places from the 1850s onward, though its philanthropy was based on the misconception that 'the poor' drank alcohol because they were thirsty rather than for much needed oblivion. Huge fountain in Aspatria (Cumbria) commemorates Sir Wilfred Lawson, who, it says, championed the movement 'with Gay Wisdom and Perseverance'. Bath temperance society put up a Rebecca at the well statue outside the Abbey in 1861, but her pitcher is broken and the water turned off.

Original street lighting of the 19th c is harder to find, though there are still about 1,000 gas lamps surviving in London, mostly round Covent Garden, Westminster Abbey, St James and the Temple off Fleet St. The dolphin lamps along the Victoria Embankment were put up between 1864–70. York has large Gothic lamps with double lanterns 1862 along Lendal Bridge.

The oldest pillar box in the country stands at Barnes Cross, Holwell, Dorset, a design of about 1853. The red uniform came in some time after 1874. Dark green was a more favoured colour for the early Victorian versions. 2 very pretty fluted column pillarboxes 1856–7 still stand in Warwick beside E Gate and W Gate.

BIBLIOGRAPHY
and
PICTURE CREDITS

The Tribal Islands
Burgess, Colin, *The Age of Stonehenge* (Dent)
Burl, A. & Piper, E., *Rings of Stone* (Frances Lincoln)
Cunliffe, Barry, *Iron Age Communities in Britain* (Routledge & Kegan Paul)
Dyer, James, *Southern England: an archaeological guide* (Faber)
Houlder, Christopher, *Wales: an archaeological guide* (Faber)
Mackie, Euan W., *Scotland: an archaeological guide* (Faber)

The Romans
Birley, Anthony R., *Life in Roman Britain* (Batsford)
Birley, Anthony R., *The People of Roman Britain* (Batsford)
Frere, Sheppard, *Britannia* (Routledge & Kegan Paul)
Todd, Malcolm, *Roman Britain, 55BC–AD400* (Fontana)
Wacher, John, *Roman Britain* (Dent)
Wilson, R. J. A., *A Guide to the Roman Remains in Britain* (Constable)

The Dark Ages
Bede, trans. L. Shirley-Price, *A History of the English Church and People* (Penguin)
Bruce-Mitford, Rupert, *The Sutton Hoo Ship Burial* (British Museum Publications)
Hunter-Blair, P., *Introduction to Anglo-Saxon England* (CUP)
Loyn, H. R., *Anglo-Saxon England and the Norman Conquest* (Longman)
Sawyer, P. H., *From Roman Britain to Norman England* (Methuen)
Stenton, F. M., *Anglo-Saxon England* (OUP)

The Normans
Barlow, F., *The Feudal Kingdom of England* (Longman)
Barrow, G. W. S., *Feudal Britain* (Arnold)
Davis, R. H. C., *King Stephen* (Longman)
Loyn, H. R., *Anglo-Saxon England and the Norman Conquest* (Longman)

The Plantagenets
Harvey, J., *Plantagenets* (Fontana)
Holmes, G., *The Later Middle Ages* (Nelson)
Keen, M., *England in the Later Middle Ages* (Methuen)
Myers, A. R., *England in the Later Middle Ages* (Penguin)

The Tudors
Bindoff, S. T., *Tudor England* (Pelican)
Loades, D. M., *Politics and the Nation 1450–1660* (Fontana)
Rowse, A. L., *The Elizabethan Renaissance; the Life of the Society* (Macmillan)
Strong, Roy, *The Renaissance Garden in England* (Thames & Hudson)
Williams, P., *The Tudor Regime* (OUP)

The Stuarts
Coward, B., *The Stuart Age* (Longman)
Kenyon, J. P., *Stuart England* (Penguin)
Summerson, J., *Architecture in Britain 1530–1830* (Pelican)
Waterhouse, E. K., *Painting in Britain 1530–1790* (Pelican)

The Georgians
Hudson, Kenneth, *Industrial Archaeology: a new introduction* (A. C. Black)
Mingay, G. E., *English Landed Society in the 18th Century* (Routledge & Kegan Paul)
Owen, J. B., *The 18th Century, 1714–1815* (Nelson)
Plumb, J. H., *Georgian Delights* (Weidenfeld & Nicolson)
Speck, W. A., *Stability and Strife: England 1714–60* (Arnold)

The Victorians
Best, G. F. A., *Mid-Victorian Britain 1851–70* (Fontana)
Briggs, A., *The Age of Improvement 1783–1867* (Longman)
Girouard, Mark, *The Victorian Country House* (Yale University Press)
Harrison, J. F. C., *Early Victorian Britain 1832–51* (Fontana)

General
The Past All Around Us (Reader's Digest)
The National Trust Guide (Jonathan Cape)
Historic Houses, Castles and Gardens (ABC Publications)
Fellows, A., *England and Wales: a Traveller's Guide* (Batsford)
Girouard, Mark, *Life in the English Country House* (Penguin)
Hoskins, W. G., *The Making of the English Landscape* (Pelican)
Pevsner, Nikolaus, *The Buildings of England series* (Penguin)
Trevelyan, G. M., *English Social History* (Pelican)

Picture Agency credits:
Bodleian Library; Bridgeman Art Library; British Library; British Museum; Clive Friend; Durham Cathedral Treasury; ET Archive; Mansell Collection; Marquis of Bath, Longleat House; Mary Evans Picture Library; Michael Holford; Museum of London; National Maritime Museum; National Trust; National Trust for Scotland; Nicholas Servian; Painton Cowen; Platt Hall, Gallery of English Costume; Robert Harding; Tate Gallery; The Suffolk Collection, Ranger's House, Blackheath (GLC); Victoria and Albert Museum; Werner Forman; William Morris Gallery, Walthamstow; Woodmansterne Ltd.
All other photographs: *The Observer* by Christopher Cormack, Alain le Garsmeur, Tim Graham, Conrad Hafenrichter, Steve Herr, Colin Molyneux, Dave Paterson, Brian Shuel, Pamela Toler, Denis Waugh, George Wright.

INDEX

Numerals in **bold** type refer to captions